THE HEART OF WILLIAM JAMES

THE HEART OF
WILLIAM JAMES

Edited and with an Introduction by

Robert Richardson

Harvard University Press

Cambridge, Massachusetts

London, England

2010

Library of Congress Cataloging-in-Publication Data

James, William, 1842–1910.
The heart of William James / edited and with an introduction
by Robert Richardson.
p.   cm.
Includes bibliographical references (p.   ) and index.
ISBN 978-0-674-05561-2 (cloth : alk. paper)
1. Philosophy.   2. Psychology.   I. Richardson, Robert D., 1934–   II. Title.
B945.J21R53   2010
191—dc22   2010009406

Contents

Introduction

Opening an Eye of the World

The World According to James

William James was in England in late 1899 and early 1900, trying to write the lectures that would become *The Varieties of Religious Experience,* when the Boer War broke out. The war went badly for the English at first, and, hoping to persuade the Christian God to intervene on the English side, an interdenominational church group declared January 7, 1900, as a "Day of Humiliation and Prayer." James wrote a letter to the London *Times* to suggest that "both sides to the controversy might be satisfied by a service arranged on principles suggested by the anecdote of the Montana settler who met a grizzly so formidable that he fell on his knees, saying, 'Oh Lord, I hain't never yet asked ye for help, and aint agoin to ask ye for none now. But for pity's sake O Lord, don't help the Bear'" (*Correspondence*, vol. 9).

He had a point, he understood that there exist points of view other than one's own, and he had a sense of humor. The *Times* declined to print his letter. James was ahead of his time on many issues, and we are fortunate that most of his views did get printed. From our current point of view, in 2010, a hundred years after his death, James looks very much the prophet, and his work is as relevant and life-changing in our times as it was in his. James chose Darwin, chemistry, physiology, and neurology over traditional metaphysics and theology, and his work marked the real beginning of our age of neurophysiology and neurobiology. It is James who first and most convincingly taught us that the mind is *always* active, even in sleep or hypnosis, that rationality not only follows feeling, but it *is* a feeling, that many emotions follow rather than lead to physiological responses and physical actions, that we can no longer draw a clear line between the mind and the body, and that the mind is largely brain function and is rooted in physiology. James did not think consciousness exists as a thing or as a place, but only as a function. It may be, he proposed, that the furthest we can get is to suggest that thoughts follow from one another, that the thought is itself the thinker. James understood that the fringes of consciousness are as important as the centers, that "attention is the same fact as belief." He also understood that chance is the same fact as freedom, that "chance begets order" (as his friend Charles Sanders Peirce put it), and that evolution needs us as much as we need it. Every choice we make is one more specific nomination for one particular useful adaptation instead of another. The father of Alcoholics Anonymous, Bill Wilson, credits James with the founding insight of that organization—that self-mastery comes only after self-surrender and an admission of hopelessness and helplessness. James knew that truth is a process, that reality is experience—but *all* of experience—and that truth and reality are actually verbs, just as it can be argued that God is a verb.

The Life of William James

William James was born on January 11, 1842, at the Astor House in New York City. Family legend has it that Emerson, who was lecturing in New York in early March, came to see and give his blessing to the infant, which may or may not account for the marked streaks of Emersonian thought in William James's later work.

William's younger brother, who would become the great novelist Henry James, was born fifteen months after William. William and Henry were very close throughout their lives, as may be seen from their letters—published as volumes 1–3 of the *Correspondence of William James* by the University of Virginia Press—and from Henry's memoirs *A Small Boy and Others* (1913) and *Notes of a Son and Brother* (1914). The reason why Rebecca West's observation that Henry wrote fiction like a philosopher and William wrote philosophy like a novelist is so often and so warmly remembered is because William and Henry were very much involved with and influenced by each other's work. William read and commented on everything Henry wrote, and Henry read William's writings and proclaimed himself in close agreement, saying, for example, after *Pragma-tism* appeared, that he had all his life "unconsciously pragmatized," and telling his brother "you are immensely and universally *right.*"

The father of this unusually accomplished family (we should not forget two other brothers, Wilky and Robertson, both of whom fought in the Civil War, and the gifted sister, Alice, the diarist, who was the youngest of the five children) was Henry James Sr., a wealthy, eccentric, brilliant Swedenborgian and Sandemanian enthusiast. (Robert Sande-man taught a strict and clergyless Calvinism; Michael Faraday was an active Sandemanian.) Henry Sr. was a spellbinding talker, a man of dis-persed, unlikely, and improvident talents held loosely together by vast personal charm. His own father had bought the upstate New York vil-lage of Syracuse in 1824 for thirty thousand dollars. Henry Sr. inherited then flung away his portion of one of the great American fortunes of his era, leaving all four of his sons in the (fortunate) position of having to work for a living. Henry Sr., described by his biographer as a "blocked and monomaniacal hierophant," wrote one unwanted, unsellable, un-read book after another. One evening when the whole family was at work in the living room, each at his or her own studies, William drew a sketch for a frontispiece for his father's next book. The sketch survives; it shows a man beating a dead horse.

The family moved constantly. In America they lived in New York City, then Newport, Boston, and Cambridge. In between American places, they lived abroad, in London, Windsor, Paris, Boulogne-sur-Mer, and Geneva. The children rarely finished a school year in one place. Be-tween the ages of ten and sixteen, William went to at least nine differ-ent schools, not counting home tutoring. Because Henry Sr. had spent his college years (before expulsion) drinking, smoking cigars, eating oysters, and avoiding bills, he assumed that college was the problem and forbade his children college education. William, like Henry, was then essentially self-educated, by which means he avoided many of the pre-conceived ideas and attitudes that come with a classical or standard edu-cation. William was allowed to attend Harvard's Lawrence Scientific School (in effect a European-style school with masters and appren-tices, super-specialized and with no general education whatever) and he eventually earned an MD at Harvard Medical School at a time when the requirements both for admission and for graduation were less than stringent. William James had no high school diploma, no college degree, and no PhD. He was nevertheless extremely fortunate in his teachers, who included Charles W. Eliot in chemistry, Jeffries Wyman in comparative anatomy, and Louis Agassiz, on whose Amazon expedition of 1865 William James was a trusted lieutenant. James revered Agassiz as a teacher, but broke sharply with Agassiz's anti-Darwinian creationism.

If William James was fortunate in his family and his teachers, he was even more fortunate in his friends and early colleagues, who included Chauncey Wright (who had reviewed Darwin so succinctly and brilliantly that Darwin had Wright's piece reprinted for general distribution in England); Charles Sanders Peirce, the great semiotician, philosopher, and, as James insisted, the father of pragmatism; and Oliver Wendell Holmes Jr., the great jurist who said "the life of the law is not logic, it is experience." All of these men, like James, were members of the celebrated Metaphysical Club in Cambridge, a group which, if we include Asa Gray, Darwin must have had in mind when he observed that "there were enough brilliant minds in the American Cambridge in the 1860s to furnish all the universities of England."

William took his MD degree in 1869. He was twenty-seven. He had intended to be a scientist, which was not a paying proposition in the America of the time, although medicine—it was thought—could give a person a steady income. But in reality William James was drifting, and had been for some time. He had no plans to practice medicine, and, with no real alternative, he felt increasingly despondent. His back went out on him while he was working without much interest as a surgical resident at Massachusetts General Hospital. The neurasthenic young man now fell into near-suicidal despair, which was only further darkened by the tragic death of his cousin Minnie Temple. Minnie had been alive to her fingertips; she was the real-life model for Henry James's Daisy Miller and Milly Theale. All the young men were in love with Minnie, William more than most.

Appointments to teach first physiology then anatomy at Harvard College in the early 1870s hauled William James out of despair and gave him the first steady work of his life. In 1876 he met Alice Howe Gibbens, whom he married in 1878, when he was thirty-six. He had begun to teach physiological psychology, and he agreed that same year to prepare a book on psychology for the publisher Henry Holt. The marriage, the regular teaching, the new subject, and the book contract cleared the dark skies over James's head and started him off on a new life.

Twelve years and four children later, in 1890, the forty-eight-year-old James published his first real work, *The Principles of Psychology.* While he had taken forever to grow up, his last twenty years were, by contrast, crowded, active, fulfilling, and rewarding. In 1890, the year of *The Principles of Psychology,* he had just built a house at 95 Irving Street in Cambridge, where he was a professor at Harvard in a department soon to be famous. His family flourished, he acquired a summer place in Chocorua, New Hampshire, book followed book. *Psychology: Briefer Course* came out in 1892, *The Will to Believe* in 1897, *Talks to Teachers* in 1899, *The Varieties of Religious Experience* in 1902, *Pragmatism* in 1907, *A Pluralistic Universe* and *The Meaning of Truth* in 1909. By the time of his death on August 26, 1910, he was widely known and admired. One French paper came out with a black border on the issue announcing his death. He had met Freud, Jung, Bergson, and Vivekananda. He had taught Theodore Roosevelt, W. E. B. Du Bois, Gertrude Stein, and George Santayana. Even his own children were fond of the man Alfred North Whitehead once called "that adorable genius."

Chance, Attention, Belief, Conversion, and Action

The writings of William James are a standing rebuke to conventional thought, received ideas, professional jargon, classical education, and all the other ways in which what James calls "the enormous fly-wheel" of habit governs our minds as well as our bodies. Reading James continues to change lives. The pieces in this volume are not intended to cement James's reputation in philosophy, psychology, or religious studies, or to sample his views; they have been chosen for their direct appeal to a general reader. Each piece is complete, and they have been arranged in chronological order, so that one may follow, though one need not, the trajectory of James's thought.

"What Is an Emotion" is James's early, notable, and still controversial argument that many of our emotions follow from (rather than cause) physical or physiological reactions. He argues, for example, that we are afraid because we run, not that we run because we are afraid. "The Dilemma of Determinism" is a dazzling attack on those who claim (and they still do) that everything we do is determined by forces outside our control. "The Perception of Reality" is a chapter from *The Principles of Psychology* that makes the still-startling contentions that "will and belief are two names for the same fact," and "attention and belief are the same fact." "The Hidden Self" takes off from the same work of Pierre Janet's that Freud's theory of the unconscious leans on, but comes to quite a different view. One learns from this essay, for example, that the point of automatic writing and hypnosis is to get in touch with the hidden self. This has a therapeutic use that is still of value today. James's chapter on "Habit" is another classic. James argues for the power of habit, but also is at pains to show how we can nibble away at habit and change it. His piece "The Will" is connected to his view of determinism. We do have an exertable will, James says, and he gives homely, detailed, persuasive examples. "The Gospel of Relaxation" is a popular piece, a sort of self-help classic that argues for the benefits of letting go of the fist-clenching self.

"On a Certain Blindness in Human Beings" was a favorite of William James himself. It sets out to show how the most difficult thing for any of us is to really understand people who are unlike ourselves. This stirring essay would serve as a Declaration of Interdependence for any society, group, or country seriously dedicated to diversity and tolerance. "What Makes a Life Significant" is another good piece to read in hard times. James's argument is thoughtful, complex, and applies mainly to the ordinary people who do most of the world's work. "Philosophical Conceptions and Practical Results" is the opening shot of the pragmatism revolution. Given at Berkeley as a talk, this essay introduces pragmatism not only in a philosophical but also in a religious context. "The Philippine Tangle" gives us William James in a blind rage at the American government's belligerent involvement in the Philippines during the Spanish-American War. It is angry enough and anti-imperialist enough to make good reading now, and it will remind many readers today of the American involvement in Iraq.

The "Sick Soul" chapters from *The Varieties of Religious Experience* give us the heart of the religious situation. They follow and explain the chapters on the religion of healthy-mindedness. The "Sick Soul" chapters explore the darker, more painful side of life, and include glimpses of both William James and his father at their lowest, most despairing ebb. "The PhD Octopus" is the work of a man who had no PhD and therefore understandably had no exalted notion of its value apart from the actual learning of a particular person. This is a great protest against mandarinism and formalism in education and an argument for the individual student. "Does 'Consciousness' Exist?" delighted Bertrand Russell and others in its radical suggestion that there is no such thing or entity as consciousness. There is only a function, a process, a stream of impressions. This is a key insight for James's concept of radical empiricism. "The Energies of Men" is one of James's links with Emerson and Emerson's belief that we habitually operate way below our full potential. This piece leads straight to the human potential movement. "Concerning Fechner" is the most intellectually daring piece here. It considers the Fechnerian (Fechner was a German physicist and thinker) panpsychic world in which everything—*every thing*—is alive. This links James with Jung and beyond, as he considers the possibility that there is a world soul and we are each connected to it through our own minds.

Finally, "The Moral Equivalent of War" is a justly celebrated piece, which will be one hundred years old in 2010. John Dewey thought we should be grateful to James for the phrase and the mere suggestion that such a thing might come into being. The essay is one of the best anti-war pieces ever written.

Ever Not Quite

One of James's most valued correspondents was an unlikely, off-center, homegrown philosopher from upstate New York named Benjamin Paul Blood. "Certainty is the root of despair," Blood had written.

> The inevitable stales, while doubt and hope are sisters. Not unfortunately the universe is wild—game flavored as a hawk's wing. Nature is miracle all. She knows no laws; the same returns not, save to bring the different. The slow round of the engraver's lathe gains but the breadth of a hair, but the difference is distributed back over the whole curve, never an instant true—ever not quite. (*Essays in Philosophy*)

James's central work was aimed at central things. What Blood presented as metaphor James sought in action. Pragmatism was, he insisted, a "doctrine of action" and "the study of all human powers and means." Radical empiricism held that while experience is all that matters, all experience must be included. In psychology James's emphasis was always on possibilities for treatment, the therapeutic imperative, the unlocking of personal energies. His self-help strain comes from his conviction that our thoughts have a shaping power over our bodies. He drew strength from knowing that rationality itself is a sentiment or feeling, and from knowing that conversion is a psychological process that sets loose new energies and leads to rebirth.

Beyond all this, but including all this, is William James's enlargement of our field of vision and our field of attention. He was drawn to edges, fringes, borders, and margins. It is significant that the greatest variety of species are found in borderlands, at the edge of the sea or the edge of the forest. James seemed to know instinctively that borders are in fact centers for life. So he avoided marginalizing himself; instead he annexed the marginal and extended his—and our—field of interest to include all the edges and fringes. He was interested in the fringes themselves, but, as often as not, the margin also provides a new approach to the central page. The main stage is accessed via the wings.

Emerson, in his essay "Experience," listed what he considered "the lords of life"; they were illusion, temperament, succession, surface, surprise, reality, and subjectiveness. Nicolas of Cusa, that pluralist in Christian clothing, thought "the precondition for the abundance of nature lies in what is restless, limited, changeable, and composite." Italo Calvino projected six lectures (and completed five) on lightness, quickness, exactitude, visibility, multiplicity, and consistency. In like manner, William James defended "incompleteness, 'more,' uncertainty, insecurity, possibility, fact, novelty, compromise, remedy and success" as being authentic realities. James further thought of the organization of the self as "a system of memories, purposes, strivings, fulfillments, and disappointments." And he declared that philosophy "has always turned on grammatical particles, 'with, near, next, like, from, towards, against, because, for, through, my.'" These words, he said, "designate types of conjunctive relations, arranged in a roughly ascending order of immediacy and inclusiveness."

William James had the most free-ranging mind of any American thinker, and the chief source of his liberty, as his student, friend, and colleague Santayana put it in *The Genteel Tradition in American Philosophy,*

was his personal spontaneity, similar to that of Emerson, and his personal vitality, similar to that of nobody else. Convictions and ideas came to him, so to speak, from the subsoil. He had a prophetic sympathy with the dawning sentiments of the age, with the moods of the dumb majority. His scattered words caught fire in many parts of the world. His way of thinking and feeling represented the true America, and represented in a measure the whole ultramodern, radical world.

William James believed, as Emerson had, that self-trust is the quality on which a good life is best built, and—again like Emerson—James gave us the reason *why* we may safely trust our best impulses: "If we survey the field of history and ask what feature all great periods of revival, of expansion of the human mind, display in common, we shall find, I think, simply this: that each and all of them have said to the human being 'The inmost nature of the reality is congenial to powers which you possess'" (*The Principles of Psychology,* vol. 2).

As neurophysiology and neurobiology make rapid strides—almost daily—in showing us precisely how the brain works, all the while reminding us just how fantastically complicated the brain really is, we see, as no previous generation has, a clearer and clearer form in the slowly dissolving mist. We see that we each have within us a something, call it brain or mind or process, that reflects, thinks about, and responds to, and thus, in a sense, contains the world. When and if there is a final reality, something on which everyone will eventually agree, it will be seen to be commensurate with powers we in fact possess.

James stood for the individual, and he argued that each individual matters. Beyond that, James believed that we are connected, though not always in ways we see or understand. "Our lives are like islands in the sea," he said in the late essay "Confidences of a Psychical Researcher,"

> or like trees in the forest. The maple and the pine may whisper to each other with their leaves, and Conanicut and Newport hear each other's fog-horns. But the trees also commingle their roots in the darkness underground, and the islands also hang together through the ocean's bottom. Just so there is a continuum of cosmic consciousness, against which our individuality builds but accidental fences, and into which our several minds plunge as into a mother-sea or reservoir.

Further yet, James refused the easy notion that man is the measure of all things. "I firmly disbelieve, myself," he wrote in the concluding paragraphs of *Pragmatism,*

> that our human experience is the highest form of experience extant in the universe. I believe rather that we stand in much the same relation to the whole of the universe as our canine and feline pets do to the whole of human life. They inhabit our drawing-rooms and librar-

ies. They take part in scenes of whose significance they have no in-kling. They are merely tangent to curves of history the beginnings and ends and forms of which pass wholly beyond their ken. So we are tangents to the wider life of things.

Emerson and James matter then not because they are part of the history of American thought, but because they are right. Right and deeply practical. William James was a teacher, and some of his best and most convincing writing came when he was talking to teachers. Here is the last paragraph of his little collection of talks to teachers, and it is every bit as applicable and practicable now as it was a hundred years ago. With his "see to it" and his "I beg you," we can actually hear the voice of the man himself as he leans over the lectern toward his hearers.

> Spinoza long ago wrote in his *Ethics* that anything that a man can avoid under the notion that it is bad he may also avoid under the notion that something else is good. He who habitually acts *sub specie mali,* under the negative notion, the notion of the bad, is called a slave by Spinoza. To him who acts habitually under the notion of good he gives the name of freeman. See to it now, I beg you, that you make freemen of your pupils by habituating them to act, whenever possible, under the notion of a good. Get them habitually to tell the truth, not so much through showing them the wickedness of lying as by arousing enthusiasm for honor and veracity. Wean them from their native cruelty by imparting to them some of your own positive sympathy with an animal's inner springs of joy.

In essay after essay, James calls us to live a fuller, richer, better life, to seek out and use our best energies and sympathies. As every day is the day of creation and of judgment, so every age was the new age once, and William James's writings are still the gateway to many a new world.

Note on the Texts

The pieces in this collection are all complete and are without exception taken from the definitive nineteen-volume *The Works of William James*, published by Harvard University Press 1975–1988 under the general editorship of Frederick H. Burkhardt, with Fredson Bowers as textual editor and Ignas K. Skrupskelis as associate editor. For more information, please see the Acknowledgments section (pp. 335–337). All quotes from James are also from the Harvard University Press edition. Irregular capitalization and spelling have been silently corrected in a few places, but otherwise the texts remain unchanged.

Chronology of William James's Life

1842 Born January 11, Astor House, New York City.

1843 Brother Henry born April 15. Family goes to London in October.

1844 Family goes to Paris, then Windsor, England. Father's vastation (devastating spiritual experience).

1845 Family returns to New York City. Brother Wilky (Garth Wilkinson) born July 21.

1846 Brother Bob (Robertson) born August 29.

1848 Sister Alice born August 7.

1855 Family moves to London, then Geneva. William attends boarding school. Family returns to London in October.

1856 Family moves to Paris in June. William attends Fourierian school.

1857 Family moves to Boulogne-sur-Mer. William attends Collège Impériale.

1858 Family returns to America, moves to Newport, Rhode Island. William takes up sketching in William Hunt's studio.

1859 Family returns to Geneva. William studies science at Geneva Academy.

1860 Family returns to Newport in October. William studies painting with Hunt.

1861 Abandons painting to enter Lawrence Scientific School at Harvard in September. Studies chemistry with Charles W. Eliot. Meets Oliver Wendell Holmes Jr. and Charles S. Peirce.

1862 William at Scientific school, Henry at Harvard Law School. Wilky enlists in Forty-fourth Massachusetts Regiment.

1863 Wilky transfers to Fifty-fourth Massachusetts. Bob enlists, joins Fifty-fifth Massachusetts. Wilky badly wounded at Fort Wagner July 18. William returns to Scientific School, studies under Wyman.

1864 Enters Harvard Medical School. Family moves to Boston.

1865   Joins Agassiz's expedition to Brazil. Sails from New York April 1.

1866   Returns to Medical School in February. Family moves to Cambridge in November.

1867   Sails for Europe in April. Attends physiology lectures in Berlin starting in September.

1868   Adrift, visits Bad Teplitz, Dresden, Heidelberg, Geneva, Paris. Returns to Cambridge in November.

1869   Takes MD degree in June.

1870   Cousin Minnie Temple dies March 22. William has major crisis, probably in April; vision of the green-skinned youth in the asylum.

1872   Appointed to teach physiology at Harvard College starting spring 1873.

1873   Appointed to teach anatomy and physiology at Harvard. Postpones the appointment and sails for Europe in October.

1874   Returns to Cambridge, teaches comparative vertebrate anatomy. Becomes part of new "Metaphysical club."

1876   Meets Alice Howe Gibbens. Teaches physiological psychology.

1877   Meets Josiah Royce.

1878   Lectures on "The Brain and the Mind" at Hopkins in February. Engaged to Alice Gibbens in May. Signs contract for book on psychology. Marries Alice July 10, honeymoon at Keene Valley, New York.

1879   Son Henry born May 18.

1880   Summer in Europe. Appointed assistant professor of philosophy at Harvard.

1882   Mother dies January 30. Son William born June 17. Travels to Europe while wife and sons stay with her mother. Father dies December 18.

1883   Returns to Cambridge in March. Wilky dies November 15.

1884   Son Herman born January 31. William edits and publishes *The Literary Remains of the Late Henry James*. Publishes "What Is an Emotion?" Writes "The Dilemma of Determinism."

1885   Herman dies July 9.

1886   Buys summer home in Chocorua, New Hampshire.

1887   Daughter Peggy born March 24.

1889   Builds house at 95 Irving Street in Cambridge, Massachusetts. Appointed Alford Professor of Psychology at Harvard. Publishes "The Perception of Reality."

1890   Publishes *The Principles of Psychology*. Son Aleck born December 22. Publishes "The Hidden Self."

1891   Trip to England to see sister Alice. Sees dramatic adaptation of brother Henry's *The American* in London.

1892   Publishes *Psychology: Briefer Course*. Sister Alice dies March 6. In May William goes abroad, with family, for sabbatical.

1893   Returns to Cambridge in August.

1895   Writes "The Gospel of Relaxation."

1896   Presents Lowell Lectures on "Exceptional Mental States" in Boston.

1897   Publishes *The Will to Believe*. In August, appointment changed to professor of philosophy.

1898   Misadventure while hiking in the Adirondacks at Keene Valley. Overexertion and start of heart trouble. Travels to California. Delivers lecture "Philosophical Conceptions and Practical Results." Writes "On a Certain Blindness."

1899   Writes "The Philippine Tangle." Publishes *Talks to Teachers*. Goes to Bad Nauheim for heart treatments. Begins preparation for Gifford Lectures in Edinburgh.

1900   Lives abroad, working on Gifford Lectures.

1901   May–June, delivers Gifford Lectures in Edinburgh. Returns to Cambridge August 31.

1902   Sails for England April 1. Delivers second set of Gifford lectures. Both sets published as *The Varieties of Religious Experience*. Sails for America June 10.

1903   Gives talks on "radical empiricism" at Glenmore in Adirondacks. Writes "The PhD Octopus."

1904   Writes "Does Consciousness Exist?"

1905   Travels to Europe, May–June.

1906   Arrives in California January 8, to teach at Stanford. February 21, first version of "The Moral Equivalent of War" delivered as lecture. April 18, experiences earthquake in San Francisco. Returns to Cambridge at the end of April. Writes "The Energies of Men."

1907   Resigns professorship at Harvard. Last lecture given January 22. Publishes *Pragmatism* in June.

1908   Delivers Hibbert Lectures at Oxford in May.

1909   Publishes *A Pluralistic Universe* in April. Meets Freud and Jung in September. Publishes *The Meaning of Truth* in October.

1910   Publishes "The Moral Equivalent of War." March 29, sails to England with Alice to nurse brother Henry. Returns to United States August 18. Dies in Chocorua August 26.

THE HEART OF WILLIAM JAMES

1

———⊷◦⊶———

What Is an Emotion?

"What Is an Emotion?" puts forward one of William James's most original and striking contributions to psychology. Examining the bodily changes usually thought to be *produced* by emotion, James argues that they *are* the emotion. The usual view is that "the mental perception of some fact excites the mental affection called the emotion, and that this latter state of mind gives rise to the bodily expression." James says it is the other way around: "My thesis on the contrary is that the bodily changes follow directly the *perception* of the exciting fact, and that our feeling of the changes as they occur *is* the emotion." We are accustomed to think that "we lose our fortune, are sorry and weep; we meet a bear, are frightened and run; we are insulted by a rival, are angry and strike. The hypothesis here to be defended says that this order of sequence is incorrect . . . we feel sorry because we cry, angry because we strike, afraid because we tremble, and not that we cry, strike, or tremble because we are sorry, angry, or fearful."

The piece was published in 1884 in the English journal *Mind*. The Danish psychologist Carl Lange independently developed the same hypothesis. The idea, which is currently thought applicable to some if not all emotions, is still known as the James-Lange theory of emotion.

If we provisionally accept this earliest of all of James's great insights, we can see, as James himself could see, the practical, therapeutic use. The test of any theory or any insight was, for James, its "fruits for life," its actual usefulness. If the James-Lange theory is right, then "a necessary corollary of it ought to be that any voluntary arousal of the so-called manifestations of a special emotion ought to give us the emotion itself . . . Smooth the brow, brighten the eye, contract the dorsal rather than the ventral aspect of the frame, and speak in a major key, pass the genial compliment, and your heart must be frigid indeed if it do not gradually thaw."

THE PHYSIOLOGISTS who, during the past few years, have been so industriously exploring the functions of the brain, have limited their attempts at explanation to its cognitive and volitional performances. Dividing the brain into sensorial and motor centres, they have found their division to be exactly paralleled by the analysis made by empirical psychology, of the perceptive and volitional parts of the mind into their simplest elements. But the *aesthetic* sphere of the mind, its longings, its pleasures and pains, and its emotions, have been so ignored in all these researches that one is tempted to suppose that if either Dr. Ferrier or Dr. Munk were asked for a theory in brain-terms of the latter mental facts, they might both reply, either that they had as yet bestowed no thought upon the subject, or that they had found it so difficult to make distinct hypotheses, that the matter lay for them among the problems of the future, only to be taken up after the simpler ones of the present should have been definitively solved.

And yet it is even now certain that of two things concerning the emotions, one must be true. Either separate and special centres, affected to them alone, are their brain-seat, or else they correspond to processes occurring in the motor and sensory centres, already assigned, or in others like them, not yet mapped out. If the former be the case we must deny the current view, and hold the cortex to be something more than the surface of "projection" for every sensitive spot and every muscle in the body. If the latter be the case, we must ask whether the emotional "process" in the sensory or motor centre be an altogether peculiar one, or whether it resembles the ordinary perceptive processes of which those centres are already recognized to be the seat. The purpose of the following pages is to show that the last alternative comes nearest to the truth, and that the emotional brain-processes not only resemble the ordinary sensorial brain-processes, but in very truth *are* nothing but such processes variously combined. The main result of this will be to simplify our notions of the possible complications of brain-physiology, and to make us see that we have already a brain-scheme in our hands whose applications are much wider than its authors dreamed. But although this seems to be the chief result of the arguments I am to urge, I should say that they were not originally framed for the sake of any such result. They grew out of fragmentary introspective observations, and it was only when these had already combined into a theory that the thought of the simplification the theory might bring to cerebral physiology oc-curred to me, and made it seem more important than before.

I should say first of all that the only emotions I propose expressly to consider here are those that have a distinct bodily expression. That there are feelings of pleasure and displeasure, of interest and excitement, bound up with mental operations, but having no obvious bodily expres-sion for their consequence, would, I suppose, be held true by most read-ers. Certain arrangements of sounds, of lines, of colors, are agreeable, and others the reverse, without the degree of the feeling being sufficient to quicken the pulse or breathing, or to prompt to movements of either the body or the face. Certain sequences of ideas charm us as much as others tire us. It is a real intellectual delight to get a problem solved, and a real intellectual torment to have to leave it unfinished. The first set of examples, the sounds, lines, and colors, are either bodily sensations, or the images of such. The second set seem to depend on processes in the ideational centres exclusively. Taken together, they appear to prove that there are pleasures and pains inherent in certain forms of nerve-action as such, wherever that action occur. The case of these feelings we will at present leave entirely aside, and confine our attention to the more com-plicated cases in which a wave of bodily disturbance of some kind ac-companies the perception of the interesting sights or sounds, or the pas-sage of the exciting train of ideas. Surprise, curiosity, rapture, fear, anger, lust, greed, and the like, become then the names of the mental states with which the person is possessed. The bodily disturbances are said to be the "manifestation" of these several emotions, their "expression" or "natural language"; and these emotions themselves, being so strongly characterized both from within and without, may be called the *standard* emotions.

Our natural way of thinking about these standard emotions is that the mental perception of some fact excites the mental affection called the emotion, and that this latter state of mind gives rise to the bodily expression. My thesis on the contrary is that *the bodily changes follow directly the* PERCEPTION *of the exciting fact, and that our feeling of the same changes as they occur* IS *the emotion.* Common sense says, we lose our fortune, are sorry and weep; we meet a bear, are frightened and run; we are insulted by a rival, are angry and strike. The hypothesis here to be defended says that this order of sequence is incorrect, that the one mental state is not immediately induced by the other, that the bodily manifestations must first be interposed between, and that the more rational statement is that we feel sorry because we cry, angry because we strike, afraid because we tremble, and not that we cry, strike, or tremble, because we are sorry, angry, or fearful, as the case may be. Without the bodily states following on the perception, the latter would be purely cognitive in form, pale, colorless, destitute of emotional warmth. We might then see the bear, and judge it best to run, receive the insult and deem it right to strike, but we could not actually *feel* afraid or angry.

Stated in this crude way, the hypothesis is pretty sure to meet with immediate disbelief. And yet neither many nor far-fetched considerations are required to mitigate its paradoxical character, and possibly to produce conviction of its truth.

To begin with, readers of this Journal do not need to be reminded that the nervous system of every living thing is but a bundle of predispositions to react in particular ways upon the contact of particular features of the environment. As surely as the hermit-crab's abdomen presupposes the existence of empty whelk-shells somewhere to be found, so surely do the hound's olfactories imply the existence, on the one hand, of deer's or foxes' feet, and on the other, the tendency to follow up their tracks. The neural machinery is but a hyphen between determinate arrangements of matter outside the body and determinate impulses to inhibition or discharge within its organs. When the hen sees a white oval object on the ground, she cannot leave it; she must keep upon it and return to it, until at last its transformation into a little mass of moving chirping down elicits from her machinery an entirely new set of performances. The love of man for woman, or of the human mother for her babe, our wrath at snakes and our fear of precipices, may all be described similarly, as instances of the way in which peculiarly conformed pieces of the world's furniture will fatally call forth most particular mental and bodily reactions, in advance of, and often in direct opposition to, the verdict of our deliberate reason concerning them. The labors of Darwin and his successors are only just beginning to reveal the universal parasitism of each special creature upon other special things, and the way in which each creature brings the signature of its special relations stamped on its nervous system with it upon the scene.

Every living creature is in fact a sort of lock, whose wards and springs presuppose special forms of key—which keys however are not born attached to the locks, but are sure to be found in the world near by as life goes on. And the locks are indifferent to any but their own keys. The egg fails to fascinate the hound, the bird does not fear the precipice, the snake waxes not wroth at his kind, the deer cares nothing for the woman or the human babe. Those who wish for a full development of this point of view, should read Schneider's *Der thierische Wille*—no other book shows how accurately anticipatory are the actions of animals, of the specific features of the environment in which they are to live.

Now among these nervous anticipations are of course to be reckoned the emotions, so far as these may be called forth directly by the perception of certain facts. In advance of all experience of elephants no child can but be frightened if he suddenly find one trumpeting and charging upon him. No woman can see a handsome little naked baby without delight, no man in the wilderness see a human form in the distance without excitement and curiosity. I said I should consider these emotions only so far as they have bodily movements of some sort for their accompaniments. But my first point is to show that their bodily accompaniments are much more far-reaching and complicated than we ordinarily suppose.

In the earlier books on Expression, written mostly from the artistic point of view, the signs of emotion visible from without were the only ones taken account of. Sir Charles Bell's celebrated *Anatomy of Expression* noticed the respiratory changes; and Bain's and Darwin's treatises went more thoroughly still into the study of the visceral factors involved— changes in the functioning of glands and muscles, and in that of the circulatory apparatus. But not even a Darwin has exhaustively enumerated *all* the bodily affections characteristic of any one of the standard emotions. More and more, as physiology advances, we begin to discern how almost infinitely numerous and subtle they must be. The researches of Mosso with the plethysmograph have shown that not only the heart, but the entire circulatory system, forms a sort of sounding-board, which every change of our consciousness, however slight, may make reverberate. Hardly a sensation comes to us without sending waves of alternate constriction and dilatation down the arteries of our arms. The blood-vessels of the abdomen act reciprocally with those of the more outward parts. The bladder and bowels, the glands of the mouth, throat, and skin, and the liver, are known to be affected gravely in certain severe emotions, and are unquestionably affected transiently when the emotions are of a lighter sort. That the heartbeats and the rhythm of breathing play a leading part in all emotions whatsoever, is a matter too notorious for proof. And what is really equally prominent, but less likely to be admitted until special attention is drawn to the fact, is the continuous co-operation of the voluntary muscles in our emotional states. Even when no change of outward attitude is produced, their inward tension alters to suit each varying mood, and is felt as a difference of tone or of strain. In depression the flexors tend to prevail; in elation or belligerent excitement the extensors take the lead. And the various permutations and combinations of which these organic activities are susceptible, make it abstractly possible that no shade of emotion, however slight, should be without a bodily reverberation as unique, when taken in its totality, as is the mental mood itself.

The immense number of parts modified in each emotion is what makes it so difficult for us to reproduce in cold blood the total and integral expression of any one of them. We may catch the trick with the voluntary muscles, but fail with the skin, glands, heart, and other viscera. Just as an artificially imitated sneeze lacks something of the reality, so the attempt to imitate an emotion in the absence of its normal instigating cause is apt to be rather "hollow."

The next thing to be noticed is this, that every one of the bodily changes, whatsoever it be, is *felt*, acutely or obscurely, the moment it occurs. If the reader has never paid attention to this matter, he will be both interested and astonished to learn how many different local bodily feelings he can detect in himself as characteristic of his various emotional moods. It would be perhaps too much to expect him to arrest the tide of any strong gust of passion for the sake of any such curious analysis as this; but he can observe more tranquil states, and that may be assumed here to be true of the greater which is shown to be true of the less. Our whole cubic capacity is sensibly alive; and each morsel of it contributes its pulsations of feeling, dim or sharp, pleasant, painful, or dubious, to that sense of personality that every one of us unfailingly carries with him. It is surprising what little items give accent to these complexes of sensibility. When worried by any slight trouble, one may find that the focus of one's bodily consciousness is the contraction, often quite inconsiderable, of the eyes and brows. When momentarily embarrassed, it is something in the pharynx that compels either a swallow, a clearing of the throat, or a slight cough; and so on for as many more instances as might be named. Our concern here being with the general view rather than with the details, I will not linger to discuss these but, assuming the point admitted that every change that occurs must be felt, I will pass on.[1]

I now proceed to urge the vital point of my whole theory, which is this. If we fancy some strong emotion, and then try to abstract from our consciousness of it all the feelings of its characteristic bodily symptoms, we find we have nothing left behind, no "mind-stuff" out of which the emotion can be constituted, and that a cold and neutral state of intellectual perception is all that remains. It is true, that although most people, when asked, say that their introspection verifies this statement, some persist in saying theirs does not. Many cannot be made to understand the question. When you beg them to imagine away every feeling of laughter and of tendency to laugh from their consciousness of the ludicrousness of an object, and then to tell you what the feeling of its ludicrousness would be like, whether it be anything more than the perception that the object belongs to the class "funny," they persist in replying that the thing proposed is a physical impossibility, and that they always *must* laugh, if they see a funny object. Of course the task proposed is not the practical one of seeing a ludicrous object and annihilating one's tendency to laugh. It is the purely speculative one of subtracting certain elements of feeling from an emotional state supposed to exist in its fulness, and saying what the residual elements are. I cannot help thinking that all who rightly apprehend this problem will agree with the proposition above laid down. What kind of an emotion of fear would be left, if the feelings neither of quickened heart-beats nor of shallow breathing, neither of trembling lips nor of weakened limbs, neither of goose-flesh nor of visceral stirrings, were present, it is quite impossible to think. Can one fancy the state of rage and picture no ebullition of it in the chest, no flushing of the face, no dilatation of the nostrils, no clenching of the teeth, no impulse to vigorous action, but in their stead limp muscles, calm breathing, and a placid face? The present writer, for one, certainly cannot. The rage is as completely evaporated as the sensation of its so-called manifestations, and the only thing that can possibly be supposed to take its place is some cold-blooded and dispassionate judicial sentence, confined entirely to the intellectual realm, to the effect that a certain person or persons merit chastisement for their sins. In like manner of grief: what would it be without its tears, its sobs, its suffocation of the heart, its pang in the breast-bone? A feelingless cognition that certain circumstances are deplorable, and nothing more. Every passion in turn tells the same story. A purely disembodied human emotion is a nonentity. I do not say that it is a contradiction in the nature of things, or that pure spirits are necessarily condemned to cold intellectual lives; but I say that for *us*, emotion dissociated from all bodily feeling is inconceivable. The more closely I scrutinize my states, the more persuaded I become, that whatever moods, affections, and passions I have, are in very truth constituted by, and made up of, those bodily changes we ordinarily call their expression or consequence; and the more it seems to me that if I were to become corporeally anaesthetic, I should be excluded from the life of the affections, harsh and tender alike, and drag out an existence of merely cognitive or intellectual form. Such an existence, although it seems to have been the ideal of ancient sages, is too apathetic to be keenly sought after by those born after the revival of the worship of sensibility, a few generations ago.

But if the emotion is nothing but the feeling of the reflex bodily effects of what we call its "object," effects due to the connate adaptation of the nervous system to that object, we seem immediately faced by this objection: most of the objects of civilized men's emotions are things to which it would be preposterous to suppose their nervous systems connately adapted. Most occasions of shame and many insults are purely conventional, and vary with the social environment. The same is true of many matters of dread and of desire, and of many occasions of melancholy and regret. In these cases, at least, it would seem that the ideas of shame, desire, regret, etc., must first have been attached by education and association to these conventional objects before the bodily changes could possibly be awakened. And if in *these* cases the bodily changes follow the ideas, instead of giving rise to them, why not then in all cases?

To discuss thoroughly this objection would carry us deep into the study of purely intellectual Aesthetics. A few words must here suffice. We will say nothing of the argument's failure to distinguish between the idea of an emotion and the emotion itself. We will only recall the well-known evolutionary principle that when a certain power has once been fixed in an animal by virtue of its utility in presence of certain features of the environment, it may turn out to be useful in presence of other features of the environment that had originally nothing to do with either producing or preserving it. A nervous tendency to discharge being once there, all sorts of unforeseen things may pull the trigger and let loose the effects. That among these things should be conventionalities of man's contriving is a matter of no psychological consequence whatever. The most important part of my environment is my fellow-man. The consciousness of his attitude towards me is the perception that normally unlocks most of my shames and indignations and fears. The extraordinary sensitiveness of this consciousness is shown by the bodily modifications wrought in us by the awareness that our fellow-man is noticing us *at all*. No one can walk across the platform at a public meeting with just the same muscular innervation he uses to walk across his room at home. No one can give a message to such a meeting without organic excitement. "Stage-fright" is only the extreme degree of that wholly irrational personal self-consciousness which everyone gets in some measure, as soon as he feels the eyes of a number of strangers fixed upon him, even though he be inwardly convinced that their feeling towards him is of no practical account.[2] This being so, it is not surprising that the additional persuasion that my fellow-man's attitude means either well or ill for me, should awaken stronger emotions still. In primitive societies "Well" may mean handing me a piece of beef, and "Ill" may mean aiming a blow at my skull. In our "cultured age," "Ill" may mean cutting me in the street, and "Well," giving me an honorary degree. What the action itself may be is quite insignificant, so long as I can perceive in it intent or *animus. That* is the emotion-arousing perception; and may give rise to as strong bodily convulsions in me, a civilized man experiencing the treatment of an artificial society, as in any savage prisoner of war, learning whether his captors are about to eat him or to make him a member of their tribe.

But now, this objection disposed of, there arises a more general doubt. Is there any evidence, it may be asked, for the assumption that particular perceptions *do* produce wide-spread bodily effects by a sort of immediate physical influence, antecedent to the arousal of an emotion or emotional idea?

The only possible reply is, that there is most assuredly such evidence. In listening to poetry, drama, or heroic narrative, we are often surprised at the cutaneous shiver which like a sudden wave flows over us, and at the heart-swelling and the lachrymal effusion that unexpectedly catch us at intervals. In listening to music, the same is even more strikingly true. If we abruptly see a dark moving form in the woods, our heart stops beating, and we catch our breath instantly and before any articulate idea of danger can arise. If our friend goes near to the edge of a precipice, we get the well-known feeling of "all-overishness," and we shrink back, although we positively *know* him to be safe, and have no distinct imagination of his fall. The writer well remembers his astonishment, when a boy of seven or eight, at fainting when he saw a horse bled. The blood was in a bucket, with a stick in it, and, if memory does not deceive him, he stirred it round and saw it drip from the stick with no feeling save that of childish curiosity. Suddenly the world grew black before his eyes, his ears began to buzz, and he knew no more. He had never heard of the sight of blood producing faintness or sickness, and he had so little repugnance to it, and so little apprehension of any other sort of danger from it, that even at that tender age, as he well remembers, he could not help wondering how the mere physical presence of a pailful of crimson fluid could occasion in him such formidable bodily effects.

Imagine two steel knife-blades with their keen edges crossing each other at right angles, and moving to and fro. Our whole nervous organization is "on-edge" at the thought; and yet what emotion can be there except the unpleasant nervous feeling itself, or the dread that more of it may come? The entire fund and capital of the emotion here is the senseless bodily effect the blades immediately arouse. This case is typical of a class: where an ideal emotion seems to precede the bodily symptoms, it is often nothing but a representation of the symptoms themselves. One who has already fainted at the sight of blood may witness the preparations for a surgical operation with uncontrollable heart-sinking and anxiety. He anticipates certain feelings, and the anticipation precipitates their arrival. I am told of a case of morbid terror, of which the subject confessed that what possessed her seemed, more than anything, to be the fear of fear itself. In the various forms of what Professor Bain calls "tender emotion," although the appropriate object must usually be directly contemplated before the emotion can be aroused, yet sometimes thinking of the symptoms of the emotion itself may have the same effect. In sentimental natures, the thought of "yearning" will produce real "yearning." And, not to speak of coarser examples, a mother's imagination of the caresses she bestows on her child may arouse a spasm of parental longing.

In such cases as these, we see plainly how the emotion both begins and ends with what we call its effects or manifestations. It has no mental *status* except as either the presented feeling, or the idea, of the manifestations; which latter thus constitute its entire material, its sum and substance, and its stock-in-trade. And these cases ought to make us see how in all cases the feeling of the manifestations may play a much deeper part in the constitution of the emotion than we are wont to suppose.

If our theory be true, a necessary corollary of it ought to be that any voluntary arousal of the so-called manifestations of a special emotion ought to give us the emotion itself. Of course in the majority of emotions, this test is inapplicable; for many of the manifestations are in organs over which we have no volitional control. Still, within the limits in which it can be verified, experience fully corroborates this test. Everyone knows how panic is increased by flight, and how the giving way to the symptoms of grief or anger increases those passions themselves. Each fit of sobbing makes the sorrow more acute, and calls forth another fit stronger still, until at last repose only ensues with lassitude and with the apparent exhaustion of the machinery. In rage, it is notorious how we "work ourselves up" to a climax by repeated outbreaks of expression. Refuse to express a passion, and it dies. Count ten before venting your anger, and its occasion seems ridiculous. Whistling to keep up courage is no mere figure of speech. On the other hand, sit all day in a moping posture, sigh, and reply to everything with a dismal voice, and your melancholy lingers. There is no more valuable precept in moral education than this, as all who have experience know: if we wish to conquer undesirable emotional tendencies in ourselves, we must assiduously, and in the first instance cold-bloodedly, go through the *outward motions* of those contrary dispositions we prefer to cultivate. The reward of persistency will infallibly come, in the fading out of the sullenness or depression, and the advent of real cheerfulness and kindliness in their stead. Smooth the brow, brighten the eye, contract the dorsal rather than the ventral aspect of the frame, and speak in a major key, pass the genial compliment, and your heart must be frigid indeed if it do not gradually thaw!

The only exceptions to this are apparent, not real. The great emotional expressiveness and mobility of certain persons often lead us to say "They would feel more if they talked less." And in another class of persons, the explosive energy with which passion manifests itself on critical occasions, seems correlated with the way in which they bottle it up during the intervals. But these are only eccentric types of character, and within each type the law of the last paragraph prevails. The sentimentalist is so constructed that "gushing" is his or her normal mode of expression. Putting a stopper on the "gush" will only to a limited extent cause more "real" activities to take its place; in the main it will simply produce listlessness. On the other hand the ponderous and bilious "slumbering volcano," let him repress the expression of his passions as he will, will find them expire if they get no vent at all; whilst if the rare occasions multiply which he deems worthy of their outbreak, he will find them grow in intensity as life proceeds.

I feel persuaded there is no real exception to the law. The formidable effects of suppressed tears might be mentioned, and the calming results of speaking out your mind when angry and having done with it. But these are also but specious wanderings from the rule. Every perception must lead to *some* nervous result. If this be the normal emotional expression, it soon expends itself, and in the natural course of things a calm succeeds. But if the normal issue be blocked from any cause, the currents may under certain circumstances invade other tracts, and there work different and worse effects. Thus vengeful brooding may replace a burst of indignation; a dry heat may consume the frame of one who fain would weep, or he may, as Dante says, turn to stone within; and then tears or a storming-fit may bring a grateful relief. When we teach children to repress their emotions, it is not that they may *feel* more, quite the reverse. It is that they may *think* more; for to a certain extent whatever nerve-currents are diverted from the regions below, must swell the activity of the thought-tracts of the brain.[3]

The last great argument in favor of the priority of the bodily symptoms to the felt emotion, is the ease with which we formulate by its means pathological cases and normal cases under a common scheme. In every asylum we find examples of absolutely unmotived fear, anger, melancholy, or conceit; and others of an equally unmotived apathy which persists in spite of the best of outward reasons why it should give way. In the former cases we must suppose the nervous machinery to be so "labile" in some one emotional direction, that almost every stimulus, however inappropriate, will cause it to upset in that way, and as a consequence to engender the particular complex of feelings of which the psychic body of the emotion consists. Thus, to take one special instance, if inability to draw deep breath, fluttering of the heart, and that peculiar epigastric change felt as "precordial anxiety," with an irresistible tendency to take a somewhat crouching attitude and to sit still, and with perhaps other visceral processes not now known, all spontaneously occur together in a certain person; his feeling of their combination *is* the emotion of dread, and he is the victim of what is known as morbid fear. A friend who has had occasional attacks of this most evil of all maladies, tells me that in his case the whole drama seems to centre about the region of the heart and respiratory apparatus, that his main effort during the attacks is to get control of his inspirations and to slow his heart, and that the moment he attains to breathing deeply and to holding himself erect, the dread, *ipso facto,* seems to depart.[4]

The account given to Brachet by one of his own patients of her opposite condition, that of emotional insensibility, has been often quoted, and deserves to be quoted again:—

"I still continue (she says) to suffer constantly; I have not a moment of comfort, and no human sensations. Surrounded by all that can render life happy and agreeable, still to me the faculty of enjoyment and of feeling is wanting—both have become physical impossibilities. . . . In everything, even in the most tender caresses of my children, I find only bitterness. I cover them with kisses, but there is something between their lips and mine; and this horrid something is between me and all the enjoyments of life. My existence is incomplete. The functions and acts of ordinary life, it is true, still remain to me; but in every one of them there is something wanting—to wit, the feeling which is proper to them, and the pleasure which follows them. . . . *Each of my senses, each part of my proper self, is as it were separated from me and can no longer afford me any feeling; this impossibility seems to depend upon a void which I feel in the front of my head, and to be due to the diminution of the sensibility over the whole surface of my body, for it seems to me that I never actually reach the objects which I touch. . . . I feel well enough the changes of temperature on my skin, but I no longer experience the internal feeling of the air when I breathe. . . .* All this would be a small matter enough, but for

its frightful result, which is that of the impossibility of any other kind
of feeling and of any sort of enjoyment, although I experience a need
and desire of them that render my life an incomprehensible torture.
Every function, every action of my life remains, but deprived of the
feeling that belongs to it, of the enjoyment that should follow it. My
feet are cold, I warm them, but gain no pleasure from the warmth. I
recognize the taste of all I eat, without getting any pleasure from
it. . . . My children are growing handsome and healthy, everyone tells
me so, I see it myself, but the delight, the inward comfort I ought to
feel, I fail to get. Music has lost all charm for me, I used to love it
dearly. My daughter plays very well, but for me it is mere noise. That
lively interest which a year ago made me hear a delicious concert in
the smallest air their fingers played—that thrill, that general vibration
which made me shed such tender tears—all that exists no more."[5]

Other victims describe themselves as closed in walls of ice or covered with an india-rubber integument, through which no impression
penetrates to the sealed-up sensibility.

If our hypothesis be true, it makes us realize more deeply than ever
how much our mental life is knit up with our corporeal frame, in the
strictest sense of the term. Rapture, love, ambition, indignation, and
pride, considered as feelings, are fruits of the same soil with the grossest
bodily sensations of pleasure and of pain. But it was said at the outset
that this would be affirmed only of what we then agreed to call the
"standard" emotions; and that those inward sensibilities that appeared
devoid at first sight of bodily results should be left out of our account.
We had better, before closing, say a word or two about these latter feelings.

They are, the reader will remember, the moral, intellectual, and aesthetic feelings. Concords of sounds, of colors, of lines, logical consisten-
cies, teleological fitnesses, affect us with a pleasure that seems ingrained
in the very form of the representation itself, and to borrow nothing from
any reverberation surging up from the parts below the brain. The Her-
bartian psychologists have tried to distinguish feelings due to the *form* in
which ideas may be arranged. A geometrical demonstration may be as
"pretty," and an act of justice as "neat" as a drawing or a tune, although
the prettiness and neatness seem here to be a pure matter of sensation,
and there to have nothing to do with sensation. We have then, or some
of us seem to have, genuinely *cerebral* forms of pleasure and displeasure,
apparently not agreeing in their mode of production with the so-called

"standard" emotions we have been analyzing. And it is certain that readers whom our reasons have hitherto failed to convince, will now start up at this admission, and consider that by it we give up our whole case. Since musical perceptions, since logical ideas, can immediately arouse a form of emotional feeling, they will say, is it not more natural to suppose that in the case of the so-called "standard" emotions, prompted by the presence of objects or the experience of events, the emotional feeling is equally immediate, and the bodily expression something that comes later and is added on?

But a sober scrutiny of the cases of pure cerebral emotion gives little force to this assimilation. Unless in them there actually be coupled with the intellectual feeling a bodily reverberation of some kind, unless we actually laugh at the neatness of the mechanical device, thrill at the justice of the act, or tingle at the perfection of the musical form, our mental condition is more allied to a judgment of *right* than to anything else. And such a judgment is rather to be classed among awarenesses of truth: it is a *cognitive* act. But as a matter of fact the intellectual feeling hardly ever does exist thus unaccompanied. The bodily sounding-board is at work, as careful introspection will show, far more than we usually suppose. Still, where long familiarity with a certain class of effects has blunted emotional sensibility thereto as much as it has sharpened the taste and judgment, we do get the intellectual emotion, if such it can be called, pure and undefiled. And the dryness of it, the paleness, the absence of all glow, as it may exist in a thoroughly expert critic's mind, not only shows us what an altogether different thing it is from the "standard" emotions we considered first, but makes us suspect that almost the entire difference lies in the fact that the bodily sounding-board, vibrating in the one case, is in the other mute. "Not so very bad" is, in a person of consummate taste, apt to be the highest limit of approving expression. *"Rien ne me choque"* is said to have been Chopin's superlative of praise of new music. A sentimental layman would feel, and ought to feel, horrified, on being admitted into such a critic's mind, to see how cold, how thin, how void of human significance, are the motives for favor or disfavor that there prevail. The capacity to make a nice spot on the wall will outweigh a picture's whole content; a foolish trick of words will preserve a poem; an utterly meaningless fitness of sequence in one musical composition set at naught any amount of "expressiveness" in another.

I remember seeing an English couple sit for more than an hour on a piercing February day in the Academy at Venice before the celebrated "Assumption" by Titian; and when I, after being chased from room to room by the cold, concluded to get into the sunshine as fast as possible and let the pictures go, but before leaving drew reverently near to them to learn with what superior forms of susceptibility they might be endowed, all I overhead was the woman's voice murmuring: "What a *deprecatory* expression her face wears! What self-abne*gation*! How *unworthy* she feels of the honor she is receiving!" Their honest hearts had been kept warm all the time by a glow of spurious sentiment that would have fairly made old Titian sick. Mr. Ruskin somewhere makes the (for him) terrible admission that religious people as a rule care little for pictures, and that when they do care for them they generally prefer the worst ones to the best. Yes! in every art, in every science, there is the keen perception of certain relations being *right* or not, and there is the emotional flush and thrill consequent thereupon. And these are two things, not one. In the former of them it is that experts and masters are at home. The latter accompaniments are bodily commotions that they may hardly feel, but that may be experienced in their fulness by *Crétins* and Philistines in whom the critical judgment is at its lowest ebb. The "marvels" of Science, about which so much edifying popular literature is written, are apt to be "caviare" to the men in the laboratories. Cognition and emotion are parted even in this last retreat—who shall say that their antagonism may not just be one phase of the world-old struggle known as that between the spirit and the flesh?—a struggle in which it seems pretty certain that neither party will definitively drive the other off the field.

To return now to our starting-point, the physiology of the brain. If we suppose its cortex to contain centres for the perception of changes in each special sense-organ, in each portion of the skin, in each muscle, each joint, and each viscus, and to contain absolutely nothing else, we still have a scheme perfectly capable of representing the process of the emotions. An object falls on a sense-organ and is apperceived by the appropriate cortical centre; or else the latter, excited in some other way, gives rise to an idea of the same object. Quick as a flash, the reflex currents pass down through their pre-ordained channels, alter the condition of muscle, skin and viscus; and these alterations, apperceived like the original object, in as many specific portions of the cortex, combine with it in consciousness and transform it from an object-simply-apprehended into an object-emotionally-felt. No new principles have to be invoked, nothing is postulated beyond the ordinary reflex circuit, and the topical centres admitted in one shape or another by all to exist.

It must be confessed that a crucial test of the truth of the hypothesis is quite as hard to obtain as its decisive refutation. A case of complete internal and external corporeal anaesthesia, without motor alteration or alteration of intelligence except emotional apathy, would afford, if not a crucial test, at least a strong presumption, in favor of the truth of the view we have set forth; whilst the persistence of strong emotional feeling in such a case would completely overthrow our case. Hysterical anaesthesias seem never to be complete enough to cover the ground. Complete anaesthesias from organic disease, on the other hand, are excessively rare. In the famous case of Remigius Leims, no mention is made by the reporters of his emotional condition, a circumstance which by itself affords no presumption that it was normal, since as a rule nothing ever *is* noticed without a pre-existing question in the mind. Dr. Georg Winter has recently described a case somewhat similar,[6] and in reply to a question, kindly writes to me as follows:—"The case has been for a year and a half entirely removed from my observation. But so far as I am able to state, the man was characterized by a certain mental inertia and indolence. He was tranquil, and had on the whole the temperament of a phlegmatic. He was not irritable, not quarrelsome, went quietly about his farm-work, and left the care of his business and housekeeping to other people. In short, he gave one the impression of a placid countryman, who has no interests beyond his work." Dr. Winter adds that in studying the case he paid no particular attention to the man's psychic condition, as this seemed *"nebensächlich"* to his main purpose. I should add that the form of my question to Dr. Winter could give him no clue as to the kind of answer I expected.

Of course, this case proves nothing, but it is to be hoped that asylum-physicians and nervous specialists may begin methodically to study the relation between anaesthesia and emotional apathy. If the hypothesis here suggested is ever to be definitively confirmed or disproved it seems as if it must be by them, for they alone have the data in their hands.

P.S.—By an unpardonable forgetfulness at the time of dispatching my MS. to the Editor, I ignored the existence of the extraordinary case of total anaesthesia published by Professor Strümpell in Ziemssen's *Deutsches Archiv für klinische Medicin,* xxii, 321, of which I had nevertheless read reports at the time of its publication. [*Cf.* first report of the case in MIND, III (No. 10), 263, translated from Pflüger's *Archiv.* ED.] I believe that it constitutes the only remaining case of the sort in medical literature, so that with it our survey is complete. On referring to the original, which is important in many connections, I found that the patient, a shoemaker's apprentice of 15, entirely anaesthetic, inside and out, with the exception of one eye and one ear, had shown *shame* on the occasion of soiling his bed, and *grief,* when a formerly favorite dish was set before him, at the thought that he could no longer taste its flavor. As Dr. Strümpell seemed however to have paid no special attention to his psychic states, so far as these are matter for our theory, I wrote to him in a few words what the essence of the theory was, and asked him to say whether he felt sure the grief and shame mentioned were real feelings in the boy's mind, or only the reflex manifestations provoked by certain perceptions, manifestations that an outside observer might note, but to which the boy himself might be insensible.

Dr. Strümpell has sent me a very obliging reply, of which I translate the most important passage.

"I must indeed confess that I naturally failed to institute with my *Anaesthetiker* observations as special as the sense of your theory would require. Nevertheless I think I can decidedly make the statement, that he was by no means completely lacking in emotional affections. In addition to the feelings of *grief* and *shame* mentioned in my paper, I recall distinctly that he showed *e.g., anger,* and frequently quarrelled with the hospital attendants. He also manifested *fear* lest I should punish him. In short, I do not think that my case speaks exactly in favor of your theory. On the other hand, I will not affirm that it positively refutes your theory. For my case was certainly one of a very centrally conditioned anaesthesia (perception-anaesthesia, like that of hysterics) and therefore the conduction of outward impressions may in him have been undisturbed."

I confess that I do not see the relevancy of the last consideration, and this makes me suspect that my own letter was too briefly or obscurely expressed to put my correspondent fully in possession of my own thought. For his reply still makes no explicit reference to anything but the outward manifestations of emotion in the boy. Is it not at least conceivable that, just as a stranger, brought into the boy's presence for the first time, and seeing him eat and drink and satisfy other natural necessities, would suppose him to have the feelings of hunger, thirst, etc., until informed by the boy himself that he did all these things with no feeling at all but that of sight and sound—is it not, I say, at least possible, that Dr. Strümpell, addressing no direct introspective questions to his patient, and the patient not being of a class from which one could expect voluntary revelations of that sort, should have similarly omitted to discriminate between a feeling and its habitual motor accompaniment, and erroneously taken the latter as proof that the former was there? Such a mistake is of course possible, and I must therefore repeat Dr. Strümpell's own words, that his case does not yet refute my theory. Should a similar case recur, it ought to be interrogated as to the inward emotional state that coexisted with the outward expressions of shame, anger, etc. And if it then turned out that the patient recognized explicitly the same mood of feeling known under those names in his former normal state, my theory would of course fall. It is, however, to me incredible that the patient should have an *identical* feeling, for the dropping out of the organic sounding-board would necessarily diminish its volume in some way. The teacher of Dr. Strümpell's patient found a mental deficiency in him during his anaesthesia, that may possibly have been due to the consequences resulting to his general intellectual vivacity from the subtraction of so important a mass of feelings, even though they were not the whole of his emotional life. Whoever wishes to extract from the next case of total anaesthesia the maximum of knowledge about the emotions, will have to interrogate the patient with some such notion as that of my article in his mind. We can define the pure psychic emotions far better by starting from such an hypothesis and modifying it in the way of restriction and subtraction, than by having no definite hypothesis at all. Thus will the publication of my article have been justified, even though the theory it advocates, rigorously taken, be erroneous. The best thing I can say for it is, that in writing it, I have almost persuaded *myself* it may be true.

2

The Dilemma of Determinism

First given as a talk at the Harvard Divinity School in March 1884, "The Dilemma of Determinism" is a clever and hard-to-dislodge argument that in many, perhaps most, of our life situations, we are free to choose between alternatives. James means to attack all forms of determinism, such as the philosophic-theological (everything has been preordained), the behavioral (we are automata ruled by reflex action), or the genetic (we are born with certain predispositions). Not content with demolition, James champions and celebrates the alternative to determinism, which is, he says, the role of chance.

He begins with verve, and with the disarming confession that he has no desire to coerce the reader into accepting his argument. If we are truly free, we should feel free to accept or reject his argument. James carries the day—and the reader—when he says, "our first act of freedom, if we are free, ought . . . to be to affirm that we are free." Chance, a key Darwinian force, is the opposite of determinism. If everything were predetermined, there would be no role for chance at all. As he does so often, James presses his case in narrative, testimonial fashion, making his point with a story. He cites "the confession of the murderer at Brockton the other day: how, to get rid of the wife whose continued existence bored him, he inveigled her into a desert spot, shot her four times, and then, as she lay on the ground and said to him, 'You didn't do it on purpose, did you, dear?' replied, 'No, I didn't do it on purpose,' as he raised a rock and smashed her skull."

For a determinist, this was all preordained, unchangeable, fated, determined, "all necessary from eternity; and nothing else for a moment had a ghost of a chance of being put into their place." We are reluctant, James says, to go along with this, preferring to believe that there was at least a chance of things turning out better. Accepting the possibility of chance does not mean accepting a world that is random. It means realizing that chance is another word for freedom, for the view that things can go this way or that way. James lowers the heat from his murderous example to declare mildly that his listeners are free to leave by either of the doors to the auditorium. At worst, we can live as if free. Freedom is the same thing as chance, and chance, says James, is the same thing as gift, meaning "anything on which we have no effective *claim*."

James's Divinity School audience might reasonably have concluded from his talk that chance was not only a gift, it was *the* gift, perhaps resembling grace too much to really be anything else.

—————◆—————

A COMMON opinion prevails that the juice has ages ago been pressed out of the free-will controversy, and that no new champion can do more than warm up stale arguments which everyone has heard. This is a radical mistake. I know of no subject less worn out, or in which inventive genius has a better chance of breaking open new ground—not, perhaps, of forcing a conclusion or of coercing assent, but of deepening our sense of what the issue between the two parties really is, of what the ideas of fate and of free-will imply. At our very side almost, in the past few years, we have seen falling in rapid succession from the press works that present the alternative in entirely novel lights. Not to speak of the English disciples of Hegel, such as Green and Bradley; not to speak of Hinton and Hodgson, nor of Hazard here—we see in the writings of Renouvier, Fouillée, and Delboeuf[1] how completely changed and refreshed is the form of all the old disputes. I cannot pretend to vie in originality with any of the masters I have named, and my ambition limits itself to just one little point. If I can make two of the necessarily implied corollaries of determinism clearer to you than they have been made before, I shall have made it possible for you to decide for or against that doctrine with a better understanding of what you are about. And if you prefer not to decide at all, but to remain doubters, you will at least see more plainly what the subject of your hesitation is. I thus disclaim openly on the threshold all pretension to prove to you that the freedom of the will is true. The most I hope is to induce some of you to follow my own ex-ample in assuming it true, and acting as if it were true. If it be true, it seems to me that this is involved in the strict logic of the case. Its truth ought not to be forced willy-nilly down our indifferent throats. It ought to be freely espoused by men who can equally well turn their backs upon it. In other words, our first act of freedom, if we are free, ought in all inward propriety to be to affirm that we are free. This should ex-clude, it seems to me, from the free-will side of the question all hope of a coercive demonstration—a demonstration which I, for one, am per-fectly contented to go without.

With thus much understood at the outset, we can advance. But not without one more point understood as well. The arguments I am about to urge all proceed on two suppositions: first, when we make theories about the world and discuss them with one another, we do so in order to attain a conception of things which shall give us subjective satisfac-tion; and, second, if there be two conceptions, and the one seems to us, on the whole, more rational than the other, we are entitled to suppose that the more rational one is the truer of the two. I hope that you are all willing to make these suppositions with me; for I am afraid that if there be any of you here who are not, they will find little edification in the rest of what I have to say. I cannot stop to argue the point; but I myself believe that all the magnificent achievements of mathematical and phys-ical science—our doctrines of evolution, of uniformity of law, and the rest—proceed from our indomitable desire to cast the world into a more rational shape in our minds than the shape into which it is thrown there by the crude order of our experience. The world has shown itself, to a great extent, plastic to this demand of ours for rationality. How much farther it will show itself plastic no one can say. Our only means of find-ing out is to try; and I, for one, feel as free to try conceptions of moral as of mechanical or of logical rationality. If a certain formula for expressing the nature of the world violates my moral demand, I shall feel as free to throw it overboard, or at least to doubt it, as if it disappointed my de-mand for uniformity of sequence, for example; the one demand being, so far as I can see, quite as subjective and emotional as the other is. The principle of causality, for example—what is it but a postulate, an empty name covering simply a demand that the sequence of events shall some day manifest a deeper kind of belonging of one thing with another than the mere arbitrary juxtaposition which now phenomenally appears? It is as much an altar to an unknown god as the one that Saint Paul found at Athens. All our scientific and philosophic ideals are altars to unknown gods. Uniformity is as much so as is free-will. If this be admitted, we can debate on even terms. But if anyone pretends that while freedom and variety are, in the first instance, subjective demands, necessity and uniformity are something altogether different, I do not see how we can debate at all.[2]

To begin, then, I must suppose you acquainted with all the usual arguments on the subject. I cannot stop to take up the old proofs from causation, from statistics, from the certainty with which we can foretell one another's conduct, from the fixity of character, and all the rest. But there are two *words* which usually encumber these classical arguments, and which we must immediately dispose of if we are to make any progress. One is the eulogistic word *freedom,* and the other is the opprobrious word *chance.* The word "chance" I wish to keep, but I wish to get rid of the word "freedom." Its eulogistic associations have so far overshadowed all the rest of its meaning that both parties claim the sole right to use it, and determinists to-day insist that they alone are freedom's champions. Old-fashioned determinism was what we may call *hard* determinism. It did not shrink from such words as fatality, bondage of the will, necessitation, and the like. Nowadays, we have a *soft* determinism which abhors harsh words, and, repudiating fatality, necessity, and even predetermination, says that its real name is freedom; for freedom is only necessity understood, and bondage to the highest is identical with true freedom. Even a writer as little used to making capital out of soft words as Mr. Hodgson hesitates not to call himself a "free-will determinist."

Now, all this is a quagmire of evasion under which the real issue of fact has been entirely smothered. Freedom in all these senses presents simply no problem at all. No matter what the soft determinist mean by it—whether he mean the acting without external constraint, whether he mean the acting rightly, or whether he mean the acquiescing in the law of the whole—who cannot answer him that sometimes we are free and sometimes we are not? But there *is* a problem, an issue of fact and not of words, an issue of the most momentous importance, which is often decided without discussion in one sentence—nay, in one clause of a sentence—by those very writers who spin out whole chapters in their efforts to show what "true" freedom is; and that is the question of determinism, about which we are to talk to-night.

Fortunately, no ambiguities hang about this word or about its opposite, indeterminism. Both designate an outward way in which things may happen, and their cold and mathematical sound has no sentimental associations that can bribe our partiality either way in advance. Now, evidence of an external kind to decide between determinism and indeterminism is, as I intimated a while back, strictly impossible to find. Let us look at the difference between them and see for ourselves. What does determinism profess?

It professes that those parts of the universe already laid down absolutely appoint and decree what the other parts shall be. The future has no ambiguous possibilities hidden in its womb: the part we call the present is compatible with only one totality. Any other future complement than the one fixed from eternity is impossible. The whole is in each and every part, and welds it with the rest into an absolute unity, an iron block, in which there can be no equivocation or shadow of turning.

> "With Earth's first Clay They did the Last Man knead,
> And there of the Last Harvest sow'd the Seed;
>   And the first Morning of Creation wrote
> What the Last Dawn of Reckoning shall read."

Indeterminism, on the contrary, says that the parts have a certain amount of loose play on one another, so that the laying down of one of them does not necessarily determine what the others shall be. It admits that possibilities may be in excess of actualities, and that things not yet revealed to our knowledge may really in themselves be ambiguous. Of two alternative futures which we conceive, both may now be really possible; and the one become impossible only at the very moment when the other excludes it by becoming real itself. Indeterminism thus denies the world to be one unbending unit of fact. It says there is a certain ultimate pluralism in it; and, so saying, it corroborates our ordinary unsophisticated view of things. To that view, actualities seem to float in a wider sea of possibilities from out of which they are chosen; and, *somewhere*, indeterminism says, such possibilities exist, and form a part of truth.

Determinism, on the contrary, says they exist *nowhere*, and that necessity on the one hand and impossibility on the other are the sole categories of the real. Possibilities that fail to get realized are, for determinism, pure illusions: they never were possibilities at all. There is nothing inchoate, it says, about this universe of ours, all that was or is or shall be actual in it having been from eternity virtually there. The cloud of alternatives our minds escort this mass of actuality withal is a cloud of sheer deceptions, to which "impossibilities" is the only name that rightfully belongs.

The issue, it will be seen, is a perfectly sharp one, which no eulogistic terminology can smear over or wipe out. The truth *must* lie with one side or the other, and its lying with one side makes the other false.

The question relates solely to the existence of possibilities, in the strict sense of the term, as things that may, but need not, be. Both sides admit that a volition, for instance, has occurred. The indeterminists say another volition might have occurred in its place: the determinists swear that nothing could possibly have occurred in its place. Now can science be called in to tell us which of these two point-blank contradicters of each other is right? Science professes to draw no conclusions but such as are based on matters of fact, things that have actually happened; but how can any amount of assurance that something actually happened give us the least grain of information as to whether another thing might or might not have happened in its place? Only facts can be proved by other facts. With things that are possibilities and not facts, facts have no concern. If we have no other evidence than the evidence of existing facts, the possibility-question must remain a mystery never to be cleared up.

And the truth is that facts practically have hardly anything to do with making us either determinists or indeterminists. Sure enough, we make a flourish of quoting facts this way or that; and if we are determinists, we talk about the infallibility with which we can predict one another's conduct; while if we are indeterminists, we lay great stress on the fact that it is just because we cannot foretell one another's conduct, either in war or statecraft or in any of the great and small intrigues and businesses of men, that life is so intensely anxious and hazardous a game. But who does not see the wretched insufficiency of this so-called objective testimony on both sides? What fills up the gaps in our minds is something not objective, not external. What divides us into possibility men and anti-possibility men is different faiths or postulates—postulates of rationality. To this man the world seems more rational with possibilities in it—to that man more rational with possibilities excluded; and talk as we will about having to yield to evidence, what makes us monists or pluralists, determinists or indeterminists, is at bottom always some sentiment like this.

The stronghold of the deterministic sentiment is the antipathy to the idea of chance. As soon as we begin to talk indeterminism to our friends, we find a number of them shaking their heads. This notion of alternative possibility, they say, this admission that any one of several things may come to pass, is, after all, only a roundabout name for chance; and chance is something the notion of which no sane mind can for an instant tolerate in the world. What is it, they ask, but barefaced crazy unreason, the negation of intelligibility and law? And if the slightest particle of it exist anywhere, what is to prevent the whole fabric from falling together, the stars from going out, and chaos from recommencing her topsy-turvy reign?

Remarks of this sort about chance will put an end to discussion as quickly as anything one can find. I have already told you that "chance" was a word I wished to keep and use. Let us then examine exactly what it means, and see whether it ought to be such a terrible bugbear to us. I fancy that squeezing the thistle boldly will rob it of its sting.

The sting of the word "chance" seems to lie in the assumption that it means something positive, and that if anything happens by chance, it must needs be something of an intrinsically irrational and preposterous sort. Now chance means nothing of the kind. It is a purely negative and relative term,[3] giving us no information about that of which it is predicated, except that it happens to be disconnected with something else—not controlled, secured, or necessitated by other things in advance of its own actual presence. As this point is the most subtle one of the whole lecture, and at the same time the point on which all the rest hinges, I beg you to pay particular attention to it. What I say is that it tells us nothing about what a thing may be in itself to call it "chance." It may be a bad thing, it may be a good thing. It may be lucidity, transparency, fitness incarnate, matching the whole system of other things, when it has once befallen, in an unimaginably perfect way. All you mean by calling it "chance" is that this is not guaranteed, that it may also fall out otherwise. For the system of other things has no positive hold on the chance-thing. Its origin is in a certain fashion negative: it escapes, and says, Hands off! coming, when it comes, as a free gift, or not at all.

This negativeness, however, and this opacity of the chance-thing when thus considered *ab extra*, or from the point of view of previous things or distant things, do not preclude its having any amount of positiveness and luminosity from within, and at its own place and moment. All that its chance-character asserts about it is that there is something in it really of its own, something that is not the unconditional property of the whole. If the whole wants this property, the whole must wait till it can get it, if it be a matter of chance. That the universe may actually be a sort of joint-stock society of this sort, in which the sharers have both limited liabilities and limited powers, is of course a simple and conceivable notion.

Nevertheless, many persons talk as if the minutest dose of disconnectedness of one part with another, the smallest modicum of independence, the faintest tremor of ambiguity about the future, for example, would ruin everything, and turn this goodly universe into a sort of insane sand-heap or nulliverse, no universe at all. Since future human volitions are as a matter of fact the only ambiguous things we are tempted to believe in, let us stop for a moment to make ourselves sure whether their independent and accidental character need be fraught with such direful consequences to the universe as these.

What is meant by saying that my choice of which way to walk home after the lecture is ambiguous and matter of chance as far as the present moment is concerned? It means that both Divinity Avenue and Oxford Street are called; but that only one, and that one *either* one, shall be chosen. Now, I ask you seriously to suppose that this ambiguity of my choice is real; and then to make the impossible hypothesis that the choice is made twice over, and each time falls on a different street. In other words, imagine that I first walk through Divinity Avenue, and then imagine that the powers governing the universe annihilate ten minutes of time with all that it contained, and set me back at the door of this hall just as I was before the choice was made. Imagine then that, everything else being the same, I now make a different choice and traverse Oxford

Street. You, as passive spectators, look on and see the two alternative universes—one of them with me walking through Divinity Avenue in it, the other with the same me walking through Oxford Street. Now, if you are determinists you believe one of these universes to have been from eternity impossible: you believe it to have been impossible because of the intrinsic irrationality or accidentality somewhere involved in it. But looking outwardly at these universes, can you say which is the impossible and accidental one, and which the rational and necessary one? I doubt if the most iron-clad determinist among you could have the slightest glimmer of light on this point. In other words, either universe *after the fact* and once there would, to our means of observation and understanding, appear just as rational as the other. There would be absolutely no criterion by which we might judge one necessary and the other matter of chance. Suppose now we relieve the gods of their hypothetical task and assume my choice, once made, to be made forever. I go through Divinity Avenue for good and all. If, as good determinists, you now begin to affirm, what all good determinists punctually do affirm, that in the nature of things I *couldn't* have gone through Oxford Street—had I done so it would have been chance, irrationality, insanity, a horrid gap in nature—I simply call your attention to this, that your affirmation is what the Germans call a *Machtspruch*, a mere conception fulminated as a dogma and based on no insight into details. Before my choice, either street seemed as natural to you as to me. Had I happened to take Oxford Street, Divinity Avenue would have figured in your philosophy as the gap in nature; and you would have so proclaimed it with the best deterministic conscience in the world.

But what a hollow outcry, then, is this against a chance which, if it were present to us, we could by no character whatever distinguish from a rational necessity! I have taken the most trivial of examples, but no possible example could lead to any different result. For what are the alternatives which, in point of fact, offer themselves to human volition? What are those futures that now seem matters of chance? Are they not one and all like the Divinity Avenue and Oxford Street of our example? Are they not all of them *kinds* of things already here and based in the existing frame of nature? Is anyone ever tempted to produce an *absolute* accident, something utterly irrelevant to the rest of the world? Do not all the motives that assail us, all the futures that offer themselves to our choice, spring equally from the soil of the past; and would not either one of them, whether realized through chance or through necessity, the moment it was realized, seem to us to fit that past, and in the completest and most continuous manner to interdigitate with the phenomena already there?[4]

The more one thinks of the matter, the more one wonders that so empty and gratuitous a hubbub as this outcry against chance should have found so great an echo in the hearts of men. It is a word which tells us absolutely nothing about what chances, or about the *modus operandi* of the chancing; and the use of it as a war-cry shows only a temper of intellectual absolutism, a demand that the world shall be a solid block, subject to one control—which temper, which demand, the world may not be bound to gratify at all. In every outwardly verifiable and practical respect, a world in which the alternatives that now actually distract *your* choice were decided by pure chance would be by *me* absolutely undistinguished from the world in which I now live. I am, therefore, entirely willing to call it, so far as your choices go, a world of chance for me. To *yourselves*, it is true, those very acts of choice, which to me are so blind, opaque, and external, are the opposites of this, for you are within them and effect them. To you they appear as decisions; and decisions, for him who makes them, are altogether peculiar psychic facts. Self-luminous and self-justifying at the living moment at which they occur, they appeal to no outside moment to put its stamp upon them or make them continuous with the rest of nature. Themselves it is rather who seem to make nature continuous; and in their strange and intense function of granting consent to one possibility and withholding it from another, to transform an equivocal and double future into an inalterable and simple past.

But with the psychology of the matter we have no concern this evening. The quarrel which determinism has with chance fortunately has nothing to do with this or that psychological detail. It is a quarrel altogether metaphysical. Determinism denies the ambiguity of future volitions, because it affirms that nothing future can be ambiguous. But we have said enough to meet the issue. Indeterminate future volitions *do* mean chance. Let us not fear to shout it from the house-tops if need be; for we now know that the idea of chance is, at bottom, exactly the same thing as the idea of gift—the one simply being a disparaging, and the other a eulogistic, name for anything on which we have no effective *claim*. And whether the world be the better or the worse for having either chances or gifts in it will depend altogether on *what* these uncertain and unclaimable things turn out to be.

And this at last brings us within sight of our subject. We have seen what determinism means: we have seen that indeterminism is rightly described as meaning chance; and we have seen that chance, the very name of which we are urged to shrink from as from a metaphysical pestilence, means only the negative fact that no part of the world, however big, can claim to control absolutely the destinies of the whole. But although, in discussing the word "chance," I may at moments have seemed to be arguing for its real existence, I have not meant to do so yet. We have not yet ascertained whether this be a world of chance or no; at most, we have agreed that it seems so. And I now repeat what I said at the outset, that, from any strict theoretical point of view, the question is insoluble. To deepen our theoretic sense of the *difference* between a world with chances in it and a deterministic world is the most I can hope to do; and this I may now at last begin upon, after all our tedious clearing of the way.

I wish first of all to show you just what the notion that this is a deterministic world implies. The implications I call your attention to are all bound up with the fact that it is a world in which we constantly have to make what I shall, with your permission, call judgments of regret. Hardly an hour passes in which we do not wish that something might be otherwise; and happy indeed are those of us whose hearts have never echoed the wish of Omar Khayyam,

> "That we might catch ere closed the Book of Fate,
>   And make The Writer on a fairer leaf
> Inscribe our names, or quite obliterate!
>
> "Ah Love! could you and I with Fate conspire
> To grasp this sorry Scheme of Things entire,
>   Would not we shatter it to bits—and then
> Re-mould it nearer to the Heart's Desire!"

Now, it is undeniable that most of these regrets are foolish, and quite on a par in point of philosophic value with the criticisms on the universe of that friend of our infancy, the hero of the fable "The Atheist and the Acorn,"

> "Fool! had that bough a pumpkin bore,
> Thy whimsies would have worked no more," etc.

Even from the point of view of our own ends, we should probably make a botch of remodelling the universe. How much more then from the point of view of ends we cannot see! Wise men therefore regret as little as they can. But still some regrets are pretty obstinate and hard to stifle—regrets for acts of wanton cruelty or treachery, for example, whether performed by others or by ourselves. Hardly anyone can remain *entirely* optimistic after reading the confession of the murderer at Brockton the other day: how, to get rid of the wife whose continued existence bored him, he inveigled her into a desert spot, shot her four times, and then, as she lay on the ground and said to him, "You didn't do it on purpose, did you, dear?" replied, "No, I didn't do it on purpose," as he raised a rock and smashed her skull. Such an occurrence, with the mild sentence and self-satisfaction of the prisoner, is a field for a crop of regrets, which one need not take up in detail. We feel that, although a perfect mechanical fit to the rest of the universe, it is a bad moral fit, and that something else would really have been better in its place.

But for the deterministic philosophy the murder, the sentence, and the prisoner's optimism were all necessary from eternity; and nothing else for a moment had a ghost of a chance of being put into their place. To admit such a chance, the determinists tell us, would be to make a suicide of reason; so we must steel our hearts against the thought. And here our plot thickens, for we see the first of those difficult implications of determinism and monism which it is my purpose to make you feel. If this Brockton murder was called for by the rest of the universe, if it had to come at its preappointed hour, and if nothing else would have been consistent with the sense of the whole, what are we to think of the universe? Are we stubbornly to stick to our judgment of regret, and say, though it *couldn't* be, yet it *would* have been a better universe with something different from this Brockton murder in it? That, of course, seems the natural and spontaneous thing for us to do; and yet it is nothing short of deliberately espousing a kind of pessimism. The judgment of regret calls the murder bad. Calling a thing bad means, if it means any-thing at all, that the thing ought not to be, that something else ought to be in its stead. Determinism, in denying that anything else can be in its stead, virtually defines the universe as a place in which what ought to be is impossible—in other words, as an organism whose constitution is afflicted with an incurable taint, an irremediable flaw. The pessimism of a Schopenhauer says no more than this—that the murder is a symptom; and that it is a vicious symptom because it belongs to a vicious whole, which can express its nature no otherwise than by bringing forth just such a symptom as that at this particular spot. Regret for the murder must transform itself, if we are determinists and wise, into a larger re-gret. It is absurd to regret the murder alone. Other things being what they are, *it* could not be different. What we should regret is that whole frame of things of which the murder is one member. I see no escape whatever from this pessimistic conclusion, if, being determinists, our judgment of regret is to be allowed to stand at all.

The only deterministic escape from pessimism is everywhere to abandon the judgment of regret. That this can be done, history shows to be not impossible. The devil, *quoad existentiam,* may be good. That is, al-though he be a *principle* of evil, yet the universe, with such a principle in it, may practically be a better universe than it could have been without. On every hand, in a small way, we find that a certain amount of evil is a condition by which a higher form of good is bought. There is nothing to prevent anybody from generalizing this view, and trusting that if we could but see things in the largest of all ways, even such matters as this Brockton murder would appear to be paid for by the uses that follow in their train. An optimism *quand même,* a systematic and infatuated opti-mism like that ridiculed by Voltaire in his *Candide,* is one of the possible ideal ways in which a man may train himself to look on life. Bereft of dogmatic hardness and lit up with the expression of a tender and pa-thetic hope, such an optimism has been the grace of some of the most religious characters that ever lived.

> "Throb thine with Nature's throbbing breast,
> And all is clear from east to west."

Even cruelty and treachery may be among the absolutely blessed fruits of time, and to quarrel with any of their details may be blasphemy.

The only real blasphemy, in short, may be that pessimistic temper of the soul which lets it give way to such things as regrets, remorse, and grief.

Thus, our deterministic pessimism may become a deterministic optimism at the price of extinguishing our judgments of regret.

But does not this immediately bring us into a curious logical predicament? Our determinism leads us to call our judgments of regret wrong, because they are pessimistic in implying that what is impossible yet ought to be. But how then about the judgments of regret themselves? If they are wrong, other judgments, judgments of approval presumably, ought to be in their place. But as they are necessitated, nothing else *can* be in their place; and the universe is just what it was before—namely, a place in which what ought to be appears impossible. We have got one foot out of the pessimistic bog, but the other one sinks all the deeper. We have rescued our actions from the bonds of evil, but our judgments are now held fast. When murders and treacheries cease to be sins, regrets are theoretic absurdities and errors. The theoretic and the active life thus play a kind of see-saw with each other on the ground of evil. The rise of either sends the other down. Murder and treachery cannot be good without regret being bad: regret cannot be good without treachery and murder being bad. Both, however, are supposed to have been foredoomed; so something must be fatally unreasonable, absurd, and wrong in the world. It must be a place of which either sin or error forms a necessary part. From this dilemma there seems at first sight no escape. Are we then so soon to fall back into the pessimism from which we thought we had emerged? And is there no possible way by which we may, with good intellectual consciences, call the cruelties and the treacheries, the reluctances and the regrets, *all* good together?

Certainly there is such a way, and you are probably most of you ready to formulate it yourselves. But, before doing so, remark how inevitably the question of determinism and indeterminism slides us into the question of optimism and pessimism, or, as our fathers called it, "the question of evil." The theological form of all these disputes is the simplest and the deepest, the form from which there is the least escape—not because, as some have sarcastically said, remorse and regret are clung to with a morbid fondness by the theologians as spiritual luxuries, but because they are existing facts of the world, and as such must be taken into account in the deterministic interpretation of all that is fated to be. If they are fated to be error, does not the bat's wing of irrationality still cast its shadow over the world?

The refuge from the quandary lies, as I said, not far off. The necessary acts we erroneously regret may be good, and yet our error in so regretting them may be also good, on one simple condition; and that condition is this: The world must not be regarded as a machine whose final purpose is the making real of any outward good, but rather as a contrivance for deepening the theoretic consciousness of what goodness and evil in their intrinsic natures are. Not the doing either of good or of evil is what nature cares for, but the knowing of them. Life is one long eating of the fruit of the tree of *knowledge*. I am in the habit, in thinking to myself, of calling this point of view the *gnostical* point of view. According to it, the world is neither an optimism nor a pessimism, but a *gnosticism*. But as this term may perhaps lead to some misunderstandings, I will use it as little as possible here, and speak rather of *subjectivism,* and the *subjectivistic* point of view.

Subjectivism has three great branches—we may call them scientificism, sentimentalism, and sensualism, respectively. They all agree essentially about the universe, in deeming that what happens there is subsidiary to what we think or feel about it. Crime justifies its criminality by awakening our intelligence of that criminality, and eventually our remorses and regrets; and the error included in remorses and regrets, the error of supposing that the past could have been different, justifies itself by its use. Its use is to quicken our sense of *what* the irretrievably lost is. When we think of it as that which might have been ("the saddest words of tongue or pen"), the quality of its worth speaks to us with a wilder sweetness; and, conversely, the dissatisfaction wherewith we think of what seems to have driven it from its natural place gives us the severer pang. Admirable artifice of nature! we might be tempted to exclaim—deceiving us in order the better to enlighten us, and leaving nothing undone to accentuate to our consciousness the yawning distance of those opposite poles of good and evil between which creation swings.

We have thus clearly revealed to our view what may be called the dilemma of determinism, so far as determinism pretends to think things out at all. A merely mechanical determinism, it is true, rather rejoices in not thinking them out. It is very sure that the universe must satisfy its postulate of a physical continuity and coherence, but it smiles at anyone who comes forward with a postulate of moral coherence as well. I may suppose, however, that the number of purely mechanical or hard determinists among you this evening is small. The determinism to whose seductions you are most exposed is what I have called soft determinism—the determinism which allows considerations of good and bad to mingle with those of cause and effect in deciding what sort of a universe this may rationally be held to be. The dilemma of this determinism is one whose left horn is pessimism and whose right horn is subjectivism. In other words, if determinism is to escape pessimism, it must leave off looking at the goods and ills of life in a simple objective way, and regard them as materials, indifferent in themselves, for the production of consciousness, scientific and ethical, in us.

To escape pessimism is, as we all know, no easy task. Your own studies have sufficiently shown you the almost desperate difficulty of making the notion that there is a single principle of things, and that principle absolute perfection, rhyme together with our daily vision of the facts of life. If perfection be the principle, how comes there any imperfection here? If God be good, how came he to create—or, if he did not create, how comes he to permit—the devil? The evil facts must be explained as seeming: the devil must be whitewashed, the universe must be disinfected, if neither God's goodness nor his unity and power are to remain impugned. And of all the various ways of operating the disinfection, and making bad seem less bad, the way of subjectivism appears by far the best.[5]

For, after all, is there not something rather absurd in our ordinary notion of external things being good or bad in themselves? Can murders and treacheries, considered as mere outward happenings, or motions of matter, be bad without anyone to feel their badness? And could paradise properly be good in the absence of a sentient principle by which the goodness was perceived? Outward goods and evils seem practically indistinguishable except in so far as they result in getting moral judgments made about them. But then the moral judgments seem the main thing, and the outward facts mere perishing instruments for their production. This is subjectivism. Everyone must at some time have wondered at that strange paradox of our moral nature, that, though the pursuit of outward good is the breath of its nostrils, the attainment of outward good would seem to be its suffocation and death. Why does the painting of any paradise or Utopia, in heaven or on earth, awaken such yawnings for nirvana and escape? The white-robed harp-playing heaven of our sabbath-schools, and the ladylike tea-table elysium represented in Mr. Spencer's *Data of Ethics,* as the final consummation of progress, are exactly on a par in this respect—lubberlands, pure and simple, one and all.[6] We look upon them from this delicious mess of insanities and realities, strivings and deadnesses, hopes and fears, agonies and exultations, which forms our present state, and *tedium vitae* is the only sentiment they awaken in our breasts. To our crepuscular natures, born for the conflict, the Rembrandtesque moral chiaroscuro, the shifting struggle of the sunbeam in the gloom, such pictures of light upon light are vacuous and expressionless, and neither to be enjoyed nor understood. If *this* be the whole fruit of the victory, we say; if the generations of mankind suffered and laid down their lives; if prophets confessed and martyrs sang in the fire, and all the sacred tears were shed for no other end than that a race of creatures of such unexampled insipidity should succeed, and protract *in saecula saeculorum* their contented and inoffensive lives—why, at such a rate, better lose than win the battle, or at all events better ring down the curtain before the last act of the play, so that a business that began so importantly may be saved from so singularly flat a winding-up.

All this is what I should instantly say, were I called on to plead for gnosticism; and its real friends, of whom you will presently perceive I am not one, would say without difficulty a great deal more. Regarded as a stable finality, every outward good becomes a mere weariness to the flesh. It must be menaced, be occasionally lost, for its goodness to be fully felt as such. Nay, more than occasionally lost. No one knows the worth of innocence till he knows it is gone forever, and that money cannot buy it back. Not the saint, but the sinner that repenteth, is he to whom the full length and breadth, and height and depth, of life's meaning is revealed. Not the absence of vice, but vice there, and virtue holding her by the throat, seems the ideal human state. And there seems no reason to suppose it not a permanent human state. There is a deep truth in what the school of Schopenhauer insists on—the illusoriness of the notion of moral progress. The more brutal forms of evil that go are replaced by others more subtle and more poisonous. Our moral horizon moves with us as we move, and never do we draw nearer to the far-off line where the black waves and the azure meet. The final purpose of our creation seems most plausibly to be the greatest possible enrichment of our ethical consciousness, through the intensest play of contrasts and the widest diversity of characters. This of course obliges some of us to be vessels of wrath, whilst it calls others to be vessels of honor. But the subjectivist point of view reduces all these outward distinctions to a common denominator. The wretch languishing in the felon's cell may be drinking draughts of the wine of truth that will never pass the lips of the so-called favorite of fortune. And the peculiar consciousness of each of them is an indispensable note in the great ethical concert which the centuries as they roll are grinding out of the living heart of man.

So much for subjectivism! If the dilemma of determinism be to choose between it and pessimism, I see little room for hesitation from the strictly theoretical point of view. Subjectivism seems the more rational scheme. And the world may, possibly, for aught I know, be nothing else. When the healthy love of life is on one, and all its forms and its appetites seem so unutterably real; when the most brutal and the most spiritual things are lit by the same sun, and each is an integral part of the total richness—why, then it seems a grudging and sickly way of meeting so robust a universe to shrink from any of its facts and wish them not to be. Rather take the strictly dramatic point of view, and treat the whole thing as a great unending romance which the spirit of the universe, striving to realize its own content, is eternally thinking out and representing to itself.[7]

No one, I hope, will accuse me, after I have said all this, of underrating the reasons in favor of subjectivism. And now that I proceed to say why those reasons, strong as they are, fail to convince my own mind, I trust the presumption may be that my objections are stronger still.

I frankly confess that they are of a practical order. If we practically take up subjectivism in a sincere and radical manner and follow its consequences, we meet with some that make us pause. Let a subjectivism begin in never so severe and intellectual a way, it is forced by the law of its nature to develop another side of itself and end with the corruptest curiosity. Once dismiss the notion that certain duties are good in themselves, and that we are here to do them, no matter how we feel about them; once consecrate the opposite notion that our performances and our violations of duty are for a common purpose, the attainment of subjective knowledge and feeling, and that the deepening of these is the chief end of our lives—and at what point on the downward slope are we to stop? In theology, subjectivism develops as its "left wing" antinomianism. In literature, its left wing is romanticism. And in practical life it is either a nerveless sentimentality or a sensualism without bounds.

Everywhere it fosters the fatalistic mood of mind. It makes those who are already too inert more passive still; it renders wholly reckless those whose energy is already in excess. All through history we find how subjectivism, as soon as it has a free career, exhausts itself in every sort of spiritual, moral, and practical license. Its optimism turns to an ethical indifference, which infallibly brings dissolution in its train. It is perfectly safe to say now that if the hegelian gnosticism, which has begun to show itself here and in Great Britain, were to become a popular philosophy, as it once was in Germany, it would certainly develop its left wing here as there, and produce a reaction of disgust. Already I have heard a graduate of this very school express in the pulpit his willingness to sin like David, if only he might repent like David. You may tell me he was only sowing his wild, or rather his tame, oats; and perhaps he was. But the point is that in the subjectivistic or gnostical philosophy oatsowing, wild or tame, becomes a systematic necessity and the chief function of life. After the pure and classic truths, the exciting and rancid ones must be experienced; and if the stupid virtues of the philistine herd do not then come in and save society from the influence of the children of light, a sort of inward putrefaction becomes its inevitable doom.

Look at the last runnings of the romantic school, as we see them in that strange contemporary Parisian literature, with which we of the less clever countries are so often driven to rinse out our minds after they have become clogged with the dulness and heaviness of our native pursuits. The romantic school began with the worship of subjective sensibility and the revolt against legality of which Rousseau was the first great prophet; and through various fluxes and refluxes, right wings and left wings, it stands to-day with two men of genius, M. Renan and M. Zola, as its principal exponents—one speaking with its masculine, and the other with what might be called its feminine, voice. I prefer not to think now of less noble members of the school, and the Renan I have in mind is of course the Renan of latest dates. As I have used the term gnostic, both he and Zola are gnostics of the most pronounced sort. Both are athirst for the facts of life, and both think the facts of human sensibility to be of all facts the most worthy of attention. Both agree, moreover, that sensibility seems to be there for no higher purpose—certainly not, as the Philistines say, for the sake of bringing mere outward rights to pass and frustrating outward wrongs. One dwells on the sensibilities for their energy, the other for their sweetness; one speaks with a voice of bronze, the other with that of an Aeolian harp; one ruggedly ignores the distinction of good and evil, the other plays the coquette between the craven unmanliness of his Philosophic Dialogues and the butterfly optimism of his *Souvenirs de jeunesse*. But under the pages of both there sounds incessantly the hoarse bass of *vanitas vanitatum, omnia vanitas*, which the reader may hear, whenever he will, between the lines. No writer of this French romantic school has a word of rescue from the hour of satiety with the things of life—the hour in which we say, "I take no pleasure in them"—or from the hour of terror at the world's vast meaningless grinding, if perchance such hours should come. For terror and satiety are facts of sensibility like any others; and at their own hour they reign in their own right. The heart of the romantic utterances, whether poetical, critical, or historical, is this inward remedilessness, what Carlyle calls this far-off whimpering of wail and woe. And from this romantic state of mind there is absolutely no possible *theoretic* escape. Whether, like Renan, we look upon life in a more refined way, as a romance of the spirit; or whether, like the friends of M. Zola, we pique ourselves on our "scientific" and "analytic" character, and prefer to be cynical, and call the world a "roman experimental" on an infinite scale—in either case the world appears to us potentially as what the same Carlyle once called it, a vast, gloomy, solitary Golgotha and mill of death.

The only escape is by the practical way. And since I have mentioned the nowadays much-reviled name of Carlyle, let me mention it once more, and say it is the way of his teaching. No matter for Carlyle's life, no matter for a great deal of his writing. What was the most important thing he said to us? He said: "Hang your sensibilities! Stop your snivelling complaints, and your equally snivelling raptures! Leave off your general emotional tomfoolery, and get to work like men!" But this means a complete rupture with the subjectivist philosophy of things. It says conduct, and not sensibility, is the ultimate fact for our recognition. With the vision of certain works to be done, of certain outward changes to be wrought or resisted, it says our intellectual horizon terminates. No matter how we succeed in doing these outward duties, whether gladly and spontaneously, or heavily and unwillingly, do them we somehow must; for the leaving of them undone is perdition. No matter how we feel; if we are only faithful in the outward act and refuse to do wrong, the world will in so far be safe, and we quit of our debt towards it. Take, then, the yoke upon our shoulders; bend our neck beneath the heavy legality of its weight; regard something else than our feeling as our limit, our master, and our law; be willing to live and die in its service—and, at a stroke, we have passed from the subjective into the objective philosophy of things, much as one awakens from some feverish dream, full of bad lights and noises, to find one's self bathed in the sacred coolness and quiet of the air of the night.

But what is the essence of this philosophy of objective conduct, so old-fashioned and finite, but so chaste and sane and strong, when compared with its romantic rival? It is the recognition of limits, foreign and opaque to our understanding. It is the willingness, after bringing about some external good, to feel at peace; for our responsibility ends with the performance of that duty, and the burden of the rest we may lay on higher powers.[8]

> "Look to thyself, O Universe!
> Thou art better, and not worse,"

we may say in that philosophy, the moment we have done our stroke of conduct, however small. For in the view of that philosophy the universe belongs to a plurality of semi-independent forces, each one of which may help or hinder, and be helped or hindered by, the operations of the rest.

But this brings us right back, after such a long detour, to the question of indeterminism and to the conclusion of all I came here to say to-night. For the only consistent way of representing a pluralism and a world whose parts may affect one another through their conduct being either good or bad is the indeterministic way. What interest, zest, or excitement can there be in achieving the right way, unless we are enabled to feel that the wrong way is also a possible and a natural way—nay, more, a menacing and an imminent way? And what sense can there be in condemning ourselves for taking the wrong way, unless we need have done nothing of the sort, unless the right way was open to us as well? I cannot understand the willingness to act, no matter how we feel, without the belief that acts are really good and bad. I cannot understand the belief that an act is bad, without regret at its happening. I cannot understand regret without the admission of real, genuine possibilities in the world. Only *then* is it other than a mockery to feel, after we have failed to do our best, that an irreparable opportunity is gone from the universe, the loss of which it must forever after mourn.

If you insist that this is all superstition, that possibility is in the eye of science and reason impossibility, and that if I act badly 'tis that the universe was foredoomed to suffer this defect, you fall right back into the dilemma, the labyrinth, of pessimism and subjectivism, from out of whose toils we have just wound our way.

Now, we are of course free to fall back, if we please. For my own part, though, whatever difficulties may beset the philosophy of objective right and wrong, and the indeterminism it seems to imply, determinism, with its alternative of pessimism or romanticism, contains difficulties that are greater still. But you will remember that I expressly repudiated awhile ago the pretension to offer any arguments which could be coercive in a so-called scientific fashion in this matter. And I consequently find myself, at the end of this long talk, obliged to state my conclusions in an altogether personal way. This personal method of appeal seems to be among the very conditions of the problem; and the most anyone can do is to confess as candidly as he can the grounds for the faith that is in him, and leave his example to work on others as it may.

Let me, then, without circumlocution say just this. The world is enigmatical enough in all conscience, whatever theory we may take up towards it. The indeterminism I defend, the free-will theory of popular sense based on the judgment of regret, represents that world as vulnerable, and liable to be injured by certain of its parts if they act wrong. And it represents their acting wrong as a matter of possibility or accident, neither inevitable nor yet to be infallibly warded off. In all this, it is a theory devoid either of transparency or of stability. It gives us a pluralistic, restless universe, in which no single point of view can ever take in the whole scene; and to a mind possessed of the love of unity at any cost, it will, no doubt, remain forever inacceptable. A friend with such a mind once told me that the thought of my universe made him sick, like the sight of the horrible motion of a mass of maggots in their carrion bed.

But whilst I freely admit that the pluralism and the restlessness are repugnant and irrational in a certain way, I find that every alternative to them is irrational in a deeper way. The indeterminism with its maggots, if you please to speak so about it, offends only the native absolutism of my intellect—an absolutism which, after all, perhaps, deserves to be snubbed and kept in check. But the determinism with its necessary carrion, to continue the figure of speech, and with no possible maggots to eat the latter up, violates my sense of moral reality through and through. When, for example, I imagine such carrion as the Brockton murder, I cannot conceive it as an act by which the universe, as a whole, logically and necessarily expresses its nature without shrinking from complicity with such a whole. And I deliberately refuse to keep on terms of loyalty with the universe by saying blankly that the murder, since it does flow from the nature of the whole, is not carrion. There are *some* instinctive reactions which I, for one, will not tamper with. The only remaining alternative, the attitude of gnostical romanticism, wrenches my personal instincts in quite as violent a way. It falsifies the simple objectivity of their deliverance. It makes the goose-flesh the murder excites in me a sufficient reason for the perpetration of the crime. It transforms life from a tragic reality into an insincere melodramatic exhibition, as foul or as tawdry as anyone's diseased curiosity pleases to carry it out. And with its consecration of the "roman naturaliste" state of mind, and its enthronement of the baser crew of Parisian *littérateurs* among the eternally indispensable organs by which the infinite spirit of things attains to that subjective illumination which is the task of its life, it leaves me in presence of a sort of subjective carrion considerably more noisome than the objective carrion I called it in to take away.

No! better a thousand times, than such systematic corruption of our moral sanity, the plainest pessimism, so that it be straightforward; but better far than that the world of chance. Make as great an uproar about chance as you please, I know that chance means pluralism and nothing more. If some of the members of the pluralism are bad, the philosophy of pluralism, whatever broad views it may deny me, permits me, at least, to turn to the other members with a clean breast of affection and an unsophisticated moral sense. And if I still wish to think of the world as a totality, it lets me feel that a world with a *chance* in it of being altogether good, even if the chance never come to pass, is better than a world with no such chance at all. That "chance" whose very notion I am exhorted and conjured to banish from my view of the future as the suicide of reason concerning it, that "chance" is—what? Just this—the chance that in moral respects the future may be other and better than the past has been. This is the only chance we have any motive for supposing to exist. Shame, rather, on its repudiation and its denial! For its presence is the vital air which lets the world live, the salt which keeps it sweet.

And here I might legitimately stop, having expressed all I care to see admitted by others to-night. But I know that if I do stop here, misapprehensions will remain in the minds of some of you, and keep all I have said from having its effect; so I judge it best to add a few more words.

In the first place, in spite of all my explanations, the word "chance" will still be giving trouble. Though you may yourselves be adverse to the deterministic doctrine, you wish a pleasanter word than "chance" to name the opposite doctrine by; and you very likely consider my preference for such a word a perverse sort of a partiality on my part. It certainly *is* a bad word to make converts with; and you wish I had not thrust it so butt-foremost at you—you wish to use a milder term.

Well, I admit there may be just a dash of perversity in its choice. The spectacle of the mere word-grabbing game played by the soft determinists has perhaps driven me too violently the other way; and, rather than be found wrangling with them for the good words, I am willing to take the first bad one which comes along, provided it be unequivocal. The question is of things, not of eulogistic names for them; and the best word is the one that enables men to know the quickest whether they disagree or not about the things. But the word "chance," with its singular negativity, is just the word for this purpose. Whoever uses it instead of "freedom," squarely and resolutely gives up all pretence to control the things he says are free. For *him*, he confesses that they are no better than mere chance would be. It is a word of *impotence*, and is therefore the only sincere word we can use, if, in granting freedom to certain things, we grant it honestly, and really risk the game. "Who chooses me must give and forfeit all he hath." Any other word permits of quibbling, and lets us, after the fashion of the soft determinists, make a pretence of restoring the caged bird to liberty with one hand, whilst with the other we anxiously tie a string to its leg to make sure it does not get beyond our sight.

But now you will bring up your final doubt. Does not the admission of such an unguaranteed chance or freedom preclude utterly the notion of a Providence governing the world? Does it not leave the fate of the universe at the mercy of the chance-possibilities, and so far insecure? Does it not, in short, deny the craving of our nature for an ultimate peace behind all tempests, for a blue zenith above all clouds?

To this my answer must be very brief. The belief in free-will is not in the least incompatible with the belief in Providence, provided you do not restrict the Providence to fulminating nothing but *fatal* decrees. If you allow him to provide possibilities as well as actualities to the universe, and to carry on his own thinking in those two categories just as we do ours, chances may be there, uncontrolled even by him, and the course of the universe be really ambiguous; and yet the end of all things may be just what he intended it to be from all eternity.

An analogy will make the meaning of this clear. Suppose two men before a chessboard—the one a novice, the other an expert player of the game. The expert intends to beat. But he cannot foresee exactly what any one actual move of his adversary may be. He knows, however, all the *possible* moves of the latter; and he knows in advance how to meet each of them by a move of his own which leads in the direction of victory. And the victory infallibly arrives, after no matter how devious a course, in the one predestined form of check-mate to the novice's king.

Let now the novice stand for us finite free agents, and the expert for the infinite mind in which the universe lies. Suppose the latter to be thinking out his universe before he actually creates it. Suppose him to say, I will lead things to a certain end, but I will not *now*[9] decide on all the steps thereto. At various points, ambiguous possibilities shall be left open, *either* of which, at a given instant, may become actual. But whichever branch of these bifurcations become real, I know what I shall do at the *next* bifurcation to keep things from drifting away from the final result I intend.[10]

The creator's plan of the universe would thus be left blank as to many of its actual details, but all possibilities would be marked down. The realization of some of these would be left absolutely to chance; that is, would only be determined when the moment of realization came. Other possibilities would be *contingently* determined; that is, their decision would have to wait till it was seen how the matters of absolute chance fell out. But the rest of the plan, including its final upshot, would be rigorously determined once for all. So the creator himself would not need to know *all* the details of actuality until they came; and at any time his own view of the world would be a view partly of facts and partly of possibilities, exactly as ours is now. Of one thing, however, he might be certain; and that is that his world was safe, and that no matter how much it might zigzag he could surely bring it home at last.

Now, it is entirely immaterial, in this scheme, whether the creator leave the absolute chance-possibilities to be decided by himself, each when its proper moment arrives, or whether, on the contrary, he alienate this power from himself, and leave the decision out and out to finite creatures such as we men are. The great point is that the possibilities are really *here*. Whether it be we who solve them, or he working through us, at those soul-trying moments when fate's scales seem to quiver, and good snatches the victory from evil or shrinks nerveless from the fight, is of small account, so long as we admit that the issue is decided nowhere else than *here* and *now*. *That* is what gives the palpitating reality to our moral life and makes it tingle, as Mr. Mallock says, with so strange and elaborate an excitement. This reality, this excitement, are what the determinisms, hard and soft alike, suppress by their denial that *anything* is decided here and now, and their dogma that all things were foredoomed and settled long ago. If it be so, may you and I then have been foredoomed to the error of continuing to believe in liberty.[11] It is fortunate for the winding up of controversy that in every discussion with determinism this *argumentum ad hominem* can be its adversary's last word.

3

The Perception of Reality

"The Perception of Reality" is a chapter from *The Principles of Psychology,* which had appeared in the journal *Mind* as "The Psychology of Belief." It is James's fullest statement on the question of belief, and it gives the word greater weight— greater positive charge—than current usage does. For James, a belief is not, as it is for so many of us, accepting "what you know ain't so," as Mark Twain puts it; belief for James is "the mental state or function of cognizing reality." What we accept as real, we may be said to believe in. Belief for James is "a sort of feeling more allied to the emotions than to anything else." This great chapter from a great book makes the still-startling assertions that "Will and Belief . . . are two names for one and the same psychological phenomenon." Even more fundamental and challenging is the formula he put in a note, saying "belief and attention are the same fact." This is one of those pieces which, if you read the first three paragraphs attentively and without substantive dissent, you will end, like the helpless yes-men in Plato's dialogues, unable to deny James his conclusions once you have granted his premises.

Belief

EVERYONE knows the difference between imagining a thing and believing in its existence, between supposing a proposition and acquiescing in its truth. In the case of acquiescence or belief, the object is not only apprehended by the mind, but is held to have reality. Belief is thus the mental state or function of cognizing reality. As used in the following pages, 'Belief' will mean every degree of assurance, including the highest possible certainty and conviction.

There are, as we know, two ways of studying every psychic state. First, the way of analysis: What does it consist in? What is its inner nature? Of what sort of mind-stuff is it composed? Second, the way of history: What are its conditions of production, and its connection with other facts?

Into the first way we cannot go very far. *In its inner nature belief, or the sense of reality, is a sort of feeling more allied to the emotions than to anything else.* Mr. Bagehot distinctly calls it the 'emotion' of conviction. I just now spoke of it as acquiescence. It resembles more than anything what in the psychology of volition we know as consent. Consent is recognized by all to be a manifestation of our active nature. It would naturally be described by such terms as 'willingness' or the 'turning of our disposition.' What characterizes both consent and belief is the cessation of theoretic agitation, through the advent of an idea which is inwardly stable, and fills the mind solidly to the exclusion of contradictory ideas. When this is the case, motor effects are apt to follow. Hence the states of consent and belief, characterized by repose on the purely intellectual side, are both intimately connected with subsequent practical activity. This inward stability of the mind's content is as characteristic of disbelief as of belief. But we shall presently see that we never disbelieve anything except for the reason that we believe something else which contradicts the first thing.[1] Disbelief is thus an incidental complication to belief, and need not be considered by itself.

The true opposites of belief, psychologically considered, *are doubt and inquiry, not disbelief.* In both these states the content of our mind is in unrest, and the emotion engendered thereby is, like the emotion of belief itself, perfectly distinct, but perfectly indescribable in words. Both sorts of emotion may be pathologically exalted. One of the charms of drunkenness unquestionably lies in the deepening of the sense of reality and truth which is gained therein. In whatever light things may then appear to us, they seem more utterly what they are, more 'utterly utter' than when we are sober. This goes to a fully unutterable extreme in the nitrous oxide intoxication, in which a man's very soul will sweat with conviction, and he be all the while unable to tell what he is convinced of at all.[2] The pathological state opposed to this solidity and deepening has been called the questioning mania (*Grübelsucht* by the Germans). It is sometimes found as a substantive affection, paroxysmal or chronic, and consists in the inability to rest in any conception, and the need of having it confirmed and explained. 'Why do I stand here where I stand?' 'Why is a glass a glass, a chair a chair?' 'How is it that men are only of the size they are? Why not as big as houses,' etc., etc.[3] There is, it is true, another pathological state which is as far removed from doubt as from belief, and which some may prefer to consider the proper contrary of the latter state of mind. I refer to the feeling that everything is hollow, unreal, dead. I shall speak of this state again upon a later page. The point I wish to notice here is simply that belief and disbelief are but two aspects of one psychic state.

John Mill, reviewing various opinions about belief, comes to the conclusion that no account of it can be given:

> "What," he says, "is the difference *to our minds* between thinking of a reality, and representing to ourselves an imaginary picture? I confess that I can perceive no escape from the opinion that the distinction is ultimate and primordial. There is no more difficulty in holding it to be so, than in holding the difference between a sensation and an idea to be primordial. It seems almost another aspect of the same difference. . . . I cannot help thinking, therefore, that there is in the remembrance of a real fact, as distinguished from that of a thought, an element which does not consist . . . in a difference between the mere ideas which are present to the mind in the two cases. This element, howsoever we define it, constitutes Belief, and is the difference between Memory and Imagination. From whatever direction we approach, this difference seems to close our path. When we arrive at it, we seem to have reached, as it were, the central point of our intellectual nature, presupposed and built upon in every attempt we make to explain the more recondite phenomena of our mental being."[4]

If the words of Mill be taken to apply to the mere subjective analysis of belief—to the question, What does it feel like when we have it?—they must be held, on the whole, to be correct. Belief, the sense of reality, feels like itself—that is about as much as we can say.

Prof. Brentano, in an admirable chapter of his *Psychologie,* expresses this by saying that conception and belief (which he names *judgment*) are two different fundamental psychic phenomena. What I myself have called (Vol. I, p. 265) the 'object' of thought may be comparatively simple, like "Ha! what a pain," or "It-thunders"; or it may be complex, like "Columbus-discovered-America-in-1492," or "There-exists-an-all-wise-Creator-of-the-world." In either case, however, the mere thought of the object may exist as something quite distinct from the belief in its reality. The belief, as Brentano says, presupposes the mere thought:

> "Every object comes into consciousness in a twofold way, as simply thought of [*vorgestellt*] and as admitted [*anerkannt*] or denied. The relation is analogous to that which is assumed by most philosophers (by Kant no less than by Aristotle) to obtain between mere thought and desire. Nothing is ever desired without being thought of; but the desiring is nevertheless a second quite new and peculiar form of relation to the object, a second quite new way of receiving it into consciousness. No more is anything judged [i.e., believed or disbelieved] which is not thought of too. But we must insist that, so soon as the object of a thought becomes the object of an assenting or rejecting judgment, our consciousness steps into an entirely new relation towards it. It is then twice present in consciousness, as thought of, and as held for real or denied; just as when desire awakens for it, it is both thought and simultaneously desired" (P. 266).

The commonplace doctrine of 'judgment' is that it consists in the combination of 'ideas' by a 'copula' into a 'proposition,' which may be of various sorts, as affirmative, negative, hypothetical, etc. But who does not see that in a disbelieved or doubted or interrogative or conditional proposition, the ideas are combined in the same identical way in which they are in a proposition which is solidly believed? *The way in which the ideas are combined is a part of the inner constitution of the thought's object or content.* That object is sometimes an articulated whole with relations between its parts, amongst which relations, that of predicate to subject may be one. But when we have got our object with its inner constitution thus defined in a proposition, then the question comes up regarding the object as a whole: 'Is it a real object? is this proposition a true proposition or not?' And in the answer *Yes* to *this* question lies that new psychic act which Brentano calls 'judgment,' but which I prefer to call 'belief.'

In every proposition, then, so far as it is believed, questioned, or disbelieved, four elements are to be distinguished, the subject, the predicate, and their relation (of whatever sort it be)—these form the *object* of
belief—and finally the psychic attitude in which our mind stands towards the proposition taken as a whole—and this is the belief itself.[5]

Admitting, then, that this attitude is a state of consciousness *sui gen-
eris*, about which nothing more can be said in the way of internal analysis, let us proceed to the second way of studying the subject of belief:
Under what circumstances do we think things real? We shall soon see how
much matter this gives us to discuss.

The Various Orders of Reality

Suppose a new-born mind, entirely blank and waiting for experience to
begin. Suppose that it begins in the form of a visual impression (whether
faint or vivid is immaterial) of a lighted candle against a dark background, and nothing else, so that whilst this image lasts it constitutes
the entire universe known to the mind in question. Suppose, moreover
(to simplify the hypothesis), that the candle is only imaginary, and that
no 'original' of it is recognized by us psychologists outside. Will this hallucinatory candle be believed in, will it have a real existence for the
mind?

What possible sense (for that mind) would a suspicion have that the
candle was not real? What would doubt or disbelief of it imply? When
we, the onlooking psychologists, say the candle is unreal, we mean
something quite definite, viz., that there is a world known to *us* which *is*
real, and to which we perceive that the candle does not belong; it belongs exclusively to that individual mind, has no *status* anywhere else,
etc. It exists, to be sure, in a fashion, for it forms the content of that
mind's hallucination; but the hallucination itself, though unquestionably it is a sort of existing fact, has no knowledge of *other* facts; and since
those *other* facts are the realities *par excellence* for us, and the only things
we believe in, the candle is simply outside of our reality and belief altogether.

By the hypothesis, however, the *mind which sees the candle* can spin
no such considerations as these about it, for of other facts, actual or possible, it has no inkling whatever. That candle is its all, its absolute. Its
entire faculty of attention is absorbed by it. It *is*, it is *that*; it is *there*; no

other possible candle, or quality of this candle, no other possible place, or possible object in the place, no alternative, in short, suggests itself as even conceivable; so how can the mind help believing the candle real? The supposition that it might possibly not do so is, under the supposed conditions, unintelligible.[6]

This is what Spinoza long ago announced:

> "Let us conceive a boy," he said, "imagining to himself a horse, and taking note of nothing else. As this imagination involves the existence of the horse, *and the boy has no perception which annuls its existence,* he will necessarily contemplate the horse as present, nor will he be able to doubt of its existence, however little certain of it he may be. I deny that a man in so far as he imagines [*percipit*] affirms nothing. For what is it to imagine a winged horse but to affirm that the horse [that horse, namely] has wings? For if the mind had nothing before it but the winged horse it would contemplate the same as present, would have no cause to doubt of its existence, nor any power of dissenting from its existence, unless the imagination of the winged horse were joined to an idea which contradicted [*tollit*] its existence." (*Ethics*, II, 49, Scholium.)

The sense that anything we think of is unreal can only come, then, when that thing is contradicted by some other thing of which we think. *Any object which remains uncontradicted is ipso facto believed and posited as absolute reality.*

Now, how comes it that one thing thought of can be contradicted by another? It cannot unless it begins the quarrel by saying something inadmissible about that other. Take the mind with the candle, or the boy with the horse. If either of them say, "That candle or that horse, even when I don't see it, exists in *the outer world,*" he pushes into 'the outer world' an object which may be incompatible with everything which he otherwise knows of that world. If so, he must take his choice of which to hold by, the present perceptions or the other knowledge of the world. If he holds to the other knowledge, the present perceptions are contradicted, *so far as their relation to that world goes.* Candle and horse, whatever they may be, are not existents in outward space. They are existents, of course; they are mental objects; mental objects have existence as mental objects. But they are situated in their own spaces, the space in which they severally appear, and neither of those spaces is the space in which the realities called 'the outer world' exist.

Take again the horse with wings. If I merely dream of a horse with wings, my horse interferes with nothing else and has not to be contradicted. That horse, its wings, and its place, are all equally real. That horse exists no otherwise than as winged, and is moreover really there, for that place exists no otherwise than as the place of that horse, and claims as yet no connection with the other places of the world. But if with this horse I make an inroad into the *world otherwise known*, and say, for example, "That is my old mare Maggie, having grown a pair of wings where she stands in her stall," the whole case is altered; for now the horse and place are identified with a horse and place otherwise known, and *what* is known of the latter objects is incompatible with what is perceived with the former. "Maggie in her stall with wings! Never!" The wings are unreal, then, visionary. I have dreamed a lie about Maggie in her stall.

The reader will recognize in these two cases the two sorts of judgment called in the logic-books existential and attributive respectively. 'The candle exists as an outer reality' is an existential, 'My Maggie has got a pair of wings' is an attributive, proposition;[7] and it follows from what was first said that *all propositions, whether attributive or existential, are believed through the very fact of being conceived, unless they clash with other propositions believed at the same time, by affirming that their terms are the same with the terms of these other propositions.* A dream-candle has existence, true enough; but not the same existence (existence for itself, namely, or *extra mentem meam*) which the candles of waking perception have. A dream-horse has wings; but then neither horse nor wings are the same with any horses or wings known to memory. That we can at any moment think of the same thing which at any former moment we thought of is the ultimate law of our intellectual constitution. But when we now think of it incompatibly with our other ways of thinking it, then we must choose which way to stand by, for we cannot continue to think in two contradictory ways at once. *The whole distinction of real and unreal, the whole psychology of belief, disbelief, and doubt, is thus grounded on two mental facts—first, that we are liable to think differently of the same; and second, that when we have done so, we can choose which way of thinking to adhere to and which to disregard.*

The subjects adhered to become real subjects, the attributes adhered to real attributes, the existence adhered to real existence; whilst the subjects disregarded become imaginary subjects, the attributes disregarded erroneous attributes, and the existence disregarded an existence in no man's land, in the limbo "where footless fancies dwell." The real things are, in M. Taine's terminology, the *reductives* of the things judged unreal.

The Many Worlds

Habitually and practically we do not *count* these disregarded things as existents at all. For them *Vae victis* is the law in the popular philosophy; they are not even treated as appearances; they are treated as if they were mere waste, equivalent to nothing at all. To the genuinely philosophic mind, however, they still have existence, though not the same existence, as the real things. *As* objects of fancy, *as* errors, *as* occupants of dreamland, etc., they are in their way as indefeasible parts of life, as undeniable features of the Universe, as the realities are in their way. The total world of which the philosophers must take account is thus composed of the realities *plus* the fancies and illusions.

Two sub-universes, at least, connected by relations which philosophy tries to ascertain! Really there are more than two sub-universes of which we take account, some of us of this one, and others of that. For there are various categories both of illusion and of reality, and alongside of the world of absolute error (i.e., error confined to single individuals) but still within the world of absolute reality (i.e., reality believed by the complete philosopher) there is the world of collective error, there are the worlds of abstract reality, of relative or practical reality, of ideal relations, and there is the supernatural world. The popular mind conceives of all these sub-worlds more or less disconnectedly; and when dealing with one of them, forgets for the time being its relations to the rest. The complete philosopher is he who seeks not only to assign to every given object of his thought its right place in one or other of these sub-worlds, but he also seeks to determine the relation of each sub-world to the others in the total world which *is*.

The most important sub-universes commonly discriminated from each other and recognized by most of us as existing, each with its own special and separate style of existence, are the following:

(1) The world of sense, or of physical 'things' as we instinctively ap-

prehend them, with such qualities as heat, color, and sound, and such 'forces' as life, chemical affinity, gravity, electricity, all existing as such within or on the surface of the things.

(2) The world of science, or of physical things as the learned conceive them, with secondary qualities and 'forces' (in the popular sense) excluded, and nothing real but solids and fluids and their 'laws' (i.e., customs) of motion.[8]

(3) The world of ideal relations, or abstract truths believed or believable by all, and expressed in logical, mathematical, metaphysical, ethical, or aesthetic propositions.

(4) The world of 'idols of the tribe,' illusions or prejudices common to the race. All educated people recognize these as forming one sub-universe. The motion of the sky round the earth, for example, belongs to this world. That motion is not a recognized item of any of the other worlds; but as an 'idol of the tribe' it really exists. For certain philosophers 'matter' exists only as an idol of the tribe. For science, the 'secondary qualities' of matter are but 'idols of the tribe.'

(5) The various supernatural worlds, the Christian heaven and hell, the world of the Hindoo mythology, the world of Swedenborg's *visa et audita*, etc. Each of these is a consistent system, with definite relations among its own parts. Neptune's trident, e.g., has no status of reality whatever in the Christian heaven; but within the classic Olympus certain definite things are true of it, whether one believe in the reality of the classic mythology as a whole or not. The various worlds of deliberate fable may be ranked with these worlds of faith—the world of the *Iliad*, that of *King Lear*, of the *Pickwick Papers*, etc.[9]

(6) The various worlds of individual opinion, as numerous as men are.

(7) The worlds of sheer madness and vagary, also indefinitely numerous.

Every object we think of gets at last referred to one world or another of this or of some similar list. It settles into our belief as a common-sense object, a scientific object, an abstract object, a mythological object, an object of someone's mistaken conception, or a madman's object; and it reaches this state sometimes immediately, but often only after being hustled and bandied about amongst other objects until it finds some which will tolerate its presence and stand in relations to it which nothing contradicts. The molecules and ether-waves of the scientific world, for example, simply kick the object's warmth and color out, they refuse to have any relations with them. But the world of 'idols of the tribe' stands ready to take them in. Just so the world of classic myth takes up the winged horse; the world of individual hallucination, the vision of the candle; the world of abstract truth, the proposition that justice is kingly, though no actual king be just. The various worlds themselves, however, appear (as aforesaid) to most men's minds in no very definitely conceived relation to each other, and our attention, when it turns to one, is apt to drop the others for the time being out of its account. Propositions concerning the different worlds are made from 'different points of view'; and in this more or less chaotic state the consciousness of most thinkers remains to the end. Each world *whilst it is attended to* is real after its own fashion; only the reality lapses with the attention.

The World of 'Practical Realities'

Each thinker, however, has dominant habits of attention; and these *practically elect from among the various worlds some one to be for him the world of ultimate realities.* From this world's objects he does not appeal. Whatever positively contradicts them must get into another world or die. The horse, e.g., may have wings to its heart's content, so long as it does not pretend to be the real world's horse—*that* horse is absolutely wingless. For most men, as we shall immediately see, the 'things of sense' hold this prerogative position, and are the absolutely real world's nucleus. Other things, to be sure, may be real for this man or for that—things of science, abstract moral relations, things of the Christian theology, or what not. But even for the special man, these things are usually real with a less real reality than that of the things of sense. They are taken less seriously; and the very utmost that can be said for anyone's belief in them is that it is as strong as his 'belief in his own senses.'[10]

In all this the everlasting partiality of our nature shows itself, our inveterate propensity to choice. For, in the strict and ultimate sense of the word existence, everything which can be thought of at all exists as *some* sort of object, whether mythical object, individual thinker's object, or object in outer space and for intelligence at large. Errors, fictions, tribal beliefs, are parts of the whole great Universe which God has made, and He must have meant all these things to be in it, each in its respective place. But for us finite creatures, "'tis to consider too curiously to consider so." The mere fact of appearing as an object at all is not enough to constitute reality. That may be metaphysical reality, reality for God; but what we need is practical reality, reality for ourselves; and, to have that, an object must not only appear, but it must appear both *interesting* and *important*. The worlds whose objects are neither interesting nor important we treat simply negatively, we brand them as *un*real.

In the relative sense, then, the sense in which we contrast reality with simple *un*reality, and in which one thing is said to have *more* reality than another, and to be more believed, *reality means simply relation to our emotional and active life*. This is the only sense which the word ever has in the mouths of practical men. *In this sense, whatever excites and stimulates our interest is real;* whenever an object so appeals to us that we turn to it, accept it, fill our mind with it, or practically take account of it, so far it is real for us, and we believe it. Whenever, on the contrary, we ignore it, fail to consider it or act upon it, despise it, reject it, forget it, so far it is unreal for us and disbelieved. Hume's account of the matter was then essentially correct, when he said that belief in anything was simply the having the idea of it in a lively and active manner:

> "I say then, that belief is nothing but a more vivid, lively, forcible, firm, steady conception of an object, than what the imagination alone is ever able to attain. . . . It consists not in the peculiar nature or order of ideas, but in the *manner* of their conception, and in their *feeling* to the mind. I confess, that it is impossible perfectly to explain this feeling or manner of conception. . . . Its true and proper name . . . is *belief;* which is a term, that every one sufficiently understands in common life. And in philosophy, we can go no farther than assert, that *belief* is something felt by the mind, which distinguishes the ideas of the judgment from the fictions of the imagination.[11] It gives them more weight and influence; makes them appear of greater importance; inforces them in the mind; gives them a superior influence on the passions, and renders them the governing principle of our actions."[12]

Or as Prof. Bain puts it: "In its essential character, Belief is a phase of our active nature,—otherwise called the Will."[13]

The object of belief, then, reality or real existence, is something quite different from all the other predicates which a subject may possess. Those are properties intellectually or sensibly intuited. When we add any one of them to the subject, we increase the intrinsic content of the latter, we enrich its picture in our mind. But adding reality does not enrich the picture in any such inward way; it leaves it inwardly as it finds it, and only fixes it and stamps it in to *us*.

> "The real," as Kant says, "contains no more than the possible. A hundred real dollars do not contain a penny more than a hundred possible dollars. . . . By whatever and by however many predicates I may think a thing . . . nothing is added to it, if I add that the thing exists. . . . Whatever therefore our concept of an object may contain, we must always step outside of it, in order to attribute to it existence."[14]

The 'stepping outside' of it is the establishment either of immediate practical relations between it and ourselves, or of relations between it and other objects with which we have immediate practical relations. Relations of this sort, which are as yet not transcended or superseded by others, are *ipso facto* real relations, and confer reality upon their objective term. *The fons et origo of all reality, whether from the absolute or the practical point of view, is thus subjective, is ourselves.* As bare logical thinkers, without emotional reaction, we give reality to whatever objects we think of, for they are really phenomena, or objects of our passing thought, if nothing more. But, *as thinkers with emotional reaction, we give what seems to us a still higher degree of reality to whatever things we select and emphasize and turn to* WITH A WILL. These are our *living* realities; and not only these, but all the other things which are intimately connected with these. Reality, starting from our Ego, thus sheds itself from point to point—first, upon all objects which have an immediate sting of interest for our Ego in them, and next, upon the objects most continuously related with these. It only fails when the connecting thread is lost. A whole system may be real, if it only hang to our Ego by one immediately *stinging* term. But what contradicts any such stinging term, even though it be another stinging term itself, is either not believed, or only believed after settlement of the dispute.

We reach thus the important conclusion that *our own reality, that sense of our own life which we at every moment possess, is the ultimate of ultimates for our belief.* 'As sure as I exist!'—this is our uttermost warrant for the being of all other things. As Descartes made the indubitable reality of the *cogito* go bail for the reality of all that the *cogito* involved, so we all of us, feeling our own present reality with absolutely coercive force, ascribe an all but equal degree of reality, first to whatever things we lay hold on with a sense of personal need, and second, to whatever farther things continuously belong with these. "Mein Jetzt und Hier," as Prof. Lipps says, "ist der letzte Angelpunkt für alle Wirklichkeit, also alle Erkenntniss."

The world of living realities as contrasted with unrealities is thus anchored in the Ego, considered as an active and emotional term.[15] That is the hook from which the rest dangles, the absolute support. And as from a painted hook it has been said that one can only hang a painted chain, so conversely, from a real hook only a real chain can properly be hung. *Whatever things have intimate and continuous connection with my life are things of whose reality I cannot doubt.* Whatever things fail to establish this connection are things which are practically no better for me than if they existed not at all.

In certain forms of melancholic perversion of the sensibilities and reactive powers, nothing touches us intimately, rouses us, or wakens natural feeling. The consequence is the complaint so often heard from melancholic patients, that nothing is believed in by them as it used to be, and that all sense of reality is fled from life. They are sheathed in india-rubber; nothing penetrates to the quick or draws blood, as it were. According to Griesinger, "I see, I hear!" such patients say, "but the objects do not reach me, it is as if there were a wall between me and the outer world!"

> "In such patients there often is an alteration of the cutaneous sensibility, such that things feel indistinct or sometimes rough and woolly. But even were this change always present, it would not completely explain the psychic phenomenon . . . which reminds us more of the alteration in our psychic relations to the outer world which advancing age on the one hand, and on the other emotions and passions, may bring about. In childhood we feel ourselves to be closer to the world of sensible phenomena, we live immediately with them and in them; an intimately vital tie binds us and them together. But with the ripening of reflection this tie is loosened, the warmth of our interest cools, things look differently to us, and we act more as foreigners to the outer world, even though we know it a great deal better. Joy and expansive emotions in general draw it nearer to us again. Everything makes a more lively impression, and with the quick immediate return of this warm receptivity for sense-impressions, joy makes us feel

young again. In depressing emotions it is the other way. Outer things, whether living or inorganic, suddenly grow cold and foreign to us, and even our favorite objects of interest feel as if they belonged to us no more. Under these circumstances, receiving no longer from any- thing a lively impression, we cease to turn towards outer things, and the sense of inward loneliness grows upon us. . . . Where there is no strong intelligence to control this *blasé* condition, this psychic coldness and lack of interest, the issue of these states in which all seems so cold and hollow, the heart dried up, the world grown dead and empty, is often suicide or the deeper forms of insanity."[16]

The Paramount Reality of Sensations

But now we are met by questions of detail. What does this stirring, this exciting power, this interest, consist in, which some objects have? which *are* those 'intimate relations' with our life which give reality? And what things stand in these relations immediately, and what others are so closely connected with the former that (in Hume's language) we 'carry our disposition' also on to them?

In a simple and direct way these questions cannot be answered at all. The whole history of human thought is but an unfinished attempt to answer them. For what have men been trying to find out, since men were men, but just those things: "Where do our true interests lie— which relations shall we call the intimate and real ones—which things shall we call living realities and which not?" A few psychological points can, however, be made clear.

Any relation to our mind at all, in the absence of a stronger contradicting relation, suffices to make an object real. The barest appeal to our attention is enough for that. Revert to the beginning of the chapter, and take the candle entering the vacant mind. The mind was waiting for just some such object to make its spring upon. It makes its spring and the candle is believed. But when the candle appears at the same time with other ob- jects, it must run the gauntlet of their rivalry, and then it becomes a question which of the various candidates for attention shall compel be- lief. As a rule we believe as much as we can. We would believe every- thing if we only could. When objects are represented by us quite unsys- tematically they conflict but little with each other, and the number of them which in this chaotic manner we can believe is limitless. The primitive savage's mind is a jungle in which hallucinations, dreams, superstitions, conceptions, and sensible objects all flourish alongside of each other, unregulated except by the attention turning in this way or in that. The child's mind is the same. It is only as objects become permanent and their relations fixed that discrepancies and contradictions are felt and must be settled in some stable way. As a rule, the success with which a contradicted object maintains itself in our belief is proportional to several qualities which it must possess. Of these the one which would be put first by most people, because it characterizes objects of sensation, is its—

(1) Coerciveness over attention, or the mere power to possess consciousness: then follow—

(2) Liveliness, or sensible pungency, especially in the way of exciting pleasure or pain;

(3) Stimulating effect upon the will, i.e., capacity to arouse active impulses, the more instinctive the better;

(4) Emotional interest, as object of love, dread, admiration, desire, etc.;

(5) Congruity with certain favorite forms of contemplation—unity, simplicity, permanence, and the like;

(6) Independence of other causes, and its own causal importance.

These characters run into each other. Coerciveness is the result of liveliness or emotional interest. What is lively and interesting stimulates *eo ipso* the will; congruity holds of active impulses as well as of contemplative forms; causal independence and importance suit a certain contemplative demand, etc. I will therefore abandon all attempt at a formal treatment, and simply proceed to make remarks in the most convenient order of exposition.

As a whole, sensations are more lively and are judged more real than conceptions; things met with every hour more real than things seen once; attributes perceived when awake, more real than attributes perceived in a dream. But, owing to the *diverse relations contracted by the various objects with each other,* the simple rule that the lively and permanent is the real is often enough disguised. A conceived thing may be deemed more real than a certain sensible thing, if it only be intimately related to other sensible things more vivid, permanent, or interesting than the first one. Conceived molecular vibrations, e.g., are by the physicist judged more real than felt warmth, because so intimately related to all those other facts of motion in the world which he has made his special study. Similarly, a rare thing may be deemed more real than a permanent thing if it be more widely related to other permanent things. All the occasional crucial observations of science are examples of this. A rare experience, too, is likely to be judged more real than a permanent one, if it be more interesting and exciting. Such is the sight of Saturn through a telescope; such are the occasional insights and illuminations which upset our habitual ways of thought.

But no mere floating conception, no mere disconnected rarity, ever displaces vivid things or permanent things from our belief. A conception, to prevail, must *terminate* in the world of orderly sensible experience. A rare phenomenon, to displace frequent ones, must belong with others more frequent still. The history of science is strewn with wrecks and ruins of theory—essences and principles, fluids and forces—once fondly clung to, but found to hang together with no facts of sense. And exceptional phenomena solicit our belief in vain until such time as we chance to conceive them as of kinds already admitted to exist. What science means by 'verification' is no more than this, that no object of conception shall be believed which sooner or later has not some permanent and vivid object of sensation for its *term*. Compare what was said in the chapter "Sensation" in *Principles of Psychology*, vol. 2.

Sensible objects are thus either our realities or the tests of our realities. Conceived objects must show sensible effects or else be disbelieved. And the effects, even though reduced to relative unreality when their causes come to view (as heat, which molecular vibrations make unreal), are yet the things on which our knowledge of the causes rests. Strange mutual dependence this, in which the appearance needs the reality in order to exist, but the reality needs the appearance in order to be known!

Sensible vividness or pungency is then the vital factor in reality when once the conflict between objects, and the connecting of them together in the mind, has begun. No object which neither possesses this vividness in its own right nor is able to borrow it from anything else has a chance of making headway against vivid rivals, or of rousing in us that reaction in which belief consists. On the vivid objects we *pin*, as the saying is, our faith in all the rest; and our belief returns instinctively even to those of them from which reflection has led it away. Witness the obduracy with which the popular world of colors, sounds, and smells holds its own against that of molecules and vibrations. Let the physicist himself but nod, like Homer, and the world of sense becomes his absolute reality again.[17]

That things originally devoid of this stimulating power should be enabled, by association with other things which have it, to compel our belief as if they had it themselves, is a remarkable psychological fact, which since Hume's time it has been impossible to overlook.

> "The vividness of the first conception," he writes, "diffuses itself along the relations, and is convey'd, as by so many pipes or canals, to every idea that has any communication with the primary one. . . . Superstitious people are fond of the relicks of saints and holy men, for the same reason that they seek after types and images, in order to inliven their devotion, and give them a more intimate and strong conception of those exemplary lives. . . . Now 'tis evident, one of the best relicks a devotee cou'd procure, wou'd be the handywork of a saint; and if his cloaths and furniture are ever to be consider'd in this light, 'tis because they were once at his disposal, and were mov'd and affected by him; in which respect they are . . . connected with him by a shorter chain of consequences than any of those, from which we learn the reality of his existence. This phaenomenon clearly proves, that a present impression with a relation of causation may inliven any idea, and consequently produce belief or assent, according to the precedent definition of it. . . . It has been remark'd among the *Mahometans* as well as *Christians*, that those *pilgrims*, who have seen Mecca or the Holy Land, are ever after more faithful and zealous believers, than those who have not had that advantage. A man, whose memory presents him with a lively image of the *Red-Sea, and the Desert, and Jerusalem, and Galilee* can never doubt of any miraculous events, which are related either by *Moses or the Evangelists*. The lively idea of the places passes by an easy transition to the facts, which are suppos'd to have been related to them by contiguity, and encreases the belief by encreasing the vivacity of the conception. The remembrance of these fields and rivers has the same influence as a new argument. . . . The ceremonies of the *Catholic* religion may be consider'd as instances of the same nature. The devotees of that strange superstition usually

plead in excuse of the mummeries, with which they are upbraided, that they feel the good effect of those external motions, and postures, and actions, in inlivening their devotion, and quickening their fervour, which otherwise wou'd decay away, if directed entirely to distant and immaterial objects. We shadow out the objects of our faith, say they, in sensible types and images, and render them more present to us by the immediate presence of these types, than 'tis possible for us to do, merely by an intellectual view and contemplation."[18]

Hume's cases are rather trivial; and the things which associated sensible objects make us believe in are supposed by him to be unreal. But all the more manifest for that is the fact of their psychological influence. Who does not 'realize' more the fact of a dead or distant friend's existence, at the moment when a portrait, letter, garment or other material reminder of him is found? The whole notion of him then grows pungent and speaks to us and shakes us, in a manner unknown at other times. In children's minds, fancies and realities live side by side. But however lively their fancies may be, they still gain help from association with reality. The imaginative child identifies its *dramatis personae* with some doll or other material object, and this evidently solidifies belief, little as it may resemble what it is held to stand for. A thing not too interesting by its own real qualities generally does the best service here. The most useful doll I ever saw was a large cucumber in the hands of a little Amazonian-Indian girl; she nursed it and washed it and rocked it to sleep in a hammock, and talked to it all day long—there was no part in life which the cucumber did not play. Says Mr. Tylor:

> "An imaginative child will . . . make a dog do duty for a horse, or a soldier for a shepherd, till at last the objective resemblance almost disappears, and a bit of wood may be dragged about, representing a ship on the sea, or a coach on the road. Here the likeness of the bit of wood to a ship or a coach is very slight indeed; but it is a thing, and can be moved about . . . and is an evident assistance to the child in enabling it to arrange and develop its ideas. . . . Of how much use . . . may be seen by taking it away and leaving the child nothing to play with. . . . In later years, and among highly educated people, the mental process which goes on in a child playing with wooden soldiers and horses, though it never disappears, must be sought for in more complex phenomena. Perhaps nothing in after life more closely resembles the effect of a doll upon a child, than the effect of the illustrations of a tale

upon a grown-up reader. Here the objective resemblance is very indefinite . . . yet what reality is given to the scene by a good picture. . . . Mr. Backhouse one day noticed in Van Diemen's Land a woman arranging several stones that were flat, oval, and about two inches wide, and marked in various directions with black and red lines. These he learned represented absent friends, and one larger than the rest stood for a fat native woman on Flinders Island, known by the name of Mother Brown. Similar practices are found among far higher races than the ill-fated Tasmanians. Among some North American tribes, a mother who has lost a child keeps its memory ever present to her by filling its cradle with black feathers and quills, and carrying it about with her for a year or more. When she stops anywhere, she sets up the cradle and talks to it as she goes about her work, just as she would have done if the dead baby had been still alive within it. Here we have no image; but in Africa we find a rude doll, representing the child, kept as a memorial. . . . Bastian saw Indian women in Peru, who had lost an infant, carrying about on their backs a wooden doll to represent it."[19]

To many persons among us, photographs of lost ones seem to be fetishes. They, it is true, resemble; but the fact that the mere materiality of the reminder is almost as important as its resemblance is shown by the popularity a hundred years ago of the black taffeta 'silhouettes' which are still found among family relics, and of one of which Fichte could write to his affianced: *"Die Farbe fehlt, das Auge fehlt, es fehlt der himmlische Ausdruck deiner lieblichen Züge"*—and yet go on worshipping it all the same. The opinion so stoutly professed by many, that language is essential to thought, seems to have this much of truth in it, that all our inward images tend invincibly to attach themselves to something sensible, so as to gain in corporeity and life. Words serve this purpose, gestures serve it, stones, straws, chalk-marks, anything will do. As soon as any one of these things stands for the idea, the latter seems to be more real. Some persons, the present writer among the number, can hardly lecture without a black-board: the abstract conceptions must be symbolized by letters, squares or circles, and the relations between them by lines. All this symbolism, linguistic, graphic, and dramatic, has other uses too, for it abridges thought and fixes terms. But one of its uses is surely to rouse the believing reaction and give to the ideas a more living reality. As, when we are told a story, and shown the very knife that did the murder, the very ring whose hiding-place the clairvoyant revealed, the whole thing passes from fairy-land to mother-earth, so here we believe all the more, if only we see that "the bricks are alive to tell the tale."

So much for the prerogative position of sensations in regard to our belief. But among the sensations themselves all are not deemed equally real. The more practically important ones, the more permanent ones, and the more aesthetically apprehensible ones are selected from the mass, to be believed in most of all; the others are degraded to the position of mere signs and suggesters of these. This fact has already been adverted to in former chapters.[20] The real color of a thing is that one color-sensation which it gives us when most favorably lighted for vision. So of its real size, its real shape, etc.—these are but optical sensations selected out of thousands of others, because they have aesthetic characteristics which appeal to our convenience or delight. But I will not repeat what I have already written about this matter, but pass on to our treatment of tactile and muscular sensations, as 'primary qualities,' more real than those 'secondary' qualities which eye and ear and nose reveal. Why do we thus so markedly select the *tangible* to be the real? Our motives are not far to seek. The tangible qualities are the least fluctuating. When we get them at all we get them the same. The other qualities fluctuate enormously as our relative position to the object changes. Then, more decisive still, the tactile properties are those most intimately connected with our weal or woe. A dagger hurts us only when in contact with our skin, a poison only when we take it into our mouths, and we can only use an object for our advantage when we have it in our muscular control. It is as tangibles, then, that things concern us most; and the other senses, so far as their practical use goes, do but warn us of what tangible things to expect. They are but organs of anticipatory touch, as Aristotle and Berkeley have with perfect clearness explained.[21]

Among all sensations, the *most* belief-compelling are those productive of pleasure or of pain. Locke expressly makes the *pleasure-* or *pain-*giving quality to be the ultimate human criterion of anything's reality. Discussing (with a supposed Berkeleyan before Berkeley) the notion that all our perceptions may be but a dream, he says:

"He may please to dream that I make him this answer . . . that I believe he will allow a very manifest difference between dreaming of
being in the fire, and being actually in it. But yet if he be resolved to
appear so sceptical as to maintain, that what I call 'being actually in
the fire' is nothing but a dream; and that we cannot thereby certainly
know that any such thing as fire actually exists without us: I answer,
that we certainly finding that pleasure or pain [or emotion of any
sort] follows upon the application of certain objects to us, whose existence we perceive, or dream that we perceive, by our senses; *this certainly is as great as our happiness or misery,* beyond which we have no
concernment to know or to be."[22]

The Influence of Emotion and Active Impulse on Belief

The quality of arousing emotion, of shaking, moving us or inciting us to
action, has as much to do with our belief in an object's reality as the
quality of giving pleasure or pain. In Chapter XXV I shall seek to show
that our emotions probably owe their pungent quality to the bodily sensations which they involve. Our tendency to believe in emotionally
exciting objects (objects of fear, desire, etc.) is thus explained without
resorting to any fundamentally new principle of choice. Speaking generally, the more a conceived object *excites* us, the more reality it has. The
same object excites us differently at different times. Moral and religious
truths come 'home' to us far more on some occasions than on others. As
Emerson says, "There is a difference between one and another hour of
life, in their authority and subsequent effect. Our faith comes in moments. . . . Yet there is a depth in those brief moments which constrains
us to ascribe more reality to them than to all other experiences." The
'depth' is partly, no doubt, the insight into wider systems of unified relation, but far more often than that it is the emotional thrill. Thus, to descend to more trivial examples, a man who has no belief in ghosts by
daylight will temporarily believe in them when, alone at midnight, he
feels his blood curdle at a mysterious sound or vision, his heart thump-
ing, and his legs impelled to flee. The thought of falling when we walk
along a curbstone awakens no emotion of dread; so no sense of reality
attaches to it, and we are sure we shall not fall. On a precipice's edge,
however, the sickening emotion which the notion of a possible fall en-

genders makes us believe in the latter's imminent reality, and quite un-fits us to proceed.

The greatest proof that a man is *sui compos* is his ability to suspend belief in presence of an emotionally exciting idea. To give this power is the highest result of education. In untutored minds the power does not exist. *Every exciting thought in the natural man carries credence with it. To conceive with passion is eo ipso to affirm.* As Bagehot says:

> "The Caliph Omar . . . burnt the Alexandrian Library, saying, 'All books which contain what is not in the Koran are dangerous; all those which contain what is in the Koran are useless!' Probably no one ever had an intenser belief in anything than Omar had in this. Yet it is impossible to imagine it preceded by an argument. His belief in Mahomet, in the Koran, and in the sufficiency of the Koran, came to him probably in spontaneous rushes of emotion; there may have been little vestiges of argument floating here and there, but they did not justify the strength of the emotion, still less did they create it, and they hardly even excused it. . . . Probably, when the subject is thoroughly examined, 'conviction' will be proved to be one of the intensest of human emotions, and one most closely connected with the bodily state . . . accompanied or preceded by the sensation that Scott makes his seer describe as the prelude to a prophecy:—
>
> > 'At length the fatal answer came,
> > In characters of living flame—
> > Not spoke in word, nor blazed in scroll,
> > But borne and branded on my soul.'
>
> A hot flash seems to burn across the brain. Men in these intense states of mind have altered all history, changed for better or worse the creed of myriads, and desolated or redeemed provinces and ages. Nor is this intensity a sign of truth, for it is precisely strongest in those points in which men differ most from each other. John Knox felt it in his anti-Catholicism; Ignatius Loyola in his anti-Protestantism; and both, I suppose, felt it as much as it is possible to feel it."[23]

The reason of the belief is undoubtedly the bodily commotion which the exciting idea sets up. 'Nothing which I can feel like *that* can be false.' All our religious and supernatural beliefs are of this order. The surest warrant for immortality is the yearning of our bowels for our dear ones; for God, the sinking sense it gives us to imagine no such Providence or help. So of our political or pecuniary hopes and fears, and things and persons dreaded and desired. "A grocer has a full creed as to foreign policy, a young lady a complete theory of the sacraments, as to which neither has any doubt. . . . A girl in a country parsonage will be sure 'that Paris never can be taken,' or that 'Bismarck is a wretch,'"—all because they have either conceived these things at some moment with passion, or associated them with other things which they have conceived with passion.

M. Renouvier calls this belief of a thing for no other reason than that we conceive it with passion, by the name of *mental vertigo*.[24] Other objects whisper doubt or disbelief; but the object of passion makes us deaf to all but itself, and we affirm it unhesitatingly. Such objects are the delusions of insanity, which the insane person can at odd moments steady himself against, but which again return to sweep him off his feet. Such are the revelations of mysticism. Such, particularly, are the sudden beliefs which animate mobs of men when frenzied impulse to action is involved. Whatever be the action in point—whether the stoning of a prophet, the hailing of a conqueror, the burning of a witch, the baiting of a heretic or Jew, the starting of a forlorn hope, or the flying from a foe—the fact that to believe a certain object will *cause that action to explode* is a sufficient reason for that belief to come. The motor impulse sweeps it unresisting in its train.

The whole history of witchcraft and early medicine is a commentary on the facility with which anything which chances to be conceived is believed the moment the belief chimes in with an emotional mood. 'The cause of sickness?' When a savage asks the cause of anything he means to ask exclusively 'What is to blame?' The theoretic curiosity starts from the practical life's demands. Let someone then accuse a necromancer, suggest a charm or spell which has been cast, and no more 'evidence' is asked for. What evidence is required beyond this intimate sense of the culprit's responsibility, to which our very viscera and limbs reply?[25]

Human credulity in the way of therapeutics has similar psychological roots. If there is anything intolerable (especially to the heart of a woman), it is to do nothing when a loved one is sick or in pain. To do anything is a relief. Accordingly, whatever remedy may be suggested is a spark on inflammable soil. The mind makes its spring towards action on that cue, sends for that remedy, and for a day at least believes the danger past. Blame, dread, and hope are thus the great belief-inspiring passions, and cover among them the future, the present, and the past.

These remarks illustrate the earlier heads of the list on pp. 53–54. Whichever represented objects give us sensations, especially interesting ones, or incite our motor impulses, or arouse our hate, desire, or fear, are real enough for us. Our requirements in the way of reality terminate in our own acts and emotions, our own pleasures and pains. These are the ultimate fixities from which, as we formerly observed, the whole chain of our beliefs depends, object hanging to object, as the bees, in swarming, hang to each other until, *de proche en proche*, the supporting branch, the Self, is reached and held.

Belief in Objects of Theory

Now the merely conceived or imagined objects which our mind represents as hanging to the sensations (causing them, etc.), filling the gaps between them, and weaving their interrupted chaos into order are innumerable. Whole systems of them conflict with other systems, and our choice of which system shall carry our belief is governed by principles which are simple enough, however subtle and difficult may be their application to details. *The conceived system, to pass for true, must at least include the reality of the sensible objects in it, by explaining them as effects on us, if nothing more. The system which includes the most of them, and definitely explains or pretends to explain the most of them, will, ceteris paribus, prevail.* It is needless to say how far mankind still is from having excogitated such a system. But the various materialisms, idealisms, and hylozoisms show with what industry the attempt is forever made. It is conceivable that several rival theories should equally well include the actual order of our sensations in their scheme, much as the one-fluid and two-fluid theories of electricity formulated all the common electrical phenomena equally well. The sciences are full of these alternatives. Which theory is then to be believed? *That theory will be most generally believed which, besides offering us objects able to account satisfactorily for our sensible experience, also offers those which are most interesting, those which appeal most urgently to our aesthetic, emotional, and active needs.* So here, in the higher intellectual life, the same selection among general conceptions goes on which went on among the sensations themselves. First, a word of their relation to our emotional and active needs—and here I can do no better than quote from an article published some years ago:[26]

> "A philosophy may be unimpeachable in other respects, but either of two defects will be fatal to its universal acceptance. First, its ultimate principle must not be one that essentially baffles and disappoints our dearest desires and most cherished powers. A pessimistic principle like Schopenhauer's incurably vicious Will-substance, or Hartmann's wicked jack-at-all-trades, the Unconscious, will perpetually call forth essays at other philosophies. Incompatibility of the future with their desires and active tendencies is, in fact, to most men a source of more fixed disquietude than uncertainty itself. Witness the attempts to overcome the 'problem of evil,' the 'mystery of pain.' There is no 'problem of good.'
>
> "But a second and worse defect in a philosophy than that of contradicting our active propensities is to give them no Object whatever to press against. A philosophy whose principle is so incommensurate with our most intimate powers as to deny them all relevancy in universal affairs, as to annihilate their motives at one blow, will be even more unpopular than pessimism. Better face the enemy than the eternal Void! This is why materialism will always fail of universal adoption, however well it may fuse things into an atomistic unity, however clearly it may prophesy the future eternity. For materialism denies reality to the objects of almost all the impulses which we most cherish. The real *meaning* of the impulses, it says, is something which has no emotional interest for us whatever. But what is called extradition is quite as characteristic of our emotions as of our senses. Both point to an Object as the cause of the present feeling. What an intensely objective reference lies in fear! In like manner an enraptured man, a dreary-feeling man, are not simply aware of their subjective states; if they were, the force of their feelings would evaporate. Both believe there is outward cause *why* they should feel as they do: either 'It is a glad world! how good is life!' or 'What a loathsome tedium is existence!' Any philosophy which annihilates the validity of the reference by explaining away its objects or translating them into terms of no emotional pertinency leaves the mind with little to care or act for. This is the opposite condition from that of nightmare, but when acutely brought home to consciousness it produces a kindred horror. In nightmare we have motives to act, but no power; here we have powers, but no motives. A nameless *Unheimlichkeit* comes over us at the thought of there being nothing eternal in our final purposes, in the objects of those loves and aspirations which are our deepest ener-

gies. The monstrously lopsided equation of the universe and its knower, which we postulate as the ideal of cognition, is perfectly paralleled by the no less lopsided equation of the universe and the *doer*. We demand in it a *character* for which our emotions and active propensities shall be a match. Small as we are, minute as is the point by which the Cosmos impinges upon each one of us, each one desires to feel that his reaction at that point is congruous with the demands of the vast whole, that he balances the latter, so to speak, and is able to do what it expects of him. But as his abilities to 'do' lie wholly in the line of his natural propensities; as he enjoys reaction with such emotions as fortitude, hope, rapture, admiration, earnestness, and the like; and as he very unwillingly reacts with fear, disgust, despair, or doubt,—a philosophy which should legitimate only emotions of the latter sort would be sure to leave the mind a prey to discontent and craving.

"It is far too little recognized how entirely the intellect is built up of practical interests. The theory of Evolution is beginning to do very good service by its reduction of all mentality to the type of reflex action. Cognition, in this view, is but a fleeting moment, a cross-section at a certain point of what in its totality is a motor phenomenon. In the lower forms of life no one will pretend that cognition is anything more than a guide to appropriate action. The germinal question concerning things brought for the first time before consciousness is not the theoretic 'What is that?' but the practical 'Who goes there?' or rather, as Horwicz has admirably put it, 'What is to be done?'—'*Was fang' ich an?*' In all our discussions about the intelligence of lower animals the only test we use is that of their *acting* as if for a purpose. Cognition, in short, is incomplete until discharged in act. And although it is true that the later mental development, which attains its maximum through the hypertrophied cerebrum of man, gives birth to a vast amount of theoretic activity over and above that which is immediately ministerial to practice, yet the earlier claim is only postponed, not effaced, and the active nature asserts its rights to the end. . . .

"If there be any truth at all in this view, it follows that however vaguely a philosopher may define the ultimate universal datum, he cannot be said to leave it unknown to us so long as he in the slightest degree pretends that our emotional or active attitude towards it should be of one sort rather than another. He who says, 'Life is real, life is earnest,' however much he may speak of the fundamental mysteriousness of things, gives a distinct definition to that mysteriousness by ascribing to it the right to claim from us the particular mood called seriousness, which means the willingness to live with energy, though energy bring pain. The same is true of him who says that all is vanity. Indefinable as the predicate vanity may be *in se,* it is clearly enough something which permits anaesthesia, mere escape from suffering, to be our rule of life. There is no more ludicrous incongruity than for agnostics to proclaim with one breath that the substance of things is unknowable, and with the next that the thought of it should inspire us with admiration of its glory, reverence, and a willingness to add our cooperative push in the direction towards which its manifestations seem to be drifting. The unknowable may be unfathomed, but if it make such distinct demands upon our activity, we surely are not ignorant of its essential quality.

"If we survey the field of history and ask what feature all great periods of revival, of expansion of the human mind, display in common, we shall find, I think, simply this: that each and all of them have said to the human being, 'The inmost nature of the reality is congenial to *powers* which you possess.' In what did the emancipating message of primitive Christianity consist, but in the announcement that God recognizes those weak and tender impulses which paganism had so rudely overlooked? Take repentance: the man who can do nothing rightly can at least repent of his failures. But for paganism this faculty of repentance was a pure supernumerary, a straggler too late for the fair. Christianity took it and made it the one power within us which appealed straight to the heart of God. And after the night of the Middle Ages had so long branded with obloquy even the generous impulses of the flesh, and defined the Reality to be such that only slavish natures could commune with it, in what did the *Sursum corda!* of the Renaissance lie but in the proclamation that the archetype of verity in things laid claim on the widest activity of our whole aesthetic being? What were Luther's mission and Wesley's but appeals to powers which even the meanest of men might carry with them, faith and self-despair, but which were personal, requiring no priestly intermediation, and which brought their owner face to face with God? What caused the wildfire influence of Rousseau but the assurance he gave that man's nature was in harmony with the nature of things, if only the paralyzing corruptions of custom would stand from between? How did Kant and Fichte, Goethe and Schiller, inspire their time with cheer, except by saying, 'Use all your powers; that is the only obedience which the universe exacts'? And Carlyle with his gospel of Work, of Fact, of Veracity, how does he move us except by saying that the universe imposes no tasks upon us but such as the most humble can perform? Emerson's creed that everything that ever was or will be is here in the enveloping Now; that man has but to obey himself—'He who will rest in what he *is*, is a part of Destiny'—is in like manner nothing but an exorcism of all scepticism as to the pertinency of one's natural faculties.

"In a word, 'Son of Man, *stand upon thy feet* and I will speak unto thee!' is the only revelation of truth to which the solving epochs have helped the disciple. But that has been enough to satisfy the greater part of his rational need. *In se* and *per se* the universal essence has hardly been more defined by any of these formulae than by the agnostic *x;* but the mere assurance that my powers, such as they are, are not irrelevant to it, but pertinent, that it speaks to them and will in some way recognize their reply, that I can be a match for it if I will, and not a footless waif, suffices to make it rational to my feeling in the sense given above. Nothing could be more absurd than to hope for the definitive triumph of any philosophy which should refuse to legitimate, and to legitimate in an emphatic manner, the more powerful of our emotional and practical tendencies. Fatalism, whose solving word in all crises of behavior is 'All striving is vain,' will never reign supreme, for the impulse to take life strivingly is indestructible in the race. Moral creeds which speak to that impulse will be widely successful in spite of inconsistency, vagueness, and shadowy determination of expectancy. Man needs a rule for his will, and will invent one if one be not given him."

After the emotional and active needs come the intellectual and aesthetic ones. The two great aesthetic principles, of richness and of ease, dominate our intellectual as well as our sensuous life. And, *ceteris paribus*, no system which should not be rich, simple, and harmonious would have a chance of being chosen for belief, if rich, simple, and harmonious systems were also there. Into the latter we should unhesitatingly settle, with that welcoming attitude of the will in which belief consists. To quote from a remarkable book:

"This law, that our consciousness constantly tends to the minimum of complexity and to the maximum of definiteness, is of great importance for all our knowledge. . . . Our own activity of attention will thus determine what we are to know and what we are to believe. If things have more than a certain complexity, not only will our limited powers of attention forbid us to unravel this complexity, but we shall strongly desire to believe the things actually much simpler than they are. For our thoughts about them will have a constant tendency to become as simple and definite as possible. Put a man into a perfect chaos of phenomena, sights, sounds, feelings; and if the man continued to exist, and to be rational at all, his attention would doubtless soon find for him a way to make up some kind of rhythmic regularity, which he would impute to the things about him, so as to imagine that he had discovered some law of sequence in this mad new world. And thus, in every case where we fancy ourselves sure of a simple law of Nature, we must remember that a good deal of the fancied simplicity may be due in the given case not to Nature, but to the ineradicable prejudice of our own minds in favor of regularity and simplicity. All our thought is determined, in great measure, by this law of least effort, as it is found exemplified in our activity of attention. . . . The aim of the whole process seems to be to reach as complete and united a conception of reality as is possible, a conception wherein the greatest fullness of data shall be combined with the greatest simplicity of conception. The effort of consciousness seems to be to combine the greatest richness of content with the greatest definiteness of organization."[27]

The richness is got by including all the facts of sense in the scheme; the simplicity, by deducing them out of the smallest possible number of permanent and independent primordial entities: the definite organization, by assimilating these latter to ideal objects between which relations of an inwardly rational sort obtain. What these ideal objects and rational relations are will require a separate chapter to show.[28] Meanwhile, enough has surely been said to justify the assertion made above that no general offhand answer can be given as to which objects mankind shall choose as its realities. The fight is still under way. Our minds are yet chaotic; and at best we make a mixture and a compromise, as we yield to the claim of this interest or that, and follow first one and then another principle in turn. It is undeniably true that materialistic, or so-called 'scientific,' conceptions of the universe have so far gratified the purely intellectual interests more than the mere sentimental conceptions have. But, on the other hand, as already remarked, they leave the emotional and active interests cold. *The perfect object of belief would be a God or 'Soul of the World,' represented both optimistically and moralistically (if such a combination could be), and withal so definitely conceived as to show us why our phenomenal experiences should be sent to us by Him in just the very way in which they come.* All Science and all History would thus be accounted for in the deepest and simplest fashion. The very room in which I sit, its sensible walls and floor, and the feeling the air and fire within it give me, no less than the 'scientific' conceptions which I am urged to frame concerning the mode of existence of all these phenomena when my back is turned, would then all be corroborated, not de-realized, by the ultimate principle of my belief. The World-soul sends me just those phenomena in order that I may react upon them; and among the reactions is the intellectual one of spinning these conceptions. What is *beyond* the crude experiences is not an *alternative* to them, but something that *means* them for me here and now. It is safe to say that, if ever such a system is satisfactorily excogitated, mankind will drop all other systems and cling to that one alone as real. Meanwhile the other systems coexist with the attempts at that one, and, all being alike fragmentary, each has its little audience and day.

I have now, I trust, shown sufficiently what the psychologic sources of the sense of reality are. Certain postulates are given in our nature; and whatever satisfies those postulates is treated as if real.[29] I might therefore finish the chapter here, were it not that a few additional words will set the truth in a still clearer light.

Doubt

There is hardly a common man who (if consulted) would not say that things come to us in the first instance *as ideas;* and that if we take them for realities, it is because we *add something to them,* namely, the predicate of having also *'real existence outside of our thought.'* This notion that a higher faculty than the mere *having* of a conscious content is needed to make us know anything real by its means has pervaded psychology from the earliest times, and is the tradition of Scholasticism, Kantism, and Common-sense. Just as sensations must come as inward affections and then be 'extradited'; as objects of memory must appear at first as present unrealities, and subsequently be 'projected' backwards as past realities; so conceptions must be *entia rationis* till a higher faculty uses them as windows to look beyond the ego, into the real *extra*-mental world;—so runs the orthodox and popular account.

And there is no question that this is a true account of the way in which many of our later beliefs come to pass. The logical distinction between the bare thought of an object and belief in the object's reality is often a chronological distinction as well. The having and the crediting of

an idea do not always coalesce; for often we first suppose and then believe; first play with the notion, frame the hypothesis, and then affirm
the existence, of an object of thought. And we are quite conscious of the
succession of the two mental acts. But these cases are none of them
primitive cases. They only occur in minds long schooled to doubt by the
contradictions of experience. *The primitive impulse is to affirm immediately
the reality of all that is conceived.*[30] When we do doubt, however, in what
does the subsequent resolution of the doubt consist? It either consists in
a purely verbal performance, the coupling of the adjectives 'real' or 'outwardly existing' (as predicates) to the thing originally conceived (as subject); or it consists in the perception in the given case of *that for which
these adjectives,* abstracted from other similar concrete cases, *stand.* But
what these adjectives stand for, we now know well. They stand for
certain relations (immediate, or through intermediaries) to ourselves.
Whatever concrete objects have hitherto stood in those relations have
been for us 'real,' 'outwardly existing.' So that when we now abstractly
admit a thing to be 'real' (without perhaps going through any definite
perception of its relations), it is as if we said "it belongs in the same
world with those other objects." Naturally enough, we have hourly opportunities for this summary process of belief. All remote objects in
space or time are believed in this way. When I believe that some prehis-
toric savage chipped this flint, for example, the reality of the savage and
of his act makes no direct appeal either to my sensation, emotion, or
volition. What I mean by my belief in it is simply my dim sense of a *continuity* between the long dead savage and his doings and the present
world of which the flint forms part. It is pre-eminently a case for applying our doctrine of the 'fringe' (see Vol. I, p. 249). When I think the savage with one fringe of relationship, I believe in him; when I think him
without that fringe, or with another one (as, e.g., if I should class him
with 'scientific vagaries' in general), I disbelieve him. The word 'real' itself is, in short, a fringe.

Relations of Belief and Will

We shall see in Chapter XXVI that will consists in nothing but a manner
of attending to certain objects, or consenting to their stable presence before the mind. The objects, in the case of will, are those whose existence
depends on our thought, movements of our own body for example, or

facts which such movements executed in future may make real. Objects of belief, on the contrary, are those which do not change according as we think regarding them. I *will* to get up early tomorrow morning; I *believe* that I got up late yesterday morning; I *will* that my foreign bookseller in Boston shall procure me a German book and write to him to that effect. I *believe* that he will make me pay three dollars for it when it comes, etc. Now the important thing to notice is that this difference between the objects of will and belief is entirely immaterial, as far as the relation of the mind to them goes. All that the mind does is in both cases the same; it looks at the object and consents to its existence, espouses it, says 'it shall be my reality.' It turns to it, in short, in the interested active emotional way. The rest is done by nature, which in some cases *makes* the objects real which we think of in this manner, and in other cases does not. Nature cannot change the past to suit our thinking. She cannot change the stars or the winds; but she *does* change our bodies to suit our thinking, and through their instrumentality changes much besides; so the great practical distinction between objects which we may will or unwill, and objects which we can merely believe or disbelieve, grows up, and is of course one of the most important distinctions in the world. Its roots, however, do not lie in psychology, but in physiology; as the chapter on Volition will abundantly make plain. *Will and Belief, in short, meaning a certain relation between objects and the Self, are two names for one and the same* PSYCHOLOGICAL *phenomenon.* All the questions which arise concerning one are questions which arise concerning the other. The causes and conditions of the peculiar relation must be the same in both. The free-will question arises as regards belief. If our wills are indeterminate, so must our beliefs be, etc. The first act of free-will, in short, would naturally be to believe in free-will, etc. In Chapter XXVI, I shall mention this again.

A practical observation may end this chapter. If belief consists in an emotional reaction of the entire man on an object, how *can* we believe at will? We cannot control our emotions. Truly enough, a man cannot believe at will abruptly. Nature sometimes, and indeed not very infrequently, produces instantaneous conversions for us. She suddenly puts us in an active connection with objects of which she had till then left us cold. "I realize for the first time," we then say, "what that means!" This happens often with moral propositions. We have often heard them; but now they shoot into our lives; they move us; we feel their living force. Such instantaneous beliefs are truly enough not to be achieved by will. But *gradually* our will can lead us to the same results by a very simple method: *we need only in cold blood* ACT *as if the thing in question were real, and keep acting as if it were real, and it will infallibly end by growing into such a connection with our life that it will become real.* It will become so knit with habit and emotion that our interests in it will be those which character-ize belief. Those to whom 'God' and 'Duty' are now mere names can make them much more than that, if they make a little sacrifice to them every day. But all this is so well known in moral and religious education that I need say no more.[31]

4

The Hidden Self

"The Hidden Self" is a little-read piece James wrote in response to the work of the French psychologist Pierre Janet, by whom Freud was greatly influenced. The piece is concerned with what used to be called "multiple personality disorder" and is now called "dissociative personality disorder." "The Hidden Self" was very much admired by William James's sister, Alice, and by his brother Henry. Alice seems to have felt that the piece described her own condition. Henry's late great story "The Jolly Corner" presents William's—and Janet's—clinical findings in fictional form.

"The Hidden Self" shows clearly how automatic writing and hypnosis were, in James's view, neither magic nor charlatanry, but ways of accessing a part of the self that has become obscured. The piece is also notable for showing James's overriding interest in the therapeutic aspect of psychology, in curing the sick.

"The Hidden Self" begins with the much-quoted statement that "the great field for new discoveries . . . is always the Unclassified Residuum." It is an observation that helps explain why the hard-to-classify writings of William James are themselves a significant field for new discoveries.

"THE GREAT field for new discoveries," said a scientific friend to me the other day, "is always the Unclassified Residuum." Round about the accredited and orderly facts of every science there ever floats a sort of dust-cloud of exceptional observations, of occurrences minute and irregular, and seldom met with, which it always proves less easy to attend to than to ignore. The ideal of every science is that of a closed and completed system of truth. The charm of most sciences to their more passive disciples consists in their appearing, in fact, to wear just this ideal form. Each one of our various *ologies* seems to offer a definite head of classification for every possible phenomenon of the sort which it professes to cover; and, so far from free is most men's fancy, that when a consistent and organized scheme of this sort has once been comprehended and assimilated, a different scheme is unimaginable. No alternative, whether to whole or parts, can any longer be conceived as possible. Phenomena unclassifiable within the system are therefore paradoxical absurdities, and must be held untrue. When, moreover, as so often happens, the reports of them are vague and indirect, when they come as mere marvels and oddities rather than as things of serious moment, one neglects or denies them with the best of scientific consciences. Only the born geniuses let themselves be worried and fascinated by these outstanding exceptions, and get no peace till they are brought within the fold. Your Galileos, Galvanis, Fresnels, Purkinjes, and Darwins are always getting confounded and troubled by insignificant things. *Anyone* will renovate his science who will steadily look after the irregular phenomena. And when the science is renewed, its new formulas often have more of the voice of the exceptions in them than of what were supposed to be the rules.

No part of the unclassed residuum has usually been treated with a more contemptuous scientific disregard than the mass of phenomena generally called *mystical*. Physiology will have nothing to do with them. Orthodox psychology turns its back upon them. Medicine sweeps them out; or, at most, when in an anecdotal vein, records a few of them as "effects of the imagination," a phrase of mere dismissal whose meaning, in this connection, it is impossible to make precise. All the while, however, the phenomena are there, lying broadcast over the surface of history. No matter where you open its pages, you find things recorded under the name of divinations, inspirations, demoniacal possessions, apparitions, trances, ecstasies, miraculous healings and productions of disease, and occult powers possessed by peculiar individuals over persons and things in their neighborhood. We suppose that mediumship originated in Rochester, N.Y., and animal magnetism with Mesmer; but once look behind the pages of official history, in personal memoirs, legal documents, and popular narratives and books of anecdote, and you will find that there never was a time when these things were not reported just as abundantly as now. We college-bred gentry, who follow the stream of cosmopolitan culture exclusively, not infrequently stumble upon some old-established journal, or some voluminous native author, whose names are never heard of in *our* circle, but who number their readers by the quarter-million. It always gives us a little shock to find this mass of human beings not only living and ignoring us and all our gods, but actually reading and writing and cogitating without ever a thought of our canons, standards, and authorities. Well, a public no less large keeps and transmits from generation to generation the traditions and practices of the occult; but academic science cares as little for its beliefs and opinions as you, gentle subscriber to this MAGAZINE, care for those of the readers of the *Waverley* and the *Fireside Companion*. To no one type of mind is it given to discern the totality of Truth. Something escapes the best of us, not accidentally, but systematically, and because we have a twist. The scientific-academic mind and the feminine-mystical mind shy from each other's facts, just as they fly from each other's temper and spirit. Facts are there only for those who have a mental affinity with them. When once they are indisputably ascertained and admitted, the academic and critical minds are by far the best fitted ones to interpret and discuss them—for surely to pass from mystical to scientific speculations is like passing from lunacy to sanity; but on the other hand if there is anything which human history demonstrates, it is the extreme slowness with which the ordinary academic and critical mind acknowledges facts to exist which present themselves as *wild* facts with no stall or pigeon-hole, or as facts which threaten to break up the accepted system. In psychology, physiology, and medicine, wherever a debate between the Mystics and the Scientifics has been once for all decided, it is the Mystics who have usually proved to be right about the *facts*, while the Scientifics had the better of it in respect to the theories. The most recent and flagrant example of this is "animal magnetism," whose facts were stoutly dismissed as a pack of lies by academic medical science the world over, until the non-mystical theory of "hypnotic suggestion" was found for them, when they were admitted to be so excessively and dangerously common that special penal laws, forsooth, must be passed to keep all persons unequipped with medical diplomas from taking part in their production. Just so stigmatizations, invulnerabilities, instantaneous cures, inspired discourses, and demoniacal possessions, the records of which were shelved in our libraries but yesterday in the alcove headed "Superstitions," now, under the brand-new title of "Cases of hystero-epilepsy," are republished, reobserved, and reported with an even too credulous avidity.

Repugnant as the mystical style of philosophizing may be (especially when self-complacent), there is no sort of doubt that it goes with a gift for meeting with certain kinds of phenomenal experience. The writer has been forced in the past few years to this admission; and he now believes that he who will pay attention to facts of the sort dear to mystics, while reflecting upon them in academic-scientific ways, will be in the best possible position to help philosophy. It is a circumstance of good augury, that scientifically trained minds in all countries seem drifting to the same conclusion. Nowhere is this the case more than in France. France always was the home of the study of character. French literature is one long loving commentary on the variations of which individual human nature is capable. It seems fitting, therefore, that where minute and faithful observation of abnormal personal peculiarities is the order of the day, French science should take the lead. The work done at Paris and Nancy on the hypnotic trance is well known. Grant any amount of imperfection, still the essential thing remains, that here we have a mass of phenomena, hitherto outlawed, brought within the pale of sober investigation—the rest is only an affair of time. Last summer there appeared a record of observations made at Havre on certain hysterical somnambulists, by M. Pierre Janet, Professor of Philosophy in the Lycée of that town, and published in a volume of five hundred pages, entitled *L'Automatisme psychologique* (Paris, Alcan), which, serving as the author's thesis for the Doctorate of Science in Paris, made quite a commotion in the world to which such things pertain.

The new light which this book throws on what has long been vaguely talked about as unconscious mental life seems so important that I propose to entertain the readers of SCRIBNER's with some account of its contents, as an example of the sort of "psychical research" which a shrewd man with good opportunities may now achieve. The work bristles with facts, and is rather deficient in form. The author aims, moreover, at generalizing only where the phenomena force him to, and abstract statements are more embedded, and, as it were, interstitial, than is the case in most Gallic performances. In all this M. Janet's mind has an

English flavor about it which it is pleasant to meet with in one otherwise so good a Frenchman. I shall also quote some of the observations of M. Binet,[1] the most ingenious and original member of the Salpêtrière school, as these two gentlemen, working independently and with different subjects, come to conclusions which are strikingly in accord.

Both may be called contributors to the comparative science of trance-states. The "Subjects" studied by both are sufferers from the most aggravated forms of hysteria, and both authors, I fancy, are consequently led to exaggerate the dependence of the trance-conditions upon this kind of disease. M. Janet's subjects, whom he calls Léonie, Lucie, Rose, Marie, etc., were patients at the Havre Hospital, in charge of doctors who were his friends, and who allowed him to make observations on them to his heart's content. One of the most constant symptoms in persons suffering from hysteric disease in its extreme forms consists in alterations of the natural sensibility of various parts and organs of the body. Usually the alteration is in the direction of defect, or anaesthesia. One or both eyes are blind, or blind over one half of the field of vision, or the latter is extremely contracted, so that its margins appear dark, or else the patient has lost all sense for color. Hearing, taste, smell may similarly disappear, in part or in totality. Still more striking are the cutaneous anaesthesias. The old witch-finders, looking for the "devil's seals," well learned the existence of those insensible patches on the skin of their victims, to which the minute physical examinations of recent medicine have but lately attracted attention again. They may be scattered anywhere, but are very apt to affect one side of the body. Not infrequently they affect an entire lateral half, from head to foot, and the insensible skin of, say the left side, will then be found separated from the naturally sensitive skin of the right by a perfectly sharp line of demarcation down the middle of the front and back. Sometimes, most remarkable of all, the entire skin, hands, feet, face, everything, and the mucous membranes, muscles, and joints, so far as they can be explored, become *completely* insensible without the other vital functions being gravely disturbed. These anaesthesias and hemianaesthesias, in all their various grades, form the nucleus of M. Janet's observations and hypotheses. And, first of all, he has an hypothesis about the anaesthesia itself, which, like all provisional hypotheses, may do excellent service while awaiting the day when a better one shall take its place.

The original sin of the hysteric mind, he thinks, is the *contractions of the field of consciousness.* The attention has not sufficient strength to take in the normal number of sensations or ideas at once. If an ordinary person can feel ten things at a time, an hysteric can feel but five. Our minds are all of them like vessels full of water, and taking in a new drop makes another drop fall out; only the hysteric mental vessel is preternaturally small. The unifying or synthetizing power which the Ego exerts over the manifold facts which are offered to it is insufficient to do its full amount of work, and an ingrained habit is formed of neglecting or overlooking certain determinate portions of the mass. Thus one eye will be ignored, one arm and hand, or one half of the body. And apart from anaesthesia, hysterics are often extremely *distraites,* and unable to attend to two things at once. When talking with you they forget everything else. When Lucie stopped conversing directly with anyone, she ceased to be able to hear anyone else. You might stand behind her, call her by name, shout abuse into her ears, without making her turn round; or place yourself before her, show her objects, touch her, etc., without attracting her notice. When finally she becomes aware of you, she thinks you have just come into the room again, and greets you accordingly. This singular forgetfulness makes her liable to tell all her secrets aloud, unrestrained by the presence of unsuitable auditors. This contracted mental field (or state of monoideism, as it has been called) characterizes also the hypnotic state of normal persons, so that in this important respect a waking hysteric is like a well person in the hypnotic trance. Both are wholly lost in their present idea, its normal "reductives" and correctives having lapsed from view.

The anaesthesias of the class of patients we are considering can be made to disappear more or less completely by various odd processes. It has been recently found that magnets, plates of metal, the electrodes of a battery, placed against the skin, have this peculiar power. And when one side is relieved in this way, the anaesthesia is often found to have transferred itself to the opposite side, which, until then, was well. Whether these strange effects of magnets and metals be due to their direct physiological action, or to a prior effect on the patient's mind ("expectant attention" or "suggestion") is still a mooted question.[2] A still better awakener of sensibility in most of these subjects is the *hypnotic state,* which M. Janet seems to have most easily induced by the orthodox "magnetic" method of "passes" made over the face and body. It was in making these passes that he first stumbled on one of the most curious facts recorded in his volume. One day, when the subject named Lucie was in the hypnotic state, he made passes over her again for half an hour, just as if she were not already "asleep." The result was to throw her into a sort of syncope from which, after another half hour, she revived in a second somnambulic condition entirely unlike that which had characterized her hitherto—different sensibilities, a different memory, a different person, in short. In the waking state the poor young woman was anaesthetic all over, nearly deaf, and with a badly contracted field of vision. Bad as it was, however, sight was her best sense, and she used it as a guide in all her movements. With her eyes bandaged she was entirely helpless, and, like other persons of a similar sort whose cases have been recorded, she almost immediately fell asleep in consequence of the withdrawal of her last sensorial stimulus. M. Janet calls this waking or primary (one can hardly, in such a connection, say "normal") state by the name of Lucie 1. In Lucie 2, her first sort of hypnotic trance, the anaesthesias were diminished but not removed. In the deeper trance, "Lucie 3," brought about as just described, no trace of them remained. Her sensibility became perfect, and instead of being an extreme example of the "visual" type, she was transformed into what, in Professor Charcot's terminology, is known as a motor. That is to say, that whereas, when awake, she had thought in visual terms exclusively, and could imagine things only by remembering how they *looked*, now, in this deeper trance, her thoughts and memories seemed largely composed of images of movement and of touch—of course I state summarily here what appears in the book as an induction from many facts.

Having discovered this deeper trance in Lucie, M. Janet naturally became eager to find it in his other subjects. He found it in Rose, in Marie, and in Léonie; and, best of all, his brother, Dr. Jules Janet, who was *interne* at the Salpêtrière Hospital, found it in the celebrated subject Witt. whose trances had been studied for years by the various doctors of that institution without any of them having happened to awaken this very peculiar modification of the personality.

With the return of all the sensibilities in the deeper trance, the subjects are transformed, as it were, into normal persons. Their memories, in particular, grow more extensive; and here comes in M. Janet's first great theoretic generalization, which is this: When a certain kind of sensation is abolished in an hysteric patient, there is also abolished along with it all recollection of past sensations of that kind. If, for example, hearing be the anaesthetic sense, the patient becomes unable even to imagine sounds and voices, and has to speak, when speech is still possible, by means of motor or articulatory cues. If the motor sense be abolished, the patient must will the movements of his limbs by first defining them to his mind in visual terms, and must innervate his voice by premonitory ideas of the way in which the words are going to sound. The practical effects of this law of M. Janet's upon the patient's recollections would necessarily be great. Take things touched and handled, for example, and bodily movements. All memories of such things, all records of such experiences, being normally stored away in tactile terms, would have to be incontinently lost and forgotten so soon as the cutaneous and muscular sensibility should come to be cut out in the course of disease. Memory of them would be restored again, on the other hand, so soon as the sense of touch came back. Experiences, again, undergone during an anaesthetic condition of touch (and stored up consequently in visual or auditory terms exclusively), can have contracted no "associations" with tactile ideas, for such ideas are, for the time being, forgotten and practically non-existent. If, however, the touch-sensibilities ever are restored, and their ideas and memories with them, it may easily happen that they, with their clustered associations, may temporarily keep out of consciousness things like the visual and other experiences accumulated during the anaesthetic period which have no connections with them. If touch be the dominant sense in childhood, it would thus be explained why hysterical anaesthetics, whose tactile sensibilities and memories are brought back again by trance, so often assume a childlike deportment, and even call themselves by baby-names. Such, at least, is a suggestion of M. Janet's to explain a not infrequent sort of observation. MM. Bourru and Burot found, for instance, in their extraordinary male somnambulist Louis V., that reviving by suggestion a certain condition of bodily feeling in him would invariably transport him back to the epoch of his life when that condition had prevailed. He forgot the later years, and resumed the character and sort of intellect which had characterized him at the earlier time.

M. Janet's theory will provoke controversy and stimulate observation. You can ask little more than that of any theory. My own impression is that the law that anaesthesias carry "amnesias" with them, will not come out distinctly in every individual case. The intricacy of the associative processes, and the fact that comparatively few experiences are stored up in one form of sensibility alone, would be sufficient to prevent this. Perfect illustrations of the law will therefore be met with only in privileged subjects like M. Janet's own. *They* indeed seem to have exemplified it beautifully. M. Janet says:

> "It seems to me, that if I were to awake some morning with no muscular or tactile feelings, if, like Rose, I should suddenly lose my sense of color, and distinguish nothing in the universe but black and white, I should be terrified, and instantly appeal for help. These women, on the contrary, find their state so natural that they never even complain. When I, after some trials, proved to Rose that she could perceive no color, I found her ignorant of the fact. When I showed Lucie that she could feel neither pain nor contact, she answered, 'All the better!' When I made her conscious that she never knew where her arms were till she saw them, and that she lost her legs when in bed, she replied, '*C'est tout naturel,* as long as I don't see them; everyone is like that.' In a word, being incapable of comparing their present state of sensibility with a former one of which all memory is lost, they suffer no more than we do at not hearing the 'music of the spheres.' "

M. Janet restored their tactile sense temporarily by means of electric currents, passes, etc., and then made them handle various objects, such as keys and pencils, or make particular movements, like the sign of the cross. The moment the anaesthesia returned, they found it impossible to recollect the objects or the acts. "They had had nothing in their hands, they had done nothing," etc. The next day, however, sensibility being again restored by similar processes, they remembered perfectly the circumstance, and told what they had handled or had done.

It is in this way that M. Janet explains the general law that persons forget in the waking state what has happened to them in trance. There are differences of sensibility, and consequently breaches in the association of ideas. Certain of his hysterics (as we have seen) regained complete sensibility in their deeper trance. The result was such an enlargement of their power of recollecting that they could then go back and explain the origin of many of their peculiarities which would else be inexplicable. One stage in the great convulsive attack of hystero-epilepsy is what the French writers call *la phase des attitudes passionnelles,* in which the patient, without speaking or giving any account of herself, will go through the outward movements of fear, anger, or some other emotional state of mind. Usually this phase is, with each patient, a thing so stereotyped as to seem automatic, and doubts have even been expressed as to whether any consciousness exists whilst it lasts. When, however, the patient Lucie's tactile sensibility came back in her state of Lucie 3, she explained the origin of her hysteric crises in a great fright which she had had when a child, on a day when certain men, hid behind the curtains, had jumped out upon her; she told how she went through this scene again in all her crises; she told of her sleep-walking fits through the house when a child, and how, for several months, she had been shut in a dark room because of a disorder of the eyes. All these were things of which she recollects nothing when awake, because they were records of experiences mainly of motion and of touch, and when awake her feelings of touch and movement disappeared.

But the case of Léonie is the most interesting, and shows beautifully how, with the sensibilities and motor impulses, the memories and character will change.

> "This woman, whose life sounds more like an improbable romance than a genuine history, has had attacks of natural somnambulism since the age of three years. She has been hypnotized constantly, by all sorts of persons, from the age of sixteen upwards, and she is now forty-five. Whilst her normal life developed in one way in the midst of her poor country surroundings, her second life was passed in drawing-rooms and doctors' offices, and naturally took an entirely different direction. To-day, when in her normal state, this poor peasant-woman is a serious and rather sad person, calm and slow, very mild with everyone, and extremely timid; to look at her one would never suspect the personage which she contains. But hardly is she put to sleep hypnotically than a metamorphosis occurs. Her face is no longer the same. She keeps her eyes closed, it is true, but the acuteness of her other senses supplies their place. She is gay, noisy, restless, sometimes insupportably so. She remains good-natured, but has acquired a singular tendency to irony and sharp jesting. Nothing is more curious than to hear her, after a sitting when she has received a visit from strangers who wished to see her asleep. She gives a word-portrait of them, apes their manners, pretends to know their little ridiculous aspects and passions, and for each invents a romance. To this character must be added the possession of an enormous number of recollections whose existence she does not even suspect when awake, for her amnesia is then complete. . . . She refuses the name of Léonie, and takes that of Léontine (Léonie 2), to which her first magnetizers had accustomed her. 'That good woman is not myself,' she says, 'she is too

stupid.' . . . To herself Léontine (or Léonie 2), she attributes all the
sensations and all the actions; in a word, all the conscious experiences, which she has undergone *in somnambulism,* and knits them together to make the history of her already long life. To Léonie 1, on the
other hand, she exclusively ascribes the events lived through in waking hours. I was at first struck by an important exception to the rule,
and was disposed to think that there might be something arbitrary in
this partition of her recollections. In the normal state Léonie has a
husband and children. But Léonie 2, the somnambulist, whilst acknowledging the children as her own, attributes the husband to 'the
other.' This choice was perhaps explicable, but it followed no rule. It
was not till later that I learned that her magnetizers in early days, as
audacious as certain hypnotizers of recent date, had somnambulized
her for her first *accouchements,* and that she had lapsed into that state
spontaneously in the later ones. Léonie 2 was thus quite right in ascribing to herself the children—since it was she who had had them—
and the rule that her first trance-state forms a different personality
was not broken. But it is the same with her second state of trance.
When after the renewed passes, syncope, etc., she reaches the condition which I have called Léonie 3, she is another person still. Serious
and grave, instead of being a restless child, she speaks slowly and
moves but little. Again she separates herself from the waking Léonie
1. 'A good but rather stupid woman,' she says, 'and not me.' And she
also separates herself from Léonie 2. 'How can you see anything of
me in that crazy creature?' she says. 'Fortunately I am nothing for
her!'"

Léonie 1 knows only of herself; Léonie 2 of herself and of Léonie 1;
Léonie 3 knows of herself and of both the others. Léonie 1 has a visual
consciousness; Léonie 2 has one both visual and auditory; in Léonie 3 it
is at once visual, auditory, and tactile. Professor Janet thought at first
that he was Léonie 3's discoverer. But she told him that she had been
frequently in that condition before. Dr. Perrier, a former magnetizer,
had hit upon her just as M. Janet had, in seeking by means of passes to
deepen the sleep of Léonie 2. "This resurrection of a somnambulic personage, who had been extinct for twenty years, is curious enough; and
in speaking to Léonie 3 I naturally now adopt the name of Léonore,
which was given her by her first master."

The reader easily sees what surprises the trance-state may prepare,
not only for the subject but for the operator. For the subject the surprises are often inconvenient enough, especially when the trance comes

and goes spontaneously. Thus Léonie 1 is overwhelmed with embarrass-
ment when, in the street, Léonie 2's gentlemen-friends (who are not
hers) accost her. Léonie 2 spontaneously writes letters, which Léonie 1,
not understanding, destroys when she finds them. Léonie 2 proceeds to
thereupon hide them in a photograph album, into which she knows
Léonie 1 will never look, because it contains the portrait of her former
magnetizer, the sight of whom may put her to sleep again, which she
dislikes. Léonie 1 finds herself in places known only to Léonie 2, to
which the latter has led her, and then taken flight, etc. One sees the possibility of a new kind of "Comedy of Errors," to which it would take the
skill of a Parisian *vaudevilliste* to do justice.

I fear that the reader unversed in this sort of lore will here let his
growing impatience master him, and throw away my article as the work
of either a mystifier or a dupe. These facts seem so silly and unreal,
these "subjects" so contrary to all that our education has led us to expect
our fellow-creatures to be! Well, our education has been too narrow,
that is all. Let one but once become familiar with the behavior of that
not very rare personage, a good hypnotic subject, and the entire class of
phenomena which I am recording come to seem not only possible but
probable. It is, after all, only the fulfilment of what Locke's speculative
genius suggested long ago, when, in that famous chapter on "Identity
and Diversity" which occasioned such scandal in its day, after saying
that personality extended no farther than consciousness, he went on to
affirm that there would be two different selves or persons in one man, if
the experiences undergone by that man should fall into two groups,
each gathered into a distinct focus of recollection.

But still more remarkable things are to come, so I pray the reader to
be patient and hear me a little longer, even if he means to give me up at
last. These different personalities, admitted as possible by Locke, which
we, under M. Janet's guidance, have seen actually succeeding each
other under the names of Lucie 1, 2, and 3; and under those of Léonie 1,
2, and 3 mutually disowning and despising each other; are proved by M.
Janet not only to exist in the successive forms in which we have seen
them, but to *coexist*, to exist simultaneously; in such wise that while Lucie 1, for example, is apparently the only Lucie, anaesthetic, helpless,
yet absorbed in conversation, that other Lucie—Lucie 3—is all the time
"alive and kicking" inside of the same woman, and fully sensible and

wide awake, and occupied with her own quite different concerns. This simultaneous coexistence of the different personages into which one human being may be split is the *great* thesis of M. Janet's book. Others, as Edmund Gurney, Bernheim, Binet, and more besides, have had the same idea, and proved it for certain cases; but M. Janet has emphasized and generalized it, and shown it to be true universally. He has been enabled to do this by *tapping* the submerged consciousness and making it respond in certain peculiar ways of which I now proceed to give a brief account. He found in several subjects, when the ordinary or primary consciousness was fully absorbed in conversation with a visitor (and the reader will remember how absolutely these hysterics then lapse into oblivion of surrounding things), that the submerged self would hear his voice if he came up and addressed the subject in a whisper; and would respond either by obeying such orders as he gave, or by gestures, or, finally, by pencil-writing on a sheet of paper placed under the hand. The *ostensible* consciousness, meanwhile, would go on with the conversation, entirely unaware of the gestures, acts, or writing performances of the hand. These latter, in turn, appeared quite as little disturbed by the upper consciousness's concerns. This proof by automatic writing of the secondary consciousness's existence is the most cogent and striking one; but a crowd of other facts prove the same thing. If I run through them all rapidly, the reader will probably be convinced.

The apparently anaesthetic hand of these subjects, for one thing, will often adapt itself discriminatingly to whatever object may be put into it. With a pencil it will make writing movements; into a pair of scissors it will put its fingers, and will open and shut them, etc. The primary consciousness, so to call it, is meanwhile unable to say whether or no *anything* is in the hand, if the latter be hidden from sight. "I put a pair of eye-glasses into Léonie's anaesthetic hand; this hand opens it and raises it towards the nose, but halfway thither it enters the field of vision of Léonie, who sees it and stops stupefied. 'Why,' says she, 'I have an eye-glass in my left hand!'" M. Binet found a very curious sort of connection between the apparently anaesthetic skin and the mind in some Salpêtrière subjects. Things placed in the hand were not felt, but *thought* of (apparently in visual terms), and in no wise referred by the subject to their starting-point in the hand's sensation. A key, a knife, placed in the hand occasioned *ideas* of a key or a knife, but the hand felt nothing.

Similarly the subject thought of the number 3, 6, etc., if the hand or finger was bent three or six times by the operator, or if he stroked it three, six, etc., times.

In certain individuals there was found a still odder phenomenon, which reminds one of that curious idiosyncrasy of "colored hearing" of which a few cases have been lately described with great care by foreign writers. These individuals, namely, *saw* the impression received by the hand, but could not feel it; and the things seen appeared by no means associated with the hand, but more like an independent vision, which usually interested and surprised the patient. Her hand being hidden by a screen, she was ordered to look at another screen and to tell of any visual image which might project itself thereon. Numbers would then come, corresponding to the number of times the insensible member was raised, touched, etc. Colored lines and figures would come, corresponding to similar ones traced on the palm; the hand itself, or its fingers, would come when manipulated; and, finally, objects placed in it would come; but on the hand itself nothing could ever be felt. Of course, simulation would not be hard here; but M. Binet disbelieves this (usually very shallow) explanation to be a probable one of the cases in question.[3]

The usual way in which doctors measure the delicacy of our touch is by the compass-points. Two points are normally felt as one whenever they are too close together for discrimination; but what is "too close" on one part of the skin may seem very far apart on another. In the middle of the back or on the thigh less than three inches may be too close; on the finger-tip a tenth of an inch is far enough apart. Now, as tested in this way, with the appeal made to the primary consciousness, which talks through the mouth, and seems to hold the field alone, a certain person's skin may be entirely anaesthetic and not feel the compass-points at all; and yet this same skin will prove to have a perfectly normal sensibility if the appeal be made to that other secondary or sub-consciousness which expresses itself automatically by writing or by movements of the hand. M. Binet, M. Pierre Janet, and M. Jules Janet have all found this. The subject, whenever touched, would signify "one point" or "two points," as accurately as if she were a normal person. But she would signify it only by these movements; and of the movements themselves her primary self would be as unconscious as of the facts they signified, for what the submerged consciousness makes the hand do automatically is unknown to the upper consciousness, which uses the mouth.

Messrs. Bernheim and Pitres have also proved, by observations too complicated to be given here, that the hysterical blindness is no real blindness at all. The eye of an hysteric which is totally blind when the other, or seeing eye, is shut, will do its share of vision perfectly well when *both* eyes are open together. But even where both eyes are semi-blind from hysterical disease, the method of automatic writing proves that their perceptions exist, only cut off from communication with the upper consciousness. M. Binet has found the hand of his patients un-consciously writing down words which their eyes were vainly endeav-oring to "see," *i.e.*, to bring to the upper consciousness. Their submerged consciousness was, of course, seeing them, or the hand couldn't have written as it did. Similarly the sub-conscious self perfectly well perceives colors which the hysterically color-blind eyes cannot bring to the nor-mal consciousness. Again, pricks, burns, and pinches on the anaesthetic skin, all unnoticed by the upper self, are recollected to have been suf-fered, and complained of, as soon as the under self gets a chance to ex-press itself by the passage of the subject into hypnotic trance.

It must be admitted therefore that, in certain persons at least, the total possible consciousness may be split into parts which coexist, but mutually ignore each other and share the objects of knowledge between them, and—more remarkable still—are complementary. Give an object to one of the consciousnesses, and by that fact you remove it from the other or others. Barring a certain common fund of information, like the command of language, etc., what the upper self knows, the under self is ignorant of, and *vice versa*. M. Janet has proved this beautifully in his subject Lucie. The following experiment will serve as the type of the rest: In her trance he covered her lap with cards, each bearing a num-ber. He then told her that on waking she should *not see* any card whose number was a multiple of three. This is the ordinary so-called "post-hypnotic suggestion," now well known, and for which Lucie was a well-adapted subject. Accordingly, when she was awakened and asked about the papers on her lap, she counted and picked up only those whose number was not a multiple of 3. To the 12, 18, 9, etc., she was blind. But the hand, when the sub-conscious self was interrogated by the usual method of engrossing the upper self in another conversation, wrote that the only cards in Lucie's lap were those numbered 12, 18, 9, etc., and on being asked to pick up all the cards which were there, picked up these and let the others lie. Similarly, when the sight of certain things was suggested to the sub-conscious Lucie, the normal Lucie suddenly became partially or totally blind. "What is the matter? I can't see!" the normal personage suddenly cried out in the midst of her conversation, when M. Janet whispered to the secondary personage to make use of her eyes. The anaesthesias, paralyses, contractions, and other irregularities from which hysterics suffer seem, then, to be due to the fact that their secondary personage has enriched itself by robbing the primary one of a function which the latter ought to have retained. The curative indication is evident: Get at the secondary personage by hypnotization, or in whatever other way, and make her *give up* the eye, the skin, the arm, or whatever the affected part may be. The normal self thereupon regains possession, sees, feels, and is able to move again. In this way M. Jules Janet easily cured the subject Witt. of all sorts of afflictions which, until he had discovered the secret of her deeper trance, it had been difficult to subdue. *"Cessez cette mauvaise plaisanterie"* he said to the secondary self, and the latter obeyed. The way in which the various personages share the stock of possible sensations between them seems to be amusingly illustrated in this young woman. When awake, her skin is insensible everywhere except on a zone about the arm where she habitually wears a gold bracelet. This zone has feeling; but in the deeper trance, when all the rest of her body feels, this particular zone becomes absolutely anaesthetic.

Sometimes the mutual ignorance of the selves leads to incidents which are strange enough. The acts and movements performed by the sub-conscious self are withdrawn from the conscious one, and the subject will do all sorts of incongruous things, of which he remains quite unaware.

> "I order Lucie [by the method of *distraction*] to make a *pied de nez*, and her hands go forthwith to the end of her nose. Asked what she is doing, she replies that she is doing nothing, and continues for a long time talking, with no apparent suspicion that her fingers are moving in front of her nose. I make her walk about the room, she continues to speak, and believes herself sitting down."

M. Janet observed similar acts in a man in alcoholic delirium. Whilst the doctor was questioning him, M. Janet made him, by whispered suggestion, walk, sit, kneel, and even lie down on his face on the floor, he all the while believing himself to be standing beside his bed. Such *bizarreries* sound incredible until one has seen their like. Long ago, without understanding it, I myself saw a small example of the way in which a person's knowledge may be shared by the two selves. A young woman, who had been writing automatically, was sitting with a pencil in her hand, trying to recall, at my request, the name of a gentleman whom she had once seen. She could only recollect the first syllable. *Her hand,* meanwhile, without her knowledge, wrote down the last two syllables. In a perfectly healthy young man who can write with the planchette, I lately found the hand to be entirely anaesthetic during the writing act. I could prick it severely without the subject knowing the fact. The planchette, however, accused me in strong terms of hurting the hand. Pricks on the *other* (non-writing) hand, meanwhile, which awakened strong protest from the young man's vocal organs, were denied to exist by the self which made the planchette go.

We get exactly similar results in post-hypnotic suggestion. It is a familiar fact that certain subjects, when told during a trance to perform an act or to experience an hallucination after waking, will, when the time comes, obey the command. How is the command registered? How is its performance so accurately timed? These problems were long a mystery, for the primary personality remembers nothing of the trance or the suggestion, and will often trump up an improvised pretext for yielding to the unaccountable impulse which comes over him so suddenly, and which he cannot resist. Edmund Gurney was the first to discover, by means of automatic writing, that the secondary self was awake, keeping its attention constantly fixed on the command and watching for the signal of its execution. Certain trance-subjects, who were also automatic writers, when roused from trance and put to the planchette—not knowing then what they wrote, and having their upper attention fully engrossed by reading aloud, talking, or solving problems in mental arithmetic—would inscribe the orders they had received, together with notes relative to the time elapsed and the time yet to run before the execution. It is therefore to no "automatism," in the mechanical sense, that such acts are due: a self presides over them, a split-off, limited, and buried, but yet a fully conscious self. More than this, the buried self often comes to the surface and drives out the other self whilst the acts are performing. In other words, the subject lapses into trance again when the moment arrives for execution, and has no subsequent recollection of the act which he has done. Gurney and Beaunis established this fact, which has since been verified on a large scale; and Gurney also showed that the patient became *suggestible* again during the brief time of the performance. M. Janet's observations, in their turn, well illustrate the phenomenon.

"I tell Lucie to keep her arms raised after she shall have awakened. Hardly is she in the normal state when up go her arms above her head, but she pays no attention to them. She goes, comes, converses, holding her arms high in the air. If asked what her arms are doing, she is surprised at such a question and says, very sincerely: 'My hands are doing nothing; they are just like yours.' . . . I command her to weep, and when awake she really sobs, but continues in the midst of her tears to talk of very gay matters. The sobbing over, there remains no trace of this grief, which seemed to have been quite sub-conscious.'

The primary self often has to invent an hallucination by which to mask and hide from its own view the deeds which the other self is enacting. Léonie 3 writes real letters, whilst Léonie 1 believes that she is knitting; or Lucie 3 really comes to the doctor's office, whilst Lucie 1 believes herself to be at home. This is a sort of delirium. The alphabet, or the series of numbers, when handed over to the attention of the secondary personage, may, for the time being, be lost to the normal self. Whilst the hand writes the alphabet, obediently to command, the "subject," to her great stupefaction, finds herself unable to recall it, etc. Few things are more curious than these relations of mutual exclusion, of which all gradations exist, between the several partial consciousnesses.

How far this splitting up of the mind into separate consciousnesses may obtain in each one of us is a problem. M. Janet holds that it is only possible where there is abnormal weakness, and consequently a defect of unifying or co-ordinating power. An hysteric woman abandons part of her consciousness because she is too weak nervously to hold it all together. The abandoned part, meanwhile, may solidify into a secondary or sub-conscious self. In a perfectly sound subject, on the other hand, what is dropped out of mind at one moment keeps coming back at the next. The whole fund of experiences and knowledges remains integrated, and no split-off portions of it can get organized stably enough to form subordinate selves. The stability, monotony, and stupidity of these latter is often very striking. The post-hypnotic self-consciousness seems to think of nothing but the order which it last received; the cataleptic sub-consciousness, of nothing but the last position imprinted on the limb. M. Janet could cause definitely circumscribed reddening and tumefaction of the skin, on two of his subjects, by suggesting to them in hypnotism the hallucination of a mustard-poultice of any special shape. *"J'ai tout le temps pensé à votre sinapisme,"* says the subject, when put back into trance after the suggestion has taken effect. A man, N——, whom M. Janet operated on at long intervals, was between whiles tampered with by another operator, and when put to sleep again by M. Janet, said he was "too far away to receive orders, being in Algiers." The other operator, having suggested that hallucination, had forgotten to remove it before waking the subject from his trance, and the poor, passive, trance-personality had stuck for weeks in the stagnant dream. Léonie's sub-conscious performances having been illustrated to a caller by a *pied de nez*, executed with her left hand in the course of conversation, when, a year later, she meets him again up goes the same hand to her nose again, without Léonie 1 suspecting the fact.

And this leads me to what, after all, is the really important part of these investigations—I mean their possible application to the relief of human misery. Let one think and say what one will about the crudity and intellectual barbarism of much of the philosophizing of our contemporary nerve-doctors; let one dislike as much as one may please the thoroughly materialistic attitude of mind which many of them show; still, their work, as a whole, is sanctified by its positive, practical fertility. Theorems about the unity of the thinking principle will always be, as they always have been, *barren;* but observations of fact lead to new issues *in infinitum.* And when one reflects that nothing less than the cure of insanity—that direst of human afflictions—lies possibly at the end of such inquiries as those which M. Janet and his *confrères* are beginning, one feels as if the disdain which some spiritualistic psychologists exhibit for such researches were very poorly placed. The way to redeem people from barbarism is not to stand aloof and sneer at their awkward attempts, but to show them how to do the same things better. Ordinary hypnotic suggestion is proving itself immensely fertile in the therapeutic field; and the subtler knowledge of sub-conscious states which we are now gaining will certainly increase our powers in this direction many fold. Who knows how many pathological states (not simply nervous

and functional ones, but organic ones too) may be due to the existence
of some perverse buried fragment of consciousness obstinately nourishing its narrow memory or delusion, and thereby inhibiting the normal
flow of life? A concrete case will best exhibit what I mean. On the whole,
it is more deeply suggestive to me than anything in Janet's book.

The story is that of a young girl of nineteen named Marie, who came
to the hospital in an almost desperate condition, with monthly convulsive crises, chill, fever, delirium, attacks of terror, etc., lasting for days,
together with various shifting anaesthesias and contractures all the time,
and a fixed blindness of the left eye. At first M. Janet, divining no particular psychological factor in the case, took little interest in the patient,
who remained in the hospital for seven months, and had all the usual
courses of treatment applied, including water-cure and ordinary hypnotic suggestions, without the slightest good effect.

She then fell into a sort of despair, of which the result was to make
M. Janet try to throw her into a deeper trance, so as to get, if possible,
some knowledge of her remoter psychologic antecedents, and of the
original causes of the disease, of which, in the waking state and in ordinary hypnotism, she could give no definite account. He succeeded even
beyond his expectations; for both her early memories and the internal
memory of her crises returned in the deep somnambulism, and she explained three things: Her periodical chill, fever, and delirium were due
to a foolish immersion of herself in cold water at the age of thirteen. The
chill, fever, etc., were consequences which then ensued; and now, years
later, the experience then stamped in upon the brain for the first time
was *repeating itself* at regular intervals in the form of an hallucination
undergone by the sub-conscious self, and of which the primary personality only experienced the outer results. The attacks of terror were accounted for by another shocking experience. At the age of sixteen she
had seen an old woman killed by falling from a height; and the sub-
conscious self, for reasons best known to itself, saw fit to believe itself
present at this experience also whenever the other crises came on. The
hysterical blindness of her left eye had the same sort of origin, dating
back to her sixth year, when she had been forced, in spite of her cries, to
sleep in the same bed with another child, the left half of whose face bore
a disgusting eruption. The result was an eruption on the same parts of
her own face, which came back for several years before it disappeared

entirely, and left behind it an anaesthesia of the skin and the blindness of the eye.

So much for the origin of the poor girl's various afflictions. Now for the cure! The thing needed was, of course, to get the subconscious personality to leave off having these senseless hallucinations. But they had become so stereotyped and habitual that this proved no easy task to achieve. Simple commands were fruitless; but M. Janet at last hit upon an artifice, which shows how many resources the successful mind-doctor must possess. He carried the poor Marie back in imagination to the earlier dates. It proved as easy with her as with many others when entranced, to produce the hallucination that she was again a child, all that was needed being an impressive affirmation to that effect. Accordingly M. Janet, replacing her in this wise at the age of six, made her go through the bed-scene again, but gave it a different *dénouement*. He made her believe that the horrible child had no eruption and was charming, so that she was finally convinced, and caressed without fear this new object of her imagination. He made her re-enact the scene of the cold immersion, but gave it also an entirely different result. He made her live again through the old woman's accident, but substituted a comical issue for the old tragical one which had made so deep an impression. The subconscious Marie, passive and docile as usual, adopted these new versions of the old tales; and was apparently either living in monotonous contemplation of them or had become extinct altogether when M. Janet wrote his book. For all morbid symptoms ceased as if by magic. "It is five months," our author says, "since these experiments were performed. Marie shows no longer the slightest mark of hysteria. She is well; and, in particular, has grown quite stout. Her physical aspect has absolutely changed." Finally, she is no longer hypnotizable, as often happens in these cases when the health returns.

The mind-curers and Christian scientists, of whom we have lately heard so much, unquestionably get, by widely different methods, results, in certain cases, no less remarkable than this. The ordinary medical man, if he believes the facts at all, dismisses them from his attention with the cut-and-dried remark that they are "only effects of the imagination." It is the great merit of these French investigators, and of Messrs. Myers, Gurney, and the "psychical researchers," that they are for the first time trying to read some sort of a definite meaning into this vaguest of phrases. Little by little the meaning will grow more precise. It seems to me a very great step to have ascertained that the secondary self, or selves, coexist with the primary one, the trance-personalities with the normal one, during the waking state. But just what these secondary selves may be, and what are their remoter relations and conditions of existence, are questions to which the answer is anything but clear. My own decided impression is that M. Janet's generalizations are based on too limited a number of cases to cover the whole ground. He would have it that the secondary self is always a symptom of hysteria, and that the essential fact about hysteria is the lack of synthetizing power and consequent disintegration of the field of consciousness into mutually exclusive parts. The secondary and the primary consciousnesses added together can, on M. Janet's theory, never exceed the normally total consciousness of the individual. This theory certainly expresses pretty well the facts which have fallen under its author's own observation, though even here, if this were a critical article, I might have something to say. But there are trances which obey another type. I know a non-hysterical woman who, in her trances, knows facts which altogether transcend her *possible* normal consciousness, facts about the lives of people whom she never saw or heard of before. I am well aware of all the liabilities to which this statement exposes me, and I make it deliberately, having practically no doubt whatever of its truth. My *own* impression is that the trance-condition is an immensely complex and fluctuating thing, into the understanding of which we have hardly begun to penetrate, and concerning which any very sweeping generalization is sure to be premature. *A comparative study of trances and subconscious states* is meanwhile of the most urgent importance for the comprehension of our nature. It often happens that scattered facts of a certain kind float around for a long time, but that nothing scientific or solid comes of them until some man writes just enough of a book to give them a possible body and meaning. Then they shoot together, as it were, from all directions, and that book becomes the centre of crystallization of a rapid accumulation of new knowledge. Such a book I am sure that M. Janet's ought to be; and I confidently prophesy that anyone who may be induced by this article to follow the path of study in which it is so brilliant a pioneer will reap a rich reward.

5

Habit

Habit is one of William James's favorite subjects, and a subject to the understanding of which he made a major contribution. As a young man he had read Sydney Smith on habit and had come to agree with Smith that there is scarcely anything habit cannot accomplish. "There is no degree of disguise or distortion which human nature may not be made to assume from habit," wrote Smith in his *Elementary Sketches of Moral Philosophy*. "It grows in every direction in which it is trained, and accommodates itself to every circumstance which caprice or design places in its way. There is not a single principle of our nature, which may not be cherished to the complete exclusion and subjugation of all the rest." James likens the power of habit to the fold in a sheet of paper. Once folded, the paper can be much more easily folded along the same line the second time. The first time we react to a stimulus is an act, says James, and the second and all subsequent times are habit. James agrees with the Duke of Wellington's saying "habit is a second nature! habit is ten times nature."

Gordon Allport, the father of modern personality theory, has observed, in an introduction to a 1961 reprint of James's *Psychology: Briefer Course*, that "habit, for James, is the structural unit of mental life." James treats the subject in several places; the piece included here is from *Psychology: Briefer Course*, which James originally published in 1892. Here he gives a pronounced physiological account. A new habit, he says, is "a new pathway of discharge formed in the brain, by which certain incoming currents ever after tend to escape." This is the essay where James speaks of habit as the "enormous fly-wheel of society" and where he makes a personal appeal that "the great thing, then, in all education, is to *make our nervous system our ally instead of our enemy*" (his italics).

⟫⟩◆⟨⟪

Its Importance for Psychology.—There remains a condition of general neural activity so important as to deserve a chapter by itself—I refer to the aptitude of the nerve-centres, especially of the hemispheres, for acquiring habits. *An acquired habit, from the physiological point of view, is nothing but a new pathway of discharge formed in the brain, by which certain incoming currents ever after tend to escape.* That is the thesis of this chapter; and we shall see in the later and more psychological chapters that such functions as the association of ideas, perception, memory, reasoning, the education of the will, etc. etc., can best be understood as results of the formation *de novo* of just such pathways of discharge.

Habit has a physical basis. The moment one tries to define what habit is, one is led to the fundamental properties of matter. The laws of Nature are nothing but the immutable habits which the different elementary sorts of matter follow in their actions and reactions upon each other. In the organic world, however, the habits are more variable than this. Even instincts vary from one individual to another of a kind; and are modified in the same individual, as we shall later see, to suit the exigencies of the case. On the principles of the atomistic philosophy the habits of an elementary particle of matter cannot change, because the particle is itself an unchangeable thing; but those of a compound mass of matter can change, because they are in the last instance due to the structure of the compound, and either outward forces or inward tensions can, from one hour to another, turn that structure into something different from what it was. That is, they can do so if the body be plastic enough to maintain its integrity, and be not disrupted when its structure yields. The change of structure here spoken of need not involve the outward shape; it may be invisible and molecular, as when a bar of iron becomes magnetic or crystalline through the action of certain outward causes, or india-rubber becomes friable, or plaster 'sets.' All these changes are rather slow; the material in question opposes a certain resistance to the modifying cause, which it takes time to overcome, but the gradual yielding whereof often saves the material from being disintegrated altogether. When the structure has yielded, the same inertia becomes a condition of its comparative permanence in the new form, and of the new habits the body then manifests. *Plasticity,* then, in the wide sense of the word, means the possession of a structure weak enough to yield to an influence, but strong enough not to yield all at once. Each relatively stable phase of equilibrium in such a structure is marked by what we may call a new set of habits. Organic matter, especially nervous tissue, seems endowed with a very extraordinary degree of plasticity of this sort; so that we may without hesitation lay down as our first proposition the following: that *the phenomena of habit in living beings are due to the plasticity of the organic materials of which their bodies are composed.*

The philosophy of habit is thus, in the first instance, a chapter in physics rather than in physiology or psychology. That it is at bottom a physical principle is admitted by all good recent writers on the subject. They call attention to analogues of acquired habits exhibited by dead matter. Thus, M. Léon Dumont writes:

"Everyone knows how a garment, after having been worn a certain time, clings to the shape of the body better than when it was new; there has been a change in the tissue, and this change is a new habit of cohesion. A lock works better after being used some time; at the outset more force was required to overcome certain roughnesses in the mechanism. The overcoming of their resistance is a phenomenon of habituation. It costs less trouble to fold a paper when it has been folded already; . . . and just so the impressions of outer objects fashion for themselves in the nervous system more and more appropriate paths, and these vital phenomena recur under similar excitements from without, when they have been interrupted a certain time."

Not in the nervous system alone. A scar anywhere is a *locus minoris resistentiae,* more liable to be abraded, inflamed, to suffer pain and cold, than are the neighboring parts. A sprained ankle, a dislocated arm, are in danger of being sprained or dislocated again; joints that have once been attacked by rheumatism or gout, mucous membranes that have been the seat of catarrh, are with each fresh recurrence more prone to a relapse, until often the morbid state chronically substitutes itself for the sound one. And in the nervous system itself it is well known how many so-called functional diseases seem to keep themselves going simply because they happen to have once begun; and how the forcible cutting short by medicine of a few attacks is often sufficient to enable the physiological forces to get possession of the field again, and to bring the or-

gans back to functions of health. Epilepsies, neuralgias, convulsive affections of various sorts, insomnias, are so many cases in point. And, to
take what are more obviously habits, the success with which a 'weaning'
treatment can often be applied to the victims of unhealthy indulgence
of passion, or of mere complaining or irascible disposition, shows us
how much the morbid manifestations themselves were due to the mere
inertia of the nervous organs, when once launched on a false career.

Habits are due to pathways through the nerve-centres. If habits are due to the plasticity of materials to outward agents, we can immediately see to what outward influences, if to any, the brain-matter is
plastic. Not to mechanical pressures, not to thermal changes, not to any
of the forces to which all the other organs of our body are exposed; for,
as we saw in the chapter "Sensation in General" in *Psychology: Briefer
Course,* Nature has so blanketed and wrapped the brain about that the
only impressions that can be made upon it are through the blood, on
the one hand, and the sensory nerve-roots, on the other; and it is to the
infinitely attenuated currents that pour in through these latter channels
that the hemispherical cortex shows itself to be so peculiarly susceptible.
The currents, once in, must find a way out. In getting out they leave
their traces in the paths which they take. The only thing they *can* do, in
short, is to deepen old paths or to make new ones; and the whole plasticity of the brain sums itself up in two words when we call it an organ
in which currents pouring in from the sense-organs make with extreme
facility paths which do not easily disappear. For, of course, a simple
habit, like every other nervous event—the habit of snuffling, for example, or of putting one's hands into one's pockets, or of biting one's nails—
is, mechanically, nothing but a reflex discharge; and its anatomical sub-
stratum must be a path in the system. The most complex habits, as we
shall presently see more fully, are, from the same point of view, nothing
but *concatenated* discharges in the nerve-centres, due to the presence
there of systems of reflex paths, so organized as to wake each other up
successively—the impression produced by one muscular contraction
serving as a stimulus to provoke the next, until a final impression inhibits the process and closes the chain.

It must be noticed that the growth of structural modification in living matter may be more rapid than in any lifeless mass, because the incessant nutritive renovation of which the living matter is the seat tends
often to corroborate and fix the impressed modification, rather than to

counteract it by renewing the original constitution of the tissue that has been impressed. Thus, we notice after exercising our muscles or our brain in a new way, that we can do so no longer at that time; but after a day or two of rest, when we resume the discipline, our increase in skill not seldom surprises us. I have often noticed this in learning a tune; and it has led a German author to say that we learn to swim during the winter, and to skate during the summer.

Practical Effects of Habit.—First, habit simplifies our movements, makes them accurate, and diminishes fatigue.

Man is born with a tendency to do more things than he has ready-made arrangements for in his nerve-centres. Most of the performances of other animals are automatic. But in him the number of them is so enormous that most of them must be the fruit of painful study. If practice did not make perfect, nor habit economize the expense of nervous and muscular energy, he would be in a sorry plight. As Dr. Maudsley says:[1]

"If an act became no easier after being done several times, if the careful direction of consciousness were necessary to its accomplishment on each occasion, it is evident that the whole activity of a lifetime might be confined to one or two deeds—that no progress could take place in development. A man might be occupied all day in dressing and undressing himself; the attitude of his body would absorb all his attention and energy; the washing of his hands or the fastening of a button would be as difficult to him on each occasion as to the child on its first trial; and he would furthermore be completely exhausted by his exertions. Think of the pains necessary to teach a child to stand, of the many efforts which it must make, and of the ease with which it at last stands, unconscious even of an effort. For while secondary automatic acts are accomplished with comparatively little weariness—in this regard approaching the organic movements, or the original reflex movements—the conscious efforts of the will soon produce exhaustion. A spinal cord without . . . memory would simply be an idiotic spinal cord. . . . It is impossible for an individual to realise how much he owes to its automatic agency until disease has impaired its functions."

Secondly, *habit diminishes the conscious attention with which our acts are performed.*

One may state this abstractly thus: If an act require for its execution a chain, *A,B,C,D,E,F,G,* etc., of successive nervous events, then in the first performances of the action the conscious will must choose each of these events from a number of wrong alternatives that tend to present themselves; but habit soon brings it about that each event calls up its own appropriate successor without any alternative offering itself, and without any reference to the conscious will, until at last the whole chain, *A,B,C,D,E,F,G,* rattles itself off as soon as *A* occurs, just as if *A* and the rest of the chain were fused into a continuous stream. Whilst we are learning to walk, to ride, to swim, skate, fence, write, play, or sing, we interrupt ourselves at every step by unnecessary movements and false notes. When we are proficients, on the contrary, the results follow not only with the very minimum of muscular action requisite to bring them forth, but they follow from a single instantaneous 'cue.' The marksman sees the bird, and, before he knows it, he has aimed and shot. A gleam in his adversary's eye, a momentary pressure from his rapier, and the fencer finds that he has instantly made the right parry and return. A glance at the musical hieroglyphics, and the pianist's fingers have rippled through a shower of notes. And not only is it the right thing at the right time that we thus involuntarily do, but the wrong thing also, if it be an habitual thing. Who is there that has never wound up his watch on taking off his waistcoat in the daytime, or taken his latch-key out on arriving at the door-step of a friend? Persons in going to their bedroom to dress for dinner have been known to take off one garment after another and finally to get into bed, merely because that was the habitual issue of the first few movements when performed at a later hour. We all have a definite routine manner of performing certain daily offices connected with the toilet, with the opening and shutting of familiar cupboards, and the like. But our higher thought-centres know hardly anything about the matter. Few men can tell off-hand which sock, shoe, or trousers-leg they put on first. They must first mentally rehearse the act; and even that is often insufficient—the act must be *performed.* So of the questions, Which valve of the shutters opens first? Which way does my door swing? etc. I cannot *tell* the answer; yet my *hand* never makes a mistake. No one can *describe* the order in which he brushes his hair or teeth; yet it is likely that the order is a pretty fixed one in all of us.

These results may be expressed as follows:

In action grown habitual, what instigates each new muscular contraction to take place in its appointed order is not a thought or a perception, but the *sensation occasioned by the muscular contraction just finished.* A strictly voluntary act has to be guided by idea, perception, and volition, throughout its whole course. In habitual action, mere sensation is a sufficient guide, and the upper regions of brain and mind are set comparatively free. A diagram will make the matter clear:

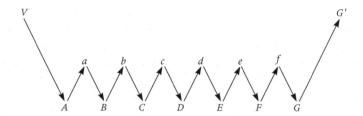

Let A,B,C,D,E,F,G represent an habitual chain of muscular contractions, and let a,b,c,d,e,f stand for the several sensations which these contractions excite in us when they are successively performed. Such sensations will usually be in the parts moved, but they may also be effects of the movement upon the eye or the ear. Through them, and through them alone, we are made aware whether or not the contraction has occurred. When the series, A,B,C,D,E,F,G, is being learned, each of these sensations becomes the object of a separate act of attention by the mind. We test each movement intellectually, to see if it have been rightly performed, before advancing to the next. We hesitate, compare, choose, revoke, reject, etc.; and the order by which the next movement is discharged is an express order from the ideational centres after this deliberation has been gone through.

In habitual action, on the contrary, the only impulse which the intellectual centres need send down is that which carries the command to *start*. This is represented in the diagram by V; it may be a thought of the first movement or of the last result, or a mere perception of some of the habitual conditions of the chain, the presence, e.g., of the keyboard near the hand. In the present example, no sooner has this conscious thought or volition instigated movement A, than A, through the sensation a of its own occurrence, awakens B reflexly; B then excites C through b, and so on till the chain is ended, when the intellect generally takes cognizance of the final result. The intellectual perception at the end is indicated in the diagram by the sensible effect of the movement G being represented at G', in the ideational centres above the merely sensational line. The sensational impressions, *a,b,c,d,e,f,* are all supposed to have their seat below the ideational level.

Habits depend on sensations not attended to. We have called *a,b,c,d,e,f* by the name of 'sensations.' If sensations, they are sensations to which we are usually inattentive; but that they are more than unconscious nerve-currents seems certain, for they catch our attention if they go wrong. Schneider's account of these sensations deserves to be quoted. In the act of walking, he says, even when our attention is entirely absorbed elsewhere, "it is doubtful whether we could preserve equilibrium if no sensation of our body's attitude were there, and doubtful whether we should advance our leg if we had no sensation of its movement as executed, and not even a minimal feeling of impulse to set it down. Knitting appears altogether mechanical, and the knitter keeps up her knitting even while she reads or is engaged in lively talk. But if we ask her how this is possible, she will hardly reply that the knitting goes on of itself. She will rather say that she has a feeling of it, that she feels in her hands that she knits and how she must knit, and that therefore the movements of knitting are called forth and regulated by the sensations associated therewithal, even when the attention is called away. . . ." Again: "When a pupil begins to play on the violin, to keep him from raising his right elbow in playing a book is placed under his right armpit, which he is ordered to hold fast by keeping the upper arm tight against his body. The muscular feelings, and feelings of contact connected with the book, provoke an impulse to press it tight. But often it happens that the beginner, whose attention gets absorbed in the production of the notes, lets drop the book. Later, however, this never happens; the faintest sensations of contact suffice to awaken the impulse to keep it in its place, and the attention may be wholly absorbed by the notes and the fingering with the left hand. *The simultaneous combination of movements is thus in the first instance conditioned by the facility with which in us, alongside of intellectual processes, processes of inattentive feeling may still go on.*"

Ethical and Pedagogical Importance of the Principle of Habit.—"Habit a second nature! Habit is ten times nature," the Duke of Wellington is said to have exclaimed; and the degree to which this is true no one probably can appreciate as well as one who is a veteran soldier himself. The daily drill and the years of discipline end by fashioning a man completely over again, as to most of the possibilities of his conduct.

"There is a story," says Prof. Huxley, "which is credible enough, though it may not be true, of a practical joker, who, seeing a discharged veteran carrying home his dinner, suddenly called out 'Attention!' whereupon the man instantly brought his hands down, and lost his mutton and potatoes in the gutter. The drill had been thorough, and its effects had become embodied in the man's nervous structure."

Riderless cavalry-horses, at many a battle, have been seen to come together and go through their customary evolutions at the sound of the bugle-call. Most domestic beasts seem machines almost pure and simple, undoubtingly, unhesitatingly doing from minute to minute the duties they have been taught, and giving no sign that the possibility of an alternative ever suggests itself to their mind. Men grown old in prison have asked to be readmitted after being once set free. In a railroad accident a menagerie-tiger, whose cage had broken open, is said to have emerged, but presently crept back again, as if too much bewildered by his new responsibilities, so that he was without difficulty secured.

Habit is thus the enormous fly-wheel of society, its most precious conservative agent. It alone is what keeps us all within the bounds of ordinance, and saves the children of fortune from the envious uprisings of the poor. It alone prevents the hardest and most repulsive walks of life from being deserted by those brought up to tread therein. It keeps the fisherman and the deck-hand at sea through the winter; it holds the miner in his darkness, and nails the countryman to his log-cabin and his lonely farm through all the months of snow; it protects us from invasion by the natives of the desert and the frozen zone. It dooms us all to fight out the battle of life upon the lines of our nurture or our early choice, and to make the best of a pursuit that disagrees, because there is no other for which we are fitted, and it is too late to begin again. It keeps different social strata from mixing. Already at the age of twenty-five you see the professional mannerism settling down on the young commercial traveller, on the young doctor, on the young minister, on the young counsellor-at-law. You see the little lines of cleavage running through the character, the tricks of thought, the prejudices, the ways of the 'shop,' in a word, from which the man can by-and-by no more escape than his coat-sleeve can suddenly fall into a new set of folds. On the whole, it is best he should not escape. It is well for the world that in most of us, by the age of thirty, the character has set like plaster, and will never soften again.

If the period between twenty and thirty is the critical one in the formation of intellectual and professional habits, the period below twenty is more important still for the fixing of *personal* habits, properly so called, such as vocalization and pronunciation, gesture, motion, and address. Hardly ever is a language learned after twenty spoken without a foreign accent; hardly ever can a youth transferred to the society of his betters unlearn the nasality and other vices of speech bred in him by the associations of his growing years. Hardly ever, indeed, no matter how much money there be in his pocket, can he even learn to *dress* like a gentleman-born. The merchants offer their wares as eagerly to him as to the veriest 'swell,' but he simply *cannot* buy the right things. An invisible law, as strong as gravitation, keeps him within his orbit, arrayed this year as he was the last; and how his better-clad acquaintances contrive to get the things they wear will be for him a mystery till his dying day.

The great thing, then, in all education, is to *make our nervous system our ally instead of our enemy.* It is to fund and capitalize our acquisitions, and live at ease upon the interest of the fund. *For this we must make automatic and habitual, as early as possible, as many useful actions as we can,* and guard against the growing into ways that are likely to be disadvantageous to us, as we should guard against the plague. The more of the details of our daily life we can hand over to the effortless custody of automatism, the more our higher powers of mind will be set free for their own proper work. There is no more miserable human being than one in whom nothing is habitual but indecision, and for whom the lighting of every cigar, the drinking of every cup, the time of rising and going to bed every day, and the beginning of every bit of work, are subjects of express volitional deliberation. Full half the time of such a man goes to the deciding, or regretting, of matters which ought to be so ingrained in him as practically not to exist for his consciousness at all. If there be such daily duties not yet ingrained in any one of my readers, let him begin this very hour to set the matter right.

In Professor Bain's chapter on "The Moral Habits" there are some admirable practical remarks laid down. Two great maxims emerge from his treatment. The first is that in the acquisition of a new habit, or the leaving off of an old one, we must take care to *launch ourselves with as strong and decided an initiative as possible.* Accumulate all the possible circumstances which shall re-enforce the right motives; put yourself assiduously in conditions that encourage the new way; make engagements incompatible with the old; take a public pledge, if the case allows; in short, envelop your resolution with every aid you know. This will give your new beginning such a momentum that the temptation to break down will not occur as soon as it otherwise might; and every day during which a breakdown is postponed adds to the chances of its not occurring at all.

The second maxim is: *Never suffer an exception to occur till the new habit is securely rooted in your life.* Each lapse is like the letting fall of a ball of string which one is carefully winding up; a single slip undoes more than a great many turns will wind again. *Continuity* of training is the great means of making the nervous system act infallibly right. As Professor Bain says:

"The peculiarity of the moral habits, contra-distinguishing them from the intellectual acquisitions, is the presence of two hostile powers, one to be gradually raised into the ascendant over the other. It is necessary, above all things, in such a situation, never to lose a battle. Every gain on the wrong side undoes the effect of many conquests on the right. The essential precaution, therefore, is, so to regulate the two opposing powers that the one may have a series of uninterrupted successes, until repetition has fortified it to such a degree as to enable it to cope with the opposition, under any circumstances. This is the theoretically best career of mental progress."

The need of securing success at the *outset* is imperative. Failure at first is apt to damp the energy of all future attempts, whereas past experiences of success nerve one to future vigor. Goethe says to a man who consulted him about an enterprise but mistrusted his own powers: "Ach! you need only blow on your hands!" And the remark illustrates the effect on Goethe's spirits of his own habitually successful career.

The question of 'tapering-off,' in abandoning such habits as drink and opium-indulgence, comes in here, and is a question about which experts differ within certain limits, and in regard to what may be best for an individual case. In the main, however, all expert opinion would agree that abrupt acquisition of the new habit is the best way, *if there be a real possibility of carrying it out.* We must be careful not to give the will so stiff a task as to insure its defeat at the very outset; but, *provided one can stand it,* a sharp period of suffering, and then a free time, is the best thing to aim at, whether in giving up a habit like that of opium, or in simply changing one's hours of rising or of work. It is surprising how soon a desire will die of inanition if it be *never* fed.

"One must first learn, unmoved, looking neither to the right nor left, to walk firmly on the straight and narrow path, before one can begin 'to make one's self over again.' He who every day makes a fresh resolve is like one who, arriving at the edge of the ditch he is to leap, forever stops and returns for a fresh run. Without *unbroken* advance there is no such thing as *accumulation* of the ethical forces possible, and to make this possible, and to exercise us and habituate us in it, is the sovereign blessing of regular work."[2]

A third maxim may be added to the preceding pair: *Seize the very first possible opportunity to act on every resolution you make, and on every emotional prompting you may experience in the direction of the habits you aspire to gain.* It is not in the moment of their forming, but in the moment of their producing *motor effects*, that resolves and aspirations communicate the new 'set' to the brain. As the author last quoted remarks:

"The actual presence of the practical opportunity alone furnishes the fulcrum upon which the lever can rest, by means of which the moral will may multiply its strength, and raise itself aloft. He who has no solid ground to press against will never get beyond the stage of empty gesture-making."

No matter how full a reservoir of *maxims* one may possess, and no matter how good one's *sentiments* may be, if one have not taken advantage of every concrete opportunity to *act*, one's character may remain entirely unaffected for the better. With mere good intentions, hell is proverbially paved. And this is an obvious consequence of the principles we have laid down. A 'character,' as J. S. Mill says, 'is a completely fashioned will'; and a will, in the sense in which he means it, is an aggregate of tendencies to act in a firm and prompt and definite way upon all the principal emergencies of life. A tendency to act only becomes effectively ingrained in us in proportion to the uninterrupted frequency with which the actions actually occur, and the brain 'grows' to their use. When a resolve or a fine glow of feeling is allowed to evaporate without bearing practical fruit it is worse than a chance lost; it works so as positively to hinder future resolutions and emotions from taking the normal path of discharge. There is no more contemptible type of human character than that of the nerveless sentimentalist and dreamer, who spends his life in a weltering sea of sensibility and emotion, but who never does a manly concrete deed. Rousseau, inflaming all the mothers of France, by his eloquence, to follow Nature and nurse their babies themselves, while he sends his own children to the foundling hospital, is the classical example of what I mean. But every one of us in his measure, whenever, after glowing for an abstractly formulated Good, he practically ignores some actual case, among the squalid 'other particulars' of which that same Good lurks disguised, treads straight on Rousseau's path. All Goods are disguised by the vulgarity of their concomitants, in this work-a-day world; but woe to him who can only recognize them when he thinks them in their pure and abstract form! The habit of excessive novel-reading and theatre-going will produce true monsters in this line. The weeping of the Russian lady over the fictitious personages in the play, while her coachman is freezing to death on his seat outside, is the sort of thing that everywhere happens on a less glaring scale. Even the habit of excessive indulgence in music, for those who are neither performers themselves nor musically gifted enough to take it in a purely intellectual way, has probably a relaxing effect upon the character. One becomes filled with emotions which habitually pass without prompting to any deed, and so the inertly sentimental condition is kept up. The remedy would be, never to suffer one's self to have an emotion at a concert, without expressing it afterwards in *some* active way. Let the expression be the least thing in the world—speaking genially to one's grandmother, or giving up one's seat in a horse-car, if nothing more heroic offers—but let it not fail to take place.

These latter cases make us aware that it is not simply *particular lines* of discharge, but also *general forms* of discharge, that seem to be grooved out by habit in the brain. Just as, if we let our emotions evaporate, they get into a way of evaporating; so there is reason to suppose that if we often flinch from making an effort, before we know it the effort-making capacity will be gone; and that, if we suffer the wandering of our attention, presently it will wander all the time. Attention and effort are, as we shall see later, but two names for the same psychic fact. To what brain-processes they correspond we do not know. The strongest reason for believing that they do depend on brain-processes at all, and are not pure acts of the spirit, is just this fact, that they seem in some degree subject to the law of habit, which is a material law. As a final practical maxim, relative to these habits of the will, we may, then, offer something like this: *Keep the faculty of effort alive in you by a little gratuitous exercise every day.* That is, be systematically ascetic or heroic in little unnecessary points, do every day or two something for no other reason than that you would rather not do it, so that when the hour of dire need draws nigh, it may find you not unnerved and untrained to stand the test. Asceticism of this sort is like the insurance which a man pays on his house and goods. The tax does him no good at the time, and possibly may never bring him a return. But if the fire *does* come, his having paid it will be his salvation from ruin. So with the man who has daily inured himself to habits of concentrated attention, energetic volition, and self-denial in unnecessary things. He will stand like a tower when everything rocks around him, and when his softer fellow-mortals are winnowed like chaff in the blast.

The physiological study of mental conditions is thus the most powerful ally of hortatory ethics. The hell to be endured hereafter, of which theology tells, is no worse than the hell we make for ourselves in this world by habitually fashioning our characters in the wrong way. Could the young but realize how soon they will become mere walking bundles of habits, they would give more heed to their conduct while in the plastic state. We are spinning our own fates, good or evil, and never to be undone. Every smallest stroke of virtue or of vice leaves its never so little scar. The drunken Rip Van Winkle, in Jefferson's play, excuses himself for every fresh dereliction by saying, 'I won't count this time!' Well! he may not count it, and a kind Heaven may not count it; but it is being counted none the less. Down among his nerve-cells and fibres the molecules are counting it, registering and storing it up to be used against him when the next temptation comes. Nothing we ever do is, in strict scientific literalness, wiped out. Of course this has its good side as well as its bad one. As we become permanent drunkards by so many separate drinks, so we become saints in the moral, and authorities and experts in the practical and scientific spheres, by so many separate acts and hours of work. Let no youth have any anxiety about the upshot of his education, whatever the line of it may be. If he keep faithfully busy each hour of the working day, he may safely leave the final result to itself. He can with perfect certainty count on waking up some fine morning, to find himself one of the competent ones of his generation, in whatever pursuit he may have singled out. Silently, between all the details of his business, the *power of judging* in all that class of matter will have built itself up within him as a possession that will never pass away. Young people should know this truth in advance. The ignorance of it has probably engendered more discouragement and faint-heartedness in youths embarking on arduous careers than all other causes put together.

6

The Will

When James published *Talks to Teachers,* which was, in effect, his third try at putting forth his comprehensive views on psychology, he closed the volume with the chapter "The Will," because he understood will to be the bridge between mental activity and outward conduct. But James was not inclined to underestimate either reflex action or the power of habit, and he believed we should understand "will" to apply to "such acts only as cannot be inattentively performed." Further, he understood the power of inhibition, and that "voluntary action, then, is at all times a resultant of the compounding of our impulsions with our inhibitions." He distinguished, crucially, between "inhibition by repression or by negation, and inhibition by substitution" and came to greatly prefer the latter. The chapter and the book thus end with a stirring appeal in which we can hear the living voice of the man as he urges teachers to consider that "anything that a man can avoid under the notion that it is bad he may also avoid under the notion that something else is good." Don't, for example, stop drinking because it is bad to be a drunk, stop because it is good to be healthy.

SINCE MENTALITY terminates naturally in outward conduct, the final chapter in psychology has to be the chapter on the will. But the word 'will' can be used in a broader and in a narrower sense. In the broader sense, it designates our entire capacity for impulsive and active life, including our instinctive reactions and those forms of behavior that have become secondarily automatic and semi-unconscious through frequent repetition. In the narrower sense, acts of will are such acts only as cannot be inattentively performed. A distinct idea of what they are, and a deliberate *fiat* on the mind's part, must precede their execution.

Such acts are often characterized by hesitation, and accompanied by a feeling, altogether peculiar, of resolve, a feeling which may or may not carry with it a farther feeling of effort. In my earlier talks, I said so much of our impulsive tendencies that I will restrict myself in what follows to volition in this narrower sense of the term.

All our deeds were considered by the early psychologists to be due to a peculiar faculty called the will, without whose fiat action could not occur. Thoughts and impressions, being intrinsically inactive, were supposed to produce conduct only through the intermediation of this superior agent. Until they twitched its coat-tails, so to speak, no outward behavior could occur. This doctrine was long ago exploded by the discovery of the phenomena of reflex action, in which sensible impressions, as you know, produce movement immediately and of themselves. The doctrine may also be considered exploded as far as ideas go.

The fact is that there is no sort of consciousness whatever, be it sensation, feeling, or idea, which does not directly and of itself tend to discharge into some motor effect. The motor effect need not always be an outward stroke of behavior. It may be only an alteration of the heartbeats or breathing, or a modification in the distribution of blood, such as blushing or turning pale; or else a secretion of tears, or what not. But in any case, it is there in some shape when any consciousness is there; and a belief as fundamental as any in modern psychology is the belief at last attained that conscious processes of any sort, conscious processes merely as such, *must* pass over into motion, open or concealed.

The least complicated case of this tendency is the case of a mind possessed by only a single idea. If that idea be of an object connected with a native impulse, the impulse will immediately proceed to discharge. If it be the idea of a movement, the movement will occur. Such a case of action from a single idea has been distinguished from more complex cases by the name of 'ideo-motor' action, meaning action without express decision or effort. Most of the habitual actions to which we are trained are of this ideo-motor sort. We perceive, for instance, that the door is open, and we rise and shut it; we perceive some raisins in a dish before us, and extend our hand and carry one of them to our mouth without interrupting the conversation; or, when lying in bed, we suddenly think that we shall be late for breakfast, and instantly we get up with no particular exertion or resolve. All the ingrained procedures by which life is carried on—the manners and customs, dressing and undressing, acts of salutation, etc.—are executed in this semi-automatic way unhesitatingly and efficiently, the very outermost margin of consciousness seeming to be concerned in them, whilst the focus may be occupied with widely different things.

But now turn to a more complicated case. Suppose two thoughts to be in the mind together, of which one, A, taken alone, would discharge itself in a certain action; but of which the other, B, suggests an action of a different sort, or a consequence of the first action calculated to make us shrink. The psychologists now say that the second idea, B, will probably arrest or *inhibit* the motor effects of the first idea, A. One word, then, about 'inhibition' in general, to make this particular case more clear.

One of the most interesting discoveries of physiology was the discovery, made simultaneously in France and Germany fifty years ago, that nerve currents do not only start muscles into action, but may check action already going on or keep it from occurring as it otherwise might. *Nerves of arrest* were thus distinguished alongside of motor nerves. The pneumogastric nerve, for example, if stimulated, arrests the movements of the heart; the splanchnic nerve arrests those of the intestines, if already begun. But it soon appeared that this was too narrow a way of looking at the matter, and that arrest is not so much the specific function of certain nerves as a general function which any part of the nervous system may exert upon other parts under the appropriate conditions. The higher centres, for example, seem to exert a constant inhibitive influence on the excitability of those below. The reflexes of an animal with its hemispheres wholly or in part removed become exaggerated. You all know that common reflex in dogs whereby, if you scratch the animal's side, the corresponding hind leg will begin to make scratching movements, usually in the air. Now in dogs with mutilated hemispheres this scratching reflex is so incessant that, as Goltz first described them, the hair gets all worn off their sides. In idiots, the functions of the hemispheres being largely in abeyance, the lower impulses, not inhibited, as they would be in normal human beings, often express themselves in most odious ways. You know also how any higher emotional tendency will quench a lower one. Fear arrests appetite, maternal love annuls fear, respect checks sensuality, and the like; and in the more subtle manifestations of the moral life, whenever an ideal stirring is suddenly quickened into intensity, it is as if the whole scale of values of our motives changed its equilibrium. The force of old temptations vanishes, and what a moment ago was impossible is now not only possible, but easy, because of their inhibition. This has been well called the 'expulsive power of the higher emotion.'

It is easy to apply this notion of inhibition to the case of our ideational processes. I am lying in bed, for example, and think it is time to get up; but alongside of this thought there is present to my mind a realization of the extreme coldness of the morning and the pleasantness of the warm bed. In such a situation the motor consequences of the first idea are blocked; and I may remain for half an hour or more with the two ideas oscillating before me in a kind of deadlock, which is what we call the state of hesitation or deliberation. In a case like this the deliberation can be resolved and the decision reached in either of two ways:

(1) I may forget for a moment the thermometric conditions, and then the idea of getting up will immediately discharge into act: I shall suddenly find that I have got up—or

(2) Still mindful of the freezing temperature, the thought of the duty of rising may become so pungent that it determines action in spite of inhibition. In the latter case, I have a sense of energetic moral effort, and consider that I have done a virtuous act.

All cases of wilful action properly so called, of choice after hesitation and deliberation, may be conceived after one of these latter patterns. So you see that volition, in the narrower sense, takes place only when there are a number of conflicting systems of ideas, and depends on our having a complex field of consciousness. The interesting thing to note is the extreme delicacy of the inhibitive machinery. A strong and urgent motor idea in the focus may be neutralized and made inoperative by the presence of the very faintest contradictory idea in the margin. For instance, I hold out my forefinger, and with closed eyes try to realize as vividly as possible that I hold a revolver in my hand and am pulling the trigger. I can even now fairly feel my finger quivering with the tendency to contract; and if it were hitched to a recording apparatus, it would certainly betray its state of tension by registering incipient movements. Yet it does not actually crook, and the movement of pulling the trigger is not performed. Why not? Simply because, all concentrated though I am upon the idea of the movement, I nevertheless also realize the total conditions of the experiment, and in the back of my mind, so to speak, or in its fringe and margin, have the simultaneous idea that the movement is not to take place. The mere presence of that marginal intention, without effort, urgency, or emphasis, or any special reinforcement from my attention, suffices to the inhibitive effect.

And this is why so few of the ideas that flit through our minds do, in point of fact, produce their motor consequences. Life would be a curse and a care for us if every fleeting fancy were to do so. Abstractly, the law of ideo-motor action is true; but in the concrete our fields of consciousness are always so complex that the inhibiting margin keeps the centre inoperative most of the time. In all this, you see, I speak as if ideas by their mere presence or absence determined behavior, and as if between the ideas themselves on the one hand and the conduct on the other there were no room for any third intermediate principle of activity, like that called 'the will.'

If you are struck by the materialistic or fatalistic doctrines which seem to follow this conception, I beg you to suspend your judgment for a moment, as I shall soon have something more to say about the matter. But, meanwhile yielding one's self to the mechanical conception of the psychophysical organism, nothing is easier than to indulge in a picture of the fatalistic character of human life. Man's conduct appears as the mere resultant of all his various impulsions and inhibitions. One object, by its presence, makes us act; another object checks our action. Feelings aroused and ideas suggested by objects sway us one way and another; emotions complicate the game by their mutual inhibitive effects, the higher abolishing the lower or perhaps being itself swept away. The life in all this becomes prudential and moral; but the psychologic agents in the drama may be described, you see, as nothing but the 'ideas' themselves—ideas for the whole system of which what we call the 'soul' or 'character' or 'will' of the person is nothing but a collective name. As Hume said, the ideas are themselves the actors, the stage, the theatre, the spectators, and the play. This is the so-called 'associationist' psychology, brought down to its radical expression: it is useless to ignore its power as a conception. Like all conceptions, when they become clear and lively enough, this conception has a strong tendency to impose itself upon belief; and psychologists trained on biological lines usually adopt it as the last word of science on the subject. No one can have an adequate notion of modern psychological theory unless he has at some time apprehended this view in the full force of its simplicity.

Let us humor it for a while, for it has advantages in the way of exposition.

Voluntary action, then, is at all times a resultant of the compounding of our impulsions with our inhibitions.

From this it immediately follows that there will be two types of will, in one of which impulsions will predominate, in the other inhibitions. We may speak of them, if you like, as the precipitate and the obstructed will, respectively. When fully pronounced, they are familiar to everybody. The extreme example of the precipitate will is the maniac; his ideas discharge into action so rapidly, his associative processes are so extravagantly lively, that inhibitions have no time to arrive, and he says and does whatever pops into his head without a moment of hesitation.

Certain melancholiacs furnish the extreme example of the over-inhibited type. Their minds are cramped in a fixed emotion of fear or helplessness, their ideas confined to the one thought that for them life is impossible. So they show a condition of perfect 'abulia,' or inability to will or act. They cannot change their posture or speech or execute the simplest command.

The different races of men show different temperaments in this regard. The Southern races are commonly accounted the more impulsive and precipitate; the English race, especially our New England branch of it, is supposed to be all sicklied over with repressive forms of self-consciousness, and condemned to express itself through a jungle of scruples and checks.

The highest form of character, however, abstractly considered, must be full of scruples and inhibitions. But action, in such a character, far from being paralyzed, will succeed in energetically keeping on its way, sometimes overpowering the resistances, sometimes steering along the line where they lie thinnest.

Just as our extensor muscles act most firmly when a simultaneous contraction of the flexors guides and steadies them; so the mind of him whose fields of consciousness are complex, and who, with the reasons for the action, sees the reasons against it, and yet, instead of being palsied, acts in the way that takes the whole field into consideration—so, I say, is such a mind the ideal sort of mind that we should seek to reproduce in our pupils. Purely impulsive action, or action that proceeds to extremities regardless of consequences, on the other hand, is the easiest action in the world, and the lowest in type. Anyone can show energy when made quite reckless. An oriental despot requires but little ability: as long as he lives he succeeds, for he has absolutely his own way; and when the world can no longer endure the horror of him, he is assassinated. But not to proceed immediately to extremities, to be still able to act energetically under an array of inhibitions—that indeed is rare and difficult. Cavour, when urged to proclaim martial law in 1859, refused to do so, saying: "Anyone can govern in that way. I will be constitutional." Your parliamentary rulers, your Lincoln, your Gladstone, are the strongest type of man, because they accomplish results under the most intricate possible conditions. We think of Napoleon Bonaparte as a colossal monster of will-power, and truly enough he was so. But from the point of view of the psychological machinery, it would be hard to say whether he or Gladstone was the larger volitional quantity; for Napoleon disregarded all the usual inhibitions, and Gladstone, passionate as he was, scrupulously considered them in his statesmanship.

A familiar example of the paralyzing power of scruples is the inhibitive effect of conscientiousness upon conversation. Nowhere does conversation seem to have flourished as brilliantly as in France during the last century. But if we read old French memoirs, we see how many brakes of scrupulosity which tie our tongues to-day were then removed. Where mendacity, treachery, obscenity, and malignity find unhampered expression, talk can be brilliant indeed; but its flame waxes dim where the mind is stitched all over with conscientious fear of violating the moral and social proprieties.

The teacher often is confronted in the school-room with an abnormal type of will, which we may call the 'balky will.' Certain children, if they do not succeed in doing a thing immediately, remain completely inhibited in regard to it; it becomes literally impossible for them to understand it if it be an intellectual problem, or to do it if it be an outward operation, as long as this particular inhibited condition lasts. Such children are usually treated as sinful, and are punished; or else the teacher pits his or her will against the child's will, considering that the latter must be 'broken.' "Break your child's will, in order that it may not perish," wrote John Wesley. "Break its will as soon as it can speak plainly— or even before it can speak at all. It should be forced to do as it is told, even if you have to whip it ten times running. Break its will, in order that its soul may live." Such will-breaking is always a scene with a great deal of nervous wear and tear on both sides, a bad state of feeling left behind it, and the victory not always with the would-be will-breaker.

When a situation of the kind is once fairly developed, and the child is all tense and excited inwardly, nineteen times out of twenty it is best for the teacher to apperceive the case as one of neural pathology rather than as one of moral culpability. So long as the inhibiting sense of impossibility remains in the child's mind, he will continue unable to get beyond the obstacle. The aim of the teacher should then be to make him simply forget. Drop the subject for the time, divert the mind to something else; then, leading the pupil back by some circuitous line of association, spring it on him again before he has time to recognize it, and as likely as not he will go over it now without any difficulty. It is in no other way that we overcome balkiness in a horse: we divert his attention, do something to his nose or ear, lead him round in a circle, and thus get him over a place where flogging would only have made him more invincible. A tactful teacher will never let these strained situations come up at all.

You perceive now, my friends, what your general or abstract duty is as teachers. Although you have to generate in your pupils a large stock of ideas, any one of which may be inhibitory, yet you must also see to it that no habitual hesitancy or paralysis of the will ensues, and that the pupil still retains his power of vigorous action. Psychology can state your problem in these terms, but you see how impotent she is to furnish the elements of its practical solution. When all is said and done, and your best efforts are made, it will probably remain true that the result will depend more on a certain native tone or temper in the pupil's psychological constitution than on anything else. Some persons appear to have a naturally poor focalization of the field of consciousness; and in such persons actions hang slack, and inhibitions seem to exert peculiarly easy sway.

But let us now close in a little more closely on this matter of the education of the will. Your task is to build up a *character* in your pupils; and a character, as I have so often said, consists in an organized set of habits of reaction. Now of what do such habits of reaction themselves consist? They consist of tendencies to act characteristically when certain ideas possess us, and to refrain characteristically when possessed by other ideas.

Our volitional habits depend, then, first, on what the stock of ideas is which we have; and second, on the habitual coupling of the several ideas with action or inaction respectively. How is it when an alternative is presented to you for choice, and you are uncertain what you ought to do? You first hesitate, and then you deliberate. And in what does your deliberation consist? It consists in trying to apperceive the case successively by a number of different ideas, which seem to fit it more or less, until at last you hit on one which seems to fit it exactly. If that be an idea which is a customary forerunner of action in you, which enters into one of your maxims of positive behavior, your hesitation ceases, and you act immediately. If, on the other hand, it be an idea which carries inaction as its habitual result, if it ally itself with *prohibition*, then you unhesitatingly refrain. The problem is, you see, to find the right idea or conception for the case. This search for the right conception may take days or weeks.

I spoke as if the action were easy when the conception once is found. Often it is so, but it may be otherwise; and when it is otherwise, we find ourselves at the very centre of a moral situation, into which I should now like you to look with me a little nearer.

The proper conception, the true head of classification, may be hard to attain; or it may be one with which we have contracted no settled habits of action. Or again, the action to which it would prompt may be dangerous and difficult; or else inaction may appear deadly cold and negative when our impulsive feeling is hot. In either of these latter cases it is hard to hold the right idea steadily enough before the attention to let it exert its adequate effects. Whether it be stimulative or inhibitive, it is *too reasonable* for us; and the more instinctive passional propensity then tends to extrude it from our consideration. We shy away from the thought of it; it twinkles and goes out the moment it appears in the margin of our consciousness; and we need a resolute effort of voluntary attention to drag it into the focus of the field, and to keep it there long enough for its associative and motor effects to be exerted. Everyone knows only too well how the mind flinches from looking at considerations hostile to the reigning mood of feeling.

Once brought, however, in this way to the centre of the field of consciousness, and held there, the reasonable idea will exert these effects inevitably; for the laws of connection between our consciousness and our nervous system provide for the action then taking place. Our moral effort, properly so called, terminates in our holding fast to the appropriate idea.

If, then, you are asked, "*In what does a moral act consist* when reduced to its simplest and most elementary form?" you can make only one reply. You can say that *it consists in the effort of attention by which we hold fast to an idea* which but for that effort of attention would be driven out of the mind by the other psychological tendencies that are there. *To think,* in short, is the secret of will, just as it is the secret of memory.

This comes out very clearly in the kind of excuse which we most frequently hear from persons who find themselves confronted by the sinfulness or harmfulness of some part of their behavior. "I never *thought*" they say. "I never *thought* how mean the action was, I never *thought* of these abominable consequences." And what do we retort when they say this? We say: "Why *didn't* you think? What were you there for but to think?" And we read them a moral lecture on their irreflectiveness.

The hackneyed example of moral deliberation is the case of an habitual drunkard under temptation. He has made a resolve to reform, but he is now solicited again by the bottle. His moral triumph or failure literally consists in his finding the right *name* for the case. If he says that it is a case of not wasting good liquor already poured out, or a case of not being churlish and unsociable when in the midst of friends, or a case of learning something at last about a brand of whiskey which he never met before, or a case of celebrating a public holiday, or a case of stimulating himself to a more energetic resolve in favor of abstinence than any he has ever yet made, then he is lost; his choice of the wrong name seals his doom. But if, in spite of all the plausible good names with which his thirsty fancy so copiously furnishes him, he unwaveringly clings to the truer bad name, and apperceives the case as that of "being a drunk-ard, being a drunkard, being a drunkard," his feet are planted on the road to salvation; he saves himself by thinking rightly.

Thus are your pupils to be saved: first, by the stock of ideas with which you furnish them; second, by the amount of voluntary attention that they can exert in holding to the right ones, however unpalatable; and third, by the several habits of acting definitely on these latter to which they have been successfully trained.

In all this the power of voluntarily attending is the point of the whole procedure. Just as a balance turns on its knife-edges, so on it our moral destiny turns. You remember that, when we were talking of the subject of attention, we discovered how much more intermittent and brief our acts of voluntary attention are than is commonly supposed. If they were all summed together, the time that they occupy would cover an almost incredibly small portion of our lives. But I also said, you will remember, that their brevity was not in proportion to their significance, and that I should return to the subject again. So I return to it now. It is not the mere size of a thing which constitutes its importance; it is its po-sition in the organism to which it belongs. Our acts of voluntary atten-tion, brief and fitful as they are, are nevertheless momentous and criti-cal, determining us, as they do, to higher or lower destinies. The exercise of voluntary attention in the school-room must therefore be counted one of the most important points of training that take place there; and the first-rate teacher, by the keenness of the remoter interests which he is able to awaken, will provide abundant opportunities for its occur-rence. I hope that you appreciate this now without any farther explana-tion.

I have been accused of holding up before you, in the course of these talks, a mechanical and even a materialistic view of the mind. I have called it an organism and a machine; I have spoken of its reaction on the environment as the essential thing about it; and I have referred this, ei-ther openly or implicitly, to the construction of the nervous system. I have, in consequence, received notes from some of you, begging me to be more explicit on this point; and to let you know frankly whether I am a complete materialist, or not.

Now in these lectures I wish to be strictly practical and useful, and to keep free from all speculative complications. Nevertheless, I do not wish to leave any ambiguity about my own position; and I will therefore say, in order to avoid all misunderstanding, that in no sense do I count myself a materialist. I cannot see how such a thing as our consciousness can possibly be *produced* by a nervous machinery, though I can perfectly well see how, if 'ideas' do accompany the workings of the machinery, the *order* of the ideas might very well follow exactly the *order* of the machine's operations. Our habitual associations of ideas, trains of thought, and sequences of action might thus be consequences of the succession of currents in our nervous systems. And the possible stock of ideas which a man's free spirit would have to choose from might depend exclusively on the native and acquired powers of his brain. If this were all, we might indeed adopt the fatalist conception which I sketched for you but a short while ago. Our ideas would be determined by brain currents, and these by purely mechanical laws.

But after what we have just seen—namely, the part played by voluntary attention in volition—a belief in free will and purely spiritual causation is still open to us. The duration and amount of this attention *seem* within certain limits indeterminate. We *feel* as if we could make it really more or less, and as if our free action in this regard were a genuine critical point in nature, a point on which our destiny and that of others might hinge. The whole question of free will concentrates itself, then, at this same small point: "Is or is not the appearance of indetermination at this point an illusion?"

It is plain that such a question can be decided only by general analogies, and not by accurate observations. The free-willist believes the appearance to be a reality; the determinist believes that it is an illusion. I myself hold with the free-willists—not because I cannot conceive the fatalist theory clearly, or because I fail to understand its plausibility, but simply because, if free will *were* true, it would be absurd to have the belief in it fatally forced on our acceptance. Considering the inner fitness of things, one would rather think that the very first act of a will endowed with freedom should be to sustain the belief in the freedom itself. I accordingly believe freely in my freedom; I do so with the best of scientific consciences, knowing that the predetermination of the amount of my effort of attention can never receive objective proof, and hoping that, whether you follow my example in this respect or not, it will at least make you see that such psychological and psychophysical theories

as I hold do not necessarily force a man to become a fatalist or a materialist.

Let me say one more final word now about the will, and therewith conclude both that important subject and these lectures.

There are two types of will; there are also two types of inhibition.
We may call them inhibition by repression or by negation, and inhibition by substitution, respectively. The difference between them is that,
in the case of inhibition by repression, both the inhibited idea and the
inhibiting idea, the impulsive idea and the idea that negates it, remain
along with each other in consciousness, producing a certain inward
strain or tension there; whereas, in inhibition by substitution, the inhibiting idea supersedes altogether the idea which it inhibits, and the latter
quickly vanishes from the field.

For instance, your pupils are wandering in mind, are listening to a
sound outside the window, which presently grows interesting enough
to claim all their attention. You can call the latter back again by bellow-
ing at them not to listen to those sounds, but to keep their minds on
their books or on what you are saying. And by thus keeping them conscious that your eye is sternly on them, you may produce a good effect.
But it will be a wasteful effect and an inferior effect; for the moment
you relax your supervision the attractive disturbance, always there so-
liciting their curiosity, will overpower them, and they will be just as they
were before; whereas if, without saying anything about the street disturbances, you open a counter-attraction by starting some very interesting talk or demonstration yourself, they will altogether forget the dis-
tracting incident, and without any effort follow you along. There are
many interests that can never be inhibited by the way of negation. To a
man in love, for example, it is literally impossible, by any effort of will,
to annul his passion; but let 'some new planet swim into his ken,' and
the former idol will immediately cease to engross his mind.

It is clear that in general we ought, whenever we can, to employ the
method of inhibition by substitution. He whose life is based upon the
word 'no,' who tells the truth because a lie is wicked, and who has constantly to grapple with his envious and cowardly and mean propensities, is in an inferior situation in every respect to what he would be if
the love of truth and magnanimity positively possessed him from the

outset, and he felt no inferior temptations. Your born gentleman is certainly, for this world's purposes, a more valuable being than your "Crump, with his grunting resistance to his native devils," even though in God's sight the latter may, as the Catholic theologians say, be rolling up great stores of 'merit.'

Spinoza long ago wrote in his *Ethics* that anything that a man can avoid under the notion that it is bad he may also avoid under the notion that something else is good. He who habitually acts *sub specie mali,* under the negative notion, the notion of the bad, is called a slave by Spinoza. To him who acts habitually under the notion of good he gives the name of freeman. See to it now, I beg you, that you make freemen of your pupils by habituating them to act, whenever possible, under the notion of a good. Get them habitually to tell the truth, not so much through showing them the wickedness of lying as by arousing their enthusiasm for honor and veracity. Wean them from their native cruelty by imparting to them some of your own positive sympathy with an animal's inner springs of joy. And in the lessons which you may be legally obliged to conduct upon the bad effects of alcohol, lay less stress than the books do on the drunkard's stomach, kidneys, nerves, and social miseries, and more on the blessings of having an organism kept in lifelong possession of its full youthful elasticity by a sweet, sound blood, to which stimulants and narcotics are unknown, and to which the morning sun and air and dew will daily come as sufficiently powerful intoxicants.

Conclusion

I have now ended these talks. If to some of you the things I have said seem obvious or trivial, it is possible that they may appear less so when, in the course of a year or two, you find yourselves noticing and apperceiving events in the school-room a little differently, in consequence of some of the conceptions I have tried to make more clear. I cannot but think that to apperceive your pupil as a little sensitive, impulsive, associative, and reactive organism, partly fated and partly free, will lead to a better intelligence of all his ways. Understand him, then, as such a subtle little piece of machinery. And if, in addition, you can also see him *sub specie boni,* and love him as well, you will be in the best possible position for becoming perfect teachers.

7

The Gospel of Relaxation

"The Gospel of Relaxation" shows us the side of William James that embraced popular psychology and self-help—the practical application of psychology to American life. Here he argues that we should "pay primary attention to what we do and express, and not . . . care too much for what we feel." This is one of the practical consequences of the James-Lange theory of emotion, which holds that, in many but not all cases, we act first and feeling follows. "Brighten the eye," says James, smile, "pass the genial compliment," and you will find yourself feeling better about the person you are with. When James refers on this point to Hannah Whitall Smith's *The Christian's Secret of a Happy Life*, we may well suspect that psychological self-help books had come by 1900 to serve the function once performed only by manuals of practical piety. In so much of daily life, it is what you do, not what you feel, that matters. James also reaches out to and embraces the then-current self-help manual by Annie Payson Call called *Power through Repose*, which argues that Americans in particular are too tensed up and need to let go a little more, rather than to clench the fist and struggle harder.

I WISH in the following hour to take certain psychological doctrines and show their practical applications to mental hygiene—to the hygiene of our American life more particularly. Our people, especially in academic circles, are turning towards psychology nowadays with great expectations; and if psychology is to justify them, it must be by showing fruits in the paedagogic and therapeutic lines.

The reader may possibly have heard of a peculiar theory of the emotions, commonly referred to in psychological literature as the Lange-James theory. According to this theory, our emotions are mainly due to those organic stirrings that are aroused in us in a reflex way by the stimulus of the exciting object or situation. An emotion of fear, for example, or surprise, is not a direct effect of the object's presence on the mind, but an effect of that still earlier effect, the bodily commotion which the object suddenly excites; so that, were this bodily commotion suppressed, we should not so much *feel* fear as call the situation fearful; we should not feel surprise, but coldly recognize that the object was indeed astonishing. One enthusiast has even gone so far as to say that when we feel sorry it is because we weep, when we feel afraid it is because we run away, and not conversely. Some of you may perhaps be acquainted with the paradoxical formula. Now, whatever exaggeration may possibly lurk in this account of our emotions (and I doubt myself whether the exaggeration be very great), it is certain that the main core of it is true, and that the mere giving way to tears, for example, or to the outward expression of an anger-fit, will result for the moment in making the inner grief or anger more acutely felt. There is, accordingly, no better known or more generally useful precept in the moral training of youth, or in one's personal self-discipline, than that which bids us pay primary attention to what we do and express, and not to care too much for what we feel. If we only check a cowardly impulse in time, for example; or if we only *don't* strike the blow or rip out with the complaining or insulting word that we shall regret as long as we live, our feelings themselves will presently be the calmer and better, with no particular guidance from us on their own account. Action seems to follow feeling, but really action and feeling go together; and by regulating the action, which is under the more direct control of the will, we can indirectly regulate the feeling, which is not.

Thus the sovereign voluntary path to cheerfulness, if our spontaneous cheerfulness be lost, is to sit up cheerfully, to look round cheerfully, and to act and speak as if cheerfulness were already there. If such conduct does not make you soon feel cheerful, nothing else on that occasion can. So to feel brave, act as if we *were* brave, use all our will to that end, and a courage-fit will very likely replace the fit of fear. Again, in order to feel kindly towards a person to whom we have been inimical, the only way is more or less deliberately to smile, to make sympathetic inquiries, and to force ourselves to say genial things. One hearty laugh together will bring enemies into a closer communion of heart than hours spent on both sides in inward wrestling with the mental demon of uncharitable feeling. To wrestle with a bad feeling only pins our attention on it, and keeps it still fastened in the mind; whereas if we act as if from some better feeling, the old bad feeling soon folds its tent like an Arab and silently steals away.

The best manuals of religious devotion accordingly reiterate the maxim that we must let our feelings go and pay no regard to them whatever. In an admirable and widely successful little book called *The Christian's Secret of a Happy Life*, by Mrs. Hannah Whitall Smith, I find this lesson on almost every page. *Act* faithfully, and you really have faith, no matter how cold and even how dubious you may feel. "It is your purpose God looks at," writes Mrs. Smith, "not your feelings about that purpose; and your purpose, or will, is therefore the only thing you need attend to. . . . Let your emotions come or let them go, just as God pleases, and make no account of them either way. . . . They really have nothing to do with the matter. They are not the indicators of your spiritual state, but are merely the indicators of your temperament or of your present physical condition."

But you all know these facts already, so I need no longer press them on your attention. From our acts and from our attitudes ceaseless inpouring currents of sensation come, which help to determine from moment to moment what our inner states shall be—that is a fundamental law of psychology which I will therefore proceed to assume.

A Viennese neurologist of considerable reputation has recently written about the *Binnenleben*, as he terms it, or buried life of human beings. No doctor, this writer says, can get into really profitable relations with a nervous patient until he gets some sense of what the patient's *Binnenleben* is, of the sort of unuttered inner atmosphere in which his consciousness dwells alone with the secrets of its prison-house. This inner personal tone is what we can't communicate or describe articulately to others; but the wraith and ghost of it, so to speak, are often what our friends and intimates feel as our most characteristic quality. In the unhealthy-minded, apart from all sorts of old regrets, ambitions checked by shames and aspirations obstructed by timidities, it consists mainly of bodily discomforts not distinctly localized by the sufferer, but breeding a general self-mistrust and sense that things are not as they should be with him. Half the thirst for alcohol that exists in the world exists simply because alcohol acts as a temporary anaesthetic and effacer to all these morbid feelings that never ought to be in a human being at all. In the healthy-minded, on the contrary, there are no fears or shames to discover; and the sensations that pour in from the organism only help to swell the general vital sense of security and readiness for anything that may turn up.

Consider, for example, the effects of a well-toned *motor-apparatus,* nervous and muscular, on our general personal self-consciousness, the sense of elasticity and efficiency that results. They tell us that in Norway the life of the women has lately been entirely revolutionized by the new order of muscular feelings with which the use of the *ski,* or long snow-shoes, as a sport for both sexes, has made the women acquainted. Fifteen years ago the Norwegian women were even more than the women of other lands votaries of the old-fashioned ideal of femininity, the 'domestic angel,' the 'gentle and refining influence' sort of thing. Now these sedentary fireside tabby-cats of Norway have been trained, they say, by the snow-shoes into lithe and audacious creatures for whom no night is too dark or height too giddy; and who are not only saying good-bye to the traditional feminine pallor and delicacy of constitution, but actually taking the lead in every educational and social reform. I cannot but think that the tennis and tramping and skating habits and the bicycle-craze which are so rapidly extending among our dear sisters and daughters in this country are going also to lead to a sounder and heartier moral tone, which will send its tonic breath through all our American life.

I hope that here in America more and more the ideal of the well-trained and vigorous body will be maintained neck by neck with that of the well-trained and vigorous mind as the two coequal halves of the higher education for men and women alike. The strength of the British Empire lies in the strength of character of the individual Englishman,

taken all alone by himself; and that strength, I am persuaded, is perennially nourished and kept up by nothing so much as by the national
worship, in which all classes meet, of athletic outdoor life and sport.

I recollect, years ago, reading a certain work by an American doctor
on hygiene and the laws of life and the type of future humanity. I have
forgotten its author's name and its title, but I remember well an awful
prophecy that it contained about the future of our muscular system.
Human perfection, the writer said, means ability to cope with the environment; but the environment will more and more require mental
power from us, and less and less will ask for bare brute strength. Wars
will cease, machines will do all our heavy work, man will become more
and more a mere director of nature's energies, and less and less an ex-
erter of energy on his own account. So that if the *homo sapiens* of the
future can only digest his food and think, what need will he have of
well-developed muscles at all? And why, pursued this writer, should we
not even now be satisfied with a more delicate and intellectual type of
beauty than that which pleased our ancestors? Nay, I have heard a fanciful friend make a still farther advance in this 'new-man' direction.
With our future food, he says, itself prepared in liquid form from the
chemical elements of the atmosphere, pepsinated or half-digested in advance, and sucked up through a glass tube from a tin can, what need
shall we have of teeth, or stomachs even? They may go, along with our
muscles and our physical courage, whilst, challenging ever more and
more our proper admiration, will grow the gigantic domes of our crania,
arching over our spectacled eyes, and animating our flexible little lips to
those floods of learned and ingenious talk which will constitute our
most congenial occupation.

I am sure that your flesh creeps at this apocalyptic vision. Mine certainly did so; and I cannot believe that our muscular vigor will ever be a
superfluity. Even if the day ever dawns in which it will not be needed
for fighting the old heavy battles against Nature, it will still always be
needed to furnish the background of sanity, serenity, and cheerfulness
to life, to give moral elasticity to our disposition, to round off the wiry
edge of our fretfulness, and make us good-humored and easy of approach. Weakness is too apt to be what the doctors call irritable weakness. And that blessed internal peace and confidence, that *acquiescentia
in seipso*, as Spinoza used to call it, that wells up from every part of the

body of a muscularly well-trained human being, and soaks the indwelling soul of him with satisfaction, is, quite apart from every consideration of its mechanical utility, an element of spiritual hygiene of supreme significance.

And now let me go a step deeper into mental hygiene, and try to enlist your insight and sympathy in a cause which I believe is one of paramount patriotic importance to us Yankees. Many years ago a Scottish medical man, Dr. Clouston, a mad-doctor as they call him there, or what we should call an asylum physician (the most eminent one in Scotland), visited this country and said something that has remained in my memory ever since. "You Americans," he said, "wear too much expression on your faces. You are living like an army with all its reserves engaged in action. The duller countenances of the British population betoken a better scheme of life. They suggest stores of reserved nervous force to fall back upon, if any occasion should arise that requires it. This inexcitability, this presence at all times of power not used, I regard," continued Dr. Clouston, "as the great safeguard of our British people. The other thing in you gives me a sense of insecurity, and you ought somehow to tone yourselves down. You really do carry too much expression, you take too intensely the trivial moments of life."

Now Dr. Clouston is a trained reader of the secrets of the soul as expressed upon the countenance, and the observation of his which I quote seems to me to mean a great deal. And all Americans who stay in Europe long enough to get accustomed to the spirit that reigns and expresses itself there, so unexcitable as compared with ours, make a similar observation when they return to their native shores. They find a wild-eyed look upon their compatriots' faces, either of too desperate eagerness and anxiety or of too intense responsiveness and good-will. It is hard to say whether the men or the women show it most. It is true that we do not all feel about it as Dr. Clouston felt. Many of us, far from deploring it, admire it. We say: "What intelligence it shows! How different from the stolid cheeks, the codfish eyes, the slow, inanimate demeanor we have been seeing in the British Isles!" Intensity, rapidity, vivacity of appearance, are indeed with us something of a nationally accepted ideal; and the medical notion of 'irritable weakness' is not the first thing suggested by them to our mind, as it was to Dr. Clouston's. In a weekly paper not very long ago I remember reading a story in which, after describing the beauty and interest of the heroine's personality, the author summed up her charms by saying that to all who looked upon her an impression as of 'bottled lightning' was irresistibly conveyed.

Bottled lightning, in truth, is one of our American ideals, even of a young girl's character! Now it is most ungracious, and it may seem to some persons unpatriotic, to criticise in public the physical peculiarities of one's own people, of one's own family, so to speak. Besides, it may be said, and said with justice, that there are plenty of bottled-lightning temperaments in other countries, and plenty of phlegmatic temperaments here; and that when all is said and done the more or less of tension about which I am making such a fuss is a very small item in the sum total of a nation's life, and not worth solemn treatment at a time when agreeable rather than disagreeable things should be talked about. Well, in one sense the more or less of tension in our faces and in our unused muscles *is* a small thing; not much mechanical work is done by these contractions. But it is not always the material size of a thing that measures its importance; often it is its place and function. One of the most philosophical remarks I ever heard made was by an unlettered workman who was doing some repairs at my house many years ago. "There is very little difference between one man and another," he said, "when you go to the bottom of it. But what little there is, is very important." And the remark certainly applies to this case. The general overcontraction may be small when estimated in foot-pounds, but its importance is immense on account of its *effects on the over-contracted person's spiritual life.* This follows as a necessary consequence from the theory of our emotions to which I made reference at the beginning of this article. For by the sensations that so incessantly pour in from the over-tense excited body the over-tense and excited habit of mind is kept up; and the sultry, threatening, exhausting, thunderous inner atmosphere never quite clears away. If you never wholly give yourself up to the chair you sit in, but always keep your leg- and body-muscles half contracted for a rise; if you breathe eighteen or nineteen instead of sixteen times a minute, and never quite breathe out at that—what mental mood *can* you be in but one of inner panting and expectancy, and how can the future and its worries possibly forsake your mind? On the other hand, how can they gain admission to your mind if your brow be unruffled, your respiration calm and complete, and your muscles all relaxed?

Now what is the cause of this absence of repose, this bottled-lightning quality in us Americans? The explanation of it that is usually given is that it comes from the extreme dryness of our climate and the acrobatic performances of our thermometer, coupled with the extraordinary progressiveness of our life, the hard work, the railroad speed, the rapid success, and all the other things we know so well by heart. Well, our climate is certainly exciting, but hardly more so than that of many parts of Europe, where nevertheless no bottled-lightning girls are found. And the work done and the pace of life are as extreme in every great capital of Europe as they are here. To me both of these pretended causes are utterly insufficient to explain the facts.

To explain them, we must go not to physical geography, but to psychology and sociology. The latest chapter both in sociology and in psychology to be developed in a manner that approaches adequacy is the chapter on the imitative impulse. First Bagehot, then Tarde, then Royce and Baldwin here, have shown that invention and imitation, taken together, form, one may say, the entire warp and woof of human life, in so far as it is social. The American over-tension and jerkiness and breathlessness and intensity and agony of expression are primarily social, and only secondarily physiological, phenomena. They are *bad habits*, nothing more or less, bred of custom and example, born of the imitation of bad models and the cultivation of false personal ideals. How are idioms acquired, how do local peculiarities of phrase and accent come about? Through an accidental example set by someone, which struck the ears of others, and was quoted and copied till at last everyone in the locality chimed in. Just so it is with national tricks of vocalization or intonation, with national manners, fashions of movement and gesture, and habitual expressions of face. We, here in America, through following a succession of pattern-setters whom it is now impossible to trace, and through influencing each other in a bad direction, have at last settled down collectively into what, for better or worse, is our own characteristic national type—a type with the production of which, so far as these habits go, the climate and conditions have had practically nothing at all to do.

This type, which we have thus reached by our imitativeness, we now have fixed upon us, for better or worse. Now no type can be *wholly* disadvantageous; but so far as our type follows the bottled-lightning fashion, it cannot be wholly good. Dr. Clouston was certainly right in thinking that eagerness, breathlessness, and anxiety are not signs of strength; they are signs of weakness and of bad coordination. The even forehead, the slab-like cheek, the codfish eye, may be less interesting for the moment; but they are more promising signs than intense expression is of what we may expect of their possessor in the long run. Your dull, unhurried worker gets over a great deal of ground, because he never goes backward or breaks down. Your intense, convulsive worker breaks down and has bad moods so often that you never know where he may be when you most need his help—he may be having one of his 'bad days.' We say that so many of our fellow-countrymen collapse, and have to be sent abroad to rest their nerves, because they work so hard. I suspect that this is an immense mistake. I suspect that neither the nature nor the amount of our work is accountable for the frequency and severity of our breakdowns, but that their cause lies rather in those absurd feelings of hurry and having no time, in that breathlessness and tension, that anxiety of feature and that solicitude for results, that lack of inner harmony and ease, in short, by which with us the work is so apt to be accompanied, and from which a European who should do the same work would nine times out of ten be free. These perfectly wanton and unnecessary tricks of inner attitude and outer manner in us, caught from the social atmosphere, kept up by tradition, and idealized by many as the admirable way of life, are the last straws that break the American camel's back, the final overflowers of our measure of wear and tear and fatigue.

The voice, for example, in a surprisingly large number of us has a tired and plaintive sound. Some of us are really tired (for I do not mean absolutely to deny that our climate has a tiring quality); but far more of us are not tired at all, or would not be tired at all unless we had got into a wretched trick of feeling tired by following the prevalent habits of vocalization and expression. And if talking high and tired, and living excitedly and hurriedly, would only enable us to *do* more by the way, even whilst breaking us down in the end, it would be different. There would be some compensation, some excuse, for going on so. But the exact reverse is the case: It is your relaxed and easy worker, who is in no hurry, and quite thoughtless most of the while of consequences, who is your efficient worker; and tension and anxiety, and present and future, all mixed up together in our mind at once, are the surest drags upon steady progress and hindrances to our success. My colleague, Professor Münsterberg, an excellent observer, who came here recently, has written some notes on America to German papers. He says in substance that the appearance of unusual energy in America is superficial and illusory, being really due to nothing but the habits of jerkiness and bad co-ordination for which we have to thank the defective training of our people. I think myself that it is high time for old legends and traditional opinions to be changed; and that if anyone should begin to write about Yankee inefficiency and feebleness, and inability to do anything with time except to waste it, he would have a very pretty paradoxical little thesis to sustain, with a great many facts to quote, and a great deal of experience to appeal to in its proof.

Well, my friends, if our dear American character is weakened by all this over-tension—and I think, whatever reserves you may make, that you will agree as to the main facts—where does the remedy lie? It lies, of course, where lay the origins of the disease. If a vicious fashion and taste are to blame for the thing, the fashion and taste must be changed. And though it is no small thing to inoculate seventy millions of people with new standards, yet, if there is to be any relief, that will have to be done. We must change ourselves from a race that admires jerk and snap for their own sakes, and looks down upon low voices and quiet ways as dull, to one that, on the contrary, has calm for its ideal, and for their own sakes loves harmony, dignity, and ease.

So we go back to the psychology of imitation again. There is only one way to improve ourselves, and that is by some of us setting an ex-ample which the others may pick up and imitate till the new fashion spreads from east to west. Some of us are in more favorable positions than others to set new fashions. Some are much more striking person-ally and imitable, so to speak. But no living person is sunk so low as not to be imitated by somebody. Thackeray somewhere says of the Irish na-tion that there never was an Irishman so poor that he didn't have a still poorer Irishman living at his expense; and surely there is no human be-ing whose example doesn't work contagiously in *some* particular. The very idiots at our public institutions imitate each other's peculiarities. And if you should individually achieve calmness and harmony in your own person, you may depend upon it that a wave of imitation will spread from you, as surely as the circles spread outward when a stone is dropped into a lake.

Fortunately, we shall not have to be absolute pioneers. Even now in New York they have formed a society for the improvement of our na-tional vocalization, and one perceives its machinations already in the shape of various newspaper paragraphs intended to stir up dissatisfaction with the awful thing that it is. And better still than that, because more radical and general, is the gospel of relaxation, as one may call it, preached by Miss Annie Payson Call, of Boston, in her admirable little volume called *Power through Repose,* a book that ought to be in the hands of every teacher and student in America of either sex. You need only be followers, then, on a path already opened up by others. But of one thing be confident—others still will follow you.

And this brings me to one more application of psychology to practical life, to which I will call attention briefly, and then close. If one's example of easy and calm ways is to be effectively contagious, one feels by instinct that the less voluntarily one aims at getting imitated, the more unconscious one keeps in the matter, the more likely one is to succeed. *Become the imitable thing,* and you may then discharge your minds of all responsibility for the imitation. The laws of social nature will take care of that result. Now the psychological principle on which this precept reposes is a law of very deep and wide-spread importance in the conduct of our lives, and at the same time a law which we Americans most grievously neglect. Stated technically, the law is this, that *strong feeling about one's self tends to arrest the free association of one's objective ideas and motor processes.* We get the extreme example of this in the mental disease called melancholia.

A melancholic patient is filled through and through with intensely painful emotion about himself. He is threatened, he is guilty, he is doomed, he is annihilated, he is lost. His mind is fixed as if in a cramp on these feelings of his own situation; and in all the books on insanity you may read that the usual varied flow of his thoughts has ceased. His associative processes, to use the technical phrase, are inhibited; and his ideas stand stock-still, shut up to their one monotonous function of reiterating inwardly the fact of the man's desperate estate. And this inhibitive influence is not due to the mere fact that his emotion is *painful.* Joyous emotions about the self also stop the association of our ideas. A saint in ecstasy is as motionless and irresponsive and one-idea'd as a melancholiac. And without going as far as ecstatic saints, we know how in everyone a great or sudden pleasure may paralyze the flow of thought. Ask young people returning from a party or a spectacle, and all excited about it, what it was. "Oh, it was *fine!* it was *fine!* it was *fine!*" is all the information you are likely to receive until the excitement has calmed down. Probably every one of my hearers has been made temporarily half-idiotic by some great success or piece of good fortune. "*Good!* GOOD! GOOD!" is all we can at such times say to ourselves until we smile at our own very foolishness.

Now from all this we can draw an extremely practical conclusion. If, namely, we wish our trains of ideation and volition to be copious and varied and effective, we must form the habit of freeing them from the inhibitive influence of reflection upon them, of egoistic preoccupation about their results. Such a habit, like other habits, can be formed. Prudence and duty and self-regard, emotions of ambition and emotions of anxiety, have, of course, a needful part to play in our lives. But confine them as far as possible to the occasions when you are making your general resolutions and deciding on your plans of campaign, and keep them out of the details. When once a decision is reached and execution is the order of the day, dismiss absolutely all responsibility and care about the outcome. *Unclamp*, in a word, your intellectual and practical machinery, and let it run free; and the service it will do you will be twice as good. Who are the scholars who get 'rattled' in the recitation-room? Those who think of the possibilities of failure and feel the great importance of the act. Who are those who do recite well? Often those who are most indifferent. *Their* ideas reel themselves out of their memory of their own accord. Why do we hear the complaint so often that social life in New England is either less rich and expressive or more fatiguing than it is in some other parts of the world? To what is the fact, if fact it be, due unless to the over-active conscience of the people, afraid of either saying something too trivial and obvious, or something insincere, or something unworthy of one's interlocutor, or something in some way or other not adequate to the occasion? How can conversation possibly steer itself through such a sea of responsibilities and inhibitions as this? On the other hand, conversation does flourish and society is refreshing, and neither dull on the one hand nor exhausting from its effort on the other, wherever people forget their scruples and take the brakes off their hearts, and let their tongues wag as automatically and irresponsibly as they will.

They talk much in paedagogic circles to-day about the duty of the teacher to prepare for every lesson in advance. To some extent this is useful. But we Yankees are assuredly not those to whom such a general doctrine should be preached. We are only too careful as it is. The advice

I should give to most teachers would be in the words of one who is herself an admirable teacher. Prepare yourself in the *subject so well that it shall be always on tap;* then in the class-room trust your spontaneity and fling away all farther care.

My advice to students, especially to girl-students, would be somewhat similar. Just as a bicycle-chain may be too tight, so may one's carefulness and conscientiousness be so tense as to hinder the running of one's mind. Take, for example, periods when there are many successive days of examination impending. One ounce of good nervous tone in an examination is worth many pounds of anxious study for it in advance. If you want really to do your best at an examination, fling away the book the day before, say to yourself, "I won't waste another minute on this miserable thing, and I don't care an iota whether I succeed or not." Say this sincerely, and feel it; and go out and play, or go to bed and sleep, and I am sure the results next day will encourage you to use the method permanently. I have heard this advice given to a student by Miss Call, whose book on muscular relaxation I quoted a moment ago. In her later book, entitled *As a Matter of Course,* the gospel of moral relaxation, of dropping things from the mind, and not 'caring,' is preached with equal success. Not only our preachers, but our friends the theosophists and mind-curers of various religious sects are also harping on this string. And with the doctors, the Delsarteans, the various mind-curing sects, and such writers as Mr. Dresser, Prentice Mulford, Mr. Horace Fletcher, and Mr. Trine to help, and the whole band of schoolteachers and magazine-readers chiming in, it really looks as if a good start might be made in the direction of changing our American mental habit into something more indifferent and strong.

Worry means always and invariably inhibition of associations and loss of effective power. Of course, the sovereign cure for worry is religious faith; and this, of course, you also know. The turbulent billows of the fretful surface leave the deep parts of the ocean undisturbed, and to him who has a hold on vaster and more permanent realities the hourly vicissitudes of his personal destiny seem relatively insignificant things. The really religious person is accordingly unshakable and full of equanimity, and calmly ready for any duty that the day may bring forth. This is charmingly illustrated by a little work with which I recently became acquainted: *The Practice of the Presence of God, the Best Rule of a Holy Life, by Brother Lawrence, Being Conversations and Letters of Nicholas Herman of Lor-*

raine, Translated from the French.[1] I extract a few passages, the conversations being given in indirect discourse. Brother Lawrence was a Carmelite friar, converted at Paris in 1666. He said "that he had been footman to M. Fieubert, the treasurer, and that he was a great awkward fellow who broke everything. That he had desired to be received into a monastery, thinking that he would there be made to smart for his awkwardness and the faults he should commit, and so he should sacrifice to GOD his life, with its pleasures; but that GOD had disappointed him, he having met with nothing but satisfaction in that state. . . .

"That he had been long troubled in mind from a certain belief that he should be damned; that all the men in the world could not have persuaded him to the contrary; but that he had thus reasoned with himself about it: *I engaged in a religious life only for the love of* GOD, *and I have endeavored to act only for Him; whatever becomes of me, whether I be lost or saved, I will always continue to act purely for the love of* GOD. *I shall have this good at least, that till death I shall have done all that is in me to love Him.* . . . That since then he had passed his life in perfect liberty and continual joy. . . .

"That when an occasion of practising some virtue offered, he addressed himself to GOD, saying, LORD, *I cannot do this unless Thou enablest me;* and that then he received strength more than sufficient. That when he had failed in his duty, he only confessed his fault, saying to GOD, *I shall never do otherwise if You leave me to myself; it is You who must hinder my falling, and mend what is amiss.* That after this he gave himself no further uneasiness about it. . . .

"That he had been lately sent into Burgundy, to buy the provision of wine for the society, which was a very unwelcome task for him, because he had no turn for business, and because he was lame and could not go about the boat but by rolling himself over the casks. That, however, he gave himself no uneasiness about it, nor about the purchase of the wine. That he said to GOD, *It was His business he was about,* and that he afterward found it very well performed. That he had been sent into Auvergne, the year before, upon the same account; that he could not tell how the matter passed, but that it proved very well.

"So, likewise, in his business in the kitchen (to which he had naturally a great aversion), having accustomed himself to do everything there for the love of GOD, and with prayer, upon all occasions, for His grace to do his work well, he had found everything easy, during fifteen years that he had been employed there.

"That he was very well pleased with the post he was now in; but that he was as ready to quit that as the former, since he was always pleasing himself in every condition by doing little things for the love of GOD. . . .

"That the goodness of GOD assured him He would not forsake him utterly, and that He would give him strength to bear whatever evil He permitted to happen to him; and therefore that he feared nothing, and had no occasion to consult with anybody about his state. That when he had attempted to do it, he had always come away more perplexed."

The simple-heartedness of the good Brother Lawrence, and the relaxation of all unnecessary solicitudes and anxieties in him, is a refreshing spectacle.

The need of feeling responsible all the livelong day has been preached long enough in our New England. Long enough exclusively, at any rate—and long enough to the female sex. What our girl-students and woman-teachers most need nowadays is not the exacerbation, but rather the toning-down of their moral tensions. Even now I fear that some one of my fair hearers may be making an undying resolve to become strenuously relaxed, cost what it will, for the remainder of her life. It is needless to say that that is not the way to do it. The way to do it, paradoxical as it may seem, is genuinely not to care whether you are doing it or not. Then, possibly, by the grace of God, you may all at once find that you *are* doing it; and, having learned what the trick feels like, you may (again by the grace of God) be enabled to go on.

And that something like this may be the happy experience of all my hearers is, in closing, my most earnest wish.

8

On a Certain Blindness in Human Beings

"On a Certain Blindness in Human Beings" was William James's own favorite among his short pieces of writing. On April 24, 1899, he wrote to one correspondent that the piece contained "the perception on which my whole individualistic philosophy is based." To another he wrote on April 18 of the same year, "I care very much indeed for the truth it so inadequately tries by dint of innumerable quotations to express." The blindness he has in mind, the sorry truth, as James put it in "Human Immortality," is "that we are doomed, by the fact that we are practical beings with very limited tasks to attend to, and special ideals to look after, to be absolutely blind and insensible to the inner feelings, and to the whole inner significance of lives that are different from our own."

James aims to set this right, to restore our sight. What "Self-Reliance" is to the work of Emerson, what "Song of Myself" is to the work of Whitman, "On a Certain Blindness" is to the work of James. The piece deserves a place among the defining documents of American democracy. In it, James quotes, at length, Robert Louis Stevenson, Wordsworth, Whitman, Tolstoy, and others. The use of skillfully edited lengthy quotations is a technique James also employed in *The Varieties of Religious Experience.* Here as there, readers have the feeling that they are hearing one witness after another give personal testimony. Each is allowed his or her own voice for his or her own experience. Perhaps great writers, like all great artists, can, if they try, enter into other lives by a sort of imaginative sympathy or negative (in the sense of self-forgetting) capability. It is worth noting that the English word "empathy," from the German "Einfuhlung," only appeared in the first decade of the twentieth century. But most of us cannot, or cannot easily, enter into the lives and points of view of people unlike ourselves. So James is daringly open to stating his conclusion in negative as well as in positive terms. Our blindness as to the lives of others, he says, "absolutely forbids us to be forward in pronouncing on the meaninglessness of forms of existence other than our own; and it commands us to tolerate, respect, and indulge those whom we see harmlessly interested and happy in their own ways, however unintelligible these may be to us. Hands off: neither the whole of truth, nor the whole of good, is revealed to any single observer."

⟫⟩◈⟨⟪

OUR JUDGMENTS concerning the worth of things, big or little, depend on the *feelings* the things arouse in us. Where we judge a thing to be precious in consequence of the *idea* we frame of it, this is only because the idea is itself associated already with a feeling. If we were radically feelingless, and if ideas were the only things our mind could entertain, we should lose all our likes and dislikes at a stroke, and be unable to point to any one situation or experience in life more valuable or significant than any other.

Now the blindness in human beings of which this discourse will treat is the blindness with which we all are afflicted in regard to the feelings of creatures and people different from ourselves.

We are practical beings, each of us with limited functions and duties to perform. Each is bound to feel intensely the importance of his own duties and the significance of the situations that call these forth. But this feeling is in each of us a vital secret, for sympathy with which we vainly look to others—the others are too much absorbed in their own vital secrets to take an interest in ours. Hence the stupidity and injustice of our opinions, so far as they deal with the significance of alien lives. Hence the falsity of our judgments, so far as they presume to decide in an absolute way on the value of other persons' conditions or ideals.

Take our dogs and ourselves, connected as we are by a tie more intimate than most ties in this world; and yet, outside of that tie of friendly fondness, how insensible, each of us, to all that makes life significant for the other!—we to the rapture of bones under hedges, or smells of trees and lamp-posts, they to the delights of literature and art. As you sit reading the most moving romance you ever fell upon, what sort of a judge is your fox-terrier of your behavior? With all his good will towards you, the nature of your conduct is absolutely excluded from his comprehension. To sit there like a senseless statue, when you might be taking him to walk and throwing sticks for him to catch! What queer disease is this that comes over you every day, of holding things and staring at them like that for hours together, paralyzed of motion and vacant of all conscious life? The African savages came nearer the truth; but they, too, missed it, when they gathered wonderingly round one of our American travellers who in the interior had just come into possession of a stray copy of the New York *Commercial Advertiser,* and was devouring it column by column. When he got through, they offered him a high price for the mysterious object; and being asked for what they wanted it, they said: "For an eye-medicine"—that being the only reason they could conceive of for the protracted bath which he had given his eyes upon its surface.

The spectator's judgment is sure to miss the root of the matter and to possess no truth. The subject judged knows a part of the world of reality which the judging spectator fails to see, knows more whilst the spectator knows less; and wherever there is conflict of opinion and difference of vision, we are bound to believe that the truer side is the side that feels the more and not the side that feels the less.

Let me take a personal example of the kind that befalls each one of us daily.

Some years ago, whilst journeying in the mountains of North Carolina, I passed by a large number of 'coves,' as they call them there, or heads of small valleys between the hills, which had been newly cleared and planted. The impression on my mind was one of unmitigated squalor. The settler had in every case cut down the more manageable trees, and left their charred stumps standing. The larger trees he had girdled and killed, in order that their foliage should not cast a shade. He had then built a log cabin, plastering its chinks with clay, and had set up a tall zigzag rail fence around the scene of his havoc, to keep the pigs and cattle out. Finally, he had irregularly planted the intervals between the stumps and trees with Indian corn, which grew among the chips; and there he dwelt with his wife and babes—an axe, a gun, a few utensils, and some pigs and chickens feeding in the woods, being the sum total of his possessions.

The forest had been destroyed; and what had 'improved' it out of existence was hideous, a sort of ulcer, without a single element of artificial grace to make up for the loss of Nature's beauty. Ugly indeed seemed the life of the squatter, scudding, as the sailors say, under bare poles, beginning again away back where our first ancestors started, and by hardly a single item the better off for all the achievements of the intervening generations.

Talk about going back to Nature! I said to myself, oppressed by the dreariness, as I drove by. Talk of a country life for one's old age and for one's children! Never thus, with nothing but the bare ground and one's bare hands to fight the battle! Never, without the best spoils of culture woven in! The beauties and commodities gained by the centuries are sacred. They are our heritage and birthright. No modern person ought to be willing to live a day in such a state of rudimentariness and denudation.

Then I said to the mountaineer who was driving me: "What sort of people are they who have to make these new clearings?" "All of us," he replied; "why, we ain't happy here unless we are getting one of these coves under cultivation." I instantly felt that I had been losing the whole inward significance of the situation. Because to me the clearings spoke of naught but denudation, I thought that to those whose sturdy arms and obedient axes had made them they could tell no other story. But when *they* looked on the hideous stumps, what they thought of was personal victory. The chips, the girdled trees and the vile split rails spoke of honest sweat, persistent toil and final reward. The cabin was a warrant of safety for self and wife and babes. In short, the clearing, which to me was a mere ugly picture on the retina, was to them a symbol redolent with moral memories and sang a very paean of duty, struggle, and success.

I had been as blind to the peculiar ideality of their conditions as they certainly would also have been to the ideality of mine, had they had a peep at my strange indoor academic ways of life at Cambridge.

Wherever a process of life communicates an eagerness to him who lives it, there the life becomes genuinely significant. Sometimes the eagerness is more knit up with the motor activities, sometimes with the perceptions, sometimes with the imagination, sometimes with reflective thought. But wherever it is found, there is the zest, the tingle, the excitement, of reality; and there *is* 'importance' in the only real and positive sense in which importance ever anywhere can be.

Robert Louis Stevenson has illustrated this by a case drawn from the sphere of the imagination, in an essay which I really think deserves to become immortal, both for the truth of its matter and the excellence of its form.

"Toward the end of September," Stevenson writes, "when schooltime was drawing near and the nights were already black, we would begin to sally from our respective villas, each equipped with a tin bull's-eye lantern. The thing was so well known that it had worn a rut in the commerce of Great Britain; and the grocers, about the due time, began to garnish their windows with our particular brand of luminary. We wore them buckled to the waist upon a cricket belt, and over them, such was the rigour of the game, a buttoned top-coat. They smelled noisomely of blistered tin; they never burned aright, though they would always burn our fingers; their use was naught; the pleasure of them merely fanciful; and yet a boy with a bull's-eye under his top-coat asked for nothing more. The fishermen used lanterns about their boats, and it was from them, I suppose, that we had got the hint; but theirs were not bull's-eyes, nor did we ever play at being fishermen. The police carried them at their belts, and we had plainly copied them in that; yet we did not pretend to be policemen. Burglars, indeed, we may have had some haunting thoughts of; and we had certainly an eye to past ages when lanterns were more common, and to certain story-books in which we had found them to figure very largely. But take it for all in all, the pleasure of the thing was substantive; and to be a boy with a bull's-eye under his top-coat was good enough for us.

"When two of these asses met, there would be an anxious 'Have you got your lantern?' and a gratified 'Yes!' That was the shibboleth, and very needful too; for, as it was the rule to keep our glory contained, none could recognise a lantern-bearer, unless (like the polecat) by the smell. Four or five would sometimes climb into the belly of a ten-man lugger, with nothing but the thwarts above them—for the cabin was usually locked, or choose out some hollow of the links where the wind might whistle overhead. There the coats would be unbuttoned and the bull's-eyes discovered; and in the chequering glimmer, under the huge windy hall of the night, and cheered by a rich steam of toasting tinware, these fortunate young gentlemen would crouch together in the cold sand of the links or on the scaly bilges of the fishing-boat, and delight themselves with inappropriate talk. Woe is me that I may not give some specimens. . . . But the talk was but a condiment; and these gatherings themselves only accidents in the career of the lantern-bearer. The essence of this bliss was to walk by yourself in the black night; the slide shut, the top-coat buttoned; not a ray escaping, whether to conduct your footsteps or to make your glory public: a mere pillar of darkness in the dark; and all the while, deep down in the privacy of your fool's heart, to know you had a bull's-eye at your belt, and to exult and sing over the knowledge.

"It is said that a poet has died young in the breast of the most stolid. It may be contended, rather, that this (somewhat minor) bard in almost every case survives, and is the spice of life to his possessor. Justice is not done to the versatility and the unplumbed childishness of man's imagination. His life from without may seem but a rude mound of mud; there will be some golden chamber at the heart of it, in which he dwells delighted; and for as dark as his pathway seems to the observer, he will have some kind of a bull's-eye at his belt.

". . . There is one fable that touches very near the quick of life: the fable of the monk who passed into the woods, heard a bird break into song, hearkened for a trill or two, and found himself on his return a stranger at his convent gates; for he had been absent fifty years, and of all his comrades there survived but one to recognise him. It is not only in the woods that this enchanter carols, though perhaps he is native there. He sings in the most doleful places. The miser hears him and chuckles, and the days are moments. With no more apparatus than an ill-smelling lantern I have evoked him on the naked links. All life that is not merely mechanical is spun out of two strands: seeking for that bird and hearing him. And it is just this that makes life so hard to value, and the delight of each so incommunicable. And just a knowledge of this, and a remembrance of those fortunate hours in which the bird *has* sung to *us*, that fills us with such wonder when we turn the pages of the realist. There, to be sure, we find a picture of life in so far as it consists of mud and of old iron, cheap desires and cheap fears, that which we are ashamed to remember and that which we are careless whether we forget; but of the note of that time-devouring nightingale we hear no news.

". . . Say that I came [in such a realistic romance] on some such business as that of my lantern-bearers on the links; and described the boys as very cold, spat upon by flurries of rain, and drearily surrounded, all of which they were; and their talk as silly and indecent, which it certainly was. . . . To the eye of the observer they *are* wet and cold and drearily surrounded; but ask themselves, and they are in the heaven of a recondite pleasure, the ground of which is an ill-smelling lantern.

"For, to repeat, the ground of a man's joy is often hard to hit. It may hinge at times upon a mere accessory, like the lantern, it may reside in the mysterious inwards of psychology. . . . It has so little bond with externals . . . that it may even touch them not; and the man's true life, for which he consents to live, lie altogether in the field of fancy. . . . In such a case the poetry runs underground. The observer (poor soul, with his documents!) is all abroad. For to look at the man is but to court deception. We shall see the trunk from which he draws his nourishment; but he himself is above and abroad in the green dome of foliage, hummed through by winds and nested in by nightingales. And the true realism were that of the poets, to climb up after him like a squirrel, and catch some glimpse of the heaven for which he lives. And the true realism, always and everywhere, is that of the poets: to find out where joy resides, and give it a voice far beyond singing.

"For to miss the joy is to miss all. In the joy of the actors lies the sense of any action. That is the explanation, that the excuse. To one who has not the secret of the lanterns, the scene upon the links is meaningless. And hence the haunting and truly spectral unreality of realistic books. . . . In each, we miss the personal poetry, the enchanted atmosphere, that rainbow work of fancy that clothes what is naked and seems to ennoble what is base; in each, life falls dead like dough, instead of soaring away like a balloon into the colours of the sunset; each is true, each inconceivable; for no man lives in the external truth, among salts and acids, but in the warm, phantasmagoric chamber of his brain, with the painted windows and the storied walls."[1]

These paragraphs are the best thing I know in all Stevenson. "To miss the joy is to miss all." Indeed, it is. Yet we are but finite, and each one of us has some single specialized vocation of his own. And it seems as if energy in the service of its particular duties might be got only by hardening the heart towards everything unlike them. Our deadness towards all but one particular kind of joy would thus be the price we inevitably have to pay for being practical creatures. Only in some pitiful dreamer, some philosopher, poet, or romancer, or when the common practical man becomes a lover, does the hard externality give way, and a gleam of insight into the ejective world, as Clifford called it, the vast world of inner life beyond us, so different from that of outer seeming, illuminate our mind. Then the whole scheme of our customary values gets confounded, then our self is riven and its narrow interests fly to pieces, then a new centre and a new perspective must be found.

The change is well described by my colleague, Josiah Royce:

"What then is thy neighbor? Thou hast regarded his thought, his feeling, as somehow different from thine. Thou hast said: 'A pain in him is not like a pain in me, but something far easier to bear.' He seems to thee a little less living than thou. His life is dim, it is cold, it is a pale fire beside thy own burning desires. . . . So, dimly and by instinct, thou hast lived with thy neighbor, and hast known him not, being blind. Thou hast made [of him] a thing, no Self at all. Have done with this illusion and simply try to know the truth. Pain is pain, joy is joy, everywhere even as in thee. In all the songs of the forest birds; in all the cries of the wounded and dying, struggling in the captor's power; in the boundless sea, where the myriads of water-creatures strive and die; amid all the countless hordes of savage men; in all sickness and sorrow; in all exultation and hope; everywhere from the lowest to the noblest, the same conscious, burning, willful life is found, endlessly manifold as the forms of the living creatures, unquenchable as the fires of the sun, real as these impulses that even now throb in thy own little selfish heart. Lift up thy eyes, behold that life, and then turn away and forget it as thou canst; but if thou hast *known* that, thou hast begun to know thy duty."[2]

This higher vision of an inner significance in what, until then, we had realized only in the dead external way, often comes over a person suddenly; and when it does so, it makes an epoch in his history. As Emerson says, there is a depth in those moments that constrains us to ascribe more reality to them than to all other experiences. The passion of love will shake one like an explosion, or some act will awaken a remorseful compunction that hangs like a cloud over all one's later day.

This mystic sense of hidden meaning starts upon us often from non-human natural things. I take this passage from *Obermann*, a French novel that had some vogue in its day: "Paris, March 7.—It was dark and rather cold. I was gloomy, and walked because I had nothing to do. I passed by some flowers placed breast-high upon a wall. A jonquil in bloom was there. It is the strongest expression of desire: it was the first perfume of the year. I felt all the happiness destined for man. This unutterable harmony of souls, the phantom of the ideal world, arose in me complete. I never felt anything so great or so instantaneous. I know not what shape, what analogy, what secret of relation it was that made me see in this flower a limitless beauty. . . . I shall never enclose in a conception this power, this immensity that nothing will express; this form that nothing will contain; this ideal of a better world which one feels, but which it would seem that nature has not made."[3]

Wordsworth and Shelley are similarly full of this sense of a limitless significance in natural things. In Wordsworth it was a somewhat austere and moral significance, a 'lonely cheer.'

> "To every natural form, rock, fruit or flower,
> Even the loose stones that cover the high-way,
> I gave a moral life: I saw them feel,
> Or linked them to some feeling: the great mass
> Lay bedded in a quickening soul, and all
> That I beheld respired with inward meaning."[4]

"Authentic tidings of invisible things!" Just what this hidden presence in Nature was, which Wordsworth so rapturously felt, and in the light of which he lived, tramping the hills for days together, the poet never could explain logically or in articulate conceptions. Yet to the reader who may himself have had gleaming moments of a similar sort the verses in which Wordsworth simply proclaims the fact of them come with a heart-satisfying authority:

> "Magnificent
> The morning rose, in memorable pomp,
> Glorious as e'er I had beheld—in front,
> The sea lay laughing at a distance; near,
> The solid mountains shone, bright as the clouds,
> Grain-tinctured, drenched in empyrean light;
> And in the meadows and the lower grounds
> Was all the sweetness of a common dawn—

Dews, vapours, and the melody of birds,
And labourers going forth to till the fields."

"Ah! need I say, dear Friend! that to the brim
My heart was full; I made no vows, but vows
Were then made for me; bond unknown to me
Was given, that I should be, else sinning greatly,
A dedicated Spirit. On I walked
In thankful blessedness, which yet survives."[5]

As Wordsworth walked, filled with his strange inner joy, responsive thus to the secret life of Nature roundabout him, his rural neighbors, tightly and narrowly intent upon their own affairs, their crops and lambs and fences, must have thought him a very insignificant and foolish personage. It surely never occurred to any one of them to wonder what was going on inside of *him* or what it might be worth. And yet that inner life of his carried the burden of a significance that has fed the souls of others, and fills them to this day with inner joy.

Richard Jefferies has written a remarkable autobiographic document entitled *The Story of My Heart*. It tells, in many pages, of the rapture with which in youth the sense of the life of nature filled him. On a certain hill-top, he says:

"I was utterly alone with the sun and the earth. Lying down on the grass, I spoke in my soul to the earth, the sun, the air, and the distant sea far beyond sight. . . . With all the intensity of feeling which exalted me, all the intense communion I held with the earth, the sun and sky, the stars hidden by the light, with the ocean—in no manner can the thrilling depth of these feelings be written—with these I prayed, as if they were the keys of an instrument. . . . The great sun burning with light; the strong earth, dear earth; the warm sky; the pure air; the thought of ocean; the inexpressible beauty of all filled me with a rapture, an ecstasy, an inflatus. With this inflatus, too, I prayed. . . . The prayer, this soul-emotion, was in itself, not for an object; it was a passion. I hid my face in the grass, I was wholly prostrated, I lost myself in the wrestle, I was rapt and carried away. . . . Had any shepherd accidentally seen me lying on the turf, he would only have thought that I was resting a few minutes. I made no outward show. Who could have imagined the whirlwind of passion that was going on within me as I reclined there!"[6]

Surely a worthless hour of life when measured by the usual standards of commercial value. Yet in what other *kind* of value can the preciousness of any hour, made precious by any standard, consist, if it consist not in feelings of excited significance like these, engendered in someone by what the hour contains?

Yet so blind and dead does the clamor of our own practical interests make us to all other things, that it seems almost as if it were necessary to become worthless as a practical being, if one is to hope to attain to any breadth of insight into the impersonal world of worths as such, to have any perception of life's meaning on a large objective scale. Only your mystic, your dreamer, or your insolvent tramp or loafer, can afford so sympathetic an occupation, an occupation which will change the usual standards of human values in the twinkling of an eye, giving to foolishness a place ahead of power, and laying low in a minute the distinctions which it takes a hard-working conventional man a lifetime to build up. You may be a prophet at this rate; but you cannot be a worldly success.

Walt Whitman, for instance, is accounted by many of us a contemporary prophet. He abolishes the usual human distinctions, brings all conventionalisms into solution, and loves and celebrates hardly any human attributes save those elementary ones common to all members of the race. For this he becomes a sort of ideal tramp, a rider on omnibus-tops and ferry-boats, and, considered either practically or academically, a worthless unproductive being. His verses are but ejaculations—things mostly without subject or verb, a succession of interjections on an immense scale. He felt the human crowd as rapturously as Wordsworth felt the mountains, felt it as an overpoweringly significant presence, simply to absorb one's mind in which should be business sufficient and worthy to fill the days of a serious man. As he crosses Brooklyn ferry, this is what he feels:

> Flood-tide below me! I watch you face to face;
> Clouds of the west! sun there half an hour high! I see you also face
>   to face.
> Crowds of men and women attired in the usual costumes! how
>   curious you are to me!
> On the ferry-boats, the hundreds and hundreds that cross, returning
>   home, are more curious to me than you suppose;
> And you that shall cross from shore to shore years hence, are more
>   to me, and more in my meditations, than you might suppose.
> Others will enter the gates of the ferry, and cross from shore
>   to shore;

Others will watch the run of the flood-tide;
Others will see the shipping of Manhattan north and west, and the
    heights of Brooklyn to the south and east;
Others will see the islands large and small;
Fifty years hence, others will see them as they cross, the sun half
    an hour high;
A hundred years hence, or ever so many hundred years hence,
    others will see them,
Will enjoy the sunset, the pouring in of the flood-tide, the falling
    back to the sea of the ebb-tide.
It avails not, neither time or place—distance avails not;
Just as you feel when you look on the river and sky, so I felt;
Just as any of you is one of a living crowd, I was one of a crowd;
Just as you are refresh'd by the gladness of the river and the bright
    flow, I was refresh'd;
Just as you stand and lean on the rail, yet hurry with the swift
    current, I stood, yet was hurried;
Just as you look on the numberless masts of ships, and the thick-
    stem'd pipes of steamboats, I look'd.
I too many and many a time cross'd the river, the sun half an
    hour high;
I watched the Twelfth-month sea-gulls—I saw them high in the air,
    floating with motionless wings, oscillating their bodies,
I saw how the glistening yellow lit up parts of their bodies, and left
    the rest in strong shadow,
I saw the slow-wheeling circles, and the gradual edging toward the
    south.
Saw the white sails of schooners and sloops—saw the ships
    at anchor,
The sailors at work in the rigging, or out astride the spars,
The scallop-edged waves in the twilight, the ladled cups, the
    frolicsome crests and glistening,
The stretch afar growing dimmer and dimmer, the gray walls of the
    granite store-houses by the docks,
On the neighboring shore, the fires from the foundry chimneys
    burning high . . . into the night,
Casting their flicker of black . . . into the clefts of streets.
These, and all else, were to me the same as they are to you.[7]

And so on, through the rest of a divinely beautiful poem. And if you
wish to see what this hoary loafer considered the most worthy way of
profiting by life's heaven-sent opportunities, read the delicious volume
of his letters to a young car-conductor who had become his friend:

"*New York, Oct.* 9, 1868.

"DEAR PETE. It is splendid here this forenoon—bright and cool. I was out early taking a short walk by the river only two squares from where I live. . . . Shall I tell you about [my life] just to fill up? I generally spend the forenoon in my room writing, etc., then take a bath fix up and go out about 12 and loafe somewhere or call on someone down town or on business, or perhaps if it is very pleasant and I feel like it ride a trip with some driver friend on Broadway from 23rd Street to Bowling Green, three miles each way. (Every day I find I have plenty to do, every hour is occupied with something.) You know it is a never ending amusement and study and recreation for me to ride a couple of hours of a pleasant afternoon on a Broadway stage in this way. You see everything as you pass, a sort of living, endless panorama—shops and splendid buildings and great windows: and on the broad sidewalks crowds of women richly dressed continually passing altogether different, superior in style and looks from any to be seen anywhere else—in fact a perfect stream of people—men too dressed in high style, and plenty of foreigners—and then in the streets the thick crowd of carriages, stages, carts, hotel and private coaches, and in fact all sorts of vehicles and many first class teams, mile after mile, and the splendor of such a great street and so many tall, ornamental, noble buildings many of them of white marble, and the gayety and motion on every side: you will not wonder how much attraction all this is on a fine day, to a great loafer like me, who enjoys so much seeing the busy world move by him, and exhibiting itself for his amusement, while he takes it easy and just looks on and observes."[8]

Truly a futile way of passing the time, some of you may say, and not altogether creditable to a grown-up man. And yet, from the deepest point of view, who knows the more of truth, and who knows the less—Whitman on his omnibus-top, full of the inner joy with which the spectacle inspires him, or you, full of the disdain which the futility of his occupation excites?

When your ordinary Brooklynite or New Yorker, leading a life replete with too much luxury, or tired and careworn about his personal affairs, crosses the ferry or goes up Broadway, *his* fancy does not thus 'soar away into the colors of the sunset' as did Whitman's, nor does he inwardly realize at all the indisputable fact that this world never did anywhere or at any time contain more of essential divinity, or of eternal meaning, than is embodied in the fields of vision over which his eyes so carelessly pass. There is life; and there, a step away, is death. There is the only kind of beauty there ever was. There is the old human struggle and its fruits together. There is the text and the sermon, the real and the ideal in one. But to the jaded and unquickened eye it is all dead and common, pure vulgarism, flatness and disgust. "Hech! it is a sad sight!" says Carlyle, walking at night with someone who appeals to him to note the splendor of the stars. And that very repetition of the scene to new generations of men *in secula seculorum,* that eternal recurrence of the common order, which so fills a Whitman with mystic satisfaction, is to a Schopenhauer, with the emotional anaesthesia, the feeling of 'awful inner emptiness' from out of which he views it all, the chief ingredient of the tedium it instills. What is life on the largest scale, he asks, but the same recurrent inanities, the same dog barking, the same fly buzzing, forevermore? Yet of the kind of fibre of which such inanities consist is the material woven of all the excitements, joys and meanings that ever were, or ever shall be, in this world.

To be rapt with satisfied attention, like Whitman, to the mere spectacle of the world's presence, is one way, and the most fundamental way, of confessing one's sense of its unfathomable significance and importance. But how can one attain to the feeling of the vital significance of an experience, if one have it not to begin with? There is no receipt which one can follow. Being a secret and a mystery, it often comes in mysteriously unexpected ways. It blossoms sometimes from out of the very grave wherein we imagined that our happiness was buried. Benvenuto Cellini, after a life all in the outer sunshine, made of adventures and artistic excitements, suddenly finds himself cast into a dungeon in the Castle of San Angelo. The place is horrible. Rats and wet and mould possess it. His leg is broken; and his teeth fall out, apparently with scurvy. But his thoughts turn to God as they have never turned before. He gets a bible, which he reads during the one hour in the twenty-four in which a wandering ray of daylight penetrates his cavern; he has religious visions; he sings psalms to himself and composes hymns; and thinking, on the last day of July, of the festivities customary on the morrow in Rome, he says to himself: "All these past years I celebrated this holiday with the vanities of the world; from this year henceforward I will do it with the divinity of God. And then I said to myself, 'Oh, how much more happy I am for this present life of mine than for all those things remembered!'"[9]

But the great understander of these mysterious ebbs and flows is Tolstoi. They throb all through his novels. In his *War and Peace,* the hero,

Peter, is supposed to be the richest man in the Russian empire. During the French invasion he is taken prisoner, and dragged through much of the retreat. Cold, vermin, hunger, and every form of misery assail him, the result being a revelation to him of the real scale of life's values. "Here only, and for the first time, he appreciated, because he was deprived of it, the happiness of eating when he was hungry, of drinking when he was thirsty, of sleeping when he was sleepy, and of talking when he felt the desire to exchange some words. . . . Later in life he always recurred with joy to this month of captivity, and never failed to speak with enthusiasm of the powerful and ineffaceable sensations, and especially of the moral calm, which he had experienced at this epoch. When at daybreak, on the morrow of his imprisonment, he saw [I abridge here Tolstoi's description] the mountains with their wooded slopes disappearing in the grayish mist; when he felt the cool breeze caress him; when he saw the light drive away the vapors, and the sun rise majestically behind the clouds and cupolas, and the crosses, the dew, the distance, the river, sparkle in the splendid, cheerful rays; his heart overflowed with emotion. This emotion kept continually with him, and increased a hundred-fold as the difficulties of his situation grew graver. . . . He learnt that man is meant for happiness, and that this happiness is in him, in the satisfaction of the daily needs of existence, and that unhappiness is the fatal result, not of our need, but of our abundance. . . . When calm reigned in the camp, and the embers paled and little by little went out, the full moon had reached the zenith. The woods and the fields roundabout lay clearly visible; and beyond the inundation of light which filled them, the view plunged into the limitless horizon. Then Peter cast his eyes upon the firmament, filled at that hour with myriads of stars. 'All that is mine,' he thought. 'All that is in me, is me! And that is what they think they have taken prisoner! That is what they have shut up in a cabin!'—So he smiled, and turned in to sleep among his comrades."[10]

The occasion and the experience, then, are nothing. It all depends on the capacity of the soul to be grasped, to have its life-currents absorbed by what is given. "Crossing a bare common," says Emerson, "in snow puddles, at twilight, under a clouded sky, without having in my thoughts any occurrence of special good fortune, I have enjoyed a perfect exhilaration. I am glad to the brink of fear."

Life is always worth living if one have such responsive sensibilities. But we of the highly educated classes (so called) have most of us got far,

far away from Nature. We are trained to seek the choice, the rare, the exquisite, exclusively, and to overlook the common. We are stuffed with abstract conceptions, and glib with verbalities and verbosities; and in the culture of these higher functions the peculiar sources of joy connected with our simpler functions often dry up, and we grow stone-blind and insensible to life's more elementary and general goods and joys.

The remedy under such conditions is to descend to a more profound and primitive level. To be imprisoned or shipwrecked or forced into the army would permanently show the good of life to many an over-educated pessimist. Living in the open air and on the ground, the lopsided beam of the balance slowly rises to the level line; and the over-sensibilities and insensibilities even themselves out. The good of all the artificial schemes and fevers fades and pales; and that of seeing, smelling, tasting, sleeping, and daring and doing with one's body, grows and grows. The savages and children of nature to whom we deem ourselves so much superior, certainly are alive where we are often dead, along these lines; and could they write as glibly as we do, they would read us impressive lectures on our impatience for improvement and on our blindness to the fundamental static goods of life. "Ah, my brother," said a chieftain to his white guest, "thou wilt never know the happiness of both thinking of nothing and doing nothing; this, next to sleep, is the most enchanting of all things. Thus we were before our birth, and thus we shall be after death. Thy people, . . . when they have finished reaping one field, they begin to plough another, and as if the day were not enough, I have seen them plough by moonlight. What is their life to ours—their life that is as nought to them? Blind that they are, they lose it all! But we live in the present."[11]

The intense interest that life can assume when brought down to the non-thinking level, the level of pure sensorial perception, has been beautifully described by a man who *can* write, Mr. W. H. Hudson, in his volume, *Idle Days in Patagonia*.

"I spent the greater part of one winter," says this admirable author, "at a point on the Rio Negro, seventy or eighty miles from the sea. . . . It was my custom to go out every morning on horseback with my gun, and, followed by one dog, to ride away from the valley; and no sooner would I climb the terrace and plunge into the grey universal thicket, than I would find myself as completely alone as if five hundred instead of only five miles separated me from the valley and river. So wild and solitary and remote seemed that grey waste, stretching away into infinitude, a waste untrodden by man, and where the wild animals are so few that they have made no discoverable path in the wilderness of thorns. . . . Not once, nor twice, nor thrice, but day after day I returned to this solitude, going to it in the morning as if to attend a festival, and leaving it only when hunger and thirst and the westering sun compelled me. And yet I had no object in going—no motive which could be put into words; for although I carried a gun, there was nothing to shoot—the shooting was all left behind in the valley. . . . Sometimes I would pass an entire day without seeing one mammal, and perhaps not more than a dozen birds of any size. The weather at that time was cheerless, generally with a grey film of cloud spread over the sky, and a bleak wind, often cold enough to make my bridle hand quite numb. . . . At a slow pace, which would have seemed intolerable in other circumstances, I would ride about for hours at a stretch. On arriving at a hill, I would slowly ride to its summit, and stand there to survey the prospect. On every side it stretched away in great undulations, wild and irregular. How grey it all was! hardly less so near at hand than on the haze-wrapped horizon, where the hills were dim and the outline blurred by distance. Descending from my look-out, I would take up my aimless wanderings again, and visit other elevations to gaze on the same landscape from another point; and so on for hours, and at noon I would dismount and sit or lie on my folded poncho for an hour or longer. One day, in these rambles, I discovered a small grove composed of twenty to thirty trees, growing at a convenient distance apart, that had evidently been resorted to by a herd of deer or other wild animals. This grove was on a hill differing in shape from other hills in its neighbourhood; and after a time I made a point of finding and using it as a resting-place every day at noon. I did not ask myself why I made choice of that one spot, sometimes going miles out of my way to sit there, instead of sitting down under any one of the millions of trees and bushes on any other hillside. I thought nothing about it, but acted unconsciously; only afterwards it seemed to me that after having rested there once, each time I wished to rest again the wish came associated with the image of that particular clump of trees, with polished stems and clean bed of sand beneath; and in a short time I formed a habit of returning, animal-like, to repose at that same spot.

"It was perhaps a mistake to say that I would sit down and rest, since I was never tired: and yet without being tired, that noonday pause, during which I sat for an hour without moving, was strangely grateful. All day there would be no sound, not even the rustle of a leaf. One day while *listening* to the silence, it occurred to my mind to wonder what the effect would be if I were to shout aloud. This seemed at the time a horrible suggestion, which almost made me shudder. But during those solitary days it was a rare thing for any thought to cross my mind. In the state of mind I was in, thought had become impossible. My state was one of *suspense* and *watchfulness:* yet I had no expectation of meeting with an adventure, and felt as free from apprehension as I feel now when sitting in a room in London. The state seemed familiar rather than strange, and accompanied by a strong feeling of elation; and I did not know that something had come between me and my intellect until I returned to my former self—to thinking, and the old insipid existence [again].

"I had undoubtedly *gone back;* and that state of intense watchfulness, or alertness rather, with suspension of the higher intellectual faculties, represented the mental state of the pure savage. He thinks little, reasons little, having a surer guide in his [mere sensory perceptions]; he is in perfect harmony with nature, and is nearly on a level, mentally, with the wild animals he preys on, and which in their turn sometimes prey on him."[12]

For the spectator, such hours as Mr. Hudson writes of form a mere tale of emptiness, in which nothing happens, nothing is gained, and there is nothing to describe. They are meaningless and vacant tracts of time. To him who feels their inner secret, they tingle with an importance that unutterably vouches for itself. I am sorry for the boy or girl, or man or woman, who has never been touched by the spell of this mysterious sensorial life, with its irrationality, if so you like to call it, but its vigilance and its supreme felicity. The holidays of life are its most vitally significant portions, because they are, or at least should be, covered with just this kind of magically irresponsible spell.

And now what is the result of all these considerations and quotations? It is negative in one sense, but positive in another. It absolutely forbids us to be forward in pronouncing on the meaninglessness of forms of existence other than our own; and it commands us to tolerate, respect, and indulge those whom we see harmlessly interested and happy in their own ways, however unintelligible these may be to us. Hands off: neither the whole of truth, nor the whole of good, is revealed to any single observer, although each observer gains a partial superiority of insight from the peculiar position in which he stands. Even prisons and sickrooms have their special revelations. It is enough to ask of each of us that he should be faithful to his own opportunities and make the most of his own blessings, without presuming to regulate the rest of the vast field.

9

What Makes a Life Significant

"What Makes a Life Significant" is a sort of companion piece to "On a Certain Blindness." James draws the political consequences of his views, turning his back on the elitist notion that writing a book, running for high office, or getting rich is required to make a life significant. James carefully argues instead that any and all lives can be significant. "The solid meaning of life," he says, "is always the same eternal thing—the marriage, namely, of some unhabitual ideal, however special, with some fidelity, courage, and endurance; with some man's or woman's pains.—And whatever or wherever life may be, there will always be the chance for that marriage to take place." The point is there in that unexpected phrase "some unhabitual ideal." James recognizes both the power of habit and the possibility of something different and better. It is not a grand claim, perhaps, but it is a saving one.

James tells a story to illustrate his point. He says he was riding along in a train feeling the loss in modern life of "the higher heroisms and the old rare flavors" of romance, when "the sight of a workman doing something on the dizzy edge of a sky-scaling iron construction brought me to my senses very suddenly." (Henry Thoreau once woke to realize that "*this* is the heroic age," though we know it not.) James goes on, "not in clanging fights and desperate marches only is heroism to be looked for, but on every railway bridge and fireproof building that is going up to-day. On freight-trains, on the decks of vessels, in cattle-yards and mines, on lumber-rafts, among the firemen and the policemen, the demand for courage is incessant; and the supply never fails."

In my previous talk, "On a Certain Blindness," I tried to make you feel how soaked and shot-through life is with values and meanings which we fail to realize because of our external and insensible point of view. The meanings are there for the others, but they are not there for us. There lies more than a mere interest of curious speculation in understanding this. It has the most tremendous practical importance. I wish that I could convince you of it as I feel it myself. It is the basis of all our tolerance, social, religious, and political. The forgetting of it lies at the root of every stupid and sanguinary mistake that rulers over subject-peoples make. The first thing to learn in intercourse with others is non-interference with their own peculiar ways of being happy, provided those ways do not assume to interfere by violence with ours. No one has insight into all the ideals. No one should presume to judge them off-hand. The pretension to dogmatize about them in each other is the root of most human injustices and cruelties, and the trait in human character most likely to make the angels weep.

Every Jack sees in his own particular Jill charms and perfections to the enchantment of which we stolid onlookers are stone-cold. And which has the superior view of the absolute truth, he or we? Which has the more vital insight into the nature of Jill's existence, as a fact? Is he in excess, being in this matter a maniac? or are we in defect, being victims of a pathological anaesthesia as regards Jill's magical importance? Surely the latter; surely to Jack are the profounder truths revealed; surely poor Jill's palpitating little life-throbs *are* among the wonders of creation, *are* worthy of this sympathetic interest; and it is to our shame that the rest of us cannot feel like Jack. For Jack realizes Jill concretely, and we do not. He struggles towards a union with her inner life, divining her feelings, anticipating her desires, understanding her limits as manfully as he can, and yet inadequately, too; for he also is afflicted with some blindness, even here. Whilst we, dead clods that we are, do not even seek after these things, but are contented that that portion of eternal fact named Jill should be for us as if it were not. Jill, who knows her inner life, knows that Jack's way of taking it—so importantly—is the true and serious way; and she responds to the truth in him by taking him truly and seriously, too. May the ancient blindness never wrap its clouds about either of them again! Where would any of *us* be, were there no one willing to know us as we really are or ready to repay us for *our* insight by making recognizant return? We ought, all of us, to realize each other in this intense, pathetic, and important way.

If you say that this is absurd, and that we cannot be in love with everyone at once, I merely point out to you that, as a matter of fact, certain persons do exist with an enormous capacity for friendship and for taking delight in other people's lives; and that such persons know more of truth than if their hearts were not so big. The vice of ordinary Jack and Jill affection is not its intensity, but its exclusions and its jealousies. Leave those out, and you see that the ideal I am holding up before you, however impracticable to-day, yet contains nothing intrinsically absurd.

We have unquestionably a great cloud-bank of ancestral blindness weighing down upon us, only transiently riven here and there by fitful revelations of the truth. It is vain to hope for this state of things to alter much. Our inner secrets must remain for the most part impenetrable by others, for beings as essentially practical as we are are necessarily short of sight. But if we cannot gain much positive insight into one another, cannot we at least use our sense of our own blindness to make us more cautious in going over the dark places? Cannot we escape some of those hideous ancestral intolerances and cruelties, and positive reversals of the truth?

For the remainder of this hour I invite you to seek with me some principle to make our tolerance less chaotic. And as I began my previous lecture by a personal reminiscence, I am going to ask your indulgence for a similar bit of egotism now.

A few summers ago I spent a happy week at the famous Assembly Grounds on the borders of Chautauqua Lake. The moment one treads that sacred enclosure, one feels one's self in an atmosphere of success. Sobriety and industry, intelligence and goodness, orderliness and ideality, prosperity and cheerfulness, pervade the air. It is a serious and studious picnic on a gigantic scale. Here you have a town of many thousands of inhabitants, beautifully laid out in the forest and drained, and equipped with means for satisfying all the necessary lower and most of the superfluous higher wants of man. You have a first-class college in full blast. You have magnificent music—a chorus of seven hundred voices, with possibly the most perfect open-air auditorium in the world. You have every sort of athletic exercise from sailing, rowing, swimming, bicycling, to the ball-field and the more artificial doings which the gymnasium affords. You have kindergartens and model secondary schools. You have general religious services and special club-houses for the several sects. You have perpetually running soda-water fountains, and daily popular lectures by distinguished men. You have the best of company, and yet no effort. You have no zymotic diseases, no poverty, no drunkenness, no crime, no police. You have culture, you have kindness, you have cheapness, you have equality, you have the best fruits of what mankind has fought and bled and striven for under the name of civilization for centuries. You have, in short, a foretaste of what human society might be, were it all in the light, with no suffering and no dark corners.

I went in curiosity for a day. I stayed for a week, held spell-bound by the charm and ease of everything, by the middle-class paradise, without a sin, without a victim, without a blot, without a tear.

And yet what was my own astonishment, on emerging into the dark and wicked world again, to catch myself quite unexpectedly and involuntarily saying: "Ouf! what a relief! Now for something primordial and savage, even though it were as bad as an Armenian massacre, to set the balance straight again. This order is too tame, this culture too second-rate, this goodness too uninspiring. This human drama without a villain or a pang; this community so refined that ice-cream soda-water is the utmost offering it can make to the brute animal in man; this city simmering in the tepid lakeside sun; this atrocious harmlessness of all things—I cannot abide with them. Let me take my chances again in the big outside worldly wilderness with all its sins and sufferings. There are the heights and depths, the precipices and the steep ideals, the gleams of the awful and the infinite; and there is more hope and help a thousand times than in this dead level and quintessence of every mediocrity."

Such was the sudden right-about-face performed for me by my lawless fancy! There had been spread before me the realization—on a small, sample scale of course—of all the ideals for which our civilization has been striving: security, intelligence, humanity, and order; and here was the instinctive hostile reaction, not of the natural man, but of a so-called cultivated man upon such a Utopia. There seemed thus to be a self-contradiction and paradox somewhere, which I, as a professor drawing a full salary, was in duty bound to unravel and explain, if I could.

So I meditated. And, first of all, I asked myself what the thing was that was so lacking in this Sabbatical city, and the lack of which kept one forever falling short of the higher sort of contentment. And I soon recognized that it was the element that gives to the wicked outer world all its moral style, expressiveness and picturesqueness—the element of precipitousness, so to call it, of strength and strenuousness, intensity and danger. What excites and interests the looker-on at life, what the romances and the statues celebrate and the grim civic monuments remind us of, is the everlasting battle of the powers of light with those of darkness; with heroism, reduced to its bare chance, yet ever and anon snatching victory from the jaws of death. But in this unspeakable Chautauqua there was no potentiality of death in sight anywhere, and no point of the compass visible from which danger might possibly appear. The ideal was so completely victorious already that no sign of any previous battle remained, the place just resting on its oars. But what our human emotions seem to require is the sight of the struggle going on. The moment the fruits are being merely eaten, things become ignoble. Sweat and effort, human nature strained to its uttermost and on the rack, yet getting through alive, and then turning its back on its success to pursue another more rare and arduous still—this is the sort of thing the presence of which inspires us, and the reality of which it seems to be the function of all the higher forms of literature and fine art to bring home to us and suggest. At Chautauqua there were no racks, even in the place's historical museum; and no sweat, except possibly the gentle moisture on the brow of some lecturer, or on the sides of some player in the ball-field.

Such absence of human nature *in extremis* anywhere seemed, then, a sufficient explanation for Chautauqua's flatness and lack of zest.

But was not this a paradox well calculated to fill one with dismay? It looks indeed, thought I, as if the romantic idealists with their pessimism about our civilization were, after all, quite right. An irremediable flatness is coming over the world. Bourgeoisie and mediocrity, church sociables and teachers' conventions, are taking the place of the old heights and depths and romantic chiaroscuro. And to get human life in its wild intensity, we must in future turn more and more away from the actual, and forget it, if we can, in the romancer's or the poet's pages. The whole world, delightful and sinful as it may still appear for a moment to one just escaped from the Chautauquan enclosure, is nevertheless obeying more and more just those ideals that are sure to make of it in the end a mere Chautauqua Assembly on an enormous scale. *Was im Gesang soll leben muss im Leben untergehn.* Even now, in our own country, correctness, fairness, and compromise for every small advantage are crowding out all other qualities. The higher heroisms and the old rare flavors are passing out of life.[1]

With these thoughts in my mind, I was speeding with the train towards Buffalo, when, near that city, the sight of a workman doing something on the dizzy edge of a sky-scaling iron construction brought me to my senses very suddenly. And now I perceived, by a flash of insight, that I had been steeping myself in pure ancestral blindness, and looking at life with the eyes of a remote spectator. Wishing for heroism and the spectacle of human nature on the rack, I had never noticed the great fields of heroism lying roundabout me, I had failed to see it present and alive. I could only think of it as dead and embalmed, labelled and costumed, as it is in the pages of romance. And yet there it was before me in the daily lives of the laboring classes. Not in clanging fights and desperate marches only is heroism to be looked for, but on every railway bridge and fireproof building that is going up to-day. On freight-trains, on the decks of vessels, in cattle-yards and mines, on lumber-rafts, among the firemen and the policemen, the demand for courage is incessant; and the supply never fails. There, every day of the year somewhere, is human nature *in extremis* for you. And wherever a scythe, an axe, a pick, or a shovel is wielded, you have it sweating and aching and with its powers of patient endurance racked to the utmost under the length of hours of the strain.

As I awoke to all this unidealized heroic life around me, the scales seemed to fall from my eyes; and a wave of sympathy greater than anything I had ever before felt with the common life of common men began to fill my soul. It began to seem as if virtue with horny hands and dirty skin were the only virtue genuine and vital enough to take account of. Every other virtue poses; none is absolutely unconscious and simple, and unexpectant of decoration or recognition, like this. These are our soldiers, thought I, these our sustainers, these the very parents of our life.

Many years ago, when in Vienna, I had had a similar feeling of awe and reverence in looking at the peasant-women, in from the country on their business at the market for the day. Old hags many of them were, dried and brown and wrinkled, kerchiefed and short-petticoated, with thick wool stockings on their bony shanks, stumping through the glittering thoroughfares, looking neither to the right nor the left, bent on duty, envying nothing, humble-hearted, remote;—and yet at bottom, when you came to think of it, bearing the whole fabric of the splendors and corruptions of that city on their laborious backs. For where would any of it have been without their unremitting, unrewarded labor in the fields? And so with us: not to our generals and poets, I thought, but to the Italian and Hungarian laborers in the Subway, rather, ought the monuments of gratitude and reverence of a city like Boston to be reared.

If any of you have been readers of Tolstoi, you will see that I passed into a vein of feeling similar to his, with its abhorrence of all that conventionally passes for distinguished, and its exclusive deification of the bravery, patience, kindliness, and dumbness of the unconscious natural man.

Where now is *our* Tolstoi, I said, to bring the truth of all this home to our American bosoms, fill us with a better insight, and wean us away from that spurious literary romanticism on which our wretched culture—as it calls itself—is fed? Divinity lies all about us, and culture is too hidebound to even suspect the fact. Could a Howells or a Kipling be enlisted in this mission? or are they still too deep in the ancestral blindness, and not humane enough for the inner joy and meaning of the laborer's existence to be really revealed? Must we wait for someone born and bred and living as a laborer himself, but who, by grace of Heaven, shall also find a literary voice?

And there I rested on that day, with a sense of widening of vision, and with what it is surely fair to call an increase of religious insight into life. In God's eyes, the differences of social position, of intellect, of culture, of cleanliness, of dress, which different men exhibit, and all the other rarities and exceptions on which they so fantastically pin their pride, must be so small as, practically, quite to vanish; and all that should remain is the common fact that here we are, a countless multitude of vessels of life, each of us pent in to peculiar difficulties, with which we must severally struggle by using whatever of fortitude and goodness we can summon up. The exercise of the courage, patience, and kindness, must be the significant portion of the whole business; and the distinctions of position can only be a manner of diversifying the phenomenal surface upon which these underground virtues may manifest their effects. At this rate, the deepest human life is everywhere, is eternal. And if any human attributes exist only in particular individuals, they must belong to the mere trapping and decoration of the surface-show.

Thus are men's lives levelled up as well as levelled down—levelled up in their common inner meaning, levelled down in their outer gloriousness and show. Yet always, we must confess, this levelling insight tends to be obscured again; and always the ancestral blindness returns and wraps us up, so that we end once more by thinking that creation can be for no other purpose than to develop remarkable situations and conventional distinctions and merits. And then always some new leveller in the shape of a religious prophet has to arise—the Buddha, the Christ, or some Saint Francis, some Rousseau or Tolstoi—to redispel our blindness. Yet, little by little, there comes some stable gain; for the world does get more humane, and the religion of democracy tends towards permanent increase.

This, as I said, became for a time my conviction, and gave me great content. I have put the matter into the form of a personal reminiscence, so that I might lead you into it more directly and completely, and so save time. But now I am going to discuss the rest of it with you in a more impersonal way.

Tolstoi's levelling philosophy began long before he had the crisis of melancholy commemorated in that wonderful document of his entitled *My Confession,* which led the way to his more specifically religious works. In his masterpiece *War and Peace*—assuredly the greatest of human novels—the rôle of the spiritual hero is given to a poor little soldier named Karataieff, so helpful, so cheerful, and so devout that, in spite of his ignorance and filthiness, the sight of him opens the heavens, which have been closed, to the mind of the principal character of the book; and his example evidently is meant by Tolstoi to let God into the world again for the reader. Poor little Karataieff is taken prisoner by the French; and when too exhausted by hardship and fever to march, is shot as other prisoners were in the famous retreat from Moscow. The last view one gets of him is his little figure leaning against a white birch-tree, and uncomplainingly awaiting the end.

"The more," writes Tolstoi in the work *My Confession,* "the more I examined the life of these laboring folks, the more persuaded I became that they veritably have faith, and get from it alone the sense and the possibility of life. . . . Contrariwise to those of our own class, who protest against destiny and grow indignant at its rigor, these people receive maladies and misfortunes without revolt, without opposition, and with a firm and tranquil confidence that all had to be like that, could not be otherwise, and that it is all right so. . . . The more we live by our intellect, the less we understand the meaning of life. We see only a cruel jest in suffering and death, whereas these people live, suffer, and draw near to death with tranquillity, and oftener than not with joy. . . . There are enormous multitudes of them happy with the most perfect happiness, although deprived of what for us is the sole good of life. Those who understand life's meaning, and know how to live and die thus, are to be counted not by twos, threes, tens, but by hundreds, thousands, millions. They labor quietly, endure privations and pains, live and die, and throughout everything see the good without seeing the vanity. I had to love these people. The more I entered into their life, the more I loved them; and the more it became possible for me to live, too. It came about not only that the life of our society, of the learned and of the rich, disgusted me—more than that, it lost all semblance of meaning in my eyes. All our actions, our deliberations, our sciences, our arts, all appeared to me with a new significance. I understood that these things might be charming pastimes, but that one need seek in them no depth, whereas the life of the hard-working populace, of that multitude of human beings who really contribute to existence, appeared to me in its true light. I understood that there veritably is life, that the meaning which life there receives is the truth; and I accepted it."[2]

In a similar way does Stevenson appeal to our piety towards the elemental virtue of mankind.

"What a wonderful thing," he writes,[3] "is this Man! How surprising are his attributes! Poor soul, here for so little, cast among so many hardships, savagely surrounded, savagely descended, irremediably condemned to prey upon his fellow lives: who should have blamed him had he been of a piece with his destiny and a being merely barbarous? . . .

[Yet] it matters not where we look, under what climate we observe him, in what stage of society, in what depth of ignorance, burthened with what erroneous morality; in ships at sea, a man inured to hardship and vile pleasures, his brightest hope a fiddle in a tavern and a bedizened trull who sells herself to rob him, and he for all that simple, innocent, cheerful, kindly like a child, constant to toil, brave to drown, for others; in the slums of cities, moving among indifferent millions to mechanical employments, without hope of change in the future, with scarce a plea-sure in the present, and yet true to his virtues, honest up to his lights, kind to his neighbours, tempted perhaps in vain by the bright gin-palace, . . . often repaying the world's scorn with service, often standing firm upon a scruple, . . . everywhere some virtue cherished or affected, ev-erywhere some decency of thought and courage, everywhere the ensign of man's ineffectual goodness:—ah! if I could show you this! if I could show you these men and women, all the world over, in every stage of history, under every abuse of error, under every circumstance of failure, without hope, without help, without thanks, still obscurely fighting the lost fight of virtue, still clinging to some rag of honour, the poor jewel of their souls!"

All this is as true as it is splendid, and terribly do we need our Tol-stois and Stevensons to keep our sense for it alive. Yet you remember the Irishman who, when asked, "Is not one man as good as another?" replied: "Yes; and a great deal better, too!" Similarly (it seems to me) does Tolstoi overcorrect our social prejudices, when he makes his love of the peasant so exclusive, and hardens his heart towards the educated man as absolutely as he does. Grant that at Chautauqua there was little moral effort, little sweat or muscular strain in view. Still, deep down in the souls of the participants we may be sure that something of the sort was hid, some inner stress, some vital virtue not found wanting when required. And, after all, the question recurs, and forces itself upon us, Is it so certain that the surroundings and circumstances of the virtue do make so little difference in the importance of the result? Is the func-tional utility, the worth to the universe of a certain definite amount of courage, kindliness, and patience, no greater if the possessor of these virtues is in an educated situation, working out far-reaching tasks, than if he be an illiterate nobody, hewing wood and drawing water, just to keep himself alive? Tolstoi's philosophy, deeply enlightening though it certainly is, remains a false abstraction. It savors too much of that oriental pessimism and nihilism of his, which declares the whole phenomenal world and its facts and their distinctions to be a cunning fraud.

A mere bare fraud is just what our Western common sense will never believe the phenomenal world to be. It admits fully that the inner joys and virtues are the *essential* part of life's business, but it is sure that *some* positive part is also played by the adjuncts of the show. If it is idiotic in romanticism to recognize the heroic only when it sees it labelled and dressed-up in books, it is really just as idiotic to see it only in the dirty boots and sweaty shirt of someone in the fields. It is with us really under every disguise: at Chautauqua; here in your college; in the stock-yards and on the freight-trains; and in the czar of Russia's court. But, instinctively, we make a combination of two things in judging the total significance of a human being. We feel it to be some sort of a product (if such a product only could be calculated) of his inner virtue *and* his outer place—neither singly taken, but both conjoined. If the outer differences had no meaning for life, why indeed should all this immense variety of them exist? They *must* be significant elements of the world as well.

Just test Tolstoi's deification of the mere manual laborer by the facts. This is what Mr. Walter Wyckoff, after working as an unskilled laborer in the demolition of some buildings at West Point, writes of the spiritual condition of the class of men to which he temporarily chose to belong:

"The salient features of our condition are plain enough. We are grown men, and are without a trade. In the labor market we stand ready to sell to the highest bidder our mere muscular strength for so many hours each day. We are thus in the lowest grade of labor. And selling our muscular strength in the open market for what it will bring, we sell it under peculiar conditions. It is all the capital that we have. We have no reserve means of subsistence, and cannot, therefore, stand off for a 're-serve price.' We sell under the necessity of satisfying imminent hunger. Broadly speaking, we must sell our labor or starve; and as hunger is a matter of a few hours, and we have no other way of meeting this need, we must sell at once for what the market offers for our labor.

"Our employer is buying labor in a dear market, and he will certainly get from us as much work as he can at the price. The gang-boss is secured for this purpose, and thoroughly does he know his business. He has sole command of us. He never saw us before, and he will discharge us all when the débris is cleared away. In the meantime he must get from us, if he can, the utmost of physical labor which we, individually and collectively, are capable of. If he should drive some of us to exhaustion, and we should not be able to continue at work, he would not be the loser, for the market would soon supply him with others to take our places.

"We are ignorant men, but so much we clearly see: that we have sold our labor where we could sell it dearest, and our employer has bought it where he could buy it cheapest. He has paid high, and he must get all the labor that he can; and, by a strong instinct which possesses us, we shall part with as little as we can. From work like ours there seems to us to have been eliminated every element which constitutes the nobility of labor. We feel no personal pride in its progress, and no community of interest with our employer. There is none of the joy of responsibility, none of the sense of achievement, only the dull monotony of grinding toil, with the longing for the signal to quit work, and for our wages at the end.

"And being what we are, the dregs of the labor market, and having no certainty of permanent employment, and no organization among ourselves, we must expect to work under the watchful eye of a gang-boss, and be driven, like the wage-slaves that we are, through our tasks.

"All this is to tell us, in effect, that our lives are hard, barren, hopeless lives" [abridged].

And such hard, barren, hopeless lives, surely, are not lives in which one ought to be willing permanently to remain. And why is this so? Is it because they are so dirty? Well, Nansen grew a great deal dirtier on his polar expedition; and we think none the worse of his life for that. Is it the insensibility? Our soldiers have to grow vastly more insensible, and we extol them to the skies. Is it the poverty? Poverty has been reckoned the crowning beauty of many a heroic career. Is it the slavery to a task, the loss of finer pleasures? Such slavery and loss are of the very essence of the higher fortitude, and are always counted to its credit—read the records of missionary devotion all over the world. It is not any one of these things, then, taken by itself—no, nor all of them together—that make such a life undesirable. A man might in truth live like an unskilled laborer, and do the work of one, and yet count as one of the noblest of

God's creatures. Quite possibly there were some such persons in the gang that our author describes; but the current of their souls ran underground; and he was too steeped in the ancestral blindness to discern it.

If there *were* any such morally exceptional individuals, however, what made them different from the rest? It can only have been this— that their souls worked and endured in obedience to some inner *ideal,* whilst their comrades were not actuated by anything worthy of that name. These ideals of other lives are among those secrets that we can almost never penetrate, although something about the man may often tell us when they are there. In Mr. Wyckoff's own case we know exactly what the self-imposed ideal was. Partly he had stumped himself, as the boys say, to carry through a strenuous achievement; but mainly he wished to enlarge his sympathetic insight into fellow-lives. For this his sweat and toil acquire a certain heroic significance, and make us accord to him exceptional esteem. But it is easy to imagine his fellows with various other ideals. To say nothing of wives and babies, one may have been a convert of the Salvation Army, and had a nightingale singing of expiation and forgiveness in his heart all the while he labored. Or there might have been an apostle like Tolstoi himself, or his compatriot Bondareff, in the gang, voluntarily embracing labor as their religious mission. Class-loyalty was undoubtedly an ideal with many. And who knows how much of that higher manliness of poverty, of which Phillips Brooks has spoken so penetratingly, was or was not present in that gang?

"A rugged, barren land," says Phillips Brooks, "is poverty to live in,—a land where I am thankful very often if I can get a berry or a root to eat; but living in it really, letting it bear witness to me of itself, not dishonoring it all the time by judging it after the standards of the other lands, gradually there come out its qualities. Behold! no land like this barren and naked land of poverty could show the moral geology of the world. See how the hard ribs . . . stand out strong and solid. No life like poverty could so get one to the heart of things and make men know their meaning, could so let us feel life and the world with all the soft cushions stripped off and thrown away. . . . Poverty makes men come very near each other, and recognize each other's human hearts; and poverty, highest and best of all, demands and cries out for faith in God. . . . I know how superficial and unfeeling, how like mere mockery, words in praise of poverty may seem. . . . But I am sure that the poor man's dignity and freedom, his self-respect and energy, depend upon his cordial knowledge that his poverty is a true region and kind of life with its own chances of character, its own springs of happiness, and revelations of God. Let him resist the characterlessness which often comes with being poor. Let him insist on respecting the condition where he lives. Let him learn to love it so that by and by [if] he grows rich he shall go out of the low door of the old familiar poverty with a true pang of regret, and with a true honor for the narrow home where he has lived so long."[4]

The barrenness and ignobleness of the more usual laborer's life consist in the fact that it is moved by no such ideal inner springs. The backache, the long hours, the danger, are patiently endured—for what? To gain a quid of tobacco, a glass of beer, a cup of coffee, a meal, and a bed, and to begin again the next day and shirk as much as one can. This really is why we raise no monument to the laborers in the Subway, even though they be our conscripts, and even though after a fashion our city is indeed based upon their patient hearts and enduring backs and shoulders. And this is why we do raise monuments to our soldiers, whose outward conditions were even brutaller still. The soldiers are supposed to have followed an ideal, and the laborers are supposed to have followed none.

You see, my friends, how the plot now thickens; and how strangely the complexities of this wonderful human nature of ours begin to develop under our hands. We have seen the blindness and deadness to each other which are our natural inheritance; and in spite of them, we have been led to acknowledge an inner meaning which passeth show, and which may be present in the lives of others where we least descry it. And now we are led to say that such inner meaning can be *complete*, and *valid for us also*, only when the inner joy, courage, and endurance are joined with an ideal.

But what, exactly, do we mean by an ideal? Can we give no definite account of such a word?

To a certain extent we can. An ideal, for instance, must be something intellectually conceived, something of which we are not unconscious, if we have it; and it must carry with it that sort of outlook, uplift, and brightness that go with all intellectual facts. Secondly, there must be *novelty* in an ideal—novelty at least for him whom the ideal grasps. Sodden routine is incompatible with ideality, although what is sodden routine for one person may be ideal novelty for another. This shows that there is nothing absolutely ideal: ideals are relative to the lives that entertain them. To keep out of the gutter is for us here no part of consciousness at all, yet for many of our brethren it is the most legitimately engrossing of ideals.

Now, taken nakedly, abstractly, and immediately, you see that mere ideals are the cheapest things in life. Everybody has them in some shape or other, personal or general, sound or mistaken, low or high; and the most worthless sentimentalists and dreamers, drunkards, shirks and verse-makers, who never show a grain of effort, courage, or endurance, possibly have them on the most copious scale. Education, enlarging as it does our horizon and perspective, is a means of multiplying our ideals, of bringing new ones into view. And your college professor, with a starched shirt and spectacles, would, if a stock of ideals were all alone by itself enough to render a life significant, be the most absolutely and deeply significant of men. Tolstoi would be completely blind in despising him for a prig, a pedant and a parody; and all our new insight into the divinity of muscular labor would be altogether off the track of truth.

But such consequences as this, you instinctively feel, are erroneous. The more ideals a man has, the more contemptible, on the whole, do you continue to deem him, if the matter ends there for him, and if none of the laboring man's virtues are called into action on his part—no courage shown, no privations undergone, no dirt or scars contracted in the attempt to get them realized. It is quite obvious that something more than the mere possession of ideals is required to make a life significant in any sense that claims the spectator's admiration. Inner joy, to be sure, it may *have*, with its ideals; but that is its own private sentimental matter. To extort from us, outsiders as we are, with our own ideals to look after, the tribute of our grudging recognition, it must back its ideal visions with what the laborers have, the sterner stuff of manly virtue; it must multiply their sentimental surface by the dimension of the active will, if we are to have *depth*, if we are to have anything cubical and solid in the way of character.

The significance of a human life for communicable and publicly recognizable purposes is thus the offspring of a marriage of two different parents, either of whom alone is barren. The ideals taken by themselves give no reality, the virtues by themselves no novelty. And let the orientalists and pessimists say what they will, the thing of deepest—or, at any rate, of comparatively deepest—significance in life does seem to be its character of *progress*, or that strange union of reality with ideal novelty which it continues from one moment to another to present. To recognize ideal novelty is the task of what we call intelligence. Not everyone's intelligence can tell which novelties are ideal. For many the ideal thing will always seem to cling still to the older more familiar good. In this case character, though not significant totally, may be still significant pathetically. So if we are to choose which is the more essential factor of human character, the fighting virtue or the intellectual breadth, we must side with Tolstoi, and choose that simple faithfulness to his light or darkness which any common unintellectual man can show.

But with all this beating and tacking on my part, I fear you take me to be reaching a confused result. I seem to be just taking things up and dropping them again. First I took up Chautauqua, and dropped that; then Tolstoi and the heroism of common toil, and dropped them; finally, I took up ideals, and seem now almost dropping those. But please observe in what sense it is that I drop them. It is when they pretend *singly* to redeem life from insignificance. Culture and refinement all alone are not enough to do so. Ideal aspirations are not enough, when uncombined with pluck and will. But neither are pluck and will, dogged endurance and insensibility to danger enough, when taken all alone. There must be some sort of fusion, some chemical combination among these principles, for a life objectively and thoroughly significant to result.

Of course, this is a somewhat vague conclusion. But in a question of significance, of worth, like this, conclusions can never be precise. The answer of appreciation, of sentiment, is always a more or a less, a balance struck by sympathy, insight, and good will. But it is an answer, all the same, a real conclusion. And in the course of getting it, it seems to me that our eyes have been opened to many important things. Some of you are, perhaps, more livingly aware than you were an hour ago of the depths of worth that lie around you, hid in alien lives. And when you ask how much sympathy you ought to bestow, although the amount is, truly enough, a matter of ideal on your own part, yet in this notion of the combination of ideals with active virtues you have a rough standard for shaping your decision. In any case, your imagination is extended.

You divine in the world about you matter for a little more humility on your own part, and tolerance, reverence, and love for others; and you gain a certain inner joyfulness at the increased importance of our common life. Such joyfulness is a religious inspiration and an element of spiritual health, and worth more than large amounts of that sort of technical and accurate information which we professors are supposed to be able to impart.

To show the sort of thing I mean by these words, I will just make one brief practical illustration, and then close.

We are suffering to-day in America from what is called the labor-question; and when you go out into the world, you will each and all of you be caught up in its perplexities. I use the brief term labor-question to cover all sorts of anarchistic discontents and socialistic projects, and the conservative resistances which they provoke. So far as this conflict is unhealthy and regrettable—and I think it is so only to a limited extent—the unhealthiness consists solely in the fact that one-half of our fellow-countrymen remain entirely blind to the internal significance of the lives of the other half. They miss the joys and sorrows, they fail to feel the moral virtue, and they do not guess the presence of the intellectual ideals. They are at cross-purposes all along the line, regarding each other as they might regard a set of dangerously gesticulating automata, or if they seek to get at the inner motivation, making the most horrible mistakes. Often all that the poor man can think of in the rich man is a cowardly greediness for safety, luxury, and effeminacy, and a boundless affectation. What he is, is not a human being, but a pocket-book, a bank-account. And a similar greediness, turned by disappointment into envy, is all that many rich men can see in the state of mind of the dissatisfied poor. And if the rich man begins to do the sentimental act over the poor man, what senseless blunders does he make, pitying him for just those very duties and those very immunities which, rightly taken, are the condition of his most abiding and characteristic joys! Each, in short, ignores the fact that happiness and unhappiness and significance are a vital mystery; each pins them absolutely on some ridiculous feature of the external situation; and everybody remains outside of everybody else's sight.

Society has, with all this, undoubtedly got to pass towards some newer and better equilibrium, and the distribution of wealth has doubtless slowly got to change; such changes have always happened, and will happen to the end of time. But if, after all that I have said, any of you expect that they will make any *genuine vital difference*, on a large scale, to the lives of our descendants, you will have missed the significance of my entire lecture. The solid meaning of life is always the same eternal thing—the marriage, namely, of some unhabitual ideal, however special, with some fidelity, courage, and endurance; with some man's or woman's pains.—And whatever or wherever life may be, there will always be the chance for that marriage to take place.

Fitzjames Stephen wrote many years ago words to this effect more eloquent than any I can speak: "The *Great Eastern,* or some of her successors," he said, "will perhaps defy the roll of the Atlantic, and cross the seas without allowing their passengers to feel that they have left the firm land. The voyage from the cradle to the grave may come to be performed with similar facility. Progress and science may, perhaps, enable untold millions to live and die without a care, without a pang, without an anxiety. They will have a pleasant passage, and plenty of brilliant conversation. They will wonder that men ever believed at all in clanging fights, and blazing towns, and sinking ships, and praying hands; and, when they come to the end of their course, they will go their way, and the place thereof will know them no more. But it seems unlikely that they will have such a knowledge of the great ocean on which they sail, with its storms and wrecks, its currents and icebergs, its huge waves and mighty winds, as those who battled with it for years together in the little craft, which, if they had few other merits, brought those who navigated them full into the presence of time and eternity, their Maker and themselves, and forced them to have some definite views of their relations to them and to each other."[5]

In this solid and tridimensional sense, so to call it, those philosophers are right who contend that the world is a standing thing, with no progress, no real history. The changing conditions of history touch only the surface of the show. The altered equilibriums and redistributions only diversify our opportunities and open chances to us for new ideals. But with each new ideal that comes into life, the chance for a life based on some old ideal will vanish; and he would needs be a presumptuous calculator who should with confidence say that the total sum of significances is positively and absolutely greater at any one epoch than at any other of the world.

I am speaking broadly, I know, and omitting to consider certain qualifications in which I myself believe. But one can only make one point in one lecture, and I shall be well content if I have brought my point home to you this evening in even a slight degree. *There are compensations;* and no outward changes of condition in life can keep the nightingale of its eternal meaning from singing in all sorts of different men's hearts. That is the main fact to remember. If we could not only admit it with our lips, but really and truly believe it, how our convulsive insistences, how our antipathies and dreads of each other, would soften down! If the poor and the rich could look at each other in this way, *sub specie aeternitatis,* how gentle would grow their disputes! what tolerance and good humor, what willingness to live and let live, would come into the world!

10

Philosophical Conceptions and Practical Results

"Philosophical Conceptions and Practical Results" is, despite the flat-footed title, the "first blast of the trumpet of action against the abominable absolutists." It is the opening announcement, given as a talk at Berkeley, California, in 1899, of what would be elaborated on in James's *Pragmatism* in 1907. The philosophy of pragmatism, which James insisted on laying on the doorstep of his good friend and associate Charles S. Peirce, was for James a philosophy of action. He believed that the meaning of thought is "the production of belief," and that "beliefs . . . are really rules for action." He argues that we can evaluate actions better by their results than by their initial intentions or by their origins. "To develope a thought's meaning," he wrote, "we need only determine what conduct it is fitted to produce: that conduct is for us its sole significance." James's argument is "fruits not roots." He goes on: "to attain perfect clearness in our thoughts of an object, then, we need only consider what effects of a conceivably practical kind the object may involve—what sensations we are to expect from it, and what reactions we must prepare." He wanted to avoid verbal quibbles. "There can *be* no difference which doesn't *make* a difference."

Most of the Berkeley talk is, perhaps surprisingly, devoted to examining what pragmatism means for religion. If we examine "the meaning of conceptions by asking what difference they make for life," then what difference does it make whether this world was made by God or by evolution? If we love creation, should we not be as grateful to the one possible cause as to the other? Here, as in so many places, William James's way of looking at things is just as challenging now as it was a hundred years ago.

AN OCCASION like the present would seem to call for an absolutely untechnical discourse. I ought to speak of something connected with life rather than with logic. I ought to give a message with a practical outcome and an emotional musical accompaniment, so to speak, fitted to interest men as men, and yet also not altogether to disappoint philosophers—since philosophers, let them be as queer as they will, still are men in the secret recesses of their hearts, even here at Berkeley. I ought, I say, to produce something simple enough to catch and inspire the rest of you, and yet with just enough of ingenuity and oddity about it to keep the members of the Philosophical Union from yawning and letting their attention wander away.

I confess that I have something of this kind in my mind, a perfectly ideal discourse for the present occasion. Were I to set it down on paper, I verily believe it would be regarded by everyone as the final word of philosophy. It would bring theory down to a single point, at which every human being's practical life would begin. It would solve all the antinomies and contradictions, it would let loose all the right impulses and emotions; and everyone, on hearing it, would say, "Why, that *is* the truth!—*that* is what I have been believing, that is what I have really been living on all this time, but I never could find the words for it before. All that eludes, all that flickers and twinkles, all that invites and vanishes even whilst inviting, is here made a solidity and a possession. Here is the end of unsatisfactoriness, here the beginning of unimpeded clearness, joy, and power." Yes, my friends, I have such a discourse within me! But, do not judge me harshly, I cannot produce it on the present occasion. I humbly apologize; I have come across the continent to this wondrous Pacific Coast—to this Eden, not of the mythical antiquity, but of the solid future of mankind—I ought to give you something worthy of your hospitality, and not altogether unworthy of your great destiny, to help cement our rugged East and your wondrous West together in a spiritual bond,—and yet, and yet, and yet, I simply cannot. I have tried to articulate it, but it will not come. Philosophers are after all like poets. They are path-finders. What everyone can feel, what everyone can know in the bone and marrow of him, they sometimes can find words for and express. The words and thoughts of the philosophers are not exactly the words and thoughts of the poets—worse luck. But both alike have the same function. They are, if I may use a simile, so many spots, or blazes,—blazes made by the axe of the human intellect on the trees of the otherwise trackless forest of human experience. They give you somewhere to go from. They give you a direction and a place to reach. They do not give you the integral forest with all its sunlit glories and its moonlit witcheries and wonders. Ferny dells, and mossy water-falls, and secret magic nooks escape you, owned only by the wild things to whom the region is a home. Happy they without the need of blazes! But to us the blazes give a sort of ownership. We can now use the forest, wend across it with companions, and enjoy its quality. It is no longer a place merely to get lost in and never return. The poet's words and the philosopher's phrases thus are helps of the most genuine sort, giving to all of us hereafter the freedom of the trails they made. Though they create nothing, yet for this marking and fixing function of theirs we bless their names and keep them on our lips, even whilst the thin and spotty and half-casual character of their operations is most evident.

No one like the path-finder himself feels the immensity of the forest, or knows the accidentality of his own trails. Columbus, dreaming of the ancient East, is stopped by poor pristine simple America, and gets no farther on that day; and the poets and philosophers themselves know as no one else knows that what their formulas express leaves unexpressed almost everything that they organically divine and feel. So I feel that there is a center in truth's forest where I have never been: to track it out and get there is the secret spring of all my poor life's philosophic efforts; at moments I almost strike into the final valley, there is a gleam of the end, a sense of certainty, but always there comes still another ridge, so my blazes merely circle towards the true direction; and although now, if ever, would be the fit occasion, yet I cannot take you to the wondrous hidden spot to-day. To-morrow it must be, or to-morrow, or to-morrow; and pretty surely death will overtake me ere the promise is fulfilled.

Of such postponed achievements do the lives of all philosophers consist. Truth's fulness is elusive; ever not quite, not quite! So we fall back on the preliminary blazes—a few formulas, a few technical conceptions, a few verbal pointers—which at least define the initial direction of the trail. And that, to my sorrow, is all that I can do here at Berkeley to-day. Inconclusive I must be, and merely suggestive, though I will try to be as little technical as I can.

I will seek to define with you merely what seems to be the most likely direction in which to start upon the trail of truth. Years ago this direction was given to me by an American philosopher whose home is in the East, and whose published works, few as they are and scattered in periodicals, are no fit expression of his powers. I refer to Mr. Charles S. Peirce, with whose very existence as a philosopher I dare say many of you are unacquainted. He is one of the most original of contemporary thinkers; and the principle of practicalism—or pragmatism, as he called it, when I first heard him enunciate it at Cambridge in the early '70's—is the clue or compass by following which I find myself more and more confirmed in believing we may keep our feet upon the proper trail.

Peirce's principle, as we may call it, may be expressed in a variety of ways, all of them very simple. In the *Popular Science Monthly* for January, 1878, he introduces it as follows: The soul and meaning of thought, he says, can never be made to direct itself towards anything but the production of belief, belief being the demicadence which closes a musical phrase in the symphony of our intellectual life. Thought in movement has thus for its only possible motive the attainment of thought at rest. But when our thought about an object has found its rest in belief, then our action on the subject can firmly and safely begin. Beliefs, in short, are really rules for action; and the whole function of thinking is but one step in the production of habits of action. If there were any part of a thought that made no difference in the thought's practical consequences, then that part would be no proper element of the thought's significance. Thus the same thought may be clad in different words; but if the different words suggest no different conduct, they are mere outer accretions, and have no part in the thought's meaning. If, however, they determine conduct differently, they are essential elements of the significance. "Please open the door," and, *"Veuillez ouvrir la porte,"* in French, mean just the same thing; but "D—n you, open the door," although in English, *means* something very different. Thus to develope a thought's meaning we need only determine what conduct it is fitted to produce: that conduct is for us its sole significance. And the tangible fact at the root of all our thought-distinctions, however subtle, is that there is no one of them so fine as to consist in anything but a possible difference of practice. To attain perfect clearness in our thoughts of an object, then, we need only consider what effects of a conceivably practical kind the object may involve—what sensations we are to expect from it, and what reactions we must prepare. Our conception of these effects, then, is for us the whole of our conception of the object, so far as that conception has positive significance at all.

This is the principle of Peirce, the principle of pragmatism. I think myself that it should be expressed more broadly than Mr. Peirce expresses it. The ultimate test for us of what a truth means is indeed the conduct it dictates or inspires. But it inspires that conduct because it first foretells some particular turn to our experience which shall call for just that conduct from us. And I should prefer for our purposes this evening to express Peirce's principle by saying that the effective meaning of any philosophic proposition can always be brought down to some particular consequence, in our future practical experience, whether active or passive; the point lying rather in the fact that the experience must be particular, than in the fact that it must be active.

To take in the importance of this principle, one must get accustomed to applying it to concrete cases. Such use as I am able to make of it convinces me that to be mindful of it in philosophical disputations tends wonderfully to smooth out misunderstandings and to bring in peace. If it did nothing else, then, it would yield a sovereignly valuable rule of method for discussion. So I shall devote the rest of this precious hour with you to its elucidation, because I sincerely think that if you once grasp it, it will shut your steps out from many an old false opening, and head you in the true direction for the trail.

One of its first consequences is this: Suppose there are two different philosophical definitions, or propositions, or maxims, or what not, which seem to contradict each other, and about which men dispute. If, by supposing the truth of the one, you can foresee no conceivable practical consequence to anybody at any time or place, which is different from what you would foresee if you supposed the truth of the other, why then the difference between the two propositions is no difference,— it is only a specious and verbal difference, unworthy of further contention. Both formulas mean radically the same thing, although they may say it in such different words. It is astonishing to see how many philosophical disputes collapse into insignificance the moment you subject them to this simple test. There can *be* no difference which doesn't *make* a difference—no difference in abstract truth which does not express it-self in a difference of concrete fact, and of conduct consequent upon the fact, imposed on somebody, somehow, somewhere, and somewhen. It is true that a certain shrinkage of values often seems to occur in our general formulas when we measure their meaning in this prosaic and practical way. They diminish. But the vastness that is merely based on vagueness is a false appearance of importance, and not a vastness worth retaining. The x's, y's, and z's always do shrivel, as I have heard a learned friend say, whenever at the end of your algebraic computation they change into so many plain a's, b's, and c's:—but the whole function of algebra is, after all, to get them into that more definite shape; and the whole function of philosophy ought to be to find out what definite difference it will make to you and me, at definite instants of our life, if this world-formula or that world-formula be the one which is true.

If we start off with an impossible case, we shall perhaps all the more clearly see the use and scope of our principle. Let us therefore put ourselves, in imagination, in a position from which no forecasts of consequence, no dictates of conduct, can possibly be made, so that the principle of pragmatism finds no field of application. Let us, I mean, assume that the present moment is the absolutely last moment of the world, with bare nonentity beyond it, and no hereafter for either experience or conduct.

Now I say that in that case there would be no sense whatever in some of our most urgent and envenomed philosophical and religious debates. The question, "Is matter the producer of all things, or is a God there too?" would, for example, offer a perfectly idle and insignificant alternative if the world were finished and no more of it to come. Many of us, most of us I think, now feel as if a terrible coldness and deadness would come over the world were we forced to believe that no informing spirit or purpose had to do with it, but it merely accidentally had come. The actually experienced details of fact might be the same on either hypothesis, some sad, some joyous; some rational, some odd and grotesque; but without a God behind them, we think they would have something ghastly, they would tell no genuine story, there would be no speculation in those eyes that they do glare with. With the God, on the other hand, they would grow solid, warm, and altogether full of real significance.

But I say that such an alternation of feelings, reasonable enough in a consciousness that is prospective, as ours now is, and whose world is partly yet to come, would be absolutely senseless and irrational in a purely retrospective consciousness summing up a world already past. For such a consciousness, no emotional interest could attach to the alternative. The problem would be purely intellectual; and if unaided matter could, with any scientific plausibility, be shown to cipher out the actual facts, then not the faintest shadow ought to cloud the mind, of regret for the God that by the same ciphering would prove needless and disappear from our belief.

For just consider the case sincerely, and say what would be the *worth* of such a God if he *were* there, with his work accomplished and his world run down. He would be worth no more than just that world was worth. To that amount of result, with its mixed merits and defects, his creative power could attain, but go no farther. And since there is to be no future; since the whole value and meaning of the world has been already paid in and actualized in the feelings that went with it in the passing, and now go with it in the ending; since it draws no supplemental significance (such as our real world draws) from its function of preparing something yet to come; why then, by it we take God's measure, as it were. He is the Being who could once for all do *that;* and for that much we are thankful to him, but for nothing more. But now, on the contrary hypothesis, namely, that the bits of matter following their 'laws' could make that world and do no less, should we not be just as thankful to them? Wherein should we suffer loss, then, if we dropped God as an hypothesis and made the matter alone responsible? Where would the special deadness, 'crassness,' and ghastliness come in? And how, experience being what it is once for all, would God's presence in it make it any more 'living,' any richer in our sight?

Candidly, it is impossible to give any answer to this question. The actually experienced world is supposed to be the same in its details on either hypothesis, "the same, for our praise or blame," as Browning says. It stands there indefeasibly; a gift which can't be taken back. Calling matter the cause of it retracts no single one of the items that have made it up, nor does calling God the cause augment them. They are the God or the atoms, respectively, of just that and no other world. The God, if there, has been doing just what atoms could do—appearing in the character of atoms, so to speak—and earning such gratitude as is due to atoms, and no more. If his presence lends no different turn or issue to the

performance, it surely can lend it no increase of dignity. Nor would in-
dignity come to it were he absent, and did the atoms remain the only
actors on the stage. When a play is once over, and the curtain down,
you really make it no better by claiming an illustrious genius for its author, just as you make it no worse by calling him a common hack.

Thus if no future detail of experience or conduct is to be deduced
from our hypothesis, the debate between materialism and theism becomes quite idle and insignificant. Matter and God in that event mean
exactly the same thing—the power, namely, neither more nor less, that
can make just this mixed, imperfect, yet completed world—and the wise
man is he who in such a case would turn his back on such a supereroga-
tory discussion. Accordingly most men instinctively, and a large class of
men, the so-called positivists or scientists, deliberately, do turn their
backs on philosophical disputes from which nothing in the line of definite future consequences can be seen to follow. The verbal and empty
character of our studies is surely a reproach with which you of the Philosophical Union are but too sadly familiar. An escaped Berkeley student
said to me at Harvard the other day—he had never been in the philosophical department here—"Words, words, words, are all that you philosophers care for." We philosophers think it all unjust; and yet, if the
principle of pragmatism be true, it is a perfectly sound reproach unless
the metaphysical alternatives under investigation can be shown to have
alternative practical outcomes, however delicate and distant these may
be. The common man and the scientist can discover no such outcomes.
And if the metaphysician can discern none either, the common man
and scientist certainly are in the right of it, as against him. His science is
then but pompous trifling; and the endowment of a professorship for
such a being would be something really absurd.

Accordingly, in every genuine metaphysical debate some practical
issue, however remote, is really involved. To realize this, revert with me
to the question of materialism or theism; and place yourselves this time
in the real world we live in, the world that has a future, that is yet un-
completed whilst we speak. In this unfinished world the alternative of
'materialism or theism?' is intensely practical; and it is worth while for
us to spend some minutes of our hour in seeing how truly this is the
case.

How, indeed, does the programme differ for us, according as we
consider that the facts of experience up to date are purposeless configu-

rations of atoms moving according to eternal elementary laws, or that on the other hand they are due to the providence of God? As far as the past facts go, indeed there is no difference. These facts are in, are bagged, are captured; and the good that's in them is gained, be the atoms or be the God their cause. There are accordingly many materialists about us to-day who, ignoring altogether the future and practical aspects of the question, seek to eliminate the odium attaching to the word materialism, and even to eliminate the word itself, by showing that, if matter could give birth to all these gains, why then matter, functionally considered, is just as divine an entity as God, in fact coalesces with God, is what you mean by God. Cease, these persons advise us, to use either of these terms, with their outgrown opposition. Use terms free of the clerical connotations on the one hand; of the suggestion of grossness, coarseness, ignobility, on the other. Talk of the primal mystery, of the unknowable energy, of the one and only power, instead of saying either God or matter. This is the course to which Mr. Spencer urges us at the end of the first volume of his Psychology. In some well-written pages he there shows us that a 'matter' so infinitely subtile, and performing motions as inconceivably quick and fine as modern science postulates in her explanations, has no trace of grossness left. He shows that the conception of spirit, as we mortals hitherto have framed it, is itself too gross to cover the exquisite complexity of Nature's facts. Both terms, he says, are but symbols, pointing to that one unknowable reality in which their oppositions cease.

Throughout these remarks of Mr. Spencer, eloquent, and even noble in a certain sense, as they are, he seems to think that the dislike of the ordinary man to materialism comes from a purely aesthetic disdain of matter, as something gross in itself, and vile and despicable. Undoubtedly such an aesthetic disdain of matter has played a part in philosophic history. But it forms no part whatever of an intelligent modern man's dislikes. Give him a matter bound forever by its laws to lead our world nearer and nearer to perfection, and any rational man will worship that matter as readily as Mr. Spencer worships his own so-called unknowable power. It not only has made for righteousness up to date, but it will make for righteousness forever; and that is all we need. Doing practically all that a God can do, it is equivalent to God, its function is a God's function, and is exerted in a world in which a God would be superfluous; from such a world a God could never lawfully be missed.

But *is* the matter by which Mr. Spencer's process of cosmic evolution is carried on any such principle of never-ending perfection as this? Indeed it is not, for the future end of every cosmically evolved thing or system of things is tragedy; and Mr. Spencer, in confining himself to the aesthetic and ignoring the practical side of the controversy, has really contributed nothing serious to its relief. But apply now our principle of practical results, and see what a vital significance the question of materialism or theism immediately acquires.

Theism and materialism, so indifferent when taken retrospectively, point, when we take them prospectively, to wholly different practical consequences, to opposite outlooks of experience. For, according to the theory of mechanical evolution, the laws of redistribution of matter and motion, though they are certainly to thank for all the good hours which our organisms have ever yielded us and for all the ideals which our minds now frame, are yet fatally certain to undo their work again, and to redissolve everything that they have once evolved. You all know the picture of the last foreseeable state of the dead universe, as evolutionary science gives it forth. I cannot state it better than in Mr. Balfour's words: "The energies of our system will decay, the glory of the sun will be dimmed, and the earth, tideless and inert, will no longer tolerate the race which has for a moment disturbed its solitude. Man will go down into the pit, and all his thoughts will perish. The uneasy consciousness which in this obscure corner has for a brief space broken the contented silence of the universe, will be at rest. Matter will know itself no longer. 'Imperishable monuments' and 'immortal deeds,' death itself, and love stronger than death, will be as if they had not been. Nor will anything that *is*, be better or worse for all that the labour, genius, devotion, and suffering of man have striven through countless ages to effect."[1]

That is the sting of it, that in the vast driftings of the cosmic weather, though many a jewelled shore appears, and many an enchanted cloud-bank floats away, long lingering ere it be dissolved—even as our world now lingers, for our joy—yet when these transient products are gone, nothing, absolutely *nothing* remains, to represent those particular qualities, those elements of preciousness which they may have enshrined. Dead and gone are they, gone utterly from the very sphere and room of being. Without an echo; without a memory; without an influence on aught that may come after, to make it care for similar ideals. This utter final wreck and tragedy is of the essence of scientific materialism as at present understood. The lower and not the higher forces are the eternal forces, or the last surviving forces within the only cycle of evolution which we can definitely see. Mr. Spencer believes this as much as anyone; so why should he argue with us as if we were making silly aesthetic objections to the 'grossness' of 'matter and motion,'—the principles of his philosophy,—when what really dismays us in it is the disconsolateness of its ulterior practical results?

No, the true objection to materialism is not positive but negative. It would be farcical at this day to make complaint of it for what it *is*, for 'grossness.' Grossness is what grossness *does*—we now know *that*. We make complaint of it, on the contrary, for what it is *not*—not a permanent warrant for our more ideal interests, not a fulfiller of our remotest hopes.

The notion of God, on the other hand, however inferior it may be in clearness to those mathematical notions so current in mechanical philosophy, has at least this practical superiority over them, that it guarantees an ideal order that shall be permanently preserved. A world with a God in it to say the last word, may indeed burn up or freeze, but we then think of him as still mindful of the old ideals and sure to bring them elsewhere to fruition; so that, where he is, tragedy is only provisional and partial, and shipwreck and dissolution not the absolutely final things. This need of an eternal moral order is one of the deepest needs of our breast. And those poets, like Dante and Wordsworth, who live on the conviction of such an order, owe to that fact the extraordinary tonic and consoling power of their verse. Here then, in these different emotional and practical appeals, in these adjustments of our concrete attitudes of hope and expectation, and all the delicate consequences which their differences entail, lie the real meanings of materialism and theism—not in hair-splitting abstractions about matter's inner essence, or about the metaphysical attributes of God. Materialism means simply the denial that the moral order is eternal, and the cutting off of ultimate hopes; theism means the affirmation of an eternal moral order and the letting loose of hope. Surely here is an issue genuine enough, for anyone who feels it; and, as long as men are men, it will yield matter for serious philosophic debate. Concerning this question at any rate, the positivists and pooh-pooh-ers of metaphysics are in the wrong.

But possibly some of you may still rally to their defense. Even whilst admitting that theism and materialism make different prophecies of the world's future, you may yourselves pooh-pooh the difference as something so infinitely remote as to mean nothing for a sane mind. The essence of a sane mind, you may say, is to take shorter views, and to feel no concern about such chimaeras as the latter end of the world. Well, I can only say that if you say this, you do injustice to human nature. Religious melancholy is not disposed of by a simple flourish of the word insanity. The absolute things, the last things, the overlapping things, are the truly philosophic concern; all superior minds feel seriously about them, and the mind with the shortest views is simply the mind of the more shallow man.

However, I am willing to pass over these very distant outlooks on the ultimate if any of you so insist. The theistic controversy can still serve to illustrate the principle of pragmatism for us well enough, without driving us so far afield. If there be a God, it is not likely that he is confined solely to making differences in the world's latter end; he probably makes differences all along its course. Now the principle of practicalism says that the very meaning of the conception of God lies in those differences which must be made in our experience if the conception be true. God's famous inventory of perfections, as elaborated by dogmatic theology, either means nothing, says our principle, or it implies certain definite things that we can feel and do at particular moments of our lives, things which we could not feel and should not do were no God present and were the business of the universe carried on by material atoms instead. So far as our conceptions of the Deity involve no such experiences, so far they are meaningless and verbal,—scholastic entities and abstractions, as the positivists say, and fit objects for their scorn. But so far as they do involve such definite experiences, God means something for us, and may be real.

Now if we look at the definitions of God made by dogmatic theology, we see immediately that some stand and some fall when treated by this test. God, for example, as any orthodox text-book will tell us, is a being existing not only *per se,* or by himself, as created beings exist, but *a se,* or from himself; and out of this 'aseity' flow most of his perfections. He is, for example, necessary; absolute; infinite in all respects; and single. He is simple, not compounded of essence and existence, substance and accident, actuality and potentiality, or subject and attributes, as are other things. He belongs to no genus; he is inwardly and outwardly un-alterable; he knows and wills all things, and first of all his own infinite self, in one indivisible eternal act. And he is absolutely self-sufficing, and infinitely happy.—Now in which one of us practical Americans here assembled does this conglomeration of attributes awaken any sense of reality? And if in no one, then why not? Surely because such attributes awaken no responsive active feelings and call for no particular conduct of our own. How does God's 'aseity' come home to *you?* What specific thing can I do to adapt myself to his 'simplicity'? Or how determine our behavior henceforward if his 'felicity' is anyhow absolutely complete? In the '50's and '60's Captain Mayne Reid was the great writer of boys' books of out-of-door adventure. He was forever extolling the hunters and field-observers of living animals' habits, and keeping up a fire of invective against the 'closet-naturalists,' as he called them, the collec-tors and classifiers, and handlers of skeletons and skins. When I was a boy I used to think that a closet-naturalist must be the vilest type of wretch under the sun. But surely the systematic theologians are the closet-naturalists of the Deity, even in Captain Mayne Reid's sense. Their orthodox deduction of God's attributes is nothing but a shuffling and matching of pedantic dictionary-adjectives, aloof from morals, aloof from human needs, something that might be worked out from the mere word 'God' by a logical machine of wood and brass as well as by a man of flesh and blood. The attributes which I have quoted have absolutely nothing to do with religion, for religion is a living practical affair. Other parts, indeed, of God's traditional description do have practical connec-tion with life, and have owed all their historic importance to that fact. His omniscience, for example, and his justice. With the one he sees us in the dark, with the other he rewards and punishes what he sees. So do his ubiquity and eternity and unalterability appeal to our confidence, and his goodness banish our fears. Even attributes of less meaning to this present audience have in past times so appealed. One of the chief attributes of God, according to the orthodox theology, is his infinite love of himself, proved by asking the question, "By what but an infinite ob-ject can an infinite affection be appeased?" An immediate consequence of this primary self-love of God is the orthodox dogma that the manifes-tation of his own glory is God's primal purpose in creation; and that dogma has certainly made very efficient practical connection with life. It is true that we ourselves are tending to outgrow this old monarchical conception of a Deity with his 'court' and pomp—"his state is kingly, thousands at his bidding speed," etc.—but there is no denying the enormous influence it has had over ecclesiastical history, nor, by repercussion, over the history of European states. And yet even these more real and significant attributes have the trail of the serpent over them as the books on theology have actually worked them out. One feels that, in the theologians' hands, they are only a set of dictionary-adjectives, mechanically deduced; logic has stepped into the place of vision, professionalism into that of life. Instead of bread we get a stone; instead of a fish, a serpent. Did such a conglomeration of abstract general terms give really the gist of our knowledge of the Deity, divinity-schools might indeed continue to flourish, but religion, vital religion, would have taken its flight from this world. What keeps religion going is something else than abstract definitions and systems of logically concatenated adjectives, and something different from faculties of theology and their professors. All these things are after-effects, secondary accretions upon a mass of concrete religious experiences, connecting themselves with feeling and conduct, that renew themselves *in saecula saeculorum* in the lives of humble private men. If you ask what these experiences are, they are conversations with the unseen, voices and visions, responses to prayer, changes of heart, deliverances from fear, inflowings of help, assurances of support, whenever certain persons set their own internal attitude in certain appropriate ways. The power comes and goes and is lost, and can be found only in a certain definite direction, just as if it were a concrete material thing. These direct experiences of a wider spiritual life with which our superficial consciousness is continuous, and with which it keeps up an intense commerce, form the primary mass of direct religious experience on which all hearsay religion rests, and which furnishes that notion of an ever-present God, out of which systematic theology thereupon proceeds to make capital in its own unreal pedantic way. What the word 'God' means is just those passive and active experiences of your life. Now, my friends, it is quite immaterial to my purpose whether you yourselves enjoy and venerate these experiences, or whether you stand aloof and, viewing them in others, suspect them of being illusory and vain. Like all other human experiences, they too certainly share in the general liability to illusion and mistake. They need not be infallible. But they are certainly the originals of the God-idea, and theology is the translation; and you remember that I am now using the God-idea merely as an example, not to discuss as to its truth or error, but only to show how well the principle of pragmatism works. That the God of systematic theology should exist or not exist is a matter of small practical moment. At most it means that you may continue uttering certain abstract words and that you must stop using others. But if the God of these particular experiences be false, it is an awful thing for you, if you are one of those whose lives are stayed on such experiences. The theistic controversy, trivial enough if we take it merely academically and theologically, is of tremendous significance if we test it by its results for actual life.

I can best continue to recommend the principle of practicalism to you by keeping in the neighborhood of this theological idea. I reminded you a few minutes ago that the old monarchical notion of the Deity as a sort of Louis the Fourteenth of the Heavens is losing nowadays much of its ancient prestige. Religious philosophy, like all philosophy, is growing more and more idealistic. And in the philosophy of the Absolute, so called, that post-Kantian form of idealism which is carrying so many of our higher minds before it, we have the triumph of what in old times was summarily disposed of as the pantheistic heresy—I mean the conception of God, not as the extraneous creator, but as the indwelling spirit and substance of the world. I know not where one can find a more candid, more clear, or, on the whole, more persuasive statement of this theology of Absolute Idealism than in the addresses made before this very Union three years ago by your own great Californian philosopher (whose colleague at Harvard I am proud to be), Josiah Royce. His contributions to the resulting volume, *The Conception of God,* form a very masterpiece of popularization. Now you will remember, many of you, that in the discussion that followed Professor Royce's first address, the debate turned largely on the ideas of unity and plurality, and on the question whether, if God be One in All and All in All, "One with the unity of a single instant," as Royce calls it, "forming in His wholeness one luminously transparent moment," any room is left for real morality or freedom. Professor Howison, in particular, was earnest in urging that morality and freedom are relations between a manifold of selves, and that under the régime of Royce's monistic Absolute Thought "no true manifold of selves is or can be provided for." I will not go into any of the details of that particular discussion, but just ask you to consider for a moment whether, in general, any discussion about monism or pluralism, any argument over the unity of the universe, would not necessarily be brought into a shape where it tends to straighten itself out, by bringing our principle of practical results to bear.

The question whether the world is at bottom One or Many is a typical metaphysical question. Long has it raged! In its crudest form it is an exquisite example of the *loggerheads* of metaphysics. 'I say it is one great fact,' Parmenides and Spinoza exclaim. 'I say it is many little facts,' reply the atomists and associationists. 'I say it is both one and many, many in one,' say the Hegelians; and in the ordinary popular discussions we rarely get beyond this barren reiteration by the disputants of their pet adjectives of number. But is it not first of all clear that when we take such an adjective as 'One' absolutely and abstractly, its meaning is so vague and empty that it makes no difference whether we affirm or deny it? Certainly this universe is not the mere number One; and yet you can number it 'one,' if you like, in talking about it as contrasted with other possible worlds numbered 'two' and 'three' for the occasion. What exact thing do you *practically* mean by 'One,' when you call the universe One, is the first question you must ask. In what ways does the oneness come home to your own personal life? By what difference does it express itself in your experience? How can you act differently towards a universe which is one? Inquired into in this way, the unity might grow clear and be affirmed in some ways and denied in others, and so cleared up, even though a certain vague and worshipful portentousness might disappear from the notion of it in the process.

For instance, one practical result that follows when we have one thing to handle, is that we can pass from one part of it to another without letting go of the thing. In this sense oneness must be partly denied and partly affirmed of our universe. Physically we can pass continuously in various manners from one part of it to another part. But logically and psychically the passage seems less easy, for there is no obvious transition from one mind to another, or from minds to physical things. You have to step off and get on again; so that in these ways the world is not one, as measured by that practical test.

Another practical meaning of oneness is susceptibility of collection. A collection is one, though the things that compose it be many. Now, can we practically 'collect' the universe? Physically, of course we cannot. And mentally we cannot, if we take it concretely in its details. But if we take it summarily and abstractly, then we collect it mentally whenever we refer to it, even as I do now when I fling the term 'universe' at it, and so seem to leave a mental ring around it. It is plain, however, that such abstract noetic unity (as one might call it) is practically an extremely insignificant thing.

Again, oneness may mean generic sameness, so that you can treat all parts of the collection by one rule and get the same results. It is evident that in this sense the oneness of our world is incomplete, for in spite of much generic sameness in its elements and items, they still remain of many irreducible kinds. You can't pass by mere logic all over the field of it.

Its elements have, however, an affinity or commensurability with each other, are not wholly irrelevant, but can be compared, and fit together after certain fashions. This again might practically mean that they were one *in origin,* and that, tracing them backwards, we should find them arising in a single primal causal fact. Such unity of origin would have definite practical consequences, would have them for our scientific life at least.

I can give only these hasty superficial indications of what I mean when I say that it tends to clear up the quarrel between monism and pluralism to subject the notion of unity to such practical tests. On the other hand it does but perpetuate strife and misunderstanding to continue talking of it in an absolute and mystical way. I have little doubt myself that this old quarrel might be completely smoothed out to the satisfaction of all claimants, if only the maxim of Peirce were methodically followed here. The current monism on the whole still keeps talking in too abstract a way. It says the world must be either pure disconnectedness, no universe at all, or absolute unity. It insists that there is no stopping-place half way. Any connection whatever, says this monism, is only possible if there be still more connection, until at last we are driven to admit the absolutely total connection required. But this absolutely total connection either means nothing, is the mere word 'one' spelt long; or else it means the sum of all the partial connections that can possibly be conceived. I believe that when we thus attack the question, and set ourselves to search for these possible connections, and conceive each in a definite practical way, the dispute is already in a fair way to be settled beyond the chance of misunderstanding, by a compromise in which the Many and the One both get their lawful rights.

But I am in danger of becoming technical; so I must stop right here, and let you go.

I am happy to say that it is the English-speaking philosophers who first introduced the custom of interpreting the meaning of conceptions by asking what difference they make for life. Mr. Peirce has only expressed in the form of an explicit maxim what their sense for reality led them all instinctively to do. The great English way of investigating a conception is to ask yourself right off, "What is it *known as?* In what facts does it result? What is its *cash-value*, in terms of particular experience? and what special difference would come into the world according as it were true or false?" Thus does Locke treat the conception of personal identity. What you mean by it is just your chain of memories, says he. That is the only concretely verifiable part of its significance. All further ideas about it, such as the oneness or manyness of the spiritual substance on which it is based, are therefore void of intelligible meaning; and propositions touching such ideas may be indifferently affirmed or denied. So Berkeley with his 'matter.' The cash-value of matter is our physical sensations. That is what it is known as, all that we concretely verify of its conception. That therefore is the whole meaning of the word 'matter'—any other pretended meaning is mere wind of words. Hume does the same thing with causation. It is known as habitual antecedence, and tendency on our part to look for something definite to come. Apart from this practical meaning it has no significance whatever, and books about it may be committed to the flames, says Hume. Stewart and Brown, James Mill, John Mill, and Bain, have followed more or less consistently the same method; and Shadworth Hodgson has used it almost as explicitly as Mr. Peirce. These writers have many of them no doubt been too sweeping in their negations; Hume, in particular, and James Mill, and Bain. But when all is said and done, it was they, not Kant, who introduced 'the critical method' into philosophy, the one method fitted to make philosophy a study worthy of serious men. For what seriousness can possibly remain in debating philosophic propositions that will never make an appreciable difference to us in action? And what matters it, when all propositions are practically meaningless, which of them be called true or false?

The shortcomings and the negations and baldnesses of the English philosophers in question come not from their eye to merely practical results, but solely from their failure to track the practical results completely enough to see how far they extend. Hume can be corrected and built out, and his beliefs enriched, by using Humian principles exclusively, and without making any use of the circuitous and ponderous artificialities of Kant. It is indeed a somewhat pathetic matter, as it seems to me, that this is not the course which the actual history of philosophy has followed. Hume had no English successors of adequate ability to complete him and correct his negations; so it happened, as a matter of fact, that the building out of critical philosophy has mainly been left to thinkers who were under the influence of Kant. Even in England and this country it is with Kantian catch-words and categories that the fuller view of life is pursued, and in our universities it is the courses in transcendentalism that kindle the enthusiasm of the more ardent students, whilst the courses in English philosophy are committed to a secondary place. I cannot think that this is exactly as it should be. And I say this not out of national jingoism, for jingoism has no place in philosophy; or out of excitement over the great Anglo-American alliance against the world, of which we nowadays hear so much—though heaven knows that to that alliance I wish a God-speed. I say it because I sincerely believe that the English spirit in philosophy is intellectually, as well as practically and morally, on the saner, sounder, and truer path. Kant's mind is the rarest and most intricate of all possible antique bric-a-brac museums, and connoisseurs and dilettanti will always wish to visit it and see the wondrous and racy contents. The temper of the dear old man about his work is perfectly delectable. And yet he is really—although I shrink with some terror from saying such a thing before some of you here present—at bottom a mere curio, a 'specimen.' I mean by this a perfectly definite thing: I believe that Kant bequeathes to us not one single conception which is both indispensable to philosophy and which philosophy either did not possess before him, or was not destined inevitably to acquire after him through the growth of men's reflection upon the hypotheses by which science interprets nature. The true line of philosophic progress lies, in short, it seems to me, not so much *through* Kant as *round* him to the point where now we stand. Philosophy can perfectly well outflank him, and build herself up into adequate fulness by prolonging more directly the older English lines.

May I hope, as I now conclude, and release your attention from the strain to which you have so kindly put it on my behalf, that on this wonderful Pacific Coast, of which our race is taking possession, the principle of practicalism, in which I have tried so hard to interest you, and with it the whole English tradition in philosophy, will come to its rights, and in your hands help the rest of us in our struggle towards the light.

11

The Philippine Tangle

"The Philippine Tangle" appeared in the *Boston Evening Transcript* on March 1, 1899. It shows William James in a blind rage, it shows him as a citizen and an activist, and it shows him as one of the strongest anti-imperialist voices of the time. One could argue that the views expressed in this piece might be expected from the writer of "On a Certain Blindness in Human Beings," a writer whose pragmatism meant judging things by outcomes, not by intentions, but we are not, in this piece, in the realm of reasoned discourse. James is hopping mad, mad at the president, at the war spirit, at public opinion, at the newspapers. Nor was this a one-time protest. James was an active member of the Anti-Imperialist League, and he wrote at least six pieces on the Philippine question, which may be read together in the *Essays, Comments, and Reviews* volume of the Harvard edition of *The Works of William James*. Actions have consequences. Perhaps the strongest argument for James's faith—that it is what you do, not what you feel that matters—is the simple fact that American intervention in the Philippines called forth this strong public response from him. Many readers will be reminded of more recent American interventions.

To THE Editor of the Transcript:

An observer who should judge solely by the sort of evidence which the newspapers present might easily suppose that the American people felt little concern about the performances of our Government in the

Philippine Islands, and were practically indifferent to their moral aspects. The cannon of our gunboats at Manila and the ratification of the treaty have sent even the most vehement anti-imperialist journals temporarily to cover, and the bugbear of copperheadism has reduced the freest tongues for a while to silence. The excitement of battle, this time as always, has produced its cowing and disorganizing effect upon the opposition.

But it would be dangerous for the Administration to trust to these impressions. I will not say that I have been amazed, for I fully expected it; but I have been cheered and encouraged at the almost unanimous dismay and horror which I find individuals express in private conversation over the turn which things are taking. "A national infamy" is the comment on the case which I hear most commonly uttered. The fires of indignation are momentarily "banked," but they are anything but "out." They seem merely to be awaiting the properly concerted and organized signal to burst forth with far more vehemence than ever, as imperialism and the idol of a national destiny, based on martial excitement and mere "bigness," keep revealing their corrupting inwardness more and more unmistakably. The process of education has been too short for the older American nature not to feel the shock. We gave the fighting instinct and the passion of mastery their outing; we let them have the day to themselves, and temporarily committed our fortunes to their leading last spring, because we thought that, being harnessed in a cause which promised to be that of freedom, the results were fairly safe, and we could resume our permanent ideals and character when the fighting fit was done. We now see how we reckoned without our host. We see by the vividest of examples what an absolute savage and pirate the passion of military conquest always is, and how the only safeguard against the crimes to which it will infallibly drag the nation that gives way to it is to keep it chained for ever, is never to let it get its start. In the European nations it is kept chained by a greater mutual fear than they have ever before felt for one another. Here it should have been kept chained by a native wisdom nourished assiduously for a century on opposite ideals. And we can appreciate now that wisdom in those of us who, with our national Executive at their head, worked so desperately to keep it chained last spring.

But since then, Executive and all, we have been swept away by the overmastering flood. And now what it has swept us into is an adventure that in sober seriousness and definite English speech must be described as literally piratical. Our treatment of the Aguinaldo movement at Manila and at Iloilo is piracy positive and absolute, and the American people appear as pirates pure and simple, as day by day the real facts of the situation are coming to the light.

What was only vaguely apprehended is now clear with a definiteness that is startling indeed. Here was a people towards whom we felt no ill-will, against whom we had not even a slanderous rumor to bring; a people for whose tenacious struggle against their Spanish oppressors we have for years past spoken (so far as we spoke of them at all) with nothing but admiration and sympathy. Here was a leader who, as the Spanish lies about him, on which we were fed so long, drop off, and as the truth gets more and more known, appears as an exceptionally fine specimen of the patriot and national hero; not only daring, but honest; not only a fighter, but a governor and organizer of extraordinary power. Here were the precious beginnings of an indigenous national life, with which, if we had any responsibilities to these islands at all, it was our first duty to have squared ourselves. Aguinaldo's movement was, and evidently deserved to be, an ideal popular movement, which as far as it had had time to exist was showing itself "fit" to survive and likely to become a healthy piece of national self-development. It was all we had to build on, at any rate, so far—if we had any desire not to succeed to the Spaniards' inheritance of native execration.

And what did our Administration do? So far as the facts have leaked out, it issued instructions to the commanders on the ground simply to freeze Aguinaldo out, as a dangerous rival with whom all compromising entanglement was sedulously to be avoided by the great Yankee business concern. We were not to "recognize" him, we were to deny him all account of our intentions; and in general to refuse any account of our intentions to anybody, except to declare in abstract terms their "benevolence," until the inhabitants, without a pledge of any sort from us, should turn over their country into our hands. Our President's bouffe-proclamation was the only thing vouchsafed: "We are here for your own good; therefore unconditionally surrender to our tender mercies, or we'll blow you into kingdom come."

Our own people meanwhile were vaguely uneasy, for the inhuman callousness and insult shown at Paris and Washington to the officially delegated mouthpieces of the wants and claims of the Filipinos seemed simply abominable from any moral point of view. But there must be reasons of state, we assumed, and good ones. Aguinaldo is evidently a

pure adventurer "on the make," a blackmailer, sure in the end to betray
our confidence, or our Government wouldn't treat him so, for our President is essentially methodistical and moral. Mr. McKinley must be in an
intolerably perplexing situation, and we must not criticise him too soon.
We assumed this, I say, though all the while there was a horribly suspi-
cious look about the performance. On its face it reeked of the infernal
adroitness of the great department store, which has reached perfect ex-
pertness in the art of killing silently and with no public squealing or
commotion the neighboring small concern.

But that small concern, Aguinaldo, apparently not having the proper
American business education, and being uninstructed on the irresistible
character of our Republican party combine, neither offered to sell out
nor to give up. So the Administration had to show its hand without disguise. It did so at last. We are now openly engaged in crushing out the
sacredest thing in this great human world—the attempt of a people long
enslaved to attain to the possession of itself, to organize its laws and
government, to be free to follow its internal destinies according to its
own ideals. War, said Moltke, aims at destruction, and at nothing else.
And splendidly are we carrying out war's ideal. We are destroying the
lives of these islanders by the thousand, their villages and their cities; for
surely it is we who are solely responsible for all the incidental burnings
that our operations entail. But these destructions are the smallest part of
our sins. We are destroying down to the root every germ of a healthy
national life in these unfortunate people, and we are surely helping to
destroy for one generation at least their faith in God and man. No life
shall you have, we say, except as a gift from our philanthropy after your
unconditional submission to our will. So as they seem to be "slow pay"
in the matter of submission, our yellow journals have abundant time in
which to raise new monuments of capitals to the victories of Old Glory,
and in which to extol the unrestrainable eagerness of our brave soldiers
to rush into battles that remind them so much of rabbit hunts on Western plains.

It is horrible, simply horrible. Surely there cannot be many born
and bred Americans who, when they look at the bare fact of what we
are doing, the fact taken all by itself, do not feel this, and do not blush
with burning shame at the unspeakable meanness and ignominy of the
trick?

Why, then, do we go on? First, the war fever; and then the pride which always refuses to back down when under fire. But these are passions that interfere with the reasonable settlement of any affair; and in this affair we have to deal with a factor altogether peculiar with our belief, namely, in a national destiny which must be "big" at any cost, and which for some inscrutable reason it has become infamous for us to disbelieve in or refuse. We are to be missionaries of civilization, and to bear the white man's burden, painful as it often is. We must sow our ideals, plant our order, impose our God. The individual lives are nothing. Our duty and our destiny call, and civilization must go on.

Could there be a more damning indictment of that whole bloated idol termed "modern civilization" than this amounts to? Civilization is, then, the big, hollow, resounding, corrupting, sophisticating, confusing torrent of mere brutal momentum arid irrationality that brings forth fruits like this! It is safe to say that one Christian missionary, whether primitive, Protestant or Catholic, of the original missionary type, one Buddhist or Mohammedan of a genuine saintly sort, one ethical reformer or philanthropist, or one disciple of Tolstoi would do more real good in these islands than our whole army and navy can possibly effect with our whole civilization at their back. He could build up realities, in however small a degree; we can only destroy the inner realities; and indeed destroy in a year more of them than a generation can make good.

It is by their moral fruits exclusively that these benighted brown people, "half-devil and half-child" as they are, are condemned to judge a civilization. Ours is already execrated by them forever for its hideous fruits.

Shall it not in so far forth be execrated by ourselves? Shall the unsophisticated verdict upon its hideousness which the plain moral sense pronounces avail nothing to stem the torrent of mere empty "bigness" in our destiny, before which it is said we must all knock under, swallowing our higher sentiments with a gulp? The issue is perfectly plain at last. We are cold-bloodedly, wantonly and abominably destroying the soul of a people who never did us an atom of harm in their lives. It is bald, brutal piracy, impossible to dish up any longer in the cold potgrease of President McKinley's cant at the recent Boston banquet—surely as shamefully evasive a speech, considering the right of the public to know definite facts, as can often have fallen even from a professional politician's lips. The worst of our imperialists is that they do not themselves know where sincerity ends and insincerity begins. Their state of consciousness is so new, so mixed of primitively human passions and, in political circles, of calculations that are anything but primitively human; so at variance, moreover, with their former mental habits; and so empty of definite data and contents; that they face various ways at once, and their portraits should be taken with a squint. One reads the President's speech with a strange feeling—as if the very words were squinting on the page.

The impotence of the private individual, with imperialism under full headway as it is, is deplorable indeed. But every American has a voice or a pen, and may use it. So, impelled by my own sense of duty, I write these present words. One by one we shall creep from cover, and the opposition will organize itself. If the Filipinos hold out long enough, there is a good chance (the canting game being already pretty well played out, and the piracy having to show itself henceforward naked) of the older American beliefs and sentiments coming to their rights again, and of the Administration being terrified into a conciliatory policy towards the native government.

The programme for the opposition should, it seems to me, be radical. The infamy and iniquity of a war of conquest must stop. A "protectorate," of course, if they will have it, though after this they would probably rather welcome any European Power; and as regards the inner state of the island, freedom, "fit" or "unfit," that is, home rule without humbugging phrases, and whatever anarchy may go with it until the Filipinos learn from each other, not from us, how to govern themselves. Mr. Adams's programme—which anyone may have by writing to Mr. Erving Winslow, Anti-Imperialist League, Washington, D.C.—seems to contain the only hopeful key to the situation. Until the opposition newspapers seriously begin, and the mass meetings are held, let every American who still wishes his country to possess its ancient soul—soul a thousand times more dear than ever, now that it seems in danger of perdition—do what little he can in the way of open speech and writing, and above all let him give his representatives and senators in Washington a positive piece of his mind.

WILLIAM JAMES
Cambridge, Feb. 26.

12

The Sick Soul

Many people love William James for *The Varieties of Religious Experience.* This is the book that radically altered modern thinking about religion, shifting the focus away from texts, buildings, prophets, preachers, and rituals and grounding religion squarely in the religious experiences and the religious feelings of the individual. For James, it is individual experience alone that can validate religion, and when it does, nothing can invalidate it. Religion is thus "an absolute addition [James is very careful with the word 'absolute'] to the subject's range of life."

It is frequently said that William James psychologizes religion, but all that means is that James, like Emerson, thought that the universe is revealed to each individual through his or her own mind, and only in that way. James's modern democratic individualism has therefore a religious as well as a political application.

"The Sick Soul" comprises Lectures VI and VII of the Gifford Lectures James delivered at Edinburgh in 1901 and 1902, published as *The Varieties of Religious Experience* in 1902. The "Sick Soul" lectures follow immediately after the lectures on "The Religion of Healthy-Mindedness." This is where William James leaves behind the optimism of Whitman and Emerson for the darker and deeper side—the Jonathan Edwards side—of the human condition. Facing the problem of evil head-on, James acknowledges "the grisly blood-freezing heart-palsying sensation" of real fear, and concludes bluntly, "here is the real core of the religious problem: Help! help!"

"Mankind," says James, "is in a position similar to that of a set of people living on a frozen lake, surrounded by cliffs over which there is no escape, yet knowing that little by little the ice is melting, and the inevitable day drawing near when the last film of it will disappear, and to be drowned ignominiously will be the human creature's portion."

The human condition, as Edwards saw, and as James understood also, is essentially hopeless and helpless, until religion comes as a deliverance. The psychological process that does the delivering is a conversion. James saw that religious conversion is a deliverance that closes out one life to make room for a new life, and he saw that the action of conversion applies to many life situations apart from the strictly religious ones. It is only a further validation of James's ideas that the founder of Alcoholics Anonymous, Bill Wilson himself, learned from this book how to utilize James's accounts of conversion to encourage alcoholics to a new birth, by a "conversion" to a life of sobriety.

"The Sick Soul" is William James at his deepest and his most personal. The witness he calls with the passage beginning "Whilst in this state of philosophic pessimism" is not some anonymous French correspondent but in fact James himself at an earlier age. And at the end of the veiled account of his own experience, he openly footnotes a similar experience that had befallen his father, Henry James Sr. The book presents a cloud of witnesses, a many-voiced and seemingly unanswerable chorus of personal experiences. The book as a whole has the same sort of straightforward confessional power we associate with other great religious classics, like those of George Fox or John Bunyan.

—————◆————

AT OUR last meeting, we considered the healthy-minded temperament, the temperament which has a constitutional incapacity for prolonged suffering, and in which the tendency to see things optimistically is like a water of crystallization in which the individual's character is set. We saw how this temperament may become the basis for a peculiar type of religion, a religion in which good, even the good of this world's life, is regarded as the essential thing for a rational being to attend to. This religion directs him to settle his scores with the more evil aspects of the universe by systematically declining to lay them to heart or make much of them, by ignoring them in his reflective calculations, or even, on occasion, by denying outright that they exist. Evil is a disease; and worry over disease is itself an additional form of disease, which only adds to the original complaint. Even repentance and remorse, affections which come in the character of ministers of good, may be but sickly and relaxing impulses. The best repentance is to up and act for righteousness, and forget that you ever had relations with sin.

Spinoza's philosophy has this sort of healthy-mindedness woven into the heart of it, and this has been one secret of its fascination. He whom Reason leads, according to Spinoza, is led altogether by the influence over his mind of good. Knowledge of evil is an 'inadequate' knowledge, fit only for slavish minds. So Spinoza categorically condemns repentance. When men make mistakes, he says,

> "One might perhaps expect gnawings of conscience and repentance to help to bring them on the right path, and might thereupon conclude (as everyone does conclude) that these affections are good things. Yet when we look at the matter closely, we shall find that not only are they not good, but on the contrary deleterious and evil passions. For it is manifest that we can always get along better by reason and love of truth than by worry of conscience and remorse. Harmful are these and evil, inasmuch as they form a particular kind of sadness; and the disadvantages of sadness," he continues, "I have already proved, and shown that we should strive to keep it from our life. Just so we should endeavor, since uneasiness of conscience and remorse are of this kind of complexion, to flee and shun these states of mind."[1]

Within the Christian body, for which repentance of sins has from the beginning been the critical religious act, healthy-mindedness has always come forward with its milder interpretation. Repentance according to such healthy-minded Christians means *getting away from* the sin, not groaning and writhing over its commission. The Catholic practice of confession and absolution is in one of its aspects little more than a systematic method of keeping healthy-mindedness on top. By it a man's accounts with evil are periodically squared and audited, so that he may start the clean page with no old debts inscribed. Any Catholic will tell us how clean and fresh and free he feels after the purging operation. Martin Luther by no means belonged to the healthy-minded type in the radical sense in which we have discussed it, and he repudiated priestly absolution for sin. Yet in this matter of repentance he had some very healthy-minded ideas, due in the main to the largeness of his conception of God.

> "When I was a monk," he says, "I thought that I was utterly cast away, if at any time I felt the lust of the flesh: that is to say, if I felt any evil

motion, fleshly lust, wrath, hatred, or envy against any brother. I as-
sayed many ways to help to quiet my conscience, but it would not be;
for the concupiscence and lust of my flesh, did always return, so that I
could not rest, but was continually vexed with these thoughts: This or
that sin thou hast committed: thou art infected with envy, with impa-
tiency, and such other sins: therefore thou art entered into this holy
order in vain, and all thy good works are unprofitable. But if then I
had rightly understood these sentences of Paul, 'The flesh lusteth contrary to the Spirit, and the Spirit contrary to the flesh; and these two
are one against another, so that ye cannot do the things that ye would
do;' I should not have so miserably tormented myself, but should
have thought and said to myself, as now commonly I do, Martin, thou
shalt not utterly be without sin, for thou hast flesh; thou shalt therefore feel the battle thereof. I remember that Staupitz was wont to say,
'I have vowed unto God above a thousand times that I would become
a better man: but I never performed that which I vowed. Hereafter I
will make no such vow: for I have now learned by experience, that I
am not able to perform it. Unless therefore God be favourable and
merciful unto me for Christ's sake, I shall not be able with all my vows
and all my good deeds, to stand before him.' This [of Staupitz's] was
not only a true, but also a godly and a holy desperation; and this must
they all confess, both with mouth and heart, which will be saved. For
the godly trust not to their own righteousness. They look unto Christ
their reconciler, who gave his life for their sins. Moreover they know
that the remnant of sin which is in their flesh is not laid to their
charge, but freely pardoned. Notwithstanding in the mean while they
fight in spirit against the flesh, lest they should *fulfil* the lusts thereof.
And although they feel the flesh to rage and rebel, and themselves
also do fall sometimes into sin through infirmity, yet are they not dis-
couraged, nor think therefore that their state and kind of life, and the
works which are done according to their calling, displease God; but
they raise up themselves by faith."[2]

One of the heresies for which the Jesuits got that spiritual genius,
Molinos, the founder of Quietism, so abominably condemned was his
healthy-minded opinion of repentance:

"When thou fallest into a fault, in what matter soever it be, do not
trouble nor afflict thy self for it: for they are effects of our frail nature,
stained by Original Sin. The common enemy will make thee believe,
as soon as thou fallest into any fault, that thou walkest in Error, and
therefore art out of God and his favour: and herewith would he make
thee distrust of the Divine Grace, telling thee of thy misery and mak-

ing a Gyant of it, and putting into thy head, that every day thy Soul grows worse instead of better, whilst it so often repeats those failings. O blessed Soul, open thine Eyes, and shut the gate against these diabolical Suggestions, knowing thy misery, and trusting in the Mercy Divine. Would not he be a meer Fool, which running at Turneament with others, and falling in the best of the Career, should lie weeping on the ground, and afflicting himself with discourses upon his fall? Man (they would tell him) loose no time, get up and take the Course again; for he that rises again quickly, and continues his Race, is as if he had never fallen. If thou seest thy self fallen once and a thousand times, thou oughtest to make use of the Remedy which I have given thee, that is, a loving Confidence in the Divine Mercy: These are the Weapons with which thou must fight and conquer Cowardise and vain Thoughts: This is the means thou oughtest to use, not to lose time, not to disturb thy self, and reap good."[3]

Now in contrast with such healthy-minded views as these, if we treat them as a way of deliberately minimizing evil, stands a radically opposite view, a way of maximizing evil, if you please so to call it, based on the persuasion that the evil aspects of our life are of its very essence, and that the world's meaning most comes home to us when we lay them most to heart. We have now to address ourselves to this more morbid way of looking at the situation. But as I closed our last hour with a general philosophical reflection on the healthy-minded way of taking life, I should like at this point to make another philosophical reflection upon it before turning to that heavier task. You will excuse the brief delay.

If we admit that evil is an essential part of our being and the key to the interpretation of our life, we load ourselves down with a difficulty that has always proved burdensome in philosophies of religion. Theism, whenever it has erected itself into a systematic philosophy of the universe, has shown a reluctance to let God be anything less than All-in-All. In other words, philosophic theism has always shown a tendency to become pantheistic and monistic, and to consider the world as one unit of absolute fact; and this has been at variance with popular or practical theism, which latter has ever been more or less frankly pluralistic, not to say polytheistic, and shown itself perfectly well satisfied with a universe composed of many original principles, provided we be only allowed to believe that the divine principle remains supreme, and that the others are subordinate. In this latter case God is not necessarily responsible for the existence of evil; he would only be responsible if it were not finally overcome. But on the monistic or pantheistic view, evil, like everything else, must have its foundation in God; and the difficulty is to see how this can possibly be the case if God be absolutely good. This difficulty faces us in every form of philosophy in which the world appears as one flawless unit of fact. Such a unit is an *Individual,* and in it the worst parts must be as essential as the best, must be as necessary to make the individual what he is; since if any part whatever in an individual were to vanish or alter, it would no longer be *that* individual at all. The philosophy of absolute idealism, so vigorously represented both in Scotland and America to-day, has to struggle with this difficulty quite as much as scholastic theism struggled in its time; and although it would be premature to say that there is no speculative issue whatever from the puzzle, it is perfectly fair to say that there is no clear or easy issue, and that the only *obvious* escape from paradox here is to cut loose from the monistic assumption altogether, and to allow the world to have existed from its origin in pluralistic form, as an aggregate or collection of higher and lower things and principles, rather than an absolutely unitary fact. For then evil would not need to be essential; it might be, and may always have been, an independent portion that had no rational or absolute right to live with the rest, and which we might conceivably hope to see got rid of at last.

Now the gospel of healthy-mindedness, as we have described it, casts its vote distinctly for this pluralistic view. Whereas the monistic philosopher finds himself more or less bound to say, as Hegel said, that everything actual is rational, and that evil, as an element dialectically required, must be pinned in and kept and consecrated and have a function awarded to it in the final system of truth, healthy-mindedness refuses to say anything of the sort.[4] Evil, it says, is emphatically irrational, and *not* to be pinned in, or preserved, or consecrated in any final system of truth. It is a pure abomination to the Lord, an alien unreality, a waste element, to be sloughed off and negated, and the very memory of it, if possible, wiped out and forgotten. The ideal, so far from being co-extensive with the whole actual, is a mere *extract* from the actual, marked by its deliverance from all contact with this diseased, inferior, and excrementitious stuff.

Here we have the interesting notion fairly and squarely presented to us, of there being elements of the universe which may make no rational whole in conjunction with the other elements, and which, from the point of view of any system which those other elements make up, can only be considered so much irrelevance and accident—so much 'dirt,' as it were, and matter out of place. I ask you now not to forget this notion; for although most philosophers seem either to forget it or to disdain it too much ever to mention it, I believe that we shall have to admit it ourselves in the end as containing an element of truth. The mind-cure gospel thus once more appears to us as having dignity and importance. We have seen it to be a genuine religion, and no mere silly appeal to imagination to cure disease; we have seen its method of experimental verification to be not unlike the method of all science; and now here we find mind-cure as the champion of a perfectly definite conception of the metaphysical structure of the world. I hope that, in view of all this, you will not regret my having pressed it upon your attention at such length.

Let us now say good-by for a while to all this way of thinking, and turn towards those persons who cannot so swiftly throw off the burden of the consciousness of evil, but are congenitally fated to suffer from its presence. Just as we saw that in healthy-mindedness there are shallower and profounder levels, happiness like that of the mere animal, and more regenerate sorts of happiness, so also are there different levels of the morbid mind, and the one is much more formidable than the other. There are people for whom evil means only a mal-adjustment with *things,* a wrong correspondence of one's life with the environment. Such evil as this is curable, in principle at least, upon the natural plane, for merely by modifying either the self or the things, or both at once, the two terms may be made to fit, and all go merry as a marriage bell again. But there are others for whom evil is no mere relation of the subject to particular outer things, but something more radical and general, a wrongness or vice in his essential nature, which no alteration of the environment, or any superficial rearrangement of the inner self, can cure, and which requires a supernatural remedy. On the whole, the Latin races have leaned more towards the former way of looking upon evil, as made up of ills and sins in the plural, removable in detail; while the Germanic races have tended rather to think of Sin in the singular, and with a capital S, as of something ineradicably ingrained in our natural subjectivity, and never to be removed by any superficial piecemeal operations.[5] These comparisons of races are always open to exception, but undoubtedly the northern tone in religion has inclined to the more intimately pessimistic persuasion, and this way of feeling, being the more extreme, we shall find by far the more instructive for our study.

Recent psychology has found great use for the word 'threshold' as a symbolic designation for the point at which one state of mind passes into another. Thus we speak of the threshold of a man's consciousness in general, to indicate the amount of noise, pressure, or other outer stimulus which it takes to arouse his attention at all. One with a high threshold will doze through an amount of racket by which one with a low threshold would be immediately waked. Similarly, when one is sensitive to small differences in any order of sensation, we say he has a low 'difference-threshold'—his mind easily steps over it into the consciousness of the differences in question. And just so we might speak of a 'pain-threshold,' a 'fear-threshold,' a 'misery-threshold,' and find it quickly overpassed by the consciousness of some individuals, but lying too high in others to be often reached by their consciousness. The sanguine and healthy-minded live habitually on the sunny side of their misery-line, the depressed and melancholy live beyond it, in darkness and apprehension. There are men who seem to have started in life with a bottle or two of champagne inscribed to their credit; whilst others seem to have been born close to the pain-threshold, which the slightest irritants fatally send them over.

Does it not appear as if one who lived more habitually on one side of the pain-threshold might need a different sort of religion from one who habitually lived on the other? This question, of the relativity of different types of religion to different types of need, arises naturally at this point, and will become a serious problem ere we have done. But before we confront it in general terms, we must address ourselves to the unpleasant task of hearing what the sick souls, as we may call them in contrast to the healthy-minded, have to say of the secrets of their prison-house, their own peculiar form of consciousness. Let us then resolutely turn our backs on the once-born and their sky-blue optimistic gospel; let us not simply cry out, in spite of all appearances, "Hurrah for the Universe!—God's in his Heaven, all's right with the world." Let us see rather whether pity, pain, and fear, and the sentiment of human helplessness may not open a profounder view and put into our hands a more complicated key to the meaning of the situation.

To begin with, how *can* things so insecure as the successful experiences of this world afford a stable anchorage? A chain is no stronger than its weakest link, and life is after all a chain. In the healthiest and most prosperous existence, how many links of illness, danger, and disaster are always interposed? Unsuspectedly from the bottom of every fountain of pleasure, as the old poet said, something bitter rises up: a touch of nausea, a falling dead of the delight, a whiff of melancholy, things that sound a knell, for fugitive as they may be, they bring a feeling of coming from a deeper region and often have an appalling convincingness. The buzz of life ceases at their touch as a piano-string stops sounding when the damper falls upon it.

Of course the music can commence again;—and again and again— at intervals. But with this the healthy-minded consciousness is left with an irremediable sense of precariousness. It is a bell with a crack; it draws its breath on sufferance and by an accident.

Even if we suppose a man so packed with healthy-mindedness as never to have experienced in his own person any of these sobering intervals, still, if he is a reflecting being, he must generalize and class his own lot with that of others; and, doing so, he must see that his escape is just a lucky chance and no essential difference. He might just as well have been born to an entirely different fortune. And then indeed the hollow security! What kind of a frame of things is it of which the best you can say is, "Thank God, it has let me off clear this time!" Is not its blessedness a fragile fiction? Is not your joy in it a very vulgar glee, not much unlike the snicker of any rogue at his success? If indeed it were all success, even on such terms as that! But take the happiest man, the one most envied by the world, and in nine cases out of ten his inmost consciousness is one of failure. Either his ideals in the line of his achievements are pitched far higher than the achievements themselves, or else he has secret ideals of which the world knows nothing, and in regard to which he inwardly knows himself to be found wanting.

When such a conquering optimist as Goethe can express himself in this wise, how must it be with less successful men?

"I will say nothing," writes Goethe in 1824, "against the course of my existence. But at bottom it has been nothing but pain and burden, and I can affirm that during the whole of my 75 years, I have not had four weeks of genuine well-being. It is but the perpetual rolling of a rock that must be raised up again forever."

What single-handed man was ever on the whole as successful as Luther? yet when he had grown old, he looked back on his life as if it were an absolute failure.

"I am utterly weary of life. I pray the Lord will come forthwith and carry me hence. Let him come, above all, with his last Judgment: I will stretch out my neck, the thunder will burst forth, and I shall be at rest."—And having a necklace of white agates in his hand at the time he added: "O God, grant that it may come without delay. I would readily eat up this necklace to-day, for the Judgment to come tomorrow."—The Electress Dowager, one day when Luther was dining with her, said to him: "Doctor, I wish you may live forty years to come." "Madam," replied he, "rather than live forty years more, I would give up my chance of Paradise."

Failure, then, failure! so the world stamps us at every turn. We strew it with our blunders, our misdeeds, our lost opportunities, with all the memorials of our inadequacy to our vocation. And with what a damning emphasis does it then blot us out! No easy fine, no mere apology or formal expiation, will satisfy the world's demands, but every pound of flesh exacted is soaked with all its blood. The subtlest forms of suffering known to man are connected with the poisonous humiliations incidental to these results.

And they are pivotal human experiences. A process so ubiquitous and everlasting is evidently an integral part of life. "There is indeed one element in human destiny," Robert Louis Stevenson writes, "that not blindness itself can controvert: whatever else we are intended to do, we are not intended to succeed; failure is the fate allotted."[6] And our nature being thus rooted in failure, is it any wonder that theologians should have held it to be essential, and thought that only through the personal experience of humiliation which it engenders the deeper sense of life's significance is reached?[7]

But this is only the first stage of the world-sickness. Make the human being's sensitiveness a little greater, carry him a little farther over the misery-threshold, and the good quality of the successful moments themselves when they occur is spoiled and vitiated. All natural goods perish. Riches take wings; fame is a breath; love is a cheat; youth and health and pleasure vanish. Can things whose end is always dust and disappointment be the real goods which our souls require? Back of everything is the great spectre of universal death, the all-encompassing blackness:

> "What profit hath a man of all his labour which he taketh under the sun? I looked on all the works that my hands had wrought, and, behold, all *was* vanity and vexation of spirit. For that which befalleth the sons of men befalleth beasts; as the one dieth, so dieth the other; all are of the dust, and all turn to dust again. . . . The dead know not any thing, neither have they any more a reward; for the memory of them is forgotten. Also their love, and their hatred, and their envy, is now perished; neither have they any more a portion for ever in any *thing* that is done under the sun. . . . Truly the light *is* sweet, and a pleasant *thing it is* for the eyes to behold the sun: but if a man live many years, *and* rejoice in them all; yet let him remember the days of darkness; for they shall be many."

In short, life and its negation are beaten up inextricably together. But if the life be good, the negation of it must be bad. Yet the two are equally essential facts of existence; and all natural happiness thus seems infected with a contradiction. The breath of the sepulchre surrounds it.

To a mind attentive to this state of things and rightly subject to the joy-destroying chill which such a contemplation engenders, the only relief that healthy-mindedness can give is by saying: 'Stuff and nonsense, get out into the open air!' or 'Cheer up, old fellow, you'll be all right erelong, if you will only drop your morbidness!' But in all seriousness, can such bald animal talk as that be treated as a rational answer? To ascribe religious value to mere happy-go-lucky contentment with one's brief chance at natural good is but the very consecration of forgetfulness and superficiality. Our troubles lie indeed too deep for *that* cure. The fact that we *can* die, that we *can* be ill at all, is what perplexes us; the fact that we now for a moment live and are well is irrelevant to that perplexity. We need a life not correlated with death, a health not liable to illness, a kind of good that will not perish, a good in fact that flies beyond the Goods of nature.

It all depends on how sensitive the soul may become to discords. "The trouble with me is that I believe too much in common happiness and goodness," said a friend of mine whose consciousness was of this sort, "and nothing can console me for their transiency. I am appalled and disconcerted at its being possible." And so with most of us: a little cooling down of animal excitability and instinct, a little loss of animal toughness, a little irritable weakness and descent of the pain-threshold, will bring the worm at the core of all our usual springs of delight into full view, and turn us into melancholy metaphysicians. The pride of life and glory of the world will shrivel. It is after all but the standing quarrel of hot youth and hoary eld. Old age has the last word: the purely naturalistic look at life, however enthusiastically it may begin, is sure to end in sadness.

This sadness lies at the heart of every merely positivistic, agnostic, or naturalistic scheme of philosophy. Let sanguine healthy-mindedness do its best with its strange power of living in the moment and ignoring and forgetting, still the evil background is really there to be thought of, and the skull will grin in at the banquet. In the practical life of the individual, we know how his whole gloom or glee about any present fact depends on the remoter schemes and hopes with which it stands related. Its significance and framing give it the chief part of its value. Let it be known to lead nowhere, and however agreeable it may be in its immediacy, its glow and gilding vanish. The old man, sick with an insidious internal disease, may laugh and quaff his wine at first as well as ever, but he knows his fate now, for the doctors have revealed it; and the knowledge knocks the satisfaction out of all these functions. They are partners of death and the worm is their brother, and they turn to a mere flatness.

The lustre of the present hour is always borrowed from the background of possibilities it goes with. Let our common experiences be enveloped in an eternal moral order; let our suffering have an immortal significance; let Heaven smile upon the earth, and deities pay their visits; let faith and hope be the atmosphere which man breathes in;—and his days pass by with zest; they stir with prospects, they thrill with remoter values. Place round them on the contrary the curdling cold and gloom and absence of all permanent meaning which for pure naturalism and the popular science evolutionism of our time are all that is visible ultimately, and the thrill stops short, or turns rather to an anxious trembling.

For naturalism, fed on recent cosmological speculations, mankind is in a position similar to that of a set of people living on a frozen lake, surrounded by cliffs over which there is no escape, yet knowing that little by little the ice is melting, and the inevitable day drawing near when the last film of it will disappear, and to be drowned ignominiously will be the human creature's portion. The merrier the skating, the warmer and more sparkling the sun by day, and the ruddier the bonfires at night, the more poignant the sadness with which one must take in the meaning of the total situation.

The early Greeks are continually held up to us in literary works as models of the healthy-minded joyousness which the religion of nature may engender. There was indeed much joyousness among the Greeks—Homer's flow of enthusiasm for most things that the sun shines upon is steady. But even in Homer the reflective passages are cheerless,[8] and the moment the Greeks grew systematically pensive and thought of ultimates, they became unmitigated pessimists.[9] The jealousy of the gods, the nemesis that follows too much happiness, the all-encompassing death, fate's dark opacity, the ultimate and unintelligible cruelty, were the fixed background of their imagination. The beautiful joyousness of their polytheism is only a poetic modern fiction. They knew no joys comparable in quality of preciousness to those which we shall erelong see that Brahmans, Buddhists, Christians, Mohammedans, twice-born people whose religion is non-naturalistic, get from their several creeds of mysticism and renunciation.

Stoic insensibility and Epicurean resignation were the farthest advance which the Greek mind made in that direction. The Epicurean said: "Seek not to be happy, but rather to escape unhappiness; strong happiness is always linked with pain; therefore hug the safe shore, and do not tempt the deeper raptures. Avoid disappointment by expecting little, and by aiming low; and above all do not fret." The Stoic said: "The only genuine good that life can yield a man is the free possession of his own soul; all other goods are lies." Each of these philosophies is in its degree a philosophy of despair in nature's boons. Trustful self-abandonment to the joys that freely offer has entirely departed from both Epicurean and Stoic; and what each proposes is a way of rescue from the resultant dust-and-ashes state of mind. The Epicurean still awaits results from economy of indulgence and damping of desire. The Stoic hopes for no results, and gives up natural good altogether. There is dignity in both these forms of resignation. They represent distinct stages in the sobering process which man's primitive intoxication with sense-happiness is sure to undergo. In the one the hot blood has grown cool, in the other it has become quite cold; and although I have spoken of them in the past tense, as if they were merely historic, yet Stoicism and Epicureanism will probably be to all time typical attitudes, marking a certain definite stage accomplished in the evolution of the world-sick soul.[10] They mark the conclusion of what we call the once-born period, and represent the highest flights of what twice-born religion would call the purely natural man—Epicureanism, which can only by great courtesy be called a religion, showing his refinement, and Stoicism exhibiting his moral will. They leave the world in the shape of an unreconciled contradiction, and seek no higher unity. Compared with the complex ecstasies which the supernaturally regenerated Christian may enjoy, or the oriental pantheist indulge in, their receipts for equanimity are expedients which seem almost crude in their simplicity.

Please observe, however, that I am not yet pretending finally to *judge* any of these attitudes. I am only describing their variety.

The securest way to the rapturous sorts of happiness of which the twice-born make report has as an historic matter of fact been through a more radical pessimism than anything that we have yet considered. We have seen how the lustre and enchantment may be rubbed off from the goods of nature. But there is a pitch of unhappiness so great that the goods of nature may be entirely forgotten, and all sentiment of their existence vanish from the mental field. For this extremity of pessimism to be reached, something more is needed than observation of life and reflection upon death. The individual must in his own person become the prey of a pathological melancholy. As the healthy-minded enthusiast succeeds in ignoring evil's very existence, so the subject of melancholy is forced in spite of himself to ignore that of all good whatever: for him it may no longer have the least reality. Such sensitiveness and susceptibility to mental pain is a rare occurrence where the nervous constitution is entirely normal; one seldom finds it in a healthy subject even where he is the victim of the most atrocious cruelties of outward fortune. So we note here the neurotic constitution, of which I said so much in my first lecture, making its active entrance on our scene, and destined to play a part in much that follows. Since these experiences of melancholy are in the first instance absolutely private and individual, I can now help myself out with personal documents. Painful indeed they will be to listen to, and there is almost an indecency in handling them in public. Yet they lie right in the middle of our path; and if we are to touch the psychology of religion at all seriously, we must be willing to forget conventionalities, and dive below the smooth and lying official conversational surface.

One can distinguish many kinds of pathological depression. Sometimes it is mere passive joylessness and dreariness, discouragement, dejection, lack of taste and zest and spring. Professor Ribot has proposed the name *anhedonia* to designate this condition.

> "The state of *anhedonia*, if I may coin a new word to pair off with *analgesia*," he writes, "has been very little studied, but it exists. . . . A young girl was smitten with a liver disease which for some time altered her constitution. . . . She felt no longer any affection for her father and mother. She would have played with her doll, but it was impossible to find the least pleasure in the act. The same things which formerly convulsed her with laughter entirely failed to interest her now. Esquirol observed the case of a very intelligent magistrate who was also a prey to hepatic disease. Every emotion appeared dead within him. He manifested neither perversion nor violence, but complete absence of emotional reaction. If he went to the theatre, which he did out of habit, he could find no pleasure there. The thought of his house, of his home, of his wife, and of his absent children moved him as little, he said, as a theorem of Euclid."[11]

Prolonged seasickness will in most persons produce a temporary condition of anhedonia. Every good, terrestrial or celestial, is imagined only to be turned from with disgust. A temporary condition of this sort, connected with the religious evolution of a singularly lofty character, both intellectual and moral, is well described by the Catholic philosopher, Father Gratry, in his autobiographical recollections. In consequence of mental isolation and excessive study at the Polytechnic school, young Gratry fell into a state of nervous exhaustion with symptoms which he thus describes:

> "I had such a universal terror that I woke at night with a start, thinking that the Pantheon was tumbling on the Polytechnic school, or that the school was in flames, or that the Seine was pouring into the Catacombs, and that Paris was being swallowed up. And when these impressions were past, all day long without respite I suffered an incurable and intolerable desolation, verging on despair. I thought myself,

in fact, rejected by God, lost, damned! I felt something like the suffering of hell. Before that I had never even thought of hell. My mind had
never turned in that direction. Neither discourses nor reflections had
impressed me in that way. I took no account of hell. Now, and all at
once, I suffered in a measure what is suffered there.

"But what was perhaps still more dreadful is that every idea of
heaven was taken away from me: I could no longer conceive of anything of the sort. Heaven did not seem to me worth going to. It was
like a vacuum; a mythological elysium, an abode of shadows less real
than the earth. I could conceive no joy, no pleasure in inhabiting it.
Happiness, joy, light, affection, love—all these words were now devoid of sense. Without doubt I could still have talked of all these
things, but I had become incapable of feeling anything in them, of
understanding anything about them, of hoping anything from them,
or of believing them to exist. There was my great and inconsolable
grief! I neither perceived nor conceived any longer the existence of
happiness or perfection. An abstract heaven over a naked rock. Such
was my present abode for eternity."[12]

So much for melancholy in the sense of incapacity for joyous feeling. A much worse form of it is positive and active anguish, a sort of
psychical neuralgia wholly unknown to healthy life. Such anguish may
partake of various characters, having sometimes more the quality of
loathing; sometimes that of irritation and exasperation; or again of self-
mistrust and self-despair; or of suspicion, anxiety, trepidation, fear. The
patient may rebel or submit; may accuse himself, or accuse outside powers; and he may or he may not be tormented by the theoretical mystery
of why he should so have to suffer. Most cases are mixed cases, and we
should not treat our classifications with too much respect. Moreover, it
is only a relatively small proportion of cases that connect themselves
with the religious sphere of experience at all. Exasperated cases, for instance, as a rule do not. I quote now literally from the first case of melancholy on which I lay my hand. It is a letter from a patient in a French
asylum.

"I suffer too much in this hospital, both physically and morally. Besides the burnings and the sleeplessness (for I no longer sleep since I
am shut up here, and the little rest I get is broken by bad dreams, and
I am waked with a jump by nightmares, dreadful visions, lightning,
thunder, and the rest), fear, atrocious fear, presses me down, holds me
without respite, never lets me go. Where is the justice in it all! What

have I done to deserve this excess of severity? Under what form will this fear crush me? What would I not owe to anyone who would rid me of my life! Eat, drink, lie awake all night, suffer without interruption—such is the fine legacy I have received from my mother! What I fail to understand is this abuse of power. There are limits to everything, there is a middle way. But God knows neither middle way nor limits. I say God, but why? All I have known so far has been the devil. After all, I am afraid of God as much as of the devil, so I drift along, thinking of nothing but suicide, but with neither courage nor means here to execute the act. As you read this, it will easily prove to you my insanity. The style and the ideas are incoherent enough—I can see that myself. But I cannot keep myself from being either crazy or an idiot; and, as things are, from whom should I ask pity? I am defenseless against the invisible enemy who is tightening his coils around me. I should be no better armed against him even if I saw him, or had seen him. Oh, if he would but kill me, devil take him! Death, death, once for all! But I stop. I have raved to you long enough. I say raved, for I can write no otherwise, having neither brain nor thoughts left. O God! what a misfortune to be born! Born like a mushroom, doubtless between an evening and a morning; and how true and right I was when in our philosophy-year in college I chewed the cud of bitterness with the pessimists. Yes, indeed, there is more pain in life than gladness—it is one long agony until the grave. Think how gay it makes me to remember that this horrible misery of mine, coupled with this unspeakable fear, may last fifty, one hundred, who knows how many more years!"[13]

This letter shows two things. First, you see how the entire consciousness of the poor man is so choked with the feeling of evil that the sense of there being any good in the world is lost for him altogether. His attention excludes it, cannot admit it: the sun has left his heaven. And secondly you see how the querulous temper of his misery keeps his mind from taking a religious direction. Querulousness of mind tends in fact rather towards irreligion; and it has played, so far as I know, no part whatever in the construction of religious systems.

Religious melancholy must be cast in a more melting mood. Tolstoy has left us, in his book called *My Confession*, a wonderful account of the attack of melancholy which led him to his own religious conclusions. The latter in some respects are peculiar; but the melancholy presents two characters which make it a typical document for our present purpose. First it is a well-marked case of anhedonia, of passive loss of appetite for all life's values; and second, it shows how the altered and estranged aspect which the world assumed in consequence of this stimulated Tolstoy's intellect to a gnawing, carking questioning and effort for philosophic relief. I mean to quote Tolstoy at some length; but before doing so, I will make a general remark on each of these two points.

First on our spiritual judgments and the sense of value in general.

It is notorious that facts are compatible with opposite emotional comments, since the same fact will inspire entirely different feelings in different persons, and at different times in the same person; and there is no rationally deducible connexion between any outer fact and the sentiments it may happen to provoke. These have their source in another sphere of existence altogether, in the animal and spiritual region of the subject's being. Conceive yourself, if possible, suddenly stripped of all the emotion with which your world now inspires you, and try to imagine it *as it exists,* purely by itself, without your favorable or unfavorable, hopeful or apprehensive comment. It will be almost impossible for you to realize such a condition of negativity and deadness. No one portion of the universe would then have importance beyond another; and the whole collection of its things and series of its events would be without significance, character, expression, or perspective. Whatever of value, interest, or meaning our respective worlds may appear endued with are thus pure gifts of the spectator's mind. The passion of love is the most familiar and extreme example of this fact. If it comes, it comes; if it does not come, no process of reasoning can force it. Yet it transforms the value of the creature loved as utterly as the sunrise transforms Mont Blanc from a corpse-like gray to a rosy enchantment; and it sets the whole world to a new tune for the lover and gives a new issue to his life. So with fear, with indignation, jealousy, ambition, worship. If they are there, life changes. And whether they shall be there or not depends almost always upon non-logical, often on organic conditions. And as the excited interest which these passions put into the world is our gift to the world, just so are the passions themselves *gifts*—gifts to us, from sources sometimes low and sometimes high; but almost always non-logical and beyond our control. How can the moribund old man reason back to himself the romance, the mystery, the imminence of great things with which our old earth tingled for him in the days when he was young and well? Gifts, either of the flesh or of the spirit; and the spirit bloweth where it listeth; and the world's materials lend their surface passively to all the gifts alike, as the stage-setting receives indifferently whatever alternating colored lights may be shed upon it from the optical apparatus in the gallery.

Meanwhile the practically real world for each one of us, the effective world of the individual, is the compound world, the physical facts and emotional values in indistinguishable combination. Withdraw or pervert either factor of this complex resultant, and the kind of experience we call pathological ensues.

In Tolstoy's case the sense that life had any meaning whatever was for a time wholly withdrawn. The result was a transformation in the whole expression of reality. When we come to study the phenomenon of conversion or religious regeneration, we shall see that a not infrequent consequence of the change operated in the subject is a transfiguration of the face of nature in his eyes. A new heaven seems to shine upon a new earth. In melancholiacs there is usually a similar change, only it is in the reverse direction. The world now looks remote, strange, sinister, uncanny. Its color is gone, its breath is cold, there is no speculation in the eyes it glares with. "It is as if I lived in another century," says one asylum patient.—"I see everything through a cloud," says another, "things are not as they were, and I am changed."—"I see," says a third, "I touch, but the things do not come near me, a thick veil alters the hue and look of everything."—"Persons move like shadows, and sounds seem to come from a distant world."—"There is no longer any past for me; people appear so strange; it is as if I could not see any reality, as if I were in a theatre; as if people were actors, and everything were scenery; I can no longer find myself; I walk, but why? Everything floats before my eyes, but leaves no impression."—"I weep false tears, I have unreal hands: the things I see are not real things."—Such are expressions that naturally rise to the lips of melancholy subjects describing their changed state.[14]

Now there are some subjects whom all this leaves a prey to the profoundest astonishment. The strangeness is wrong. The unreality cannot be. A mystery is concealed, and a metaphysical solution must exist. If the natural world is so double-faced and unhomelike, what world, what thing is real? An urgent wondering and questioning is set up, a poring theoretic activity, and in the desperate effort to get into right relations with the matter, the sufferer is often led to what becomes for him a satisfying religious solution.

At about the age of fifty, Tolstoy relates that he began to have moments of perplexity, of what he calls arrest, as if he knew not 'how to live,' or what to do. It is obvious that these were moments in which the excitement and interest which our functions naturally bring had ceased. Life had been enchanting, it was now flat sober, more than sober, dead. Things were meaningless whose meaning had always been self-evident. The questions 'Why?' and 'What next?' began to beset him more and more frequently. At first it seemed as if such questions must be answerable, and as if he could easily find the answers if he would take the time; but as they ever became more urgent, he perceived that it was like those first discomforts of a sick man, to which he pays but little attention till they run into one continuous suffering, and then he realizes that what he took for a passing disorder means the most momentous thing in the world for him, means his death.

These questions 'Why?' 'Wherefore?' 'What for?' found no response.

"I felt," says Tolstoy, "that something had broken within me on which my life had always rested, that I had nothing left to hold on to, and that morally my life had stopped. An invincible force impelled me to get rid of my existence, in one way or another. It cannot be said exactly that I *wished* to kill myself, for the force which drew me away from life was fuller, more powerful, more general than any mere desire. It was a force like my old aspiration to live, only it impelled me in the opposite direction. It was an aspiration of my whole being to get out of life.

"Behold me then, a man happy and in good health, hiding the rope in order not to hang myself to the rafters of the room where every night I went to sleep alone; behold me no longer going shooting, lest I should yield to the too easy temptation of putting an end to myself with my gun.

"I did not know what I wanted. I was afraid of life; I was driven to leave it; and in spite of that I still hoped something from it.

"All this took place at a time when so far as all my outer circumstances went, I ought to have been completely happy. I had a good wife who loved me and whom I loved; good children and a large property which was increasing with no pains taken on my part. I was more respected by my kinsfolk and acquaintance than I had ever been; I was loaded with praise by strangers; and without exaggeration

I could believe my name already famous. Moreover I was neither insane nor ill. On the contrary, I possessed a physical and mental strength which I have rarely met in persons of my age. I could mow as well as the peasants, I could work with my brain eight hours uninterruptedly and feel no bad effects.

"And yet I could give no reasonable meaning to any actions of my life. And I was surprised that I had not understood this from the very beginning. My state of mind was as if some wicked and stupid jest was being played upon me by someone. One can live only so long as one is intoxicated, drunk with life; but when one grows sober one cannot fail to see that it is all a stupid cheat. What is truest about it is that there is nothing even funny or silly in it; it is cruel and stupid, purely and simply.

"The oriental fable of the traveler surprised in the desert by a wild beast is very old.

"Seeking to save himself from the fierce animal, the traveler jumps into a well with no water in it; but at the bottom of this well he sees a dragon waiting with open mouth to devour him. And the unhappy man, not daring to go out lest he should be the prey of the beast, not daring to jump to the bottom lest he should be devoured by the dragon, clings to the branches of a wild bush which grows out of one of the cracks of the well. His hands weaken, and he feels that he must soon give way to certain fate; but still he clings, and sees two mice, one white, the other black, evenly moving round the bush to which he hangs and gnawing off its roots.

"The traveler sees this and knows that he must inevitably perish; but while thus hanging he looks about him and finds on the leaves of the bush some drops of honey. These he reaches with his tongue and licks them off with rapture.

"Thus I hang upon the boughs of life, knowing that the inevitable dragon of death is waiting ready to tear me, and I cannot comprehend why I am thus made a martyr. I try to suck the honey which formerly consoled me; but the honey pleases me no longer, and day and night the white mouse and the black mouse gnaw the branch to which I cling. I can see but one thing: the inevitable dragon and the mice—I cannot turn my gaze away from them.

"This is no fable, but the literal incontestable truth which everyone may understand. What will be the outcome of what I do to-day? Of what I shall do to-morrow? What will be the outcome of all my life? Why should I live? Why should I do anything? Is there in life any purpose which the inevitable death which awaits me does not undo and destroy?

"These questions are the simplest in the world. From the stupid

child to the wisest old man, they are in the soul of every human being. Without an answer to them, it is impossible, as I experienced, for
life to go on.

   "'But perhaps,' I often said to myself, 'there may be something I
have failed to notice or to comprehend. It is not possible that this condition of despair should be natural to mankind.' And I sought for an
explanation in all the branches of knowledge acquired by men. I
questioned painfully and protractedly and with no idle curiosity. I
sought, not with indolence, but laboriously and obstinately for days
and nights together. I sought like a man who is lost and seeks to save
himself—and I found nothing. I became convinced, moreover, that all
those who before me had sought for an answer in the sciences have
also found nothing. And not only this, but that they have recognized
that the very thing which was leading me to despair—the meaningless absurdity of life—is the only incontestable knowledge accessible
to man" [*Ma confession,* pp. 50–70, abridged].

To prove this point, Tolstoy quotes the Buddha, Solomon, and Schopenhauer. And he finds only four ways in which men of his own class
and society are accustomed to meet the situation. Either mere animal
blindness, sucking the honey without seeing the dragon or the mice—
"and from such a way," he says, "I can learn nothing, after what I now
know"; or reflective epicureanism, snatching what it can while the day
lasts—which is only a more deliberate sort of stupefaction than the first;
or manly suicide; or seeing the mice and dragon and yet weakly and
plaintively clinging to the bush of life.

   Suicide was naturally the consistent course dictated by the logical
intellect.

   "Yet," says Tolstoy, "whilst my intellect was working, something else
   in me was working too, and kept me from the deed—a consciousness
   of life, as I may call it, which was like a force that obliged my mind to
   fix itself in another direction and draw me out of my situation of despair. . . . During the whole course of this year, when I almost unceas-
   ingly kept asking myself how to end the business, whether by the
   rope or by the bullet, during all that time, alongside of all those movements of my ideas and observations, my heart kept languishing with
   another pining emotion. I can call this by no other name than that of
   a thirst for God. This craving for God had nothing to do with the
   movement of my ideas—in fact, it was the direct contrary of that
   movement—but it came from my heart. It was like a feeling of dread
   that made me seem like an orphan and isolated in the midst of all

these things that were so foreign. And this feeling of dread was miti-
gated by the hope of finding the assistance of someone."[15]

Of the process, intellectual as well as emotional, which, starting
from this idea of God, led to Tolstoy's recovery, I will say nothing in this
lecture, reserving it for a later hour. The only thing that need interest us
now is the phenomenon of his absolute disenchantment with ordinary
life, and the fact that the whole range of habitual values may, to a man
as powerful and full of faculty as he was, come to appear so ghastly a
mockery.

When disillusionment has gone as far as this, there is seldom a *resti-
tutio ad integrum*. One has tasted of the fruit of the tree, and the happiness of Eden never comes again. The happiness that comes, when any
does come—and often enough it fails to return in an acute form, though
its form is sometimes very acute—is not the simple ignorance of ill, but
something vastly more complex, including natural evil as one of its elements, but finding natural evil no such stumbling-block and terror because it now sees it swallowed up in supernatural good. The process is
one of redemption, not of mere reversion to natural health, and the sufferer, when saved, is saved by what seems to him a second birth, a
deeper kind of conscious being than he could enjoy before.

We find a somewhat different type of religious melancholy enshrined
in literature in John Bunyan's autobiography. Tolstoy's preoccupations
were largely objective, for the purpose and meaning of life in general
was what so troubled him; but poor Bunyan's troubles were over the
condition of his own personal self. He was a typical case of the psycho-
pathic temperament, sensitive of conscience to a diseased degree, beset
by doubts, fears, and insistent ideas, and a victim of verbal automatisms,
both motor and sensory. These were usually texts of Scripture which,
sometimes damnatory and sometimes favorable, would come in a half-
hallucinatory form as if they were voices, and fasten on his mind and
buffet it between them like a shuttlecock. Added to this were a fearful
melancholy self-contempt and despair.

"Nay, thought I, now I grow worse and worse; now I am farther from
Conversion than ever I was before. If now I should have burned at
the Stake, I could not believe that Christ had love for me; alas, I could

neither hear him, nor see him, nor feel him, nor savour any of his things. Sometimes I would tell my Condition to the People of God, which, when they heard, they would pity me, and would tell me of the Promises. But they had as good have told me that I must reach the Sun with my finger as have bidden me receive or rely upon the Promise. [Yet] all this while as to the act of sinning, I never was more tender than now; I durst not take a pin or stick, though but so big as a straw, for my conscience now was sore, and would smart at every touch; I could not now tell how to speak my words, for fear I should misplace them. Oh, how gingerly did I then go in all I did or said! I found myself as on a miry Bog that shook if I did but stir; and was as there left both of God and Christ, and the Spirit, and all good things.

"But my original and inward pollution, that was my plague and my affliction. By reason of that, I was more loathsome in mine own Eyes than was a Toad; and I thought I was so in God's Eyes too. Sin and Corruption, I said, would as naturally bubble out of my Heart as Water would bubble out of a Fountain. I could have changed heart with anybody. I thought none but the Devil himself could equal me for inward wickedness and pollution of Mind. Sure, thought I, I am forsaken of God; and thus I continued a long while, even for some Years together.

"And now was I sorry that God had made me a man. The beasts, birds, fishes, etc., I blessed their condition, for they had not a sinful nature; they were not obnoxious to the wrath of God; they were not to go to Hell-fire after death. I could therefore have rejoiced, had my condition been as any of theirs. Now I blessed the condition of the Dog and Toad, yea, gladly would I have been in the condition of Dog or Horse, for I knew they had no soul to perish under the everlasting weight of Hell or Sin, as mine was like to do. Nay, and though I saw this, felt this, and was broken to pieces with it, yet that which added to my sorrow was, that I could not find that with all my Soul I did desire deliverance. My heart was, at times, exceeding hard. If I would have given a thousand Pound for a Tear, I could not shed one; no, nor sometimes scarce desire to shed one.

"I was both a burthen and a terror to myself; nor did I ever so know, as now, what it was to be weary of my life, and yet afraid to die. Oh, how gladly now would I have been anybody but myself! Anything but a man! and in any condition but mine own."[16]

Poor patient Bunyan, like Tolstoy, saw the light again, but we must also postpone that part of his story to another hour. In a later lecture I will also give the end of the experience of Henry Alline, a devoted evangelist who worked in Nova Scotia a hundred years ago, and who thus vividly describes the high-water mark of the religious melancholy which formed its beginning. The type was not unlike Bunyan's.

> "Every thing I saw seemed to be a burden to me; the earth seemed accursed for my sake: all trees, plants, rocks, hills and vales seemed to be drest in mourning, and groaning, under the weight of the curse, and every thing around me seemed to be conspiring my ruin. My sins seemed to be laid open; so that I thought that every one I saw knew them, and sometimes I was almost ready to acknowledge many things, which I thought they knew: yea sometimes it seemed to me as if every one was pointing me out as the most guilty wretch on earth. I had now so great a sense of the vanity and emptiness of all things here below, that I knew the whole world could not possibly make me happy, no, nor the whole system of creation. . . . When I waked in the morning, the first thought would be, O my wretched soul, what shall I do, where shall I go? and when I laid down, would say, I shall be perhaps in hell before morning. I would many times look on the beasts with envy, wishing with all my heart I was in their place, that I might have no soul to lose; and when I have seen birds flying over my head, have often thought within myself, O that I could fly away from my danger and distress! O how happy should I be, if I were in their place."[17]

Envy of the placid beasts seems to be a very widespread affection in this type of sadness.

The worst kind of melancholy is that which takes the form of panic fear. Here is an excellent example, for permission to print which I have to thank the sufferer. The original is in French, and though the subject was evidently in a bad nervous condition at the time of which he writes, his case has otherwise the merit of extreme simplicity. I translate freely.

> "Whilst in this state of philosophic pessimism and general depression of spirits about my prospects, I went one evening into a dressing-room in the twilight to procure some article that was there; when suddenly there fell upon me without any warning, just as if it came out of the darkness, a horrible fear of my own existence. Simultaneously there arose in my mind the image of an epileptic patient whom I had seen

in the asylum, a black-haired youth with greenish skin, entirely idiotic, who used to sit all day on one of the benches, or rather shelves against the wall, with his knees drawn up against his chin, and the coarse gray undershirt, which was his only garment, drawn over them inclosing his entire figure. He sat there like a sort of sculptured Egyptian cat or Peruvian mummy, moving nothing but his black eyes and looking absolutely non-human. This image and my fear entered into a species of combination with each other. *That shape am I*, I felt, potentially. Nothing that I possess can defend me against that fate, if the hour for it should strike for me as it struck for him. There was such a horror of him, and such a perception of my own merely momentary discrepancy from him, that it was as if something hitherto solid within my breast gave way entirely, and I became a mass of quivering fear. After this the universe was changed for me altogether. I awoke morning after morning with a horrible dread at the pit of my stomach, and with a sense of the insecurity of life that I never knew before, and that I have never felt since.[18] It was like a revelation; and although the immediate feelings passed away, the experience has made me sympathetic with the morbid feelings of others ever since. It gradually faded, but for months I was unable to go out into the dark alone.

"In general I dreaded to be left alone. I remember wondering how other people could live, how I myself had ever lived, so unconscious of that pit of insecurity beneath the surface of life. My mother in particular, a very cheerful person, seemed to me a perfect paradox in her unconsciousness of danger, which you may well believe I was very careful not to disturb by revelations of my own state of mind. I have always thought that this experience of melancholia of mine had a religious bearing."

On asking this correspondent to explain more fully what he meant by these last words, the answer he wrote was this:

"I mean that the fear was so invasive and powerful that if I had not clung to scripture-texts like 'The eternal God is my refuge,' etc., 'Come unto me, all ye that labor and are heavy-laden,' etc., 'I am the resurrection and the life,' etc., I think I should have grown really insane."[19]

There is no need of more examples. The cases we have looked at are enough. One of them gives us the vanity of mortal things; another the sense of sin; and the remaining one describes the fear of the universe;— and in one or other of these three ways it always is that man's original optimism and self-satisfaction get leveled with the dust.

In none of these cases was there any intellectual insanity or delusion about matters of fact; but were we disposed to open the chapter of really insane melancholia, with its hallucinations and delusions, it would be a worse story still—desperation absolute and complete, the whole universe coagulating about the sufferer into a material of overwhelming horror, surrounding him without opening or end. Not the conception or intellectual perception of evil, but the grisly blood-freezing heart-palsying sensation of it close upon one, and no other conception or sensation able to live for a moment in its presence. How irrelevantly remote seem all our usual refined optimisms and intellectual and moral consolations in presence of a need of help like this! Here is the real core of the religious problem: Help! help! No prophet can claim to bring a final message unless he says things that will have a sound of reality in the ears of victims such as these. But the deliverance must come in as strong a form as the complaint, if it is to take effect; and that seems a reason why the coarser religions, revivalistic, orgiastic, with blood and miracles and supernatural operations, may possibly never be displaced. Some constitutions need them too much.

Arrived at this point, we can see how great an antagonism may naturally arise between the healthy-minded way of viewing life and the way that takes all this experience of evil as something essential. To this latter way, the morbid-minded way, as we might call it, healthy-mindedness pure and simple seems unspeakably blind and shallow. To the healthy-minded way, on the other hand, the way of the sick soul seems unmanly and diseased. With their grubbing in rat-holes instead of living in the light; with their manufacture of fears, and preoccupation with every unwholesome kind of misery, there is something almost obscene about these children of wrath and cravers of a second birth. If religious intolerance and hanging and burning could again become the order of the day, there is little doubt that, however it may have been in the past, the healthy-minded would at present show themselves the less indulgent party of the two.

In our own attitude, not yet abandoned, of impartial onlookers, what are we to say of this quarrel? It seems to me that we are bound to say that morbid-mindedness ranges over the wider scale of experience, and that its survey is the one that overlaps. The method of averting one's attention from evil, and living simply in the light of good is splendid as long as it will work. It will work with many persons; it will work far more generally than most of us are ready to suppose; and within the sphere of its successful operation there is nothing to be said against it as a religious solution. But it breaks down impotently as soon as melancholy comes; and even though one be quite free from melancholy one's self, there is no doubt that healthy-mindedness is inadequate as a philosophical doctrine, because the evil facts which it refuses positively to account for are a genuine portion of reality; and they may after all be the best key to life's significance, and possibly the only openers of our eyes to the deepest levels of truth.

The normal process of life contains moments as bad as any of those which insane melancholy is filled with, moments in which radical evil gets its innings and takes its solid turn. The lunatic's visions of horror are all drawn from the material of daily fact. Our civilization is founded on the shambles, and every individual existence goes out in a lonely spasm of helpless agony. If you protest, my friend, wait till you arrive there yourself! To believe in the carnivorous reptiles of geologic times is hard for our imagination—they seem too much like mere museum specimens. Yet there is no tooth in any one of those museum-skulls that did not daily through long years of the foretime hold fast to the body struggling in despair of some fated living victim. Forms of horror just as dreadful to their victims, if on a smaller spatial scale, fill the world about us to-day. Here on our very hearths and in our gardens the infernal cat plays with the panting mouse, or holds the hot bird fluttering in her jaws. Crocodiles and rattlesnakes and pythons are at this moment vessels of life as real as we are; their loathsome existence fills every minute of every day that drags its length along; and whenever they or other wild beasts clutch their living prey, the deadly horror which an agitated melancholiac feels is the literally right reaction on the situation.[20]

It may indeed be that no religious reconciliation with the absolute totality of things is possible. Some evils, indeed, are ministerial to higher forms of good; but it may be that there are forms of evil so extreme as to enter into no good system whatsoever, and that, in respect of such evil, dumb submission or neglect to notice is the only practical resource. This question must confront us on a later day. But provisionally, and as a mere matter of program and method, since the evil facts are as genuine parts of nature as the good ones, the philosophic presumption should be that they have some rational significance, and that systematic healthy-mindedness, failing as it does to accord to sorrow, pain, and death any positive and active attention whatever, is formally less complete than systems that try at least to include these elements in their scope.

The completest religions would therefore seem to be those in which the pessimistic elements are best developed. Buddhism, of course, and Christianity are the best known to us of these. They are essentially religions of deliverance: the man must die to an unreal life before he can be born into the real life. In my next lecture, I will try to discuss some of the psychological conditions of this second birth. Fortunately from now onward we shall have to deal with more cheerful subjects than those which we have recently been dwelling on.

13

The Ph.D. Octopus

"The Ph.D. Octopus" is for anyone who has ever wondered whether the machinery of degrees and requirements originally invented to facilitate learning has come instead to replace real knowledge with meaningless little piles of credit hours.

German-style graduate education—the seminar, the departmental library, the specialized journal, and the scholarly monograph—did not come to the United States until the last two decades of the nineteenth century. As late as 1869–1870 there was a grand total of seven resident graduate students in the whole Ivy League. Of course, the Ph.D. system quickly took hold, and American graduate education rapidly became second to none, but there were doubters, and William James, who had no Ph.D., was one. He wrote "The Ph.D. Octopus" because one of his graduate students, Alfred Hodder, was initially turned down for a teaching position at Bryn Mawr because he did not have his Ph.D. diploma in hand at the time. James was irked and characteristically said what he thought. The result was a perennially valuable warning not to mistake schooling for education, not to let the requirements of a degree program take precedence over actual learning. The then-president of Bryn Mawr disputed James's version of the facts in the case. But most of what James had to say about the "three magical letters" still makes uncomfortable reading for many, including some who have those little letters and not a lot else.

⟨⟩◆⟨⟩

SOME YEARS ago we had at our Harvard Graduate School a very brilliant student of Philosophy, who, after leaving us and supporting himself by literary labor for three years, received an appointment to teach English Literature at a sister-institution of learning. The governors of this institution, however, had no sooner communicated the appointment than they made the awful discovery that they had enrolled upon their staff a person who was unprovided with the Ph.D. degree. The man in question had been satisfied to work at Philosophy for her own sweet (or bitter) sake, and had disdained to consider that an academic bauble should be his reward.

His appointment had thus been made under a misunderstanding. He was not the proper man; and there was nothing to do but to inform him of the fact. It was notified to him by his new President that his appointment must be revoked, or that a Harvard doctor's degree must forthwith be procured.

Although it was already the Spring of the year, our Subject, being a man of spirit, took up the challenge, turned his back upon literature (which in view of his approaching duties might have seemed his more urgent concern) and spent the weeks that were left him, in writing a metaphysical thesis and grinding his psychology, logic and history of philosophy up again, so as to pass our formidable ordeals.

When the thesis came to be read by our committee, we could not pass it. Brilliancy and originality by themselves won't save a thesis for the doctorate; it must also exhibit a heavy technical apparatus of learning; and this our candidate had neglected to bring to bear. So, telling him that he was temporarily rejected, we advised him to pad out the thesis properly, and return with it next year, at the same time informing his new President that this signified nothing as to his merits, that he was of ultra Ph.D. quality, and one of the strongest men with whom we had ever had to deal.

To our surprise we were given to understand in reply that the quality *per se* of the man signified nothing in this connection, and that three magical letters were the thing seriously required. The College had always gloried in a list of faculty members who bore the doctor's title, and to make a gap in the galaxy, and admit a common fox without a tail, would be a degradation impossible to be thought of. We wrote again, pointing out that a Ph.D. in philosophy would prove little anyhow as to one's ability to teach literature; we sent separate letters in which we outdid each other in eulogy of our candidate's powers, for indeed they were great; and at last, *mirabile dictu,* our eloquence prevailed. He was allowed to retain his appointment provisionally, on condition that one year later at the farthest his miserably naked name should be prolonged by the sacred appendage the lack of which had given so much trouble to all concerned.

Accordingly he came up here the following spring with an adequate thesis (known since in print as a most brilliant contribution to metaphysics), passed a first-rate examination, wiped out the stain, and brought his college into proper relations with the world again. Whether his teaching, during that first year, of English Literature was made any the better by the impending examination in a different subject, is a question which I will not try to solve.

I have related this incident at such length because it is so characteristic of American academic conditions at the present day. Graduate schools still are something of a novelty, and higher diplomas something of a rarity. The latter, therefore, carry a vague sense of preciousness and honor, and have a particularly "up-to-date" appearance, and it is no wonder if smaller institutions, unable to attract professors already eminent, and forced usually to recruit their faculties from the relatively young, should hope to compensate for the obscurity of the names of their officers of instruction by the abundance of decorative titles by which those names are followed on the pages of the catalogues where they appear. The dazzled reader of the list, the parent or student, says to himself, "this must be a terribly distinguished crowd—their titles shine like the stars in the firmament, Ph.D.'s, S.D.'s, and Litt.D.'s, bespangle the page as if they were sprinkled over it from a pepper caster."

Human nature is once for all so childish that every reality becomes a sham somewhere, and in the minds of Presidents and Trustees the Ph.D. degree is in point of fact already looked upon as a mere advertising resource, a manner of throwing dust in the Public's eyes. "No instructor who is not a Doctor" has become a maxim in the smaller institutions which represent demand; and in each of the larger ones which represent supply, the same belief in decorated scholarship expresses itself in two antagonistic passions, one for multiplying as much as possible the annual output of doctors, the other for raising the standard of difficulty in passing, so that the Ph.D. of the special institution shall carry a higher blaze of distinction than it does elsewhere. Thus we at Harvard are proud of the number of candidates whom we reject, and of the inability of men who are not *distingués* in intellect to pass our tests.

America is thus as a nation rapidly drifting towards a state of things in which no man of science or letters will be accounted respectable unless some kind of badge or diploma is stamped upon him, and in which bare personality will be a mark of outcast estate. It seems to me high time to rouse ourselves to consciousness, and to cast a critical eye upon this decidedly grotesque tendency. Other nations suffer terribly from the Mandarin disease. Are we doomed to suffer like the rest?

Our higher degrees were instituted for the laudable purpose of stimulating scholarship, especially in the form of "original research." Experience has proved that great as the love of truth may be among men, it can be made still greater by adventitious rewards. The winning of a diploma certifying mastery and marking a barrier successfully passed, acts as a challenge to the ambitious; and if the diploma will help to gain bread-winning positions also, its power as a stimulus to work is tremendously increased. So far, we are on innocent ground; it is well for a country to have research in abundance, and our graduate schools do but apply a normal psychological spur. But the institutionizing on a large scale of any natural combination of need and motive always tends to run into technicality and to develop a tyrannical Machine with unforeseen powers of exclusion and corruption. Observation of the workings of our Harvard system for 20 years past has brought some of these drawbacks home to my consciousness, and I should like to call the attention of the readers of the MONTHLY to this disadvantageous aspect of the picture, and to make a couple of remedial suggestions, if I may.

In the first place, it would seem that to stimulate study, and to increase the *gelehrtes Publikum,* the class of highly educated men in our country, is the only positive good, and consequently the sole direct end at which our graduate schools, with their diploma-giving powers, should aim. If other results have developed they should be deemed sec-

ondary incidents, and if not desirable in themselves, they should be
carefully guarded against.

To interfere with the free development of talent, to obstruct the natural play of supply and demand in the teaching profession, to foster academic snobbery by the *prestige* of certain privileged institutions, to trans-
fer accredited value from essential manhood to an outward badge, to
blight hopes and promote invidious sentiments, to divert the attention
of aspiring youth from direct dealings with truth to the passing of examinations,—such consequences, if they exist, ought surely to be regarded
as drawbacks to the system, and an enlightened public consciousness
ought to be keenly alive to the importance of reducing their amount.
Candidates themselves do seem to be keenly conscious of some of these
evils, but outside of their ranks or in the general public no such consciousness, so far as I can see, exists; or if it does exist, it fails to express
itself aloud. Schools, Colleges, and Universities, appear enthusiastic over
the entire system, just as it stands, and unanimously applaud all its de-
velopments.

I beg the reader to consider some of the secondary evils which I
have enumerated. First of all, is not our growing tendency to appoint no
instructors who are not also doctors an instance of pure sham? Will any
one pretend for a moment that the doctor's degree is a guarantee that its
possessor will be successful as a teacher? Notoriously his moral, social
and personal characteristics may utterly disqualify him for success in the
class-room; and of these characteristics his doctor's examination is unable to take any account whatever. Certain bare human beings will always be better candidates for a given place than all the doctor-applicants
on hand; and to exclude the former by a rigid rule, and in the end to
have to sift the latter by private inquiry into their personal peculiarities
among those who know them, just as if they were not doctors at all, is
to stultify one's own procedure. You may say that at least you guard
against ignorance of the subject by considering only the candidates who
are doctors; but how then about making doctors in one subject teach a
different subject? This happened in the instance by which I introduced
this article, and it happens daily and hourly in all our colleges! The truth
is that the Doctor-Monopoly in teaching, which is becoming so rooted
an American custom, can show no serious grounds whatsoever for itself
in reason. As it actually prevails and grows in vogue among us, it is due

to childish motives exclusively. In reality it is but a sham, a bauble, a dodge whereby to decorate the catalogues of schools and colleges.

Next, let us turn from the general promotion of a spirit of academic snobbery to the particular damage done to individuals by the system.

There are plenty of individuals so well endowed by nature that they pass with ease all the ordeals with which life confronts them. Such persons are born for professional success. Examinations have no terrors for them, and interfere in no way with their spiritual or worldly interests. There are others, not so gifted, who nevertheless rise to the challenge, get a stimulus from the difficulty, and become doctors, not without some baleful nervous wear and tear and retardation of their purely inner life, but on the whole successfully, and with advantage. These two classes form the natural Ph.D.'s, for whom the degree is legitimately instituted. To be sure, the degree is of no consequence one way or the other for the first sort of man, for in him the personal worth obviously outshines the title. To the second set of persons, however, the doctor-ideal may contribute a touch of energy and solidity of scholarship which otherwise they might have lacked, and were our candidates all drawn from these classes, no oppression would result from the institution.

But there is a third class of persons who are genuinely, and in the most pathetic sense, the institution's victims. For this type of character the academic life may become, after a certain point, a virulent poison. Men without marked originality or native force, but fond of truth and especially of books and study, ambitious of reward and recognition, poor often, and needing a degree to get a teaching position, weak in the eyes of their examiners,—among these we find the veritable *chair à canon* of the wars of learning, the unfit in the academic struggle for existence. There are individuals of this sort for whom to pass one degree after another seems the limit of earthly aspiration. Your private advice does not discourage them. They will fail, and go away to recuperate, and then present themselves for another ordeal, and sometimes prolong the process into middle life. Or else, if they are less heroic morally they will accept the failure as a sentence of doom that they are not fit, and are broken-spirited men thereafter.

We of the University faculties are responsible for deliberately creating this new class of American social failures, and heavy is the responsibility. We advertise our "schools" and send out our degree-requirements, knowing well that aspirants of all sorts will be attracted, and at the same time we set a standard which intends to pass no man who has not native intellectual distinction. We know that there is no test, however absurd, by which, if a title or decoration, a public badge or mark, were to be won by it, some weakly suggestible or hauntable persons would not feel challenged, and remain unhappy if they went without it. We dangle our three magic letters before the eyes of these predestined victims, and they swarm to us like moths to an electric light. They come at a time of life when failure can no longer be repaired easily and when the wounds it leaves are permanent; and we say deliberately that mere work faithfully performed, as they perform it, will not by itself save them, they must in addition put in evidence the one thing they have not got, namely this quality of intellectual distinction. Occasionally, out of sheer human pity, we ignore our high and mighty standard and pass them. Usually, however, the standard, and not the candidate, commands our fidelity. The result is caprice, majorities of one on the jury, and on the whole a confession that our pretensions about the degree cannot be lived up to consistently. Thus, partiality in the favored cases; in the unfavored, blood on our hands; and in both a bad conscience,—are the results of our administration.

The more widespread becomes the popular belief that our diplomas are indispensable hall-marks to show the sterling metal of their holders, the more widespread these corruptions will become. We ought to look to the future carefully, for it takes generations for a national custom, once rooted, to be grown away from. All the European countries are seeking to diminish the check upon individual spontaneity which state examinations with their tyrannous growth have brought in their train. We have had to institute state examinations too; and it will perhaps be fortunate if some day hereafter our descendants, comparing machine with machine, do not sigh with regret for old times and American freedom, and wish that the régime of the dear old bosses might be reinstalled, with plain human nature, the glad hand and the marble heart, liking and disliking, and man-to-man relations grown possible again. Meanwhile, whatever evolution our state-examinations are destined to undergo, our universities at least should never cease to regard themselves as the jealous custodians of personal and spiritual spontaneity. They are indeed its only organized and recognized custodians in America today. They ought to guard against contributing to the increase of officialism and snobbery and insincerity as against a pestilence; they ought to keep truth and disinterested labor always in the foreground, treat degrees as secondary incidents, and in season and out of season make it plain that what they live for is to help men's souls, and not to decorate their persons with diplomas.

There seem to be three obvious ways in which the increasing hold of the Ph.D. Octopus upon American life can be kept in check.

The first way lies with the Universities. They can lower their fantastic standards (which here at Harvard we are so proud of) and give the doctorate as a matter of course, just as they give the bachelor's degree, for a due amount of time spent in patient labor in a special department of learning, whether the man be a brilliantly gifted individual or not. Surely native distinction needs no official stamp, and should disdain to ask for one. On the other hand, faithful labor, however commonplace, and years devoted to a subject, always deserve to be acknowledged and requited.

The second way lies with both the Universities and Colleges. Let them give up their unspeakably silly ambition to bespangle their lists of officers with these doctorial titles. Let them look more to substance and less to vanity and sham.

The third way lies with the individual student, and with his personal advisers in the Faculties. Every man of native power, who might take a higher degree, and refuses to do so, because examinations interfere with the free following out of his more immediate intellectual aims, deserves well of his country, and in a rightly organized community, would not be made to suffer for his independence. With many men the passing of these extraneous tests is a very grievous interference indeed. Private letters of recommendation from their instructors, which in any event are ultimately needful, ought, in these cases, completely to offset the lack of the bread-winning degree; and instructors ought to be ready to advise students against it upon occasion, and to pledge themselves to back them later personally, in the market-struggle which they have to face.

It is indeed odd to see this love of titles—and such titles—growing up in a country of which the recognition of individuality and bare manhood have so long been supposed to be the very soul. The independence of the State, in which most of our colleges stand, relieves us of those more odious forms of academic politics which continental European countries present. Anything like the elaborate University machine of France, with its throttling influences upon individuals is unknown here. The spectacle of the "Rath" distinction in its innumerable spheres and grades, with which all Germany is crawling today, is displeasing to American eyes; and displeasing also in some respects is the institution of knighthood in England, which, aping as it does an aristocratic title, enables one's wife as well as one's self so easily to dazzle the servants at the house of one's friends. But are we Americans ourselves destined after all to hunger after similar vanities on an infinitely more contemptible scale? And is individuality with us also going to count for nothing unless stamped and licensed and authenticated by some title-giving machine? Let us pray that our ancient national genius may long preserve vitality enough to guard us from a future so unmanly and so unbeautiful!

14

Does 'Consciousness' Exist?

If Freud is the great psychologist of the unconscious, William James is the great psychologist of the conscious and of consciousness. One of his mentors, the philosopher Chauncey Wright, had published in 1871 a defense of Darwin that was so well done that Darwin himself had it reprinted and circulated in England. Darwin then invited Wright to "turn his analytic powers to work on the problem of determining, in connection with the idea of evolution, when a thing can properly be said to be effected by the will of man" (*The Life and Letters of Charles Darwin*, vol. 2). Wright's work on this question was published in 1873 as "The Evolution of Self-Consciousness." James inherited Wright's interest in the problem. If we ask what evolutionary advantage consciousness has for its possessors, James's answer, as he put it in "Are We Automata?," is that consciousness gives us the ability "always to choose out of the manifold experiences present to it at a given time some one for particular accentuation, and to ignore the rest." The evolutionary value of consciousness is that it gives its possessor a way to direct and control his attention and make it selective. Since attention is of central importance for James, so is consciousness. The piece reprinted here may seem to be knocking at an open door in its insistence that consciousness is not a thing or a place, but a process. Of course, we now say. But the implications of this are astonishing. When David Hume looked for his aboriginal central self, he found nothing more than a procession as across a stage of perceptions, memories, ideas, and feelings. What if that procession is all there is? James takes the argument a step further. Just as our feeling of selfhood is one of our strongest feelings, though we cannot point to one inner compartment where the sense of self resides, so the conscious thinker, which most of us think of ourselves as, may be no more than the previous thought, James says. It may be that we can get no further than this, he had written in *The Principles of Psychology.* "Thought is itself the thinker."

⟫·◆·⟪

'THOUGHTS' and 'things' are names for two sorts of object, which common sense will always find contrasted and will always practically oppose to each other. Philosophy, reflecting on the contrast, has varied in the past in her explanations of it, and may be expected to vary in the future. At first, 'spirit and matter,' 'soul and body,' stood for a pair of equipollent substances quite on a par in weight and interest. But one day Kant undermined the soul and brought in the transcendental ego, and ever since then the bipolar relation has been very much off its balance. The transcendental ego seems nowadays in rationalist quarters to stand for everything, in empiricist quarters for almost nothing. In the hands of such writers as Schuppe, Rehmke, Natorp, Münsterberg—at any rate in his earlier writings—Schubert-Soldern and others, the spiritual principle attenuates itself to a thoroughly ghostly condition, being only a name for the fact that the 'content' of experience *is known.* It loses personal form and activity—these passing over to the content—and becomes a bare *Bewusstheit* or *Bewusstsein überhaupt,* of which in its own right absolutely nothing can be said.

I believe that 'consciousness,' when once it has evaporated to this estate of pure diaphaneity, is on the point of disappearing altogether. It is the name of a nonentity, and has no right to a place among first principles. Those who still cling to it are clinging to a mere echo, the faint rumor left behind by the disappearing 'soul' upon the air of philosophy. During the past year, I have read a number of articles whose authors seemed just on the point of abandoning the notion of consciousness,[1] and substituting for it that of an absolute experience not due to two factors. But they were not quite radical enough, not quite daring enough in their negations. For twenty years past I have mistrusted 'consciousness' as an entity; for seven or eight years past I have suggested its nonexistence to my students, and tried to give them its pragmatic equivalent in realities of experience. It seems to me that the hour is ripe for it to be openly and universally discarded.

To deny plumply that ' consciousness' exists seems so absurd on the face of it—for undeniably 'thoughts' do exist—that I fear some readers will follow me no farther. Let me then immediately explain that I mean only to deny that the word stands for an entity, but to insist most emphatically that it does stand for a function. There is, I mean, no aboriginal stuff or quality of being, contrasted with that of which material objects are made, out of which our thoughts of them are made; but there is a function in experience which thoughts perform, and for the performance of which this quality of being is invoked. That function is *knowing.* 'Consciousness' is supposed necessary to explain the fact that things not only are, but get reported, are known. Whoever blots out the notion of consciousness from his list of first principles must still provide in some way for that function's being carried on.

I

My thesis is that if we start with the supposition that there is only one primal stuff or material in the world, a stuff of which everything is composed, and if we call that stuff 'pure experience,' then knowing can easily be explained as a particular sort of relation towards one another into which portions of pure experience may enter. The relation itself is a part of pure experience; one of its 'terms' becomes the subject or bearer of the knowledge, the knower,[2] the other becomes the object known. This will need much explanation before it can be understood. The best way to get it understood is to contrast it with the alternative view; and for that we may take the recentest alternative, that in which the evaporation of the definite soul-substance has proceeded as far as it can go without being yet complete. If neo-Kantism has expelled earlier forms of dualism, we shall have expelled all forms if we are able to expel neo-Kantism in its turn.

For the thinkers I call neo-Kantian, the word consciousness to-day does no more than signalize the fact that experience is indefeasibly dualistic in structure. It means that not subject, not object, but object-plus-subject is the minimum that can actually be. The subject-object distinction meanwhile is entirely different from that between mind and matter, from that between body and soul. Souls were detachable, had separate destinies; things could happen to them. To consciousness as such nothing can happen, for, timeless itself, it is only a witness of happenings in time, in which it plays no part. It is, in a word, but the logical correlative of 'content' in an Experience of which the peculiarity is that *fact comes to light* in it, that *awareness of content* takes place. Consciousness as such is entirely impersonal—'self' and its activities belong to the content. To say that I am self-conscious, or conscious of putting forth volition, means only that certain contents, for which 'self' and 'effort of will' are the names, are not without witness as they occur.

Thus, for these belated drinkers at the Kantian spring, we should have to admit consciousness as an 'epistemological' necessity, even if we had no direct evidence of its being there.

But in addition to this, we are supposed by almost every one to have an immediate consciousness of consciousness itself. When the world of outer fact ceases to be materially present, and we merely recall it in memory, or fancy it, the consciousness is believed to stand out and to be felt as a kind of impalpable inner flowing, which, once known in this sort of experience, may equally be detected in presentations of the outer world. "The moment we try to fix our attention upon consciousness and to see *what*, distinctly, it is," says a recent writer, "it seems to vanish: it seems as if we had before us a mere emptiness. When we try to introspect the sensation of blue, all we can see is the blue: the other element is as if it were diaphanous. Yet it *can* be distinguished if we look attentively enough, and if we know that there is something to look for."[3] "Consciousness" (Bewusstheit), says another philosopher, "is inexplicable and hardly describable, yet all conscious experiences have this in common that what we call their content has this peculiar reference to a center for which 'self' is the name, in virtue of which reference alone the content is subjectively given, or appears. . . . While in this way consciousness, or reference to a self, is the only thing which distinguishes a conscious content from any sort of being that might be there with no one conscious of it, yet this only ground of the distinction defies all closer explanations. The existence of consciousness, although it is the fundamental fact of psychology, can indeed be laid down as certain, can be brought out by analysis, but can neither be defined nor deduced from anything but itself."[4]

"Can be brought out by analysis," this author says. This supposes that the consciousness is one element, moment, factor—call it what you like—of an experience of essentially dualistic inner constitution, from which, if you abstract the content, the consciousness will remain revealed to its own eye. Experience, at this rate, would be much like a paint of which the world pictures were made. Paint has a dual constitution, involving, as it does, a menstruum[5] (oil, size or what not) and a mass of content in the form of pigment suspended therein. We can get the pure menstruum by letting the pigment settle, and the pure pigment by pouring off the size or oil. We operate here by physical subtraction; and the usual view is, that by mental subtraction we can separate the two factors of experience in an analogous way—not isolating them entirely, but distinguishing them enough to know that they are two.

II

Now my contention is exactly the reverse of this. *Experience, I believe, has no such inner duplicity; and the separation of it into consciousness and content comes, not by way of subtraction, but by way of addition*—the addition, to a given concrete piece of it, of other sets of experiences, in connection with which severally its use or function may be of two different kinds. The paint will also serve here as an illustration. In a pot in a paint-shop, along with other paints, it serves in its entirety as so much saleable matter. Spread on a canvas, with other paints around it, it represents, on the contrary, a feature in a picture and performs a spiritual function. Just so, I maintain, does a given undivided portion of experience, taken in one context of associates, play the part of a knower, of a state of mind, of 'consciousness'; while in a different context the same undivided bit of experience plays the part of a thing known, of an objective 'content.' In a word, in one group it figures as a thought, in another group as a thing. And, since it can figure in both groups simultaneously we have every right to speak of it as subjective and objective both at once. The dualism connoted by such double-barrelled terms as 'experience,' 'phenomenon,' 'datum,' '*Vorfindung*'—terms which, in philosophy at any rate, tend more and more to replace the single-barrelled terms of 'thought' and 'thing'—that dualism, I say, is still preserved in this account, but reinterpreted, so that, instead of being mysterious and elusive, it becomes verifiable and concrete. It is an affair of relations, it falls outside, not inside, the single experience considered, and can always be particularized and defined.

The entering wedge for this more concrete way of understanding the dualism was fashioned by Locke when he made the word 'idea' stand indifferently for thing and thought, and by Berkeley when he said that what common sense means by realities is exactly what the philosopher means by ideas. Neither Locke nor Berkeley thought his truth out into perfect clearness, but it seems to me that the conception I am defending does little more than consistently carry out the 'pragmatic' method which they were the first to use.

If the reader will take his own experiences, he will see what I mean. Let him begin with a perceptual experience, the 'presentation,' so called, of a physical object, his actual field of vision, the room he sits in, with the book he is reading as its center; and let him for the present treat this complex object in the common-sense way as being 'really' what it seems to be, namely, a collection of physical things cut out from an environing world of other physical things with which these physical things have actual or potential relations. Now at the same time it is just *those self-same things* which his mind, as we say, perceives; and the whole philosophy of perception from Democritus's time downwards has been just one long wrangle over the paradox that what is evidently one reality should be in two places at once, both in outer space and in a person's mind. 'Representative' theories of perception avoid the logical paradox, but on the other hand they violate the reader's sense of life, which knows no intervening mental image but seems to see the room and the book immediately just as they physically exist.

The puzzle of how the one identical room can be in two places is at bottom just the puzzle of how one identical point can be on two lines. It can, if it be situated at their intersection; and similarly, if the 'pure experience' of the room were a place of intersection of two processes, which connected it with different groups of associates respectively, it could be counted twice over, as belonging to either group, and spoken of loosely as existing in two places, although it would remain all the time a numerically single thing.

Well, the experience is a member of diverse processes that can be followed away from it along entirely different lines. The one self-identical thing has so many relations to the rest of experience that you can take it in disparate systems of association, and treat it as belonging with opposite contexts. In one of these contexts it is your 'field of consciousness'; in another it is 'the room in which you sit,' and it enters both contexts in its wholeness, giving no pretext for being said to attach itself to consciousness by one of its parts or aspects, and to outer reality by another. What are the two processes, now, into which the room-experience simultaneously enters in this way?

One of them is the reader's personal biography, the other is the history of the house of which the room is part. The presentation, the experience, the *that* in short (for until we have decided *what* it is it must be a mere *that*) is the last term of a train of sensations, emotions, decisions, movements, classifications, expectations, etc., ending in the present, and the first term of a series of similar 'inner' operations extending into the future, on the reader's part. On the other hand, the very same *that* is the *terminus ad quem* of a lot of previous physical operations, carpentering, papering, furnishing, warming, etc., and the *terminus a quo* of a lot of future ones, in which it will be concerned when undergoing the destiny of a physical room. The physical and the mental operations form curiously incompatible groups. As a room, the experience has occupied that spot and had that environment for thirty years. As your field of consciousness it may never have existed until now. As a room, attention will go on to discover endless new details in it. As your mental state merely, few new ones will emerge under attention's eye. As a room, it will take an earthquake, or a gang of men, and in any case a certain amount of time, to destroy it. As your subjective state, the closing of your eyes, or any instantaneous play of your fancy will suffice. In the real world, fire will consume it. In your mind, you can let fire play over it without effect. As an outer object, you must pay so much a month to inhabit it. As an inner content, you may occupy it for any length of time rent-free. If, in short, you follow it in the mental direction, taking it along with events of personal biography solely, all sorts of things are true of it which are false, and false of it which are true if you treat it as a real thing experienced, follow it in the physical direction, and relate it to associates in the outer world.

III

So far, all seems plain sailing, but my thesis will probably grow less plausible to the reader when I pass from percepts to concepts, or from the case of things presented to that of things remote. I believe, nevertheless, that here also the same law holds good. If we take conceptual manifolds, or memories, or fancies, they also are in their first intention mere bits of pure experience, and, as such, are single *thats* which act in one context as objects, and in another context figure as mental states. By taking them in their first intention, I mean ignoring their relation to possible perceptual experiences with which they may be connected, which they may lead to and terminate in, and which then they may be supposed to 'represent.' Taking them in this way first, we confine the problem to a world merely 'thought-of' and not directly felt or seen. This world, just like the world of percepts, comes to us at first as a chaos of experiences, but lines of order soon get traced. We find that any bit of it which we may cut out as an example is connected with distinct groups of associates, just as our perceptual experiences are, that these associates link themselves with it by different relations,[6] and that one forms the inner history of a person, while the other acts as an impersonal 'objective' world, either spatial and temporal, or else merely logical or mathematical, or otherwise 'ideal.'

The first obstacle on the part of the reader to seeing that these non-perceptual experiences have objectivity as well as subjectivity will probably be due to the intrusion into his mind of *percepts,* that third group of associates with which the non-perceptual experiences have relations, and which, as a whole, they 'represent,' standing to them as thoughts to things. This important function of the non-perceptual experiences complicates the question and confuses it; for, so used are we to treat percepts as the sole genuine realities that, unless we keep them out of the discussion, we tend altogether to overlook the objectivity that lies in non-perceptual experiences by themselves. We treat them, 'knowing' percepts as they do, as through-and-through subjective, and say that they are wholly constituted of the stuff called consciousness, using this term now for a kind of entity, after the fashion which I am seeking to refute.[7]

Abstracting, then, from percepts altogether, what I maintain is, that any single non-perceptual experience tends to get counted twice over, just as a perceptual experience does, figuring in one context as an object or field of objects, in another as a state of mind: and all this without the least internal self-diremption on its own part into consciousness and content. It is all consciousness in one taking; and, in the other, all content.

I find this objectivity of non-perceptual experiences, this complete parallelism in point of reality between the presently felt and the remotely thought, so well set forth in a page of Münsterberg's *Grundzüge,* that I will quote it as it stands.

"I may only think of my objects," says Professor Münsterberg; "yet, in my living thought they stand before me exactly as perceived objects would do, no matter how different the two ways of apprehending them may be in their genesis. The book here lying on the table before me, and the book in the next room of which I think and which I mean to get, are both in the same sense given realities for me, realities which I acknowledge and of which I take account. If you agree that the perceptual object is not an idea within me, but that percept and thing, as indistinguishably one, are really experienced *there, outside,* you ought not to believe that the merely thought-of object is hid away inside of the thinking subject. The object of which I think, and of whose existence I take cognizance without letting it now work upon my senses, occupies its definite place in the outer world as much as does the object which I directly see.

"What is true of the here and the there, is also true of the now and the then. I know of the thing which is present and perceived, but I know also of the thing which yesterday was but is no more, and which I only remember. Both can determine my present conduct, both are parts of the reality of which I keep account. It is true that of much of the past I am uncertain, just as I am uncertain of much of what is present if it be but dimly perceived. But the interval of time does not in principle alter my relation to the object, does not transform it from an object known into a mental state. . . . The things in the room here which I survey, and those in my distant home of which I think, the things of this minute and those of my long-vanished boyhood, influence and decide me alike, with a reality which my experience of them directly feels. They both make up my real world, they make it directly, they do not have first to be introduced to me and mediated by ideas which now and here arise within me. . . . This not-me character of my recollections and expectations does not imply that the external objects of which I am aware in those experiences should necessarily be there also for others. The objects of dreamers and hallucinated persons are wholly without general validity. But even were they centaurs and golden mountains, they still would be 'off there,' in fairy land, and not 'inside' of ourselves."[8]

This certainly is the immediate, primary, naïf, or practical way of taking our thought-of world. Were there no perceptual world to serve as its 'reductive,' in Taine's sense, by being 'stronger' and more genuinely 'outer' (so that the whole merely thought-of world seems weak and inner in comparison), our world of thought would be the only world, and would enjoy complete reality in our belief. This actually happens in our dreams, and in our day-dreams so long as percepts do not interrupt them.

And yet, just as the seen room (to go back to our late example) is *also* a field of consciousness, so the conceived or recollected room is *also* a state of mind; and the doubling-up of the experience has in both cases similar grounds.

The room thought-of, namely, has many thought-of couplings with many thought-of things. Some of these couplings are inconstant, others are stable. In the reader's personal history the room occupies a single date—he saw it only once perhaps, a year ago. Of the house's history, on the other hand, it forms a permanent ingredient. Some couplings have the curious stubbornness, to borrow Royce's term, of fact; others show the fluidity of fancy—we let them come and go as we please. Grouped with the rest of its house, with the name of its town, of its owner, builder, value, decorative plan, the room maintains a definite foothold, to which, if we try to loosen it, it tends to return, and to reassert itself with force.[9] With these associates, in a word, it coheres, while to other houses, other towns, other owners, etc., it shows no tendency to cohere at all. The two collections, first of its cohesive, and, second, of its loose associates, inevitably come to be contrasted. We call the first collection the system of external realities, in the midst of which the room, as 'real,' exists; the other we call the stream of our internal thinking, in which, as a 'mental image,' it for a moment floats.[10] The room thus again gets counted twice over. It plays two different rôles, being *Gedanke* and *Gedachtes,* the thought-of-an-object, and the object-thought-of, both in one; and all this without paradox or mystery, just as the same material thing may be both low and high, or small and great, or bad and good, because of its relations to opposite parts of an environing world.

As 'subjective' we say that the experience represents; as 'objective' it is represented. What represents and what is represented is here numerically the same; but we must remember that no dualism of being represented and representing resides in the experience *per se*. In its pure state, or when isolated, there is no self-splitting of it into consciousness and what the consciousness is 'of.' Its subjectivity and objectivity are functional attributes solely, realized only when the experience is 'taken,' *i.e.*, talked-of, twice, considered along with its two differing contexts respectively, by a new retrospective experience, of which that whole past complication now forms the fresh content.

The instant field of the present is at all times what I call the 'pure' experience. It is only virtually or potentially either object or subject as yet. For the time being, it is plain, unqualified actuality or existence, a simple *that*. In this *naïf* immediacy it is of course *valid*; it is *there*, we *act* upon it; and the doubling of it in retrospection into a state of mind and a reality intended thereby, is just one of the acts. The 'state of mind,' first treated explicitly as such in retrospection, will stand corrected or confirmed, and the retrospective experience in its turn will get a similar treatment; but the immediate experience in its passing is always 'truth,'[11] practical truth, *something to act on*, at its own movement. If the world were then and there to go out like a candle, it would remain truth absolute and objective, for it would be 'the last word,' would have no critic, and no one would ever oppose the thought in it to the reality intended.[12]

I think I may now claim to have made my thesis clear. Consciousness connotes a kind of external relation, and does not denote a special stuff or way of being. *The peculiarity of our experiences, that they not only are, but are known, which their 'conscious' quality is invoked to explain, is better explained by their relations—these relations themselves being experiences—to one another.*

IV

Were I now to go on to treat of the knowing of perceptual by conceptual experiences, it would again prove to be an affair of external relations. One experience would be the knower, the other the reality known; and I could perfectly well define, without the notion of 'consciousness,' what the knowing actually and practically amounts to—leading-towards, namely, and terminating-in percepts, through a series of transitional experiences which the world supplies. But I will not treat of this, space being insufficient.[13] I will rather consider a few objections that are sure to be urged against the entire theory as it stands.

V

First of all, this will be asked: "If experience has not 'conscious' existence, if it be not partly made of 'consciousness,' of what then is it made? Matter we know, and thought we know, and conscious content we know, but neutral and simple 'pure experience' is something we know not at all. Say *what* it consists of—for it must consist of something—or be willing to give it up!"

To this challenge the reply is easy. Although for fluency's sake I myself spoke early in this article of a stuff of pure experience, I have now to say that there is no *general* stuff of which experience at large is made. There are as many stuffs as there are 'natures' in the things experienced. If you ask what any one bit of pure experience is made of, the answer is always the same: "It is made of *that*, of just what appears, of space, of intensity, of flatness, brownness, heaviness, or what not." Shadworth Hodgson's analysis here leaves nothing to be desired. Experience is only a collective name for all these sensible natures, and save for time and space (and, if you like, for 'being') there appears no universal element of which all things are made.

VI

The next objection is more formidable, in fact it sounds quite crushing when one hears it first.

"If it be the self-same piece of pure experience, taken twice over, that serves now as thought and now as thing"—so the objection runs— "how comes it that its attributes should differ so fundamentally in the two takings. As thing, the experience is extended; as thought, it occupies no space or place. As thing, it is red, hard, heavy; but who ever heard of a red, hard or heavy thought? Yet even now you said that an experience is made of just what appears, and what appears is just such adjectives. How can the one experience in its thing-function be made of them, consist of them, carry them as its own attributes, while in its thought-function it disowns them and attributes them elsewhere. There is a self-contradiction here from which the radical dualism of thought and thing is the only truth that can save us. Only if the thought is one kind of being can the adjectives exist in it 'intentionally' (to use the scholastic term); only if the thing is another kind, can they exist in it constitutively and energetically. No simple subject can take the same adjectives and at one time be qualified by it, and at another time be merely 'of it, as of something only meant or known.'"

The solution insisted on by this objector, like many other commonsense solutions, grows the less satisfactory the more one turns it in one's mind. To begin with, *are* thought and thing as heterogeneous as is commonly said?

No one denies that they have some categories in common. Their relations to time are identical. Both, moreover, may have parts (for psychologists in general treat thoughts as having them); and both may be complex or simple. Both are of kinds, can be compared, added and subtracted and arranged in serial orders. All sorts of adjectives qualify our thoughts which appear incompatible with consciousness, being as such a bare diaphaneity. For instance, they are natural and easy, or laborious. They are beautiful, happy, intense, interesting, wise, idiotic, focal, marginal, insipid, confused, vague, precise, rational, casual, general, particular, and many things besides. Moreover, the chapters on 'Perception' in the Psychology-books are full of facts that make for the essential homogeneity of thought with thing. How, if 'subject' and 'object' were separated 'by the whole diameter of being,' and had no attributes in common, could it be so hard to tell, in a presented and recognized material object, what part comes in through the sense-organs and what part comes 'out of one's own head'? Sensations and apperceptive ideas fuse here so intimately that you can no more tell where one begins and the other ends, than you can tell, in those cunning circular panoramas that have lately been exhibited, where the real foreground and the painted canvas join together.[14]

Descartes for the first time defined thought as the absolutely unextended, and later philosophers have accepted the description as correct. But what possible meaning has it to say that, when we think of a foot-rule or a square yard, extension is not attributable to our thought? Of every extended object the *adequate* mental picture must have all the extension of the object itself. The difference between objective and subjective extension is one of relation to a context solely. In the mind the various extents maintain no necessarily stubborn order relatively to each other, while in the physical world they bound each other stably, and, added together, make the great enveloping Unit which we believe in and call real Space. As 'outer,' they carry themselves adversely, so to speak, to one another, exclude one another and maintain their distances; while, as 'inner,' their order is loose, and they form a *durcheinander* in which unity is lost.[15] But to argue from this that inner experience is absolutely inextensive seems to me little short of absurd. The two worlds differ, not by the presence or absence of extension, but by the relations of the extensions which in both worlds exist.

Does not this case of extension now put us on the track of truth in the case of other qualities? It does; and I am surprised that the facts should not have been noticed long ago. Why, for example, do we call a fire hot, and water wet, and yet refuse to say that our mental state, when it is 'of these objects, is either wet or hot? 'Intentionally,' at any rate, and when the mental state is a vivid image, hotness and wetness are in it just as much as they are in the physical experience. The reason is this, that, as the general chaos of all our experiences gets sifted, we find that there are some fires that will always burn sticks and always warm our bodies, and that there are some waters that will always put out fires; while there are other fires and waters that will not act at all. The general group of experiences that *act*, that do not only possess their natures intrinsically, but wear them adjectively and energetically, turning them against one another, comes inevitably to be contrasted with the group whose members, having identically the same natures, fail to manifest them in the ' energetic' way. I make for myself now an experience of blazing fire; I place it near my body; but it does not warm me in the least. I lay a stick upon it, and the stick either burns or remains green, as I please. I call up water, and pour it on the fire, and absolutely no difference ensues. I account for all such facts by calling this whole train of experiences unreal, a mental train. Mental fire is what won't burn real sticks; mental water is what won't necessarily (though of course it may) put out even a mental fire. Mental knives may be sharp, but they won't cut real wood. Mental triangles are pointed, but their points won't wound. With 'real' objects, on the contrary, consequences always accrue; and thus the real experiences get sifted from the mental ones, the things from our thoughts of them, fanciful or true, and precipitated together as the stable part of the whole experience-chaos, under the name of the physical world. Of this our perceptual experiences are the nucleus, they being the originally *strong* experiences. We add a lot of conceptual experiences to them, making these strong also in imagination, and building out the remoter parts of the physical world by their means; and around this core of reality the world of laxly connected fancies and mere rhapsodical objects floats like a bank of clouds. In the clouds, all sorts of rules are violated which in the core are kept. Extensions there can be indefinitely located; motion there obeys no Newton's laws.

VII

There is a peculiar class of experiences to which, whether we take them as subjective or as objective, we *assign* their several natures as attributes, because in both contexts they affect their associates actively, though in neither quite as 'strongly' or as sharply as things affect one another by their physical energies. I refer here to *appreciations*, which form an ambiguous sphere of being, belonging with emotion on the one hand, and having objective 'value' on the other, yet seeming not quite inner nor quite outer, as if a diremption had begun but had not made itself complete.

Experiences of painful objects, for example, are usually also painful experiences; perceptions of loveliness, of ugliness, tend to pass muster as lovely or as ugly perceptions; intuitions of the morally lofty are lofty intuitions. Sometimes the adjective wanders as if uncertain where to fix itself. Shall we speak of seductive visions or of visions of seductive things? Of wicked desires or of desires for wickedness? Of healthy thoughts or of thoughts of healthy objects? Of good impulses, or of impulses towards the good? Of feelings of anger, or of angry feelings? Both in the mind and in the thing, these natures modify their context, exclude certain associates and determine others, have their mates and incompatibles. Yet not as stubbornly as in the case of physical qualities, for beauty and ugliness, love and hatred, pleasant and painful can, in certain complex experiences, coexist.

If one were to make an evolutionary construction of how a lot of originally chaotic pure experiences became gradually differentiated into an orderly inner and outer world, the whole theory would turn upon one's success in explaining how or why the quality of an experience, once active, could become less so, and, from being an energetic attribute in some cases, elsewhere lapse into the status of an inert or merely internal 'nature.' This would be the 'evolution' of the psychical from the bosom of the physical, in which the esthetic, moral and otherwise emotional experiences would represent a halfway stage.

VIII

But a last cry of *non possumus* will probably go up from many readers. "All very pretty as a piece of ingenuity," they will say, "but our consciousness itself intuitively contradicts you. We, for our part, *know* that

we are conscious. We *feel* our thought, flowing as a life within us, in absolute contrast with the objects which it so unremittingly escorts. We
can not be faithless to this immediate intuition. The dualism is a fundamental *datum:* Let no man join what God has put asunder."

My reply to this is my last word, and I greatly grieve that to many it
will sound materialistic. I can not help that, however, for I, too, have my
intuitions and I must obey them. Let the case be what it may in others, I
am as confident as I am of anything that, in myself, the stream of thinking (which I recognize emphatically as a phenomenon) is only a careless
name for what, when scrutinized, reveals itself to consist chiefly of the
stream of my breathing. The 'I think' which Kant said must be able to
accompany all my objects, is the 'I breathe' which actually does accompany them. There are other internal facts besides breathing (intra-
cephalic muscular adjustments, etc., of which I have said a word in my
larger *Psychology*), and these increase the assets of 'consciousness,' so far
as the latter is subject to immediate perception; but breath, which was
ever the original of 'spirit,' breath moving outwards, between the glottis
and the nostrils, is, I am persuaded, the essence out of which philosophers have constructed the entity known to them as consciousness. *That
entity is fictitious, while thoughts in the concrete are fully real. But thoughts in
the concrete are made of the same stuff as things are.*

I wish I might believe myself to have made that plausible in this article. In another article I shall try to make the general notion of a world
composed of pure experiences still more clear.

15

⇒·◆·⇐

The Energies of Men

"The Energies of Men" is another piece that demonstrates the wide range of James's appeal. Given as a talk to the American Philosophical Association on December 28, 1906, in New York, it was printed as "Pamphlet no. 3" in a series sponsored by the Boston-based Emmanuel Movement (an early version of clinical pastoral counseling). The piece is a serious look at a neglected topic and, at the same time, a popular bit of self-help exhortation. But with James, as with Emerson, we are given some reason to believe that self-trust is more than wishful thinking.

In "The Energies of Men," James sets out to explore something he says psychology has overlooked, namely, the *"amount of energy available* for running one's mental and moral operations." He finds that we have in general much more than we are aware of. "We habitually live inside our limits of power," he says. "The human individual . . . possesses powers of various sorts which he habitually fails to use. He energizes below his maximum, and he behaves below his optimum."

James notes that we have mental obstructions and inhibitions of all sorts both built and trained into us. He identifies three ways we can push back and through the usual obstructions. *Excitements, ideas,* and *efforts* are the great triggers that can release new energies, and James calls the whole field "dynamogenics." Giving an example of an excitement, James says *"conversions,* whether they be political, scientific, philosophic, or religious, form [one] way in which bound energies are let loose." Here, as in so many other places, we see James's therapeutic imperative. He cares far more for outcomes than for diagnosis. The reader feels this concern and perhaps for that reason can feel an unbinding, a loosing of new energy.

—————»·•·«—————

WE HABITUALLY hear much nowadays of the difference between structural and functional psychology. I am not sure that I understand the difference, but it probably has something to do with what I have privately been accustomed to distinguish as the analytical and the clinical points of view in psychological observation. Professor Sanford, in a recently published "Sketch of a Beginner's Course in Psychology," recommended "the physician's attitude" in that subject as the thing the teacher should first of all try to impart to the pupil. I fancy that few of you can have read Professor Pierre Janet's masterly works in mental pathology without being struck by the little use he makes of the machinery usually relied on by psychologists, and by his own reliance on conceptions which in the laboratories and in scientific publications we never hear of at all.

Discriminations and associations, the rise and fall of thresholds, impulses and inhibitions, fatigue,—these are the terms into which our inner life is analyzed by psychologists who are not doctors, and in which, by hook or crook, its aberrations from normality have to be expressed. They can indeed be described, after the fact, in such terms, but always lamely; and everyone must feel how much is unaccounted for, how much left out.

When we turn to Janet's pages, we find entirely other forms of thought employed. Oscillations of the level of mental energy, differences of tension, splittings of consciousness, sentiments of insufficiency and of unreality, substitutions, agitations and anxieties, depersonalizations— such are the elementary conceptions which the total view of his patient's life imposes on this clinical observer. They have little or nothing to do with the usual laboratory categories. Ask a scientific psychologist to predict what symptoms a patient must have when his 'supply of mental energy' diminishes, and he can utter only the word 'fatigue.' He could never predict such consequences as Janet subsumes under his one term 'psychasthenia'—the most bizarre obsessions and agitations, the most complete distortions of the relation between the self and the world.

I do not vouch for Janet's conceptions being valid, and I do not say that the two ways of looking at the mind contradict each other or are mutually incongruous; I simply say that they are incongru*ent*. Each covers so little of our total mental life that they do not even interfere or jostle. Meanwhile the clinical conceptions, though they may be vaguer than the analytic ones, are certainly more adequate, give the concreter picture of the way the whole mind works, and are of far more urgent practical importance. So the 'physician's attitude,' the 'functional psychology,' is assuredly the thing most worthy of general study to-day.

I wish to spend this hour on one conception of functional psychology, a conception never once mentioned or heard of in laboratory circles, but used perhaps more than any other by common, practical men— I mean the conception of the *amount of energy available* for running one's mental and moral operations by. Practically everyone knows in his own person the difference between the days when the tide of this energy is high in him and those when it is low, though no one knows exactly what reality the term energy covers when used here, or what its tides, tensions, and levels are in themselves. This vagueness is probably the reason why our scientific psychologists ignore the conception altogether. It undoubtedly connects itself with the energies of the nervous system, but it presents fluctuations that cannot easily be translated into neural terms. It offers itself as the notion of a quantity, but its ebbs and floods produce extraordinary qualitative results. To have its level raised is the most important thing that can happen to a man, yet in all my reading I know of no single page or paragraph of a scientific psychology book in which it receives mention—the psychologists have left it to be treated by the moralists and mind-curers and doctors exclusively.

Everyone is familiar with the phenomenon of feeling more or less alive on different days. Everyone knows on any given day that there are energies slumbering in him which the incitements of that day do not call forth, but which he might display if these were greater. Most of us feel as if we lived habitually with a sort of cloud weighing on us, below our highest notch of clearness in discernment, sureness in reasoning, or firmness in deciding. Compared with what we ought to be, we are only half-awake. Our fires are damped, our drafts are checked. We are making use of only a small part of our possible mental and physical resources. In some persons this sense of being cut off from their rightful resources is extreme, and we then get the formidable neurasthenic and psychasthenic conditions, with life grown into one tissue of impossibilities, that the medical books describe.

Part of the imperfect vitality under which we labor can be explained by scientific psychology. It is the result of the inhibition exerted by one part of our ideas on other parts. Conscience makes cowards of us all. Social conventions prevent us from telling the truth after the fashion of the heroes and heroines of Bernard Shaw. Our scientific respectability keeps us from exercising the mystical portions of our nature freely. If we are doctors, our mind-cure sympathies, if we are mind-curists, our medical sympathies, are tied up. We all know persons who are models of excellence, but who belong to the extreme philistine type of mind. So deadly is their intellectual respectability that we can't converse about certain subjects at all, can't let our minds play over them, can't even mention them in their presence. I have numbered among my dearest friends persons thus inhibited intellectually, with whom I would gladly have been able to talk freely about certain interests of mine, certain authors, say, as Bernard Shaw, Chesterton, Edward Carpenter, H. G. Wells, but it wouldn't do, it made them too uncomfortable, they wouldn't play, I had to be silent. An intellect thus tied down by literality and decorum makes on one the same sort of impression that an able-bodied man would who should habituate himself to do his work with only one of his fingers, locking up the rest of his organism and leaving it unused.

In few of us are functions not tied-up by the exercise of other functions. G. T. Fechner is an extraordinary exception that proves the rule. He could use his mystical faculties while being scientific. He could be both critically keen and devout. Few scientific men can pray, I imagine. Few can carry on any living commerce with 'God.' Yet many of us are well aware how much freer in many directions and abler our lives would be, were such important forms of energizing not sealed up. There are in everyone potential forms of activity that actually are shunted out from use.

The existence of reservoirs of energy that habitually are not tapped is most familiar to us in the phenomenon of 'second wind.' Ordinarily we stop when we meet the first effective layer, so to call it, of fatigue. We have then walked, played, or worked 'enough,' and desist. That amount of fatigue is an efficacious obstruction, on this side of which our usual life is cast. But if an unusual necessity forces us to press onward, a surprising thing occurs. The fatigue gets worse up to a certain critical point, when gradually or suddenly it passes away, and we are fresher than before. We have evidently tapped a level of new energy, masked until then by the fatigue-obstacle usually obeyed. There may be layer after layer of this experience. A third and a fourth 'wind' may supervene. Mental activity shows the phenomenon as well as physical, and in exceptional cases we may find, beyond the very extremity of fatigue-distress, amounts of ease and power that we never dreamed ourselves to own, sources of strength habitually not taxed at all, because habitually we never push through the obstruction, never pass those early critical points.

When we do pass, what makes us do so?

Either some unusual stimulus fills us with emotional excitement, or some unusual idea of necessity induces us to make an extra effort of will. *Excitements, ideas, and efforts,* in a word, are what carry us over the dam.

In those hyperesthetic conditions which chronic invalidism so often brings in its train, the dam has changed its normal place. The pain-threshold is abnormally near. The slightest functional exercise gives a distress which the patient yields to and stops. In such cases of 'habit-neurosis' a new range of power often comes in consequence of the bullying-treatment, of efforts which the doctor obliges the patient, against his will, to make. First comes the very extremity of distress, then follows unexpected relief. There seems no doubt that we are each and all of us to some extent victims of habit-neurosis. We have to admit the wider potential range and the habitually narrow actual use. We live subject to inhibition by degrees of fatigue which we have come only from habit to obey. Most of us may learn to push the barrier farther off, and to live in perfect comfort on much higher levels of power.

Country people and city people, as a class, illustrate this difference. The rapid rate of life, the number of decisions in an hour, the many things to keep account of, in a busy city-man's or woman's life, seem monstrous to a country-brother. He doesn't see how we live at all. But settle him in town; and in a year or two, if not too old, he will have trained himself to keep the pace as well as any of us, getting more out of himself in any week than he ever did in ten weeks at home. The physiologists show how one can be in nutritive equilibrium, neither losing nor gaining weight, on astonishingly different quantities of food. So one can be in what I might call 'efficiency-equilibrium' (neither gaining nor losing power when once the equilibrium is reached), on astonishingly different quantities of work, no matter in what dimension the work may be measured. It may be physical work, intellectual work, moral work, or spiritual work.

Of course there are limits: the trees don't grow into the sky. But the plain fact remains that men the world over possess amounts of resource, which only very exceptional individuals push to their extremes of use.

The excitements that carry us over the usually effective dam are most often the classic emotional ones, love, anger, crowd-contagion, or despair. Life's vicissitudes bring them in abundance. A new position of responsibility, if it do not crush a man, will often, nay, one may say, will usually, show him to be a far stronger creature than was supposed. Even here we are witnessing (some of us admiring, some deploring—I must class myself as admiring) the dynamogenic effects of a very exalted political office upon the energies of an individual who had already manifested a healthy amount of energy before the office came.

Mr. Sydney Olivier has given us a fine fable of the dynamogenic effects of love in a fine story called "The Empire Builder," in the *Contemporary Review* for May, 1905. A young naval officer falls in love at sight with a missionary's daughter on a lost island, which his ship accidentally touches. From that day onward he must see her again; and he so moves Heaven and earth and the Colonial Office and the Admiralty to get sent there once more, that the island finally is annexed to the empire in consequence of the various fusses he is led to make. People must have been appalled lately in San Francisco to find the stores of bottled up energy and endurance they possessed.

Wars, of course, and shipwrecks, are the great revealers of what men and women are able to do and bear. Cromwell's and Grant's careers are the stock examples of how war will wake a man up. I owe to Professor Norton's kindness the permission to read to you part of a letter from Colonel Baird Smith, written shortly after the six weeks' siege of Delhi in 1857, for the victorious issue of which that excellent officer was chiefly to be thanked. He writes as follows:—

. . . "My poor wife had some reason to think that war and disease between them had left very little of a husband to take under nursing when she got him again. An attack of Camp Scurvy had filled my mouth with sores, shaken every joint in my body and covered me all over with livid spots so that I was marvellously unlovely to look upon. A smart knock on the ancle joint from the splinter of a shell that burst in my face, in itself a mere bagatelle of a wound, had been of necessity neglected under the pressing and incessant calls upon me and had grown worse and worse till the whole foot below the ancle became a black mass and seemed to threaten mortification. I insisted however on being allowed to use it till the place was taken, mortification or no, and tho' the pain was sometimes horrible I carried my point and kept up to the last. On the day after the assault I had an unlucky fall on some bad ground and it was an open question for a day or two whether I hadn't broken my arm at the elbow. Fortunately it turned out to be only a very severe sprain but I am still conscious of the wrench it gave me. To crown the whole pleasant catalogue I was worn to a shadow by a constant diarrhoea and consumed as much opium as would have done credit to my father-in-law.[1] However, thank God I have a good share of Tapleyism in me and come out strong under difficulties. I think I may confidently say that no man ever saw me out of heart or ever heard one croaking word from me even when our prospects were gloomiest. We were sadly scourged by the cholera and it was almost appalling to me to find that out of twenty-seven officers present I could muster only fifteen for the operations of the attack. However, it was done and after it was done came the collapse. Don't be horrified when I tell you that for the whole of the actual Siege and in truth for some little time before, I almost lived on Brandy. Appetite for food I had none but I forced myself to eat just sufficient to sustain life and I had an incessant craving for brandy as the strongest stimulant I could get. Strange to say I was quite unconscious of its affecting me in the slightest degree. *The excitement of the work was so great that no lesser one seemed to have any chance against it and I certainly never found my intellect clearer or my nerves stronger in my life.* It was only my wretched body that was weak and the moment the real work was done by our becoming complete masters of Delhi I broke down without delay and discovered that if I wished to live I must continue no longer the system that had kept me up, till the crisis was past. With it passed away as if in a moment all desire to stimulate and a perfect loathing of my late staff of life took possession of me."

Such experiences show how profound is the alteration in the manner in which, under excitement, our organism will sometimes perform its physiological work. The metabolisms become different when the reserves have to be used, and for weeks and months the deeper use may go on.

Morbid cases, here as elsewhere, lay the normal machinery bare. In the first number of Dr. Morton Prince's *Journal of Abnormal Psychology,* Dr. Janet has discussed five cases of morbid impulse, with an explanation that is precious for my present point of view. One is a girl who eats, eats, eats, all day. Another walks, walks, walks, and gets her food from an automobile that escorts her. Another is a dipsomaniac. A fourth pulls out her hair. A fifth wounds her flesh and burns her skin. Hitherto such freaks of impulse have received Greek names (as bulimia, dromomania, etc.) and been scientifically disposed of as "episodic syndromata of hereditary degeneration." But it turns out that Janet's cases are all what he calls psychasthenics, or victims of a chronic sense of weakness, torpor, lethargy, fatigue, insufficiency, impossibility, unreality, and powerlessness of will; and that in each and all of them the particular activity pursued, deleterious though it be, has the temporary result of raising the sense of vitality and making the patient feel alive again. These things reanimate; they would reanimate *us;* but it happens that in each patient the particular freak-activity chosen is the only thing that does reanimate; and therein lies the morbid state. The way to treat such persons is to discover to them more usual and useful ways of throwing their stores of vital energy into gear.

Colonel Baird Smith, needing to draw on altogether extraordinary stores of energy, found that brandy and opium were ways of throwing them into gear.

Such cases are humanly typical. We are all to some degree oppressed, unfree. We don't come to our own. It is there, but we don't get at it. The threshold must be made to shift. Then many of us find that an excentric activity—a 'spree,' say—relieves. There is no doubt that to some men sprees and excesses of almost any kind are medicinal, temporarily at any rate, in spite of what the moralists and doctors say.

But when the normal tasks and stimulations of life don't put a man's deeper levels of energy on tap, and he requires distinctly deleterious excitements, his constitution verges on the abnormal. The normal opener of deeper and deeper levels of energy is the will. The difficulty is to use it; to make the effort which the word volition implies. But if we *do* make it (or if a god, though he were only the god Chance, makes it through us), it will act dynamogenically on us for a month. It is notorious that a single successful effort of moral volition, such as saying 'no' to some habitual temptation, or performing some courageous act, will launch a man on a higher level of energy for days and weeks, will give him a new range of power.

The emotions and excitements due to usual situations are the usual inciters of the will. But these act discontinuously; and in the intervals the shallower levels of life tend to close in and shut us off. Accordingly the best practical knowers of the human soul have invented the thing known as methodical ascetic discipline to keep the deeper levels constantly in reach. Beginning with easy tasks, passing to harder ones, and exercising day by day, it is, I believe, admitted that disciples of asceticism can reach very high levels of freedom and power of will.

Ignatius Loyola's spiritual exercises must have produced this result in innumerable devotees. But the most venerable ascetic system, and the one whose results have the most voluminous experimental corroboration, is undoubtedly the Yoga system in Hindostan. From time immemorial, by Hatha Yoga, Raja Yoga, Karma Yoga, or whatever code of practice it might be, Hindu aspirants to perfection have trained themselves, month in and out, for years. The result claimed, and certainly in many cases accorded by impartial judges, is strength of character, personal power, unshakability of soul. But it is not easy to disentangle fact from tradition in Hindu affairs. So I am glad to have a European friend who has submitted to Hatha Yoga training, and whose account of the results I am privileged to quote. I think you will appreciate the light it throws on the question of our unused reservoirs of power.

My friend is an extraordinarily gifted man, both morally and intellectually, but has an instable nervous system, and for many years has lived in a circular process of alternate lethargy and over-animation: something like three weeks of extreme activity, and then a week of prostration in bed. An unpromising condition, which the best specialists in Europe had failed to relieve; so he tried Hatha Yoga, partly out of curiosity, and partly with a sort of desperate hope. What follows is a short extract from a letter sixty pages long which he addressed me a year ago.

"Thus I decided to follow Vivekananda's advice: 'Practice hard: whether you live or die by it doesn't matter.' My improvised chela and I began with starvation. I do not know whether you did try it ever . . . but voluntary starvation is very different from involuntary, and implies more temptations. We reduced first our meals to twice a day and then to once a day. The best authorities agree that in order to control the body fasting is essential, and even in the Gospel the worst spirits are said to obey only those who fast and pray. We reduced very much the amount of food, disregarding chemical theories about the need of albumen, sometimes living on olive oil and bread; or on fruits alone; or on milk and rice; in very small quantities—much less than I formerly ate at one meal. I began to get lighter every day, and lost 20 pounds in a few weeks; but this could not stop such a desperate undertaking . . . rather starve than live as a slave! Then besides we practised *asana* or postures, breaking almost our limbs. Try to sit down on the floor and to kiss your knees without bending them, or to join your hands on the usually unapproachable upper part of your back, or to bring the toe of your right foot to your left ear without bending the knees . . . these are easy samples of posture for a Yogi.

"All the time also breathing exercises: keeping the breath in and out up to two minutes, breathing in different rhythms and positions. Also very much prayer and Roman Catholic practices combined with the Yoga, in order to leave nothing untried and to be protected against the tricks of Hindu devils! Then concentration of thought on different parts of the body, and on the processes going on within them. Exclusion of all emotions, dry logical reading, as intellectual diet, and working out logical problems. . . . I wrote a Handbook of Logic as a *Nebenprodukt* of the whole experiment.[2]

"After a few weeks I broke down and had to interrupt everything, in a worse state of prostration than ever. . . . My younger chela went on unshaken by my fate; and as soon as I arose from bed I tried again, decided to fight it out, even feeling a kind of determination such as I had never felt before, a certain absolute will of victory at any price and faith in it. Whether it is my own merit or a divine grace, I cannot judge for certain, but I prefer to admit the latter. I had been ill for seven years, and some people say this is a term for many punishments. However base and vile a sinner I had been, perhaps my sins were about to be forgiven, and Yoga was only an exterior opportunity, an object for concentration of will. I do not yet pretend to explain much of what I have gone through, but the fact is that since I arose from bed on August 20, no new crisis of prostration came again, and I have now the strongest conviction that no crisis will ever return. If you consider that for the past years there has been not a single month without this lethargy, you will grant that even to an outside observer four successive months of increasing health are an objective test. In this time I underwent very severe penances, reducing sleep and food and increasing the task of work and exercise. My intuition was developed by these practices: there came a sense of certainty, never known before, as to the things needed by the body and the mind, and the body came to obey like a wild horse tamed. Also the mind learned to obey, and the current of thought and feeling was shaped according to my will. I mastered sleep and hunger, and the flights of thought, and came to know a peace never known before, an inner rhythm of unison with a deeper rhythm above or beyond. Personal wishes ceased, and the consciousness of being the instrument of a superior power arose. A calm certainty of indubitable success in every undertaking imparts great and real power. I often guessed the thoughts of my companion . . . we observed generally the greatest isolation and silence. We both felt an unspeakable joy in the simplest natural impressions, light, air, landscape, any kind of simplest food; and above everything in rhythmical respiration, which produces a state of mind without thought or feeling, and still very intense, indescribable.

"These results began to be more evident in the fourth month of uninterrupted training. We felt quite happy, never tired, sleeping only from 8 p.m. to midnight, and rising with joy from our sleep to another day's work of study and exercise. . . .

"I am now in Palermo, and have had to neglect the exercises in the last few days, but I feel as fresh as if I were in full training and see the sunny side of all things. I am not in a hurry, rushing to complete————."

And here my friend mentions a certain life-work of his own about which I had better be silent. He goes on to analyze the exercises and their effects in an extremely practical way, but at too great length for me to entertain you with. Repetition, alteration, periodicity, parallelism (or the association of the idea of some desirable vital or spiritual effect with each movement), etc., are laws which he deems highly important. "I am sure," he continues, "that everybody who is able to concentrate thought and will, and to eliminate superfluous emotions, sooner or later becomes a master of his body and can overcome every kind of illness. This is the truth at the bottom of all mind-cures. Our thoughts have a plastic power over the body."

You will be relieved, I doubt not, to hear my excentric correspondent here make connection at last with something you know by heart,
namely, 'suggestive therapeutics.' Call his whole performance, if you
like, an experiment in methodical self-suggestion. That only makes it
more valuable as an illustration of what I wish to impress in as many
ways as possible upon your minds, that we habitually live inside our
limits of power. Suggestion, especially under hypnosis, is now universally recognized as a means, exceptionally successful in certain persons,
of concentrating consciousness, and, in others, of influencing their bodies' states. It throws into gear energies of imagination, of will, and of
mental influence over physiological processes, that usually lie dormant,
and that can only be thrown into gear at all in chosen subjects. It is, in
short, dynamogenic; and the cheapest terms in which to deal with our
amateur Yogi's experience is to call it auto-suggestive.

I wrote to him that I couldn't possibly attribute any sacramental
value to the particular Hatha Yoga processes, the postures, breathings,
fastings, and the like, and that they seemed to me but so many manners, available in his case and his chela's, but not for everybody, of
breaking through the barriers which life's routine had concreted round
the deeper strata of the will, and gradually bringing its unused energies
into action.

He replied as follows: "You are quite right that the Yoga exercises
are nothing else than a methodical way of increasing our will. Because
we are unable to will at once the most difficult things, we must imagine
steps leading to them. Breathing being the easiest of the bodily activities, it is very natural that it offers a good scope for exercise of will. The
control of thought could be gained without breathing-discipline, but it is
simply easier to control thought simultaneously with the control of
breath. Anyone who can think clearly and persistently of one thing
needs not breathing exercises. You are quite right that we are not using
all our power and that we often learn how much we *can* only when we
must. . . . The power that we do not use up completely can be brought
[more and more] into use by what we call *faith*. Faith is like the manometer of the will, registering its pressure. If I could believe that I can
levitate, I could do it. But I cannot believe, and therefore I am clumsily
sticking to earth. . . . Now this faith, this power of credulity, can be educated by small efforts. I can breathe at the rate of say twelve times a
minute. I can easily believe that I can breathe ten times a minute. When
I have accustomed myself to breathe ten times a minute, I learn to be-

lieve it will be easy to breathe six times a minute. Thus I have actually learned to breathe at the rate of once a minute. How far I shall progress I do not know. . . . The Yogi goes on in his activity in an even way, without fits of too much or too little, and he is eliminating more and more every unrest, every worry—growing into the infinite by regular training, by small additions to a task which has grown familiar. . . . But you are quite right that religious-crises, love-crises, indignation-crises, may awaken in a very short time powers similar to those reached by years of patient Yoga practice. . . . The Hindus themselves admit that Samadhi can be reached in many ways and with complete disregard of every physical training."

Allowance made for every enthusiasm and exaggeration, there can be no doubt of my friend's regeneration—relatively, at any rate. The second letter, written six months later than the first (ten months after beginning Yoga practice, therefore), says the improvement holds good. He has undergone material trials with indifference, travelled third class on Mediterranean steamers, and fourth class on African trains, living with the poorest Arabs and sharing their unaccustomed food, all with equanimity. His devotion to certain interests has been put to heavy strain, and nothing is more remarkable to me than the changed moral tone with which he reports the situation. Compared with certain earlier letters, these read as if written by a different man, patient and reasonable instead of vehement, self-subordinating instead of imperious. The new tone persists in a communication received only a fortnight ago (fourteen months after beginning training)—there is, in fact, no doubt that profound modification has occurred in the running of his mental machinery. The gearing has changed, and his will is available otherwise than it was. Available without any new ideas, beliefs, or emotions, so far as I can make out, having been implanted in him. He is simply more balanced where he was more unbalanced.

You will remember that he speaks of faith, calling it a 'manometer' of the will. It sounds more natural to call our will the manometer of our faiths. Ideas set free beliefs, and the beliefs set free our wills (I use these terms with no pretension to be 'psychological'), so the will-acts register the faith-pressure within. Therefore, having considered the liberation of our stored-up energy by emotional excitements and by efforts, whether methodical or unmethodical, I must now say a word about *ideas* as our third great dynamogenic agent. Ideas contradict other ideas and keep us from believing them. An idea that thus negates a first idea may itself in turn be negated by a third idea, and the first idea may thus regain its natural influence over our belief and determine our behavior. Our philosophic and religious development proceeds thus by credulities, negations, and the negating of negations.

But whether for arousing or for stopping belief, ideas may fail to be efficacious, just as a wire at one time alive with electricity, may at another time be dead. Here our insight into causes fails us, and we can only note results in general terms. In general, whether a given idea shall be a live idea, depends more on the person into whose mind it is injected than on the idea itself. The whole history of 'suggestion' opens out here. Which are the suggestive ideas for this person, and which for that? Beside the susceptibilities determined by one's education and by one's original peculiarities of character, there are lines along which men simply as men tend to be inflammable by ideas. As certain objects naturally awaken love, anger, or cupidity, so certain ideas naturally awaken the energies of loyalty, courage, endurance, or devotion. When these ideas are effective in an individual's life, their effect is often very great indeed. They may transfigure it, unlocking innumerable powers which, but for the idea, would never have come into play. 'Fatherland,' 'The Union,' 'Holy Church,' the 'Monroe Doctrine,' 'Truth,' 'Science,' 'Liberty,' Garibaldi's phrase 'Rome or Death,' etc., are so many examples of energy-releasing abstract ideas. The *social* nature of all such phrases is an essential factor of their dynamic power. They are forces of detent in situations in which no other force produces equivalent effects, and each is a force of detent only in a specific group of men.

The memory that an oath or vow has been made will nerve one to abstinences and efforts otherwise impossible: witness the 'pledge' in the history of the temperance movement. A mere promise to his sweetheart will clean up a youth's life all over—at any rate for a time. For such effects an educated susceptibility is required. The idea of one's 'honour,' for example, unlocks energy only in those who have had the education of a gentleman, so called.

That delightful being, Prince Pückler-Muskau, writes to his wife from England that he has invented "a sort of artificial resolution respecting things which are difficult of performance." "My device," he says, "is this:—I give my word of honour most solemnly to myself, to do, or to leave undone, this or that. I am of course extremely cautious in the use of this expedient . . . but when once the word is given, even if I afterwards think I have been precipitate or mistaken, I hold it to be perfectly irrevocable, whatever inconveniences I foresee likely to result. . . . If I were capable of breaking my word after such mature consideration, I should lose all respect for myself;—and what man of sense would not prefer death to such an alternative? . . . [When the mysterious formula is pronounced,] no alteration in my own views—nothing short of physical impossibility—must, for the welfare of my soul, alter my will. . . . I find something very satisfactory in the thought, that man has the power of framing such props and weapons out of the most trivial materials, indeed out of nothing, merely by the force of his will, which thereby truly deserves the name of omnipotent."[3]

Conversions, whether they be political, scientific, philosophic, or religious, form another way in which bound energies are let loose. They unify, and put a stop to ancient mental interferences. The result is freedom, and often a great enlargement of power. A belief that thus settles upon an individual always acts as a challenge to his will. But, for the particular challenge to operate, he must be the right challeng*ee*. In religious conversions we have so fine an adjustment that the idea may be in the mind of the challengee for years before it exerts effects; and why it should do so then is often so far from obvious that the event is taken for a miracle of grace, and not a natural occurrence. Whatever it is, it may be a highwater mark of energy, in which 'noes,' once impossible, are easy, and in which a new range of 'yeses' gain the right of way.

We are just now witnessing—but our scientific education has unfitted most of us for comprehending the phenomenon—a very copious unlocking of energies by ideas, in the persons of those converts to 'New Thought,' 'Christian Science,' 'Metaphysical Healing,' or other forms of spiritual philosophy, who are so numerous among us to-day. The ideas here are healthy-minded and optimistic; and it is quite obvious that a wave of religious activity, analogous in some respects to the spread of early Christianity, Buddhism, and Mohammedanism is passing over our American world. The common feature of these optimistic faiths is that they all tend to the suppression of what Mr. Horace Fletcher has termed "fearthought." Fearthought he defines as "the self-suggestion of inferiority"; so that one may say that these systems all operate by the suggestion of power. And the power, small or great, comes in various shapes to the individual, power, as he will tell you, not to 'mind' things that used to vex him, power to concentrate his mind, good cheer, good temper; in short, to put it mildly, a firmer, more elastic moral tone. The most genuinely saintly person I have ever known is a friend of mine now suffering from cancer of the breast. I do not assume to judge of the wisdom or unwisdom of her disobedience to the doctors, and I cite her here solely as an example of what ideas can do. Her ideas have kept her a practically well woman for months after she should have given up and gone to bed. They have annulled all pain and weakness and given her a cheerful active life, unusually beneficent to others to whom she has afforded help.

How far the mind-cure movement is destined to extend its influence, or what intellectual modifications it may yet undergo, no one can foretell. Being a religious movement, it will certainly outstrip the purviews of its rationalist critics, such as we here may be supposed to be.

I have thus brought a pretty wide induction to bear upon my thesis, and it appears to hold good. The human individual lives usually far within his limits; he possesses powers of various sorts which he habitually fails to use. He energizes below his maximum, and he behaves below his optimum. In elementary faculty, in coördination, in power of inhibition and control, in every conceivable way, his life is contracted like the field of vision of an hysteric subject—but with less excuse, for the poor hysteric is diseased, while in the rest of us it is only an inveterate *habit*—the habit of inferiority to our full self—that is bad.

Expressed in this vague manner, everyone must admit my thesis to be true. The terms have to remain vague; for though every man of woman born knows what is meant by such phrases as having a good vital tone, a high tide of spirits, an elastic temper, as living energetically, working easily, deciding firmly, and the like, we should all be put to our trumps if asked to explain in terms of scientific psychology just what such expressions mean. We can draw some child-like psychophysical diagrams, and that is all. In physics the conception of 'energy' is perfectly defined. It is correlated with the conception of 'work.' But mental work and moral work, although we cannot live without talking about them, are terms as yet hardly analyzed, and doubtless mean several heterogeneous elementary things. Our muscular work is a voluminous physical quantity, but our ideas and volitions are minute forces of release, and by 'work' here we mean the substitution of higher *kinds* for lower *kinds* of detent. Higher and lower here are qualitative terms, not translatable immediately into quantities, unless indeed they should prove to mean newer or older forms of cerebral organization, and unless newer should then prove to mean cortically more superficial, older, cortically more deep. Some anatomists, as you know, have pretended this; but it is obvious that the intuitive or popular idea of mental work, fundamental and absolutely indispensable as it is in our lives, possesses no degree whatever of scientific clearness to-day.

Here, then, is the first problem that emerges from our study. Can any one of us refine upon the conceptions of mental work and mental energy, so as later to be able to throw some definitely analytic light on what we mean by 'having a more elastic moral tone,' or by 'using higher levels of power and will'? I imagine that we may have to wait long before progress in this direction is made. The problem is too homely; one doesn't see just how to get in the electric keys and revolving drums that alone make psychology scientific to-day.

My fellow-pragmatist in Florence, G. Papini, has adopted a new conception of philosophy. He calls it the *doctrine of action* in the widest sense, the study of all human powers and means (among which latter, *truths* of every kind whatsoever figure, of course, in the first rank). From this point of view philosophy is a *pragmatic,* comprehending, as tributary departments of itself, the old disciplines of logic, metaphysic, physic, and ethic.

And here, after our first problem, two other problems burst upon our view. My belief that these two problems form a program of work well worthy of the attention of a body as learned and earnest as this audience, is, in fact, what has determined me to choose this subject, and to drag you through so many familiar facts during the hour that has sped.

The first of the two problems is *that of our powers,* the second *that of our means of unlocking them or getting at them.* We ought somehow to get a topographic survey made of the limits of human power in every conceivable direction, something like an ophthalmologist's chart of the limits of the human field of vision; and we ought then to construct a methodical inventory of the paths of access, or keys, differing with the diverse types of individual, to the different kinds of power. This would be an absolutely concrete study, to be carried on by using historical and biographical material mainly. The limits of power must be limits that have been realized in actual persons, and the various ways of unlocking the reserves of power must have been exemplified in individual lives. Laboratory experimentation can play but a small part. Your psychologist's *Versuchsthier*, outside of hypnosis, can never be called on to tax his energies in ways as extreme as those which the emergencies of life will force on him.

So here is a program of concrete individual psychology, at which anyone in some measure may work. It is replete with interesting facts, and points to practical issues superior in importance to anything we know. I urge it therefore upon your consideration. In some shape we have all worked at it in a more or less blind and fragmentary way; yet before Papini mentioned it I had never thought of it, or heard it broached by anyone, in the generalized form of a program such as I now suggest, a program that might with proper care be made to cover the whole field of psychology, and might show us parts of it in a very fresh light.

It is just the generalizing of the problem that seems to me to make so strong an appeal. I hope that in some of you the conception may unlock unused reservoirs of investigating power.

16

Concerning Fechner

The drab title "Concerning Fechner" conceals the wild speculative energy of the highest point and boldest chapter of James's boldest book, *A Pluralistic Universe.* "Must we then conclude," he asks, "that the world contains nothing better in the way of consciousness than our consciousness?" Fechner's answer—and it is James's answer as well, what he calls the "daylight view of the world"—is the idea "that the whole universe in its different spans and wave-lengths, exclusions and envelopments, is everywhere alive and conscious."

Fechner was a German scientist who, like William James, had a playful streak. He did pathbreaking work in psychological measurement (psychophysics) under his own name, while under the pseudonym "Dr. Mises" he wrote satiric pieces, including one called "Proof that the Moon Is Made of Iodine." The Royal Saxon Secret Police kept an eye on Dr. Mises. William James wrote a preface for the first English translation of Fechner's *A Little Book of Life after Death* (1904). Fechner believed that "inner experience is the reality, and that matter is but a form in which inner experiences may appear to one another when they affect each other from the outside" ("Introduction to Fechner's *Life after Death,"* in *Essays in Religion and Morality*). Fechner thought, and James agreed, that we make a huge mistake in "our inveterate habit of regarding the spiritual not as the rule but as an exception in the midst of nature. Instead of believing our life to be fed at the breasts of the greater life, our individuality to be sustained by the greater individuality, which must necessarily have more consciousness and more independence than all that it brings forth, we habitually treat whatever lies outside of our life as so much slag and ashes of life only."

"Concerning Fechner" sends out sparks in all directions. There is a quick-witted rebuttal of Hegelian logic (if Hegelian logic is so great, how come scientists never use it?) and a famous if nontechnical description of "thick" versus "thin" worldviews. Fechner's is the essence of the rich, full, pluralistic openness and plenitude of the thick view. "Fechner likens our individual persons on the earth unto so many sense-organs of the earth's soul," says James. "We add to its perceptive life so long as our own life lasts. It absorbs our perceptions, just as they occur, into its larger sphere of knowledge, and combines them with the other data there. When one of us dies, it is as if an eye of the world were closed."

As if. These are some of James's most astute and useful observations. Unwilling to claim absolutely that we are free, he says we can live as if we were free. Unable to say that there is life after death or a consciousness greater than our own, he says we can live as if it were so. As Shakespeare's Touchstone remarked in *As You Like It*, "much virtue in if."

⬛◆⬛

THE PRESTIGE of the absolute has rather crumbled in our hands. The logical proofs of it miss fire; the portraits which its best court-painters show of it are featureless and foggy in the extreme; and, apart from the cold comfort of assuring us that with *it* all is well, and that to see that all is well with us also we need only rise to its eternal point of view, it yields us no relief whatever. It introduces, on the contrary, into philosophy and theology certain poisonous difficulties of which but for its intrusion we never should have heard.

But if we drop the absolute out of the world, must we then conclude that the world contains nothing better in the way of consciousness than our consciousness? Is our whole instinctive belief in higher presences, our persistent inner turning towards divine companionship, to count for nothing? Is it but the pathetic illusion of beings with incorrigibly social and imaginative minds?

Such a negative conclusion would, I believe, be desperately hasty, a sort of pouring out of the child with the bath. Logically it is possible to believe in superhuman beings without identifying them with the absolute at all. The treaty of offensive and defensive alliance which certain groups of the Christian clergy have recently made with our transcendentalist philosophers seems to me to be based on a well-meaning but baleful mistake. Neither the Jehovah of the old testament nor the heavenly father of the new has anything in common with the absolute except that they are all three greater than man; and if you say that the notion of the absolute is what the gods of Abraham, of David and of Jesus, after first developing into each other, were inevitably destined to develope into in more reflective and modern minds, I reply that altho in certain specifically philosophical minds this may have been the case, in minds more properly to be termed religious the development has followed quite another path. The whole history of evangelical Christianity is there to prove it. I propose in these lectures to plead for that other line of development. To set the doctrine of the absolute in its proper framework, so that it shall not fill the whole welkin and exclude all alternative possibilities of higher thought—as it seems to do for many students who approach it with a limited previous acquaintance with philosophy—I will contrast it with a system which, abstractly considered, seems at first to have much in common with absolutism, but which, when taken concretely and temperamentally, really stands at the opposite pole. I refer to the philosophy of Gustav Theodor Fechner, a writer but little known as yet to English readers, but destined, I am persuaded, to wield more and more influence as time goes on.

It is the intense concreteness of Fechner, his fertility of detail, which fills me with an admiration which I should like to make this audience share. Among the philosophic cranks of my acquaintance in the past was a lady all the tenets of whose system I have forgotten except one. Had she been born in the Ionian archipelago some three thousand years ago, that one doctrine would probably have made her name sure of a place in every university curriculum and examination-paper. The world, she said, is composed of only two elements, the Thick, namely, and the Thin. No one can deny the truth of this analysis, as far as it goes (tho in the light of our contemporary knowledge of nature it has itself a rather 'thin' sound), and it is nowhere truer than in that part of the world called philosophy. I am sure, for example, that many of you, listening to what poor account I have been able to give of transcendental idealism, have received an impression of its arguments being strangely thin, and of the terms it leaves us with being shiveringly thin wrappings for so thick and burly a world as this. Some of you of course will charge the thinness to my exposition; but thin as that has been, I believe the doctrines reported on to have been thinner. From Green to Haldane the absolute proposed to us to straighten out the confusions of the thicket of experience in which our life is passed remains a pure abstraction which hardly anyone tries to make a whit concreter. If we open Green, we get nothing but the transcendental ego of apperception (Kant's name for the fact that to be counted in experience a thing has to be witnessed) blown up into a sort of timeless soap-bubble large enough to mirror the whole universe. Nature, Green keeps insisting, consists only in relations, and these imply the action of a mind that is eternal; a self-distinguishing consciousness which itself escapes from the relations by which it determines other things. Present to whatever is in succession, it is not in succession itself. If we take the Cairds, they tell us little more of the principle of the universe—it is always a return into the identity of the self from the difference of its objects. It separates itself from them and so becomes conscious of them in their separation from one another, while at the same time it binds them together as elements in one higher self-consciousness.

This seems the very quintessence of thinness; and the matter hardly grows thicker when we gather, after enormous amounts of reading, that the great enveloping self in question is absolute reason as such, and that as such it is characterized by the habit of using certain jejune 'categories' with which to perform its eminent relating work. The whole active material of natural fact is tried out, and only the barest intellectualistic formalism remains.

Hegel tried, as we saw, to make the system concreter by making the relations between things 'dialectic,' but if we turn to those who use his name most worshipfully, we find them giving up all the particulars of his attempt, and simply praising his intention—much as in our manner we have praised it ourselves. Mr. Haldane, for example, in his wonderfully clever Gifford lectures, praises Hegel to the skies, but what he tells of him amounts to little more than this, that "the categories in which the mind arranges its experiences, and gives meaning to them, the universals in which the particulars are grasped in the individual, are a logical chain in which the first presupposes the last and the last is its presupposition and its truth." He hardly tries at all to thicken this thin logical scheme. He says indeed that absolute mind in itself, and absolute mind in its hetereity or otherness, under the distinction which it sets up of itself from itself, have as their real *prius* absolute mind in synthesis; and, this being absolute mind's true nature, its dialectic character must show itself in such concrete forms as Goethe's and Wordsworth's poetry, as well as in religious forms. "The nature of God, the nature of Absolute Mind, is to exhibit the triple movement of dialectic, and so the nature of God, as presented in religion, must be a triplicity, a Trinity." But beyond thus naming Goethe and Wordsworth and establishing the trinity, Mr. Haldane's Hegelianism carries us hardly an inch into the concrete detail of the world we actually inhabit.

Equally thin is Mr. Taylor, both in his principles and in their results. Following Mr. Bradley, he starts by assuring us that reality cannot be self-contradictory, but to be related to anything really outside of one's self is to be self-contradictory, so the ultimate reality must be a single all-inclusive systematic whole. Yet all he can say of this whole at the end of his excellently written book is that the notion of it "can make no addition to our information, and can of itself supply no motives for practical endeavour."

Mr. McTaggart treats us to almost as thin a fare. "The main practical interest of Hegel's philosophy," he says, "is to be found in the abstract certainty which the Logic gives us that all reality is rational and righteous, even when we cannot see in the least *how* it is so. . . . Not that it shows us how the facts around us are good, not that it shows us how we can make them better, but that it proves that they, like other reality, are, *sub specie aeternitatis*, perfectly good, and, *sub specie temporis*, destined to become perfectly good."

Here again, no detail whatever, only the abstract certainty that whatever the detail may prove to be, it will be good. Common non-dialectical men have already this certainty as a result of the generous vital enthusiasm about the universe with which they are born. The peculiarity of transcendental philosophy is its sovereign contempt for merely vital functions like enthusiasm, and its pretension to turn our simple and immediate trusts and faiths into the form of logically mediated certainties, to question which would be absurd. But the whole basis on which Mr. McTaggart's own certainty so solidly rests, settles down into the one nutshell of an assertion into which he puts Hegel's gospel, namely, that in every bit of experience and thought, however finite, the whole of reality (the absolute idea, as Hegel calls it) is 'implicitly present.'

This indeed is Hegel's *vision*, and Hegel thought that the details of his dialectic proved its truth. But disciples who treat the details of the proof as unsatisfactory and yet cling to the vision, are surely, in spite of their pretension to a more rational consciousness, no better than common men with their enthusiasms or deliberately adopted faiths. We have ourselves seen some of the weakness of the monistic proofs. Mr. McTaggart picks plenty of holes of his own in Hegel's logic, and finally concludes that "all true philosophy must be mystical, not indeed in its methods, but in its final conclusions," which is as much as to say that the rationalistic methods leave us in the lurch, in spite of all their superiority, and that in the end vision and faith must eke them out. But how abstract and thin is here the vision, to say nothing of the faith! The whole of reality, explicitly absent from our finite experiences, must nevertheless be present in them all implicitly, altho no one of us can ever see how—the bare word 'implicit' here bearing the whole pyramid of the monistic system on its slender point. Mr. Joachim's monistic system of truth rests on an even slenderer point—"*I have never doubted,*" he says, "that universal and timeless truth is a single content or significance, one and whole and complete," and he candidly confesses the failure of rationalistic attempts "to raise this immediate certainty" to the level of reflective knowledge. There is, in short, no mediation for him between the Truth in capital letters and all the little 'lower-case' truths—and errors—which life presents. The psychological fact that he never has 'doubted' is enough.

The whole monistic pyramid, resting on points as thin as these, seems to me to be a *machtspruch,* a product of will far more than one of reason. Unity is good, therefore things *shall* cohere; they *shall* be one; there *shall* be categories to make them one, no matter what empirical disjunctions may appear. In Hegel's own writings the *shall-be* temper is ubiquitous and towering; it overrides verbal and logical resistances alike. Hegel's error, as Professor Royce so well says, "lay, not in introducing logic into passion," as some people charge, "but in conceiving the logic of passion as the only logic. . . . He is [thus] suggestive," Royce says, "but never final. His system, as system, has crumbled, but his vital comprehension of our life remains forever."[1]

That vital comprehension we have already seen. It is that there is a sense in which real things are not merely their own bare selves, but may vaguely be treated as also their own others, and that ordinary logic, since it denies this, must be overcome. Ordinary logic denies this because it substitutes concepts for real things, and concepts *are* their own bare selves and nothing else. What Royce calls Hegel's 'system' was Hegel's attempt to make us believe that he was working by concepts and grinding out a higher style of logic, when in reality sensible experiences, hypotheses, and passion furnished him with all his results.

What I myself may mean by things being their own others, we shall see in a later lecture. It is now time to take our look at Fechner, whose thickness is a refreshing contrast to the thin, abstract, indigent, and threadbare appearance, the starving, school-room aspect, which the speculations of most of our absolutist philosophers present.

There is something really weird and uncanny in the contrast between the abstract pretensions of rationalism and what rationalistic methods concretely can do. If the 'logical prius' of our mind were really the 'implicit presence' of the whole 'concrete universal,' the whole of reason, or reality, or spirit, or the absolute idea, or whatever it may be called, in all our finite thinking, and if this reason worked (for example) by the dialectical method, doesn't it seem odd that in the greatest instance of rationalization mankind has known, in 'science,' namely, the dialectical method should never once have been tried? Not a solitary instance of the use of it in science occurs to my mind. Hypotheses, and deductions from these, controlled by sense-observations and analogies with what we know elsewhere, are to be thanked for all of science's results.

Fechner used no methods but these latter ones in arguing for his metaphysical conclusions about reality—but let me first rehearse a few of the facts about his life.

Born in 1801, the son of a poor country pastor in Saxony, he lived from 1817 to 1887, when he died—seventy years therefore—at Leipzig, a typical *gelehrter* of the old-fashioned German stripe. His means were always scanty, so his only extravagances could be in the way of thought, but these were gorgeous ones. He passed his medical examinations at Leipzig University at the age of twenty-one, but decided, instead of becoming a doctor, to devote himself to physical science. It was ten years before he was made professor of physics, altho he soon was authorized to lecture. Meanwhile he had to make both ends meet, and this he did by voluminous literary labors. He translated, for example, the four volumes of Biot's treatise on physics, and the six of Thénard's work on chemistry, and took care of their enlarged editions later. He edited repertories of chemistry and physics, a pharmaceutical journal, and an encyclopaedia in eight volumes, of which he wrote about one third. He published physical treatises and experimental investigations of his own, especially in electricity. Electrical measurements, as you know, are the basis of electrical science, and Fechner's measurements in galvanism, performed with the simplest self-made apparatus, are classic to this day. During this time he also published a number of half-philosophical, half-humorous writings, which have gone through several editions, under the name of Dr. Mises, besides poems, literary and artistic essays, and other occasional articles.

But overwork, poverty, and an eye-trouble produced by his observations on after-images in the retina (also a classic piece of investigation) produced in Fechner, then about thirty-eight years old, a terrific attack of nervous prostration with painful hyperaesthesia of all the functions, from which he suffered three years, cut off entirely from active life. Present day medicine would have classed poor Fechner's malady quickly enough as partly a habit-neurosis; but its severity was such that in his day it was treated as a visitation incomprehensible in its malignity, and when he suddenly began to get well, both Fechner and others treated the recovery as a sort of divine miracle. This illness, bringing Fechner face to face with inner desperation, made a great crisis in his life. "Had I not then clung to the faith," he writes, "that clinging to faith would somehow or other work its reward, *so hätte ich jene zeit nicht ausgehalten.*" His religious and cosmological faiths saved him—thenceforward one great aim with him was to work out and communicate these faiths to the world. He did so on the largest scale; but he did many other things too ere he died.

A book on the atomic theory, classic also; four elaborate mathematical and experimental volumes on what he called psychophysics—many persons consider Fechner to have practically founded scientific psychology in the first of these books; a volume on organic evolution, and two works on experimental aesthetics, in which again Fechner is considered by some judges to have laid the foundations of a new science, must be included among these other performances. Of the more religious and philosophical works I shall immediately give a further account.

All Leipzig mourned him when he died, for he was the pattern of the ideal German scholar, as daringly original in his thought as he was homely in his life, a modest, genial, laborious slave to truth and learning, and withal the owner of an admirable literary style of the vernacular sort. The materialistic generation, that in the fifties and sixties called his speculations fantastic, had been replaced by one with greater liberty of imagination, and a Preyer, a Wundt, a Paulsen, and a Lasswitz could now speak of Fechner as their master.

His mind was indeed one of those multitudinously organized crossroads of truth which are occupied only at rare intervals by children of men, and from which nothing is either too far or too near to be seen in due perspective. Patientest observation, exactest mathematics, shrewdest discrimination, humanest feeling flourished in him on the largest scale, with no apparent detriment to one another. He was in fact a philosopher in the 'great' sense, altho he cared so much less than most philosophers care for abstractions of the 'thin' order. For him the abstract lived in the concrete, and the hidden motive of all he did was to bring what he called the daylight view of this world into even greater evidence, that daylight view being this, that the whole universe in its different spans and wave-lengths, exclusions and envelopments, is everywhere alive and conscious. It has taken fifty years for his chief book, *Zendavesta,* to pass into a second edition (1901). "One swallow," he cheerfully writes, "does not make a summer. But the first swallow would not come unless the summer were coming; and for me that summer means my daylight view some time prevailing."

The original sin, according to Fechner, of both our popular and our scientific thinking, is our inveterate habit of regarding the spiritual not as the rule but as an exception in the midst of nature. Instead of believing our life to be fed at the breasts of the greater life, our individuality to be sustained by the greater individuality, which must necessarily have more consciousness and more independence than all that it brings forth, we habitually treat whatever lies outside of our life as so much slag and ashes of life only; or if we believe in a Divine Spirit, we fancy him on the one side as bodiless, and nature as soulless on the other. What comfort, or peace, Fechner asks, can come from such a doctrine? The flowers wither at its breath, the stars turn into stone; our own body grows unworthy of our spirit and sinks to a tenement for carnal senses only. The book of nature turns into a volume on mechanics, in which whatever has life is treated as a sort of anomaly; a great chasm of separation yawns between us and all that is higher than ourselves; and God becomes a thin nest of abstractions.

Fechner's great instrument for vivifying the daylight view is analogy; not a rationalistic argument is to be found in all his many pages—only reasonings like those which men continually use in practical life. For example: My house is built by someone, the world too is built by someone. The world is greater than my house, it must be a greater someone who built the world. My body moves by the influence of my feeling and will; the sun, moon, sea, and wind, being themselves more powerful, move by the influence of some more powerful feeling and will. I live now, and change from one day to another; I shall live hereafter, and change still more, etc.

Bain defines genius as the power of seeing analogies. The number that Fechner could perceive was prodigious; but he insisted on the differences as well. Neglect to make allowance for these, he said, is the common fallacy in analogical reasoning. Most of us, for example, reasoning justly that since all the minds we know are connected with bodies, therefore God's mind should be connected with a body, proceed to suppose that that body must be an animal body over again, and so paint an altogether human picture of God. But all that the analogy comports is *a* body—the particular features of *our* body are adaptations to a habitat so different from God's that if God have a physical body at all, it must be utterly different from ours in structure. Throughout his writings Fechner makes difference and analogy walk abreast, and by his extraordinary power of noticing both, he converts what would ordinarily pass for objections to his conclusions into factors of their support.

The vaster orders of mind go with the vaster orders of body. The entire earth on which we live must have, according to Fechner, its own collective consciousness. So must each sun, moon, and planet; so must the whole solar system have its own wider consciousness, in which the consciousness of our earth plays one part. So has the entire starry system as such its consciousness; and if that starry system be not the sum of all that *is*, materially considered, then that whole system, along with whatever else may be, is the body of that absolutely totalized consciousness of the universe to which men give the name of God.

Speculatively Fechner is thus a monist in his theology; but there is room in his universe for every grade of spiritual being between man and the final all-inclusive God; and in suggesting what the positive content of all this super-humanity may be, he hardly lets his imagination fly beyond simple spirits of the planetary order. The earth-soul he passionately believes in; he treats the earth as our special human guardian angel; we can pray to the earth as men pray to their saints; but I think that in his system, as in so many of the actual historic theologies, the supreme God marks only a sort of limit of enclosure of the worlds above man. He is left thin and abstract in his majesty, men preferring to carry on their personal transactions with the many less remote and abstract messengers and mediators whom the divine order provides.

I shall ask later whether the abstractly monistic turn which Fechner's speculations took was necessitated by logic. I believe it not to have been required. Meanwhile let me lead you a little more into the detail of his thought. Inevitably one does him miserable injustice by summarizing and abridging him. For altho the type of reasoning he employs is almost childlike for simplicity, and his bare conclusions can be written on a single page, the *power* of the man is due altogether to the profuseness of his concrete imagination, to the multitude of the points which he considers successively, to the cumulative effect of his learning, of his thoroughness, and of the ingenuity of his detail, to his admirably homely style, to the sincerity with which his pages glow, and finally to the impression he gives of a man who doesn't live at second-hand, but who *sees,* who in fact speaks as one having authority, and not as if he were one of the common herd of professorial philosophic scribes.

Abstractly set down, his most important conclusion for my purpose in these lectures is that the constitution of the world is identical throughout. In ourselves, visual consciousness goes with our eyes, tactile consciousness with our skin. But altho neither skin nor eye knows aught of the sensations of the other, they come together and figure in some sort of relation and combination in the more inclusive consciousness which each of us names his *self.* Quite similarly, then, says Fechner, we must suppose that my consciousness of myself and yours of yourself, altho in their immediacy they keep separate and know nothing of each other, are yet known and used together in a higher consciousness, that of the human race, say, into which they enter as constituent parts. Similarly, the whole human and animal kingdoms come together as conditions of a consciousness of still wider scope. This combines in the soul of the earth with the consciousness of the vegetable kingdom, which in turn contributes its share of experience to that of the whole solar system; and so on from synthesis to synthesis and from height to height, till an absolutely universal consciousness is reached.

A vast analogical series, in which the basis of the analogy consists of facts directly observable in ourselves.

The supposition of an earth-consciousness meets a strong instinctive prejudice which Fechner ingeniously tries to overcome. Man's mind is the highest consciousness upon the earth, we think—the earth itself being in all ways man's inferior. How should its consciousness, if it have one, be superior to his?

What are the marks of superiority which we are tempted to use here? If we look more carefully into them, Fechner points out that the earth possesses each and all of them more perfectly than we. He considers in detail the points of difference between us, and shows them all to make for the earth's higher rank. I will touch on only a few of these points.

One of them of course is independence of other external beings. External to the earth are only the other heavenly bodies. All the things on which we externally depend for life—air, water, plant and animal food, fellow men, etc.—are included in her as her constituent parts. She is self-sufficing in a million respects in which we are not so. We depend on her for almost everything, she on us for but a small portion of her history. She swings us in her orbit from winter to summer, and revolves us from day into night and from night into day.

Complexity in unity is another sign of superiority. The total earth's complexity far exceeds that of any organism, for she includes all our organisms in herself, along with an infinite number of things that our organisms fail to include. Yet how simple and massive are the phases of her own proper life! As the total bearing of any animal is sedate and tranquil compared with the agitation of its blood corpuscles, so is the earth a sedate and tranquil being compared with the animals whom she supports.

To develope from within, instead of being fashioned from without, is also counted as something superior in men's eyes. An egg is a higher style of being than a piece of clay which an external modeler makes into the image of a bird. Well, the earth's history developes from within. It is like that of a wonderful egg which the sun's heat, like that of a mother-hen, has stimulated to its cycles of evolutionary change.

Individuality of type, and difference from other beings of its type, is another mark of rank. The earth differs from every other planet, and as a class planetary beings are extraordinarily distinct from other beings.

Long ago the earth was called an animal; but a planet is a higher class of being than either man or animal; not only quantitatively greater, like a vaster and more awkward whale or elephant, but a being whose enormous size requires an altogether different plan of life. Our animal organization comes from our inferiority. Our need of moving to and fro, of stretching our limbs and bending our bodies, shows only our defect. What are our legs but crutches, by means of which, with restless efforts, we go hunting after the things we have not inside of ourselves. But the earth is no such cripple; why should she who already possesses within herself the things we so painfully pursue, have limbs analogous to ours? Shall she mimic a small part of herself? What need has she of arms, with nothing to reach for? of a neck, with no head to carry? of eyes or nose when she finds her way through space without either, and has the millions of eyes of all her animals to guide their movements on her surface, and all their noses to smell the flowers that grow? For, as we are ourselves a part of the earth, so our organs are her organs. She is, as it were, eye and ear over her whole extent, seeing and hearing at once all that we see and hear in separation. She brings forth living beings of countless kinds upon her surface, and their multitudinous conscious relations with each other she takes up into her higher and more general conscious life.

Most of us, considering the theory that the whole terrestrial mass is animated as our bodies are, make the mistake of working the analogy too literally, and allowing for no differences. If the earth be a sentient organism, we say, where are her brain and nerves? What corresponds to her heart and lungs? In other words, we expect functions which she already performs through us, to be performed outside of us again, and in just the same way. But we see perfectly well how the earth performs some of these functions in a way unlike our way. If you speak of circulation, what need has she of a heart when the sun keeps all the showers of rain that fall upon her, and all the springs and brooks and rivers that irrigate her, going? What need has she of internal lungs, when her whole sensitive surface is in living commerce with the atmosphere that clings to it?

The organ that gives us most trouble is the brain. All the consciousness we directly know seems tied to brains.—Can there be consciousness, we ask, where there is no brain? But our brain, which primarily serves to correlate our muscular reactions with the external objects on which we depend, performs a function which the earth performs in an entirely different way. She has no proper muscles or limbs of her own, and the only objects external to her are the other stars. To these her whole mass reacts by most exquisite alterations in its total gait, and by still more exquisite vibratory responses in its substance. Her ocean reflects the lights of heaven as in a mighty mirror, her atmosphere refracts them like a monstrous lens, the clouds and snowfields combine them into white, the woods and flowers disperse them into colours. Polarization, interference, absorption, awaken sensibilities in matter of which our senses are too coarse to take any note.

For these cosmic relations of hers, then, she no more needs a special brain than she needs eyes or ears. *Our* brains do indeed unify and correlate innumerable functions. Our eyes know nothing of sound, our ears nothing of light; but, having brains, we can feel sound and light together, and compare them. We account for this by the fibres which in the brain connect the optical with the acoustic centre; but just how such fibres bring together not only the centres, but the sensations, we fail to see. But if fibres are indeed all that is needed to do that trick, has not the earth pathways, by which you and I are physically continuous, more than enough to do for our two minds what the brain-fibres do for the sounds and sights in a single mind? Must every higher means of unification between things be a literal *brain-fibre*, and go by that name? Cannot the earth-mind know otherwise the contents of our minds together?

Fechner's imagination, insisting on the differences as well as on the resemblances, thus tries to make our picture of the whole earth's life more concrete. He revels in the thought of its perfections. To carry her precious freight through the hours and seasons what form could be more excellent than hers—being as it is horse, wheels and wagon all in one. Think of her beauty—a shining ball, sky-blue and sunlit over one half, the other bathed in starry night, reflecting the heavens from all her waters, myriads of lights and shadows in the folds of her mountains and windings of her valleys, she would be a spectacle of rainbow glory could one only see her from afar as we see parts of her from her own mountain-tops. Every quality of landscape that has a name would then be visible in her at once—all that is delicate or graceful, all that is quiet, or wild, or romantic, or desolate, or cheerful, or luxuriant, or fresh. That landscape is her face—a peopled landscape, too, for men's eyes would appear in it like diamonds among the dew-drops. Green would be the dominant colour, but the blue atmosphere and the clouds would enfold her as a veil enshrouds a bride—a veil the vapory transparent folds of which the earth, through her ministers the winds, never tires of laying and folding about herself anew.

Every element has its own living denizens. Can the celestial ocean of aether, whose waves are light, in which the earth herself floats, not have hers, higher by as much as their element is higher, swimming without fins, flying without wings, moving, immense and tranquil, as by a half-spiritual force through the half-spiritual sea which they inhabit, rejoicing in the exchange of luminous influence with one another, following the slightest pull of one another's attraction, and harboring, each of them, an inexhaustible inward wealth?

Men have always made fables about angels, dwelling in the light, needing no earthly food or drink, messengers between ourselves and God. Here are actually existent beings, dwelling in the light and moving through the sky, needing neither food nor drink, intermediaries between God and us, obeying his commands. So, if the heavens really are the home of angels, the heavenly bodies must be those very angels, for other creatures *there* are none. Yes! the earth is our great common guardian angel, who watches over all our interests combined.

In a striking page Fechner relates one of his moments of direct vision of this truth.

"On a certain spring morning I went out to walk. The fields were green, the birds sang, the dew glistened, the smoke was rising, here and there a man appeared; a light as of transfiguration lay on all things. It was only a little bit of the earth; it was only one moment of her existence; and yet as my look embraced her more and more it seemed to me not only so beautiful an idea, but so true and clear a fact, that she is an angel, an angel so rich and fresh and flower-like, and yet going her round in the skies so firmly and so at one with herself, turning her whole living face to Heaven, and carrying me along with her into that Heaven, that I asked myself how the opinions of men could ever have so spun themselves away from life so far as to deem the earth only a dry clod, and to seek for angels above it or about it in the emptiness of the sky—only to find them nowhere. . . . But such an experience as this passes for fantastic. The earth is a globular body, and what more she may be, one can find in mineralogical cabinets."[2]

Where there is no vision the people perish. Few professorial philosophers have any vision. Fechner had vision, and that is why one can read him over and over again, and each time bring away a fresh sense of reality.

His earliest book was a vision of what the inner life of plants may be like. He called it *Nanna*. In the development of animals the nervous system is the central fact. Plants develope centrifugally, spread their organs abroad. For that reason people suppose that they can have no consciousness, for they lack the unity which the central nervous system provides. But the plant's consciousness may be of another type, being connected with other structures. Violins and pianos give out sounds because they have strings. Does it follow that nothing but strings can give out sound? How then about flutes and organ-pipes? Of course their sounds are of a different quality, and so may the consciousness of plants be of a quality correlated exclusively with the kind of organization that they possess. Nutrition, respiration, propagation take place in them without nerves. In us these functions are conscious only in unusual states, normally their consciousness is eclipsed by that which goes with the brain. No such eclipse occurs in plants, and their lower consciousness may therefore be all the more lively. With nothing to do but to drink the light and air with their leaves, to let their cells proliferate, to feel their rootlets draw the sap, is it conceivable that they should not consciously suffer if water, light and air are suddenly withdrawn? or that when the flowering and fertilization which are the culmination of their life take place, they should not feel their own existence more intensely and enjoy something like what we call pleasure in ourselves? Does the water-lily, rocking in her triple bath of water, air and light, relish in no wise her own beauty? When the plant in our room turns to the light, closes her blossoms in the dark, responds to our watering or pruning by increase of size or change of shape and bloom, who has the right to say she does not feel, or that she plays a purely passive part? Truly plants can foresee nothing, neither the scythe of the mower, nor the hand extended to pluck their flowers. They can neither run away nor cry out. But this only proves how different their modes of feeling life must be from those of animals that live by eyes and ears and locomotive organs, it does not prove that they have no mode of feeling life at all.

How scanty and scattered would sensation be on our globe, if the feeling-life of plants were blotted from existence! Solitary would consciousness move through the woods in the shape of some deer or other quadruped, or fly about the flowers in that of some insect. But can we really suppose that the Nature through which God's breath blows is such a barren wilderness as this?

I have probably by this time said enough to acquaint those of you who have never seen these metaphysical writings of Fechner with their more general characteristics, and I hope that some of you may now feel like reading them yourselves.[3] The special thought of Fechner's with which in these lectures I have most practical concern, is his belief that the more inclusive forms of consciousness are in part *constituted* by the more limited forms. Not that they are the mere sum of the more limited forms. As our mind is not the bare sum of our sights plus our sounds plus our pains, but in adding these terms together also finds relations among them and weaves them into schemes and forms and objects of which no one sense in its separate estate knows anything, so the earth-soul traces relations between the contents of my mind and the contents of yours of which neither of our separate minds is conscious. It has schemes, forms, and objects proportionate to its wider field, which our mental fields are far too narrow to cognize. By ourselves we are simply out of relation with each other, for it we are both of us there, and *different* from each other, which is a positive relation. What we are without knowing, it knows that we are. We are closed against its world, but that world is not closed against us. It is as if the total universe of inner life had a sort of grain or direction, a sort of valvular structure permitting knowledge to flow in one way only, so that the wider might always have the narrower under observation, but never the narrower the wider.

Fechner's great analogy here is the relation of the senses to our individual minds. When our eyes are open their sensations enter into our general mental life, which grows incessantly by the addition of what they see. Close the eyes, however, and the visual additions stop, nothing but thoughts and memories of the past visual experiences remain—in combination of course with the enormous stock of other thoughts and memories, and with the data coming in from the senses not yet closed. Our eye-sensations of themselves know nothing of this enormous life into which they fall. Fechner thinks, as any common man would think, that they are taken into it directly when they occur, and form part of it just as they are. They don't stay outside and get represented inside by their copies. It is only the memories and concepts of them that are copies; the sensible perceptions themselves are taken in or walled out in their own proper persons according as the eyes are open or shut.

Fechner likens our individual persons on the earth unto so many sense-organs of the earth's soul. We add to its perceptive life so long as our own life lasts. It absorbs our perceptions, just as they occur, into its larger sphere of knowledge, and combines them with the other data there. When one of us dies, it is as if an eye of the world were closed, for all *perceptive* contributions from that particular quarter cease. But the memories and conceptual relations that have spun themselves round the perceptions of that person remain in the larger earth-life as distinct as ever, and form new relations and grow and develope throughout all the future, in the same way in which our own distinct objects of thought, once stored in memory, form new relations and develope throughout our whole finite life. This is Fechner's theory of immortality, first published in the little *Büchlein vom Leben nach dem Tode*, in 1836, and re-edited in greatly improved shape in the last volume of his *Zendavesta*.

We rise upon the earth as wavelets rise upon the ocean. We grow out of her soil as leaves grow from a tree. The wavelets catch the sun-beams separately, the leaves stir when the branches do not move. They realize their own events apart, just as in our own consciousness, when anything becomes emphatic, the background fades from observation. Yet the event works back upon the background, as the wavelet works upon the waves, or as the leaf's movements work upon the sap inside the branch. The whole sea and the whole tree are registers of what has happened, and are different for the wave's and the leaf's action having occurred. A grafted twig may modify its scion to the roots:—so our out-lived private experiences, impressed on the whole earth-mind as memories, lead the immortal life of ideas there, and become parts of the great system, fully distinguished from one another, just as we ourselves when alive were distinct, realizing themselves no longer isolatedly, but along with one another as so many partial systems, entering thus into new combinations, being affected by the perceptive experiences of those living then, and affecting the living in their turn—altho they are so seldom recognized by living men to do so.

If you imagine that this entrance after the death of the body into a common life of higher type means a merging and loss of our distinct personality, Fechner asks you whether a visual sensation of our own exists in any sense *less for itself* or *less distinctly,* when it enters into our higher relational consciousness and is there distinguished and defined.

—But here I must stop my reporting and send you to his volumes. Thus is the universe alive, according to this philosopher! I think you will admit that he makes it more *thickly* alive than do the other philosophers who, following rationalistic methods solely, gain the same results, but only in the thinnest outlines. Both Fechner and Professor Royce, for example, believe ultimately in one all-inclusive mind. Both believe that we, just as we stand here, are constituent parts of that mind. No other *content* has it than us, with all the other creatures like or unlike us, and the relations which it finds between us. Our eaches, collected into one, are substantively identical with its all, tho the all is perfect while no each is perfect, so that we have to admit that new qualities as well as unperceived relations accrue from the collective form. It is thus superior to the distributive form. But having reached this result, Royce (tho his treatment of the subject on its moral side seems to me infinitely richer and thicker than that of any other contemporary idealistic philosopher) leaves us very much to our own devices. Fechner, on the contrary, tries to trace the superiorities due to the more collective form in as much detail as he can. He marks the various intermediary stages and halting places of collectivity—as we are to our separate senses, so is the earth to us, so is the solar system to the earth, etc.—and if, in order to escape an infinitely long summation, he posits a complete God as the all-container and leaves him about as indefinite in feature as the idealists leave their absolute, he yet provides us with a very definite gate of approach to him in the shape of the earth-soul, through which in the nature of things we must first make connexion with all the more enveloping superhuman realms, and with which our more immediate religious commerce at any rate has to be carried on.

Ordinary monistic idealism leaves everything intermediary out. It recognizes only the extremes, as if, after the first rude face of the phenomenal world in all its particularity, nothing but the supreme in all its perfection could be found. First, you and I, just as we are in this room; and the moment we get below that surface, the unutterable absolute itself! Doesn't this show a singularly indigent imagination? Isn't this brave universe made on a richer pattern, with room in it for a long hierarchy of beings? Materialistic science makes it infinitely richer in terms, with its molecules and aether, and electrons, and what not. Absolute ideal-ism, thinking of reality only under intellectual forms, knows not what to do with *bodies* of any grade, and can make no use of any psychophys-ical analogy or correspondence. The resultant thinness is startling when compared with the thickness and articulation of such a universe as Fechner paints. May not satisfaction with the rationalistic absolute as the alpha and omega, and treatment of it in all its abstraction as an ade-quate religious object, argue a certain native poverty of mental demand? Things reveal themselves soonest to those who most passionately want them, for our need sharpens our wit. To a mind content with little, the much in the universe may always remain hid.

To be candid, one of my reasons for saying so much about Fechner has been to make the thinness of our current transcendentalism appear more evident by an effect of contrast. Scholasticism ran thick; Hegel himself ran thick; but English and American transcendentalisms run thin. If philosophy is more a matter of passionate vision than of logic—and I believe it is, logic only finding reasons for the vision afterwards—must not such thinness come either from the vision being defective in the disciples, or from their passion, matched with Fechner's or with He-gel's own passion, being as moonlight unto sunlight or as water unto wine?[4]

But I have also a much deeper reason for making Fechner a part of my text. His *assumption that conscious experiences freely compound and sepa-rate themselves,* the same assumption by which absolutism explains the relation of our minds to the eternal mind, and the same by which em-piricism explains the composition of the human mind out of subordi-nate mental elements, is not one which we ought to let pass without scrutiny. I shall scrutinize it in the next lecture.

17

The Moral Equivalent of War

William James thought we would not get rid of war unless we could first redirect that which is warlike in the human spirit. So he argued for inhibition by substitution rather than inhibition by prohibition. What we need then is not to just stop fighting because we want peace, but to find some morally valuable goal to fight for. The idea that there might be a "moral equivalent of war" has taken hold and shows fresh signs of life every time a war on poverty or a war on drugs is announced. In the 1930s, members of the Civilian Conservation Corps lived a barrack-room life and built hiking trails. (Fittingly enough, when a CCC leadership camp was established in Sharon, Vermont, in 1940, it was called Camp William James.) The Baptists from Hillsborough, North Carolina, and elsewhere roll their battle-ready pre-provisioned mobile kitchens onto the front lines of Hurricane Katrina and other disasters. We get it. You can't root the war spirit out. You have to find a constructive role for it.

The idea and the actual phrase were already present in *The Varieties of Religious Experience* (1902), where James is examining the practical effects of strong religious feeling. He says there, "What we now need to discover in the social realm is the moral equivalent of war: something heroic that will speak to men as universally as war does, and yet will be as compatible with their spiritual selves as war has proved itself to be incompatible . . . May not voluntarily accepted poverty be 'the strenuous life,' without the need of crushing weaker peoples?" By "voluntary poverty" James means the sort of plain living willingly undertaken for high purposes by Henry Thoreau, Mahatma Gandhi, or Dr. Paul Farmer.

By 1910, James had a new idea, which was to enlist young people in a constructive war against the soft life. "To coal and iron mines, to freight trains, to fishing fleets in December, to dish-washing, clothes-washing, and window-washing, to road-building and tunnel-making, to foundries and stoke-holes, and to the frames of skyscrapers, would our gilded youths be drafted off, according to their choice, to get the childishness knocked out of them, and to come back into society with healthier sympathies and soberer ideas."

For a hundred years now we have had the idea. Perhaps in another hundred we will have the thing itself.

———◆———

THE WAR against war is going to be no holiday excursion or camping party. The military feelings are too deeply grounded to abdicate their place among our ideals until better substitutes are offered than the glory and shame that come to nations as well as to individuals from the ups and downs of politics and the vicissitudes of trade. There is something highly paradoxical in the modern man's relation to war. Ask all our millions, north and south, whether they would vote now (were such a thing possible) to have our war for the Union expunged from history, and the record of a peaceful transition to the present time substituted for that of its marches and battles, and probably hardly a handful of ex-centrics would say yes. Those ancestors, those efforts, those memories and legends, are the most ideal part of what we now own together, a sacred spiritual possession worth more than all the blood poured out. Yet ask those same people whether they would be willing in cold blood to start another civil war now to gain another similar possession, and not one man or woman would vote for the proposition. In modern eyes, precious tho' wars may be, they must not be waged solely for the sake of the ideal harvest. Only when forced upon one, only when an enemy's injustice leaves us no alternative, is a war now thought permissible.

It was not thus in ancient times. The earlier men were hunting men; and to hunt a neighboring tribe, kill the males, loot the village and possess the females, was the most profitable, as well as the most exciting, way of living. Thus were the more martial tribes selected, and in chiefs and peoples a pure pugnacity and love of glory came to mingle with the more fundamental appetite for plunder.

Modern war is so expensive that we feel trade to be a better avenue to plunder; but modern man inherits all the innate pugnacity and all the love of glory of his ancestors. To show war's irrationality and horror has no effect upon him. The horrors make the fascination. War is the *strong* life; it is life *in extremis*. War-taxes are the only ones men never hesitate to pay, as the budgets of all nations show.

History is a bath of blood. The Iliad is one long recital of how Diomedes and Ajax, Sarpedon and Hector *killed*. No detail of the wounds they made is spared us, and the Greek mind fed upon the story. Greek history is a panorama of jingoism and imperialism—war for war's sake, all the citizens being warriors. It is horrible reading, because of the irrationality of it all—save for the purpose of making 'history'—and the history is that of the utter ruin of a civilization which in intellectual respects was perhaps the highest the earth has ever seen.

Those wars were purely piratical. Pride, gold, women, slaves, excitement, were their only motives. In the Peloponnesian war, for example, the Athenians ask the inhabitants of Melos (the island where the 'Venus of Melos' was found), hitherto neutral, to acknowledge their lordship. The envoys meet, and hold a debate which Thucydides gives in full, and which, for sweet reasonableness of form, would have satisfied a Matthew Arnold. "The powerful exact what they can," said the Athenians, "and the weak grant what they must." When the Meleans say that sooner than be slaves they will appeal to the gods, the Athenians reply: "Of the gods we believe, and of men we know, that by a law of their nature wherever they can rule they will. This law was not made by us, and we are not the first who have acted upon it; we did but inherit it, . . . and we know that you and all mankind, if you were as strong as we are, would do as we do. So much for the gods; we have told you why we expect to stand as high in their good opinion as you." Well, the Meleans still refused, and their town was taken. "The Athenians," Thucydides quietly says, "thereupon put to death all who were of military age, and made slaves of the women and children. They then colonised the island, sending thither five hundred settlers of their own."

Alexander's career was piracy pure and simple, nothing but an orgy of power and plunder, made romantic by the character of the hero. There was no rational principle in it, and the moment he died his generals and governors attacked one another. The cruelty of those times is incredible. When Rome finally conquered Greece, Paulus Aemilius was told by the Roman Senate to reward his soldiers for their toil by 'giving' them the old kingdom of Epirus. They sacked seventy cities and carried off a hundred and fifty thousand inhabitants as slaves. How many they killed I know not; but in Aetolia they killed all the senators, five hundred and fifty in number. Brutus was 'the noblest Roman of them all,' yet to reanimate his soldiers on the eve of Philippi he promises to give them the cities of Sparta and Thessalonica to ravage, if they win the fight.

Such was the gory nurse that trained societies to cohesiveness. We inherit the warlike type; and for most of the capacity of heroism of which the human race is full we have to thank this cruel history. Dead men tell no tales, and if there were tribes of other type than this, they have left no survivors. Our ancestors have bred pugnacity into our bone and marrow, and thousands of years of peace won't breed it out of us. The popular imagination fairly fattens on the thought of wars. Let public opinion once reach a certain fighting pitch, and no ruler can withstand it. In the Boer war both governments began with bluff; but they couldn't stay there—the military tension was too much for them. In 1898 our people had read the word WAR in letters three inches high in every newspaper for three months. The pliant politician McKinley was swept away by their eagerness, and our squalid war with Spain became a necessity.

At the present day, civilized opinion is a curious mental mixture. The military instincts and ideals are as strong as ever, but they are confronted by reflective criticisms which sorely curb their ancient freedom. Innumerable writers are showing up the bestial side of military service. Pure loot and mastery seem no longer morally avowable motives, and pretexts must be found for attributing them solely to the enemy. England and we, our army and navy authorities repeat without ceasing, arm solely for 'peace'; Germany and Japan it is who are bent on loot and glory. 'Peace' in military mouths to day is a synonym for 'war expected.' The word has become a pure provocative, and no government sincerely wishing peace should allow it ever to be printed in a newspaper. Every up-to-date Dictionary should say that 'peace' and 'war' mean the same thing, now *in posse,* now *in actu.* It may even reasonably be said that the intensely sharp competitive *preparation* for war by the nations is the *real war,* permanent, unceasing; and that the battles are only a sort of public verification of the military mastery gained during the 'peace'-interval.

It is plain that on this subject civilized man has developed a sort of double personality. If we take European nations, no legitimate interest of any one of them would seem to justify the tremendous destructions which a war (to compass it) would necessarily entail. It would seem as tho' common sense and reason ought to find a way to reach agreement in every conflict of honest interests. I myself think it our bounden duty to believe in international rationality as far as possible. But, as things stand, I see how desperately hard it is to bring the peace-party and the war-party together. I believe that the difficulty is due to certain deficiencies in the program of pacificism which set the militarist imagination strongly, and to a certain extent justifiably, against it. In the whole discussion both sides are on imaginative and sentimental ground. It is but one Utopia against another, and everything one says must be abstract and hypothetical. Subject to this criticism and caution, I shall try to characterize in abstract strokes the opposite imaginative forces, and point out what to my own very fallible mind seems the best Utopian hypothesis, the most promising line of conciliation.

In my remarks, pacificist tho' I am, I shall refuse to speak of the bestial side of the war-regime (already done justice to by so many writers) and consider only the higher aspects of militaristic sentiment. Patriotism no one thinks discreditable; nor does anyone deny that war is the romance of history. But inordinate ambitions are the soul of all patriotism, and the possibility of violent death the soul of all romance. The militarily patriotic and romantic-minded, and especially the professional military class, refuse to admit for a moment that war may be a transitory phenomenon in social evolution. The notion of a sheep's paradise like that revolts, they say, our higher imagination. Where then would be the steeps of life? If war had ever stopped, we should have to re-invent it, in their view, to redeem life from flat degeneration.

All reflective apologists for war at the present day take it religiously. It is to them a sort of sacrament; its profits are to the vanquished as well as to the victor; and quite apart from any question of profit, it is an absolute good, we are told, for it is human nature at its highest dynamic. Its 'horrors' are a cheap price to pay for rescue from the only alternative supposed, of a world of clerks and teachers, of co-education and zoophily, of 'consumers' leagues' and 'associated charities,' of industrialism unlimited, and feminism unabashed. No scorn, no hardness, no valor any more! Fie upon such a cattleyard of a planet!

So far as the central essence of this feeling goes, no healthy-minded person, it seems to me, can help partaking of it to some degree. Militarism is the great preserver of our ideals of hardihood, and human life without hardihood would be contemptible. Without risks or prizes for the darer, history would be insipid indeed; and there is a type of military character which everyone feels that the race should never cease to breed, for everyone is sensitive to its superiority. The duty is incumbent on mankind, of keeping military characters in stock—of keeping them, if not for use, then as ends in themselves and as pure pieces of perfection—so that Roosevelt's weaklings and mollycoddles may not end by making everything else disappear from the face of nature.

This natural feeling forms, I think, the innermost soul of army-writings. Without any exception known to me, militarist authors take a highly mystical view of their subject, and regard war as a biological or sociological necessity, uncontrolled by ordinary psychological checks and motives. When the time of development is ripe the war must come, reason or no reason, for the justifications pleaded are invariably fictitious. War is, in short, a permanent human *obligation*. General Homer Lea, in his recent book *The Valor of Ignorance,* plants himself squarely on this ground. Readiness for war is for him the essence of nationality, and ability in it the supreme measure of the health of nations.

Nations, General Lea says, are never stationary—they must necessarily expand or shrink, according to their vitality or decrepitude. Japan now is culminating; and by the fatal law in question it is impossible that her statesmen should not long since have entered, with extraordinary foresight, upon a vast policy of conquest—the game in which the first moves were her wars with China and Russia and her treaty with England, and of which the final objective is the capture of the Philippines, the Hawaiian Islands, Alaska, and the whole of our Coast west of the Sierra Passes. This will give Japan what her ineluctable vocation as a state absolutely forces her to claim, the possession of the entire Pacific Ocean; and to oppose these deep designs we Americans have, according to our author, nothing but our conceit, our ignorance, our commercialism, our corruption, and our feminism. General Lea makes a minute technical comparison of the military strength that we at present could oppose to the strength of Japan, and concludes that the Islands, Alaska, Oregon and Southern California would fall almost without resistance, that San Francisco must surrender in a fortnight to a Japanese investment, and that in three or four months the war would be over, and our republic, unable to regain what it had heedlessly neglected to protect sufficiently, would then 'disintegrate,' until perhaps some Caesar should arise to weld us again into a nation.

A dismal forecast indeed! Yet not absolutely unplausible, if the mentality of Japan's statesmen be of the Caesarian type of which history shows so many examples, and which is all that General Lea seems able to imagine. There is no reason to think, after all, that women can no longer be the mothers of Napoleonic or Alexandrian characters; and if these characters should appear in Japan and find their opportunity, just such surprises as *The Valor of Ignorance* paints may lurk in ambush for us. Ignorant as we still are of the innermost recesses of Japanese mentality, we may be foolhardy in disregarding such possibilities.

Other militarists are more complex and more moral in their considerations. The *Philosophie des Krieges* by S. R. Steinmetz is a good example. War, according to this author, is an ordeal instituted by God, who weighs the nations in its balance. It is the essential form of the State, and the only function in which peoples can employ all their powers at once and convergently. No victory is possible save as the resultant of a totality of virtues, no defeat for which some vice or weakness is not responsible. Fidelity, cohesiveness, tenacity, heroism, conscience, education, inventiveness, economy, wealth, physical health and vigor—there isn't a moral or intellectual point of superiority that doesn't tell, when God holds his assizes and hurls the peoples upon one another. *Die Weltgeschichte ist das Weltgericht;* and Dr. Steinmetz does not believe that in the long run chance and luck play any part in apportioning the issues.

The virtues that prevail, it must be noted, are virtues anyhow, superiorities that count in peaceful as well as in military competition; but the strain on them, being infinitely intenser in the latter case, makes war infinitely more searching as a trial. No ordeal, according to this author, can be comparable to its winnowings. Its dread hammer is the welder of men into cohesive states, and nowhere but in such states can human nature adequately develope its capacity. The only alternative is 'degeneration.'

Dr. Steinmetz is a conscientious thinker, and his book, short as it is, takes much into account. Its upshot, it seems to me, can be summed up in Simon Patten's word, that mankind was nursed in pain and fear, and that the transition to a 'pleasure-economy' may be fatal to a being untrained to powers of defense against its disintegrative influences. If we speak of *the fear of emancipation from the fear-regime*, we put the militarist attitude into a single phrase: fear regarding ourselves now taking the place of the ancient fear of the enemy.

Turn the fear over in my mind as I will, it all seems to lead back to two unwillingnesses of the imagination, one esthetic, and the other moral: unwillingness, first, to envisage a future in which army-life, with its many elements of charm, shall be forever impossible, and in which the destinies of peoples shall nevermore be decided quickly, thrillingly, and tragically by force, but only gradually and insipidly by 'evolution'; and, secondly, unwillingness to see the supreme theatre of human stren-uousness closed, and the splendid military aptitudes of men doomed to remain always in a state of latency and never to show themselves in ac-tion. These insistent unwillingnesses, no less than other esthetic and ethical insistencies, have, it seems to me, to be listened to and respected. One cannot meet them effectively by mere counter-insistency on war's expensiveness and horror. The horror makes the thrill; and when it is a question of getting the extremest and supremest out of human nature, talk of expense sounds ignominious. The weakness of so much merely negative criticism is evident—pacificism makes no converts from the military party. The military party denies neither the bestiality nor the horror, nor the expense; it only says that these things tell but half the story. It only says that war is *worth* these things; that, taking human nature as a whole, wars are its best protection against its weaker and more cowardly self, and that mankind cannot afford to adopt a peace-economy.

Pacificists ought to enter more deeply into the esthetical and ethical point of view of their opponents. Do that first in any controversy, says J. J. Chapman, *then move the point,* and your opponent will follow. So long as anti-militarists propose no substitutes for the disciplinary func-tion of war, no *moral equivalent* of war, analogous, as one might say, to the mechanical equivalent of heat, so long they fail to realize the full inwardness of the situation. And as a rule they do fail. The duties, pen-alties and sanctions pictured in the Utopias they paint are all too weak and tame to touch the military-minded. Tolstoy's pacificism is the only exception to this rule, for it is profoundly pessimistic as regards all this world's values, and makes the fear of the Lord furnish the moral spur provided elsewhere by the fear of the enemy. But our socialistic peace-advocates all believe absolutely in this world's values; and instead of the fear of the Lord and the fear of the enemy, the only fear they reckon with is the fear of poverty if one be lazy. This weakness pervades all the socialistic literature with which I am acquainted. Even in Lowes Dickinson's exquisite dialogue,[1] high wages and short hours are the only forces invoked for overcoming man's distaste for repulsive kinds of labor. Meanwhile men at large still live as they always have lived, under a pain-and-fear economy—for those of us who live in an ease-economy are but an island in the stormy ocean—and the whole atmosphere of present-day Utopian literature tastes mawkish and dishwatery to people who still keep a sense for life's more bitter flavors. It suggests, in truth, ubiquitous inferiority.

Inferiority is always with us, and merciless scorn of it is the keynote of the military temper. "Hounds, would you live forever?" shouted Frederick the Great. "Yes," say our Utopians, "let us live forever, and raise our level gradually." The best thing about our 'inferiors' to day is that they are as tough as nails, and physically and morally almost as insensitive. Utopianism would see them soft and squeamish, while militarism would keep their callousness, but transfigure it into a meritorious characteristic, needed by 'the service,' and redeemed by that from the suspicion of inferiority. All the qualities of a man acquire dignity when he knows that the service of the collectivity that owns him needs them. If proud of the collectivity, his own pride rises in proportion. No collectivity is like an army for nourishing such pride; but it has to be confessed that the only sentiment that the image of pacific cosmopolitan industrialism is capable of arousing in countless worthy breasts is shame at the idea of belonging to *such* a collectivity. It is obvious that the United States of America as they exist to day impress a mind like General Lea's as so much human blubber. Where is the sharpness and precipitousness, the contempt for life, whether one's own, or another's? Where is the savage 'yes' and 'no,' the unconditional duty? Where is the conscription? Where is the blood-tax? Where is anything that one feels honoured by belonging to?

Having said thus much in preparation, and by way of conciliating the side I don't belong to, I will now confess my own Utopia. I devoutly believe in the ultimate reign of peace and in the gradual advent of some sort of a socialistic equilibrium. The fatalistic view of the war-function is to me nonsense, for I know that war-making is due to definite motives and subject to prudential checks and reasonable criticisms, just like any other form of enterprise. And when whole nations are the armies, and the science of destruction vies in intellectual refinement with the sciences of production, I see that war becomes absurd and impossible from its own monstrosity. Extravagant ambitions will have to be replaced by reasonable claims, and nations must make common cause against them. I see no reason why all this should not apply to yellow as well as to white nations, and I look forward to a future when acts of war shall be formally outlawed among civilized peoples.

All these beliefs of mine put me squarely into the anti-militarist party. But I do not believe that peace either ought to be or will be permanent on this globe, unless the states pacifically organized preserve some of the old elements of army-discipline. A permanently successful peace-economy cannot be a simple pleasure-economy. In the more or less socialistic future towards which mankind seems to be drifting we must still subject ourselves collectively to those severities that answer to our real position upon this only partly hospitable globe. We must make new energies and hardihoods continue the manliness to which the military mind so faithfully clings. Martial virtues must be the enduring cement; intrepidity, contempt of softness, surrender of private interest, obedience to command, must still remain the rock upon which states are built—unless, indeed, we wish for dangerous reactions against commonwealths fit only for contempt, and liable to invite attack whenever a centre of crystallization for military-minded enterprise is formed anywhere in their neighborhood.

The war-party is assuredly right in affirming and reaffirming that the martial virtues, altho' originally gained by the race through war, are absolute and permanent human goods. Patriotic pride and ambition in their military form are, after all, only specifications of a more universal and enduring competitive passion. They are its first form, but that is no reason for supposing them to be its last form. Men now are proud of belonging to a conquering nation, and without a murmur they lay down their persons and their wealth, if by so doing they may fend off subjection. But who can be sure that *other aspects of one's country* may not, with time and education and suggestion enough, come to be regarded with similarly effective feelings of pride and shame? Why should men not some day feel that it is worth a blood-tax to belong to a collectivity superior in *any* ideal respect? Why should they not blush with indignant shame if the community that owns them is vile in any way whatsoever? Individuals, daily more numerous, now feel this civic passion. It is only a question of blowing on the spark till the whole population gets incandescent, and on the ruins of the old morals of military honour, a stable system of morals of civic honour builds itself up. What the whole community comes to believe in grasps the individual as in a vise. The war-function has graspt us so far; but constructive interests may some day seem no less imperative, and impose on the individual a hardly lighter burden.

Let me illustrate my idea more concretely. There is nothing to make one indignant in the mere fact that life is hard, that men should toil and suffer pain. The planetary conditions once for all are such, and we can stand it. But that so many men, by mere accidents of birth and opportunity, should have a life of *nothing else* but toil and pain and hardness and inferiority imposed upon them, should have *no* vacation, while others natively no more deserving get no taste of this campaigning life at all—*this* is capable of arousing indignation in reflective minds. It may end by seeming shameful to all of us that some of us have nothing but campaigning, and others have nothing but unmanly ease. If now—and this is my idea—there were, instead of military conscription a conscription of the whole youthful population to form for a certain number of years a part of the army enlisted against *nature*, the injustice would tend to be evened out, and numerous other benefits to the commonwealth would follow. The military ideals of hardihood and discipline would be wrought into the growing fibre of the people; no one would remain blind, as the luxurious classes now are blind, to man's real relations to the globe he lives on, and to the permanently solid and hard foundations of his higher life. To coal and iron mines, to freight trains, to fishing fleets in December, to dish-washing, clothes-washing, and window-washing, to road-building and tunnel-making, to foundries and stoke-holes, and to the frames of skyscrapers, would our gilded youths be drafted off, according to their choice, to get the childishness knocked out of them, and to come back into society with healthier sympathies and soberer ideas. They would have paid their blood-tax, done their own part in immemorial human warfare against nature, they would tread the earth more proudly, the women would value them more highly, they would be better fathers and teachers of the following generation.

Such a conscription, with the state of public opinion that would have required it, and the moral fruits it would bear, would preserve in the midst of a pacific civilization the manly virtues which the military party is so afraid of seeing disappear in peace. We should get toughness without callousness, authority with as little criminal cruelty as possible, and painful work done cheerily because the duty is temporary, and threatens not, as now, to degrade the whole remainder of one's life. I spoke of the 'moral equivalent' of war. So far, war has been the only force that can discipline a whole community, and until an equivalent discipline is organized, I believe that war must have its way. But I have no serious doubt that the ordinary prides and shames of social man, once developed to a certain intensity, are capable of organizing such a moral equivalent as I have sketched, or some other just as effective for preserving manliness of type. Tho' an infinitely remote Utopia just now, in the end it is but a question of time, of skilful propagandism, and of opinion-making men seizing historic opportunities.

The martial type of character can be bred without war. Strenuous honour and disinterestedness abound elsewhere. Priests and medical men are in a fashion educated to it, and we should all feel some degree of it imperative if we were conscious of our work as an obligatory service to the state. We should be *owned*, as soldiers are by the army, and our pride would rise accordingly. We could be poor, then, without humiliation, as army officers now are. The only thing needed henceforward is to inflame the civic temper as past history has inflamed the military temper.

"In many ways." says H. G. Wells, "military organisation is the most peaceful of activities. When the contemporary man steps from the street of clamorous insincere advertisement, push, adulteration, underselling and intermittent employment, into the barrack-yard, he steps on to a higher social plane, into an atmosphere of service and co-operation and of infinitely more honourable emulations. Here at least men are not flung out of employment to degenerate because there is no immediate work for them to do. They are fed and drilled and trained for better services. Here at least a man is supposed to win promotion by self-forgetfulness and not by self-seeking."[2] Bad as barrack life may be, it is very congruous with ancestral human nature, and it has the higher aspects which Wells thus emphasizes. Wells adds[3] that he thinks that the conceptions of order and discipline, the tradition of service and devotion, of physical fitness, unstinted exertion, and universal responsibility, which universal military duty is now teaching European nations, will remain a permanent acquisition, when the last ammunition has been used in the fireworks that celebrate the final peace. I believe as he does. It would be simply preposterous if the only force that could work ideals of honour and standards of efficiency into English or American natures should be the fear of being killed by the Germans or the Japanese. Great indeed is Fear; but it is not, as our military enthusiasts believe and try to make us believe, the only stimulus known for awakening the higher ranges of men's spiritual energy. The amount of alteration in public opinion that my Utopia postulates is vastly less than the difference between the mentality of those black warriors who pursued Stanley's party on the Congo with their cannibal war-cry of 'Meat! meat!' and that of the 'general-staff' of any civilized nation. History has seen the latter interval bridged over: the former one can be bridged over much more easily.

Notes

1. What Is an Emotion?

1. Of course the physiological question arises, *how* are the changes felt?—*after* they are produced, by the sensory nerves of the organs bringing back to the brain a report of the modifications that have occurred? or *before* they are produced, by our being conscious of the outgoing nerve-currents starting on their way downwards towards the parts they are to excite? I believe all the evidence we have to be in favor of the former alternative. The question is too minute for discussion here, but I have said something about it in a paper entitled "The Feeling of Effort," in the *Anniversary Memoirs of the Boston Society of Natural History,* 1880 (translated in *La Critique Philosophique* for that year, and summarized in MIND, V [No. 20], 582). See also G. E. Müller's *Grundlegung der Psychophysik,* § 110.

2. Let it be noted in passing that this personal self-consciousness seems an altogether bodily affair, largely a consciousness of our attitude, and that, like other emotions, it reacts on its physical condition, and leads to modifications of the attitude—to a certain rigidity in most men, but in children to a regular twisting and squirming fit, and in women to various gracefully shy poses.

3. This is the opposite of what happens in injuries to the brain, whether from outward violence, inward rupture or tumor, or mere starvation from disease. The cortical permeability seems reduced, so that excitement, instead of propagating itself laterally through the ideational channels as before, tends to take the downward track into the organs of the body. The consequence is that we have tears, laughter, and temper-fits, on the most insignificant provocation, accompanying a proportional feebleness in logical thought and the power of volitional attention and decision.

4. It must be confessed that there are cases of morbid fear in which objectively the heart is not much perturbed. These however fail to prove anything

against our theory, for it is of course possible that the cortical centres normally percipient of dread as a complex of cardiac and other organic sensations due to real bodily change, should become *primarily* excited in brain-disease, and give rise to an hallucination of the changes being there—an hallucination of dread, consequently, coexistent with a comparatively calm pulse, etc. I say it is possible, for I am ignorant of observations which might test the fact. Trance, ecstasy, etc., offer analogous examples—not to speak of ordinary dreaming. Under all these conditions one may have the liveliest subjective feelings, either of eye or ear, or of the more visceral and emotional sort, as a result of pure nerve-central activity, with complete peripheral repose. Whether the subjective strength of the feeling be due in these cases to the actual energy of the central disturbance, or merely to the narrowing of the field of consciousness, need not concern us. In the asylum cases of melancholy, there is usually a narrowing of the field.

5. Quoted by Semal: *De la sensibilité générale dans les affections mélancoliques,* Paris, 1875, pp. 130–134.

6. "Ein Fall von allgemeiner Anaesthesie," *Inaugural-Dissertation.* Heidelberg, Winter, 1882.

2. The Dilemma of Determinism

"The Dilemma of Determinism" was originally delivered as an address to the Harvard Divinity School students and published in the *Unitarian Review* for September 1884.

1. And I may now say Charles S. Peirce—see the *Monist,* for 1892–93.

2. "The whole history of popular beliefs about Nature refutes the notion that the thought of a universal physical order can possibly have arisen from the purely passive reception and association of particular perceptions. Indubitable as it is that men infer from known cases to unknown, it is equally certain that this procedure, if restricted to the phenomenal materials that spontaneously offer themselves, would never have led to the belief in a general uniformity, but only to the belief that law and lawlessness rule the world in motley alternation. From the point of view of strict experience, nothing exists but the sum of particular perceptions, with their coincidences on the one hand, their contradictions on the other.

"That there is more order in the world than appears at first sight is not discovered *till the order is looked for.* The first impulse to look for it proceeds from practical needs: where ends must be attained, we must know trustworthy means which infallibly possess a property, or produce a result. But the practical need is only the first occasion for our reflection on the conditions of true knowledge; and even were there no such need, motives would still be present for carrying us beyond the stage of mere association. For not with an equal interest, or rather with an equal lack of interest, does man contemplate those natural processes in which a thing is linked with its former mate, and those in which it is linked to something else. *The former processes harmonize with the conditions of his own thinking:* the latter do not. In the former, his *concepts, general judgments,* and *inferences* apply to reality: in the latter, they have no such application. And thus the intellectual satisfaction which at first comes to him without reflection, at last excites in him the conscious wish to find realized throughout the entire phenomenal world those rational continuities, uniformities, and necessities which are the fundamental element and guiding principle of his own thought." (Sigwart, *Logik*, bd. 2, s. 382.)

3. Speaking technically, it is a word with a positive denotation, but a connotation that is negative. Other things must be silent about *what* it is: it alone can decide that point at the moment in which it reveals itself.

4. A favorite argument against free-will is that if it be true, a man's murderer may as probably be his best friend as his worst enemy, a mother be as likely to strangle as to suckle her first-born, and all of us be as ready to jump from fourth-story windows as to go out of front doors, etc. Users of this argument should properly be excluded from debate till they learn what the real question is. "Free-will" does not say that everything that is physically conceivable is also morally possible. It merely says that of alternatives that really *tempt* our will more than one is really possible. Of course, the alternatives that do thus tempt our will are vastly fewer than the physical possibilities we can coldly fancy. Persons really tempted often do murder their best friends, mothers do strangle their first-born, people do jump out of fourth-story windows, etc.

5. To a reader who says he is satisfied with a pessimism, and has no objection to thinking the whole bad, I have no more to say: he makes fewer demands on the world than I, who, making them, wish to look a little farther before I give up all hope of having them satisfied. If, however, all he means is that the badness of some parts does not prevent his acceptance of a universe whose *other* parts give him satisfaction, I welcome him as an ally. He has abandoned the notion of the *Whole*, which is the essence of deterministic monism, and views things as a pluralism, just as I do in this paper.

6. Compare Sir James Stephen's *Essays by a Barrister,* London, 1862, pp. 138, 318.

7. "Cet univers est un spectacle que Dieu se donne à lui-même. Servons les intentions du grand chorège en contribuant à rendre le spectacle aussi brillant, aussi varié que possible."—RENAN.

8. The burden, for example, of seeing to it that the *end* of all our righteousness be some positive universal gain.

9. This of course leaves the creative mind subject to the law of time. And to anyone who insists on the timelessness of that mind I have no reply to make. A mind to whom all time is simultaneously present must see all things under the form of actuality, or under some form to us unknown. If he thinks certain moments as ambiguous in their content whilst future, he must simultaneously know how the ambiguity will have been decided when they are past. So that none of his mental judgments can possibly be called hypothetical, and his world is one from which chance is excluded. Is not, however, the timeless mind rather a gratuitous fiction? And is not the notion of eternity being given at a stroke to

omniscience only just another way of whacking upon us the block-universe, and of denying that possibilities exist?—just the point to be proved. To say that time is an illusory appearance is only a roundabout manner of saying there is no real plurality, and that the frame of things is an absolute unit. Admit plurality, and time may be its form.

10. And this of course means "miraculous" interposition, but not necessarily of the gross sort our fathers took such delight in representing, and which has so lost its magic for us. Emerson quotes some Eastern sage as saying that if evil were really done under the sun, the sky would incontinently shrivel to a snake-skin and cast it out in spasms. But, says Emerson, the spasms of Nature are years and centuries; and it will tax man's patience to wait so long. We may think of the reserved possibilities God keeps in his own hand, under as invisible and molecular and slowly self-summating a form as we please. We may think of them as counteracting human agencies which he inspires *ad hoc.* In short, signs and wonders and convulsions of the earth and sky are not the only neutralizers of obstruction to a god's plans of which it is possible to think.

11. As long as languages contain a future perfect tense, determinists, following the bent of laziness or passion, the lines of least resistance, can reply in that tense, saying, "It will have been fated," to the still small voice which urges an opposite course; and thus excuse themselves from effort in a quite unanswerable way.

3. The Perception of Reality

The version of "The Perception of Reality" published by Harvard University Press in *The Works of William James—The Principles of Psychology: Volumes I-III* was reprinted, with additions, from *Mind* for July 1889.

1. Compare this psychological fact with the corresponding logical truth that all negation rests on covert assertion of something else than the thing denied. (See Bradley's *Principles of Logic,* bk. I, ch. 3.)

2. See that very remarkable little work, *The Anaesthetic Revelation and the Gist of Philosophy,* by Benjamin P. Blood (Amsterdam, N.Y., 1874). Compare also *Mind,* vii, 206.

3. "To one whose mind is healthy thoughts come and go unnoticed, with me they have to be faced, thought about in a peculiar fashion, and then disposed of as finished, and this often when I am utterly wearied and would be at peace; but the call is imperative. This goes on to the hindrance of all natural action. If I were told the staircase was on fire and I had only a minute to escape, and the thought arose—'Have they sent for fire engines? It is probable the man who has the key is at hand. Is the man a careful sort of person? Will the key be hanging on a peg? Am I thinking rightly? Perhaps they don't lock the depot.' My foot would be lifted to go down. I should be conscious to excitement that I was losing my chance—but I should be unable to stir, until all these absurdities were entertained and disposed of. In the most critical moments of my life, when

I ought to have been so *engrossed as to leave no room for any secondary thoughts*, I have been oppressed by the inability to be at peace. And in the most ordinary circumstances it is all the same. Let me instance the other morning I went to walk. The day was biting cold, but I was unable to proceed except by jerks. Once I got arrested—my feet in a muddy pool. One foot was lifted to go, knowing that it was not good to be standing in water, but there I was fast, the cause of deten-tion being the discussing with myself the reasons why I should not stand in that pool." (T. S. Clouston: *Clinical Lectures on Mental Diseases,* 1883, p. 43. See also Berger, in *Archiv für Psychiatrie,* vi, 217.)

4. Note to James Mill's *Analysis,* I, 412–423.

5. For an excellent account of the history of opinion on this subject see A. Marty, in *Vierteljahrsschrift für wissenschaftliche Philosophie,* viii, 161 ff. (1884).

6. We saw near the end of Chapter XIX that a candle-image taking exclu-sive possession of the mind in this way would probably acquire the sensational vividness. But this physiological accident is logically immaterial to the argument in the text, which ought to apply as well to the dimmest sort of mental image as to the brightest sensation.

7. In both existential and attributive judgments a synthesis is represented. The syllable *ex* in the word Existence, *da* in the word *Dasein,* express it. 'The candle exists' is equivalent to 'The candle is *over there.'* And the 'over there' means real space, space related to other reals. The proposition amounts to say-ing: 'The candle is in the same space with other reals.' It affirms of the candle a very concrete predicate—namely, this relation to other particular concrete things. *Their* real existence, as we shall later see, resolves itself into their peculiar relation to *ourselves.* Existence is thus no substantive quality when we predicate it of any object; it is a relation, ultimately terminating in ourselves, and at the moment when it terminates, becoming a *practical* relation. But of this more anon. I only wish now to indicate the superficial nature of the distinction be-tween the existential and the attributive proposition.

8. I define the scientific universe here in the radical mechanical way. Prac-tically, it is oftener thought of in a mongrel way and resembles in more points the popular physical world.

9. It thus comes about that we can say such things as that Ivanhoe did not *really* marry Rebecca, as Thackeray *falsely* makes him do. The real Ivanhoe-world is the one which Scott wrote down for us. *In that world* Ivanhoe does *not* marry Rebecca. The objects within that world are knit together by perfectly definite relations, which can be affirmed or denied. Whilst absorbed in the novel, we turn our backs on all other worlds, and, for the time, the Ivanhoe-world re-mains our absolute reality. When we wake from the spell, however, we find a still more real world, which reduces Ivanhoe, and all things connected with him, to the fictive status, and relegates them to one of the sub-universes grouped under No. 5.

10. The world of dreams is our real world whilst we are sleeping, because our attention then lapses from the sensible world. Conversely, when we wake

the attention usually lapses from the dream-world and that becomes unreal. But if a dream haunts us and compels our attention during the day it is very apt to remain figuring in our consciousness as a sort of sub-universe alongside of the waking world. Most people have probably had dreams which it is hard to imagine not to have been glimpses into an actually existing region of being, perhaps a corner of the 'spiritual World.' And dreams have accordingly in all ages been regarded as revelations, and have played a large part in furnishing forth mythologies and creating themes for faith to lay hold upon. The 'larger universe,' here, which helps us to believe both in the dream and in the waking reality which is its immediate reductive, is the *total* universe, of Nature *plus* the Supernatural. The dream holds true, namely, in one half of that universe; the waking perceptions in the other half. Even to-day dream-objects figure among the realities in which some 'psychic-researchers' are seeking to rouse our belief. All our theories, not only those about the supernatural, but our philosophic and scientific theories as well, are like our dreams in rousing such different degrees of belief in different minds.

11. Distinguishes realities from unrealities, the essential from the rubbishy and neglectable.

12. *Inquiry Concerning Human Understanding*, sec. v, pt. 2 (slightly transposed in my quotation).

13. Note to James Mill's *Analysis*, ɪ, 394.

14. *Critique of Pure Reason*, trans. Müller, ɪɪ, 515–16. Hume also: "When after the simple conception of any thing we wou'd conceive it as existent, we in reality make no addition to or alteration on our first idea. Thus when we affirm, that God is existent, we simply form the idea of such a being, as he is represented to us; nor is the existence, which we attribute to him, conceiv'd by a particular idea, which we join to his other qualities, and can again separate and distinguish from them. . . . The belief of the existence joins no new ideas to those, which compose the idea of the object. When I think of God, when I think of him as existent, and when I believe him to be existent, my idea of him neither encreases nor diminishes. But as 'tis certain there is a great difference betwixt the simple conception of the existence of an object, and the belief of it, and as this difference lies not in the parts or composition of the idea, which we conceive; it follows, that it must lie in the *manner*, in which we conceive it." (*Treatise of Human Nature*, pt. ɪɪɪ, sec. 7.)

15. I use the notion of the Ego here, as common-sense uses it. Nothing is prejudged as to the results (or absence of results) of ulterior attempts to analyze the notion.

16. Griesinger: *Die Pathologie und Therapie der psychischen Krankheiten*, §§ 50, 98. See also Lotze: *Medicinische Psychologie*, p. 251. The neologism we so often hear, that an experience 'gives us a *realizing sense*' of the truth of some proposition or other, illustrates the dependence of the sense of reality upon *excitement*. Only what stirs us is 'realized.'

17. The way in which sensations are pitted against systematized concep-

tions, and in which the one or the other then prevails according as the sensations are felt by ourselves or merely known by report, is interestingly illustrated at the present day by the state of public belief about 'spiritualistic' phenomena. There exist numerous narratives of movement without contact on the part of articles of furniture and other material objects, in the presence of certain privileged individuals called mediums. Such movement violates our memories, and the whole system of accepted physical 'science.' Consequently those who have not seen it either brand the narratives immediately as lies or call the phenomena 'illusions' of sense, produced by fraud or due to hallucination. But one who has actually seen such a phenomenon, under what seems to him sufficiently 'test-conditions,' will hold to his sensible experience through thick and thin, even though the whole fabric of 'science' should be rent in twain. That man would be a weak-spirited creature indeed who should allow any fly-blown generalities about 'the liability of the senses to be deceived' to bully him out of his adhesion to what for him was an indubitable experience of sight. A man may err in this obstinacy, sure enough, in any particular case. But the spirit that animates him is that on which ultimately the very life and health of Science rest.

18. *Treatise of Human Nature*, bk. I, pt. III, sec. 8.

19. *Researches into the Early History of Mankind*, p. 108.

20. See Vol. I, pp. 274–5; Vol. II, pp. 869 ff.

21. See *An Essay towards a New Theory of Vision*, § 59.

22. *Essay*, bk. iv, chap. 2, § 14. In another place: "He that sees a candle burning, and hath experimented the force of its flame by putting his finger in it, will little doubt that this is something existing without him, which does him harm and puts him to great pain. . . . And if our dreamer pleases to try whether the glowing heat of a glass-furnace be barely a wandering imagination in a drowsy man's fancy, by putting his hand into it, he may, perhaps, be awakened into a certainty, greater than he could wish, that it is something more than bare imagination. So that this evidence is as great as we can desire, being as certain to us as our pleasure or pain, i.e. happiness or misery; beyond which we have no concernment either of knowing or being. Such an assurance of the existence of things without us is sufficient to direct us in the attaining the good and avoiding the evil which is caused by them, which is the important concernment we have of being made acquainted with them." (*Ibid.*, bk. iv, chap. 11, § 8.)

23. W. Bagehot: "On the Emotion of Conviction," *Literary Studies*, II, 412–14.

24. *Psychologie rationnelle*, ch. 12.

25. Two examples out of a thousand:

Reid: *Inquiry*, ch. II, § 9: "I remember, many years ago, a white ox was brought into this country, of so enormous a size that people came many miles to see him. There happened, some months after, an uncommon fatality among women in child-bearing. Two such uncommon events, following one another, gave a suspicion of their connection, and occasioned a common opinion among the country-people that the white ox was the cause of this fatality."

H. M. Stanley: *Through the Dark Continent,* II, 384: "On the third day of our stay at Mowa, feeling quite comfortable amongst the people, on account of their friendly bearing, I began to write down in my note-book the terms for articles in order to improve my already copious vocabulary of native words. I had proceeded only a few minutes when I observed a strange commotion amongst the people who had been flocking about me, and presently they ran away. In a short time we heard war-cries ringing loudly and shrilly over the table-land. Two hours afterwards, a long line of warriors were seen descending the table-land and advancing towards our camp. There may have been between five and six hundred of them. We, on the other hand, had made but few preparations except such as would justify us replying to them in the event of the actual commencement of hostilities. But I had made many firm friends amongst them, and I firmly believed that I would be able to avert an open rupture. When they had assembled at about a hundred yards in front of our camp, Safeni and I walked up towards them, and sat down midway. Some half-dozen of the Mowa people came near, and the shauri began.

"'What is the matter, my friends?' I asked. 'Why do you come with guns in your hands in such numbers, as though you were coming to fight? Fight! Fight us, your friends! Tut! this is some great mistake, surely.'

"'Mundelé,' replied one of them, . . . 'our people saw you yesterday make marks on some tara-tara (paper). This is very bad. Our country will waste, our goats will die, our bananas will rot, and our women will dry up. What have we done to you, that you should wish to kill us? We have sold you food, and we have brought you wine, each day. Your people are allowed to wander where they please, without trouble. Why is the Mundelé so wicked? We have gathered together to fight you if you do not burn that tara-tara now before our eyes. If you burn it we go away, and shall be friends as heretofore.'

"I told them to rest there, and left Safeni in their hands as a pledge that I should return. My tent was not fifty yards from the spot, but while going towards it my brain was busy in devising some plan to foil this superstitious madness. My notebook contained a vast number of valuable notes. . . . I could not sacrifice it to the childish caprice of savages. As I was rummaging my book box, I came across a volume of Shakespeare (Chandos edition), much worn and well thumbed, and which was of the same size as my field-book; its cover was similar also, and it might be passed for the note-book provided that no one remembered its appearance too well. I took it to them. 'Is this the tara-tara, friends, that you wish burnt?'

"'Yes, yes, that is it!'

"'Well, take it, and burn it or keep it.'

"'M—m. No, no, no. We will not touch it. It is fetish. You must burn it.'

"'I! Well, let it be so. I will do anything to please my good friends of Mowa.'

"We walked to the nearest fire. I breathed a regretful farewell to my genial companion, which during many weary hours of night had assisted to relieve my mind when oppressed by almost intolerable woes, and then gravely consigned the innocent Shakespeare to the flames, heaping the brush-fuel over it with ceremonious care.

"'Ah-h-h,' breathed the poor deluded natives, sighing their relief. . . . 'There is no trouble now.' . . . And something approaching to a cheer was shouted among them, which terminated the episode of the Burning of Shakespeare."

26. "Rationality, Activity and Faith" (*Princeton Review,* July 1882, pp. 64–9).

27. J. Royce: *The Religious Aspect of Philosophy* (Boston, 1885), pp. 316–17, 357.

28. Chapter XXVIII.

29. Prof. Royce puts this well in discussing idealism and the reality of an 'external' world. "If the history of popular speculation on these topics could be written, how much of cowardice and shuffling would be found in the behavior of the natural mind before the question: 'How dost thou know of an external reality?' Instead of simply and plainly answering: 'I mean by the external world in the first place something that I accept or demand, that I posit, postulate, actively construct on the basis of sense-data,' the natural man gives us all kinds of vague compromise answers. . . . Where shall these endless turnings and twistings have an end? . . . All these lesser motives are appealed to, and the one ultimate motive is neglected. The ultimate motive with the man of every-day life is the *will to have an external world.* Whatever consciousness contains, reason will persist in spontaneously adding the thought: 'But there *shall be* something beyond this.' . . . The popular assurance of an external world is the *fixed determination to make one,* now and henceforth." (*Religious Aspect of Philosophy,* pp. 303–4—the italics are my own.) This immixture of the will appears most flagrantly in the fact that although external matter is doubted commonly enough, minds external to our own are never doubted. We need them too much, are too essentially social to dispense with them. Semblances of matter may suffice to react upon, but not semblances of communing souls. A psychic solipsism is too hideous a mockery of our wants, and, so far as I know, has never been seriously entertained.—Chapters IX and X of Prof. Royce's work are on the whole the clearest account of the psychology of belief with which I am acquainted.

30. "The leading fact in Belief, according to my view of it, is our Primitive Credulity. We begin by believing everything; whatever is, is true. . . . The animal born in the morning of a summer day, proceeds upon the fact of daylight; assumes the perpetuity of that fact. Whatever it is disposed to do, it does without misgivings. If in the morning it began a round of operations continuing for hours, under the full benefit of daylight, it would unhesitatingly begin the same round in the evening. Its state of mind is practically one of unbounded confidence; but, as yet, it does not understand what confidence means.

"The pristine assurance is soon met by checks; a disagreeable experience leading to new insight. To be thwarted and opposed is one of our earliest and most frequent pains. It develops the sense of a distinction between free and obstructed impulses; the unconsciousness of an open way is exchanged for consciousness; we are now said properly to believe in what has never been contradicted, as we disbelieve in what has been contradicted. We believe that, after the dawn of day, there is before us a continuance of light; we do not believe that this light is to continue for ever.

"Thus, the vital circumstance in belief is never to be contradicted—never to lose *prestige*. The number of repetitions counts for little in the process: we are as much convinced after ten as after fifty; we are more convinced by ten unbroken, than by fifty for and one against." (Bain: *The Emotions and the Will,* pp. 511, 512.)

31. *Literature.* D. Hume: *Treatise of Human Nature,* part III, §§ VII–x. A. Bain: *Emotions and the Will,* chapter on Belief (also pp. 20 ff.). J. Sully: *Sensation and Intuition,* essay IV. J. Mill: *Analysis of the Human Mind,* chapter XI. Charles Renouvier: *Psychologie rationnelle,* vol. II, pt. II; and *Esquisse d'une classification systématique des doctrines philosophiques,* part VI. J. H. Newman: *A Grammar of Assent.* J. Venn: *On Some of the Characteristics of Belief.* V. Brochard: *De l'erreur,* part II, chap, VI, IX; and *Revue Philosophique,* XVIII, 1. E. Rabier: *Psychologie,* chap. XXI, Appendix. Ollé-Laprune: *De la certitude morale* (1880). G. F. Stout: "The Genesis of the Cognition of Physical Reality," in *Mind,* Jan. 1890. J. Pikler: *The Psychology of the Belief in Objective Existence* (London, 1890).—Mill says that we believe present sensations; and makes our belief in all other things a matter of *association* with these. So far so good; but as he makes no mention of emotional or volitional reaction, Bain rightly charges him with treating belief as a purely intellectual state. For Bain belief is rather an incident of our active life. When a thing is such as to make us *act* on it, then we believe it, according to Bain. "But how about past things, or remote things, upon which no reaction of ours is possible? And how about belief in things which *check* action?" says Sully, who considers that we believe a thing only when "the idea of it has an inherent tendency to approximate in character and intensity to a sensation." It is obvious that each of these authors emphasizes a true aspect of the question. My own account has sought to be more complete, sensation, association, and active reaction all being acknowledged to be concerned. The most compendious possible formula perhaps would be that *our belief and attention* are the same fact. For the moment, what we attend to is reality; Attention is a motor reaction; and we are so made that sensations force attention from us. On Belief and Conduct see an article by Leslie Stephen, *Nineteenth Century,* Sept. 1888.

A set of facts have been recently brought to my attention which I hardly know how to treat, so I say a word about them in this footnote. I refer to a type of experience which has frequently found a place amongst the 'Yes' answers to the Census of Hallucinations, and which is generally described by those who report it as an 'impression of the presence' of someone near them, although no sensation either of sight, hearing, or touch is involved. From the way in which this experience is spoken of by those who have had it, it would appear to be an extremely definite and positive state of mind, coupled with a belief in the reality of its object quite as strong as any direct sensation ever gives. And yet *no* sensation seems to be connected with it at all. Sometimes the person whose nearness is thus impressed is a known person, dead or living, sometimes an unknown one. His attitude and situation are often very definitely impressed, and so, sometimes (though not by way of hearing), are words which he wishes to say.

The phenomenon would seem to be due to a pure *conception* becoming saturated with the sort of stinging urgency which ordinarily only sensations bring. But I cannot yet persuade myself that the urgency in question consists in concomitant emotional and motor impulses. The 'impression' may come quite suddenly and depart quickly; it may carry no emotional suggestions, and wake no motor consequences beyond those involved in attending to it. Altogether, the matter is somewhat paradoxical, and no conclusion can be come to until more definite data are obtained.

Perhaps the most curious case of the sort which I have received is the following. The subject of the observation, Mr. P., is an exceptionally intelligent witness, though the words of the narrative are his wife's.

"Mr. P. has all his life been the occasional subject of rather singular delusions or impressions of various kinds. If I had belief in the existence of latent or embryo faculties, other than the five senses, I should explain them on that ground. Being totally blind, his other perceptions are abnormally keen and developed, and given the existence of a rudimentary sixth sense, it would be only natural that this also should be more acute in him than in others. One of the most interesting of his experiences in this line was the frequent apparition of a corpse some years ago, which may be worth the attention of your Committee on that subject. At the time Mr. P. had a music-room in Boston on Beacon Street, where he used to do severe and protracted practice with little interruption. Now, all one season it was a very familiar occurrence with him while in the midst of work to feel a cold draft of air suddenly upon his face, with a prickling sensation at the roots of his hair, when he would turn from the piano, and a figure which he knew to be dead would come sliding under the crack of the door from without, flattening itself to squeeze through and rounding out again to the human form. It was of a middle-aged man, and drew itself along the carpet on hands and knees, but with head thrown back till it reached the sofa, upon which it stretched itself. It remained some moments, but vanished always if Mr. P. spoke or made a decided movement. The most singular point in the occurrence was its frequent repetition. He might expect it on any day between two and four o'clock, and it came always heralded by the same sudden cold shiver, and was invariably the same figure which went through the same movements. He afterwards traced the whole experience to strong tea. He was in the habit of taking cold tea, which always stimulates him, for lunch, and on giving up this practice he never saw this or any other apparition again. However, even allowing, as is doubtless true, that the event was a delusion of nerves first fatigued by overwork and then excited by this stimulant, there is one point which is still wholly inexplicable and highly interesting to me. Mr. P. has no memory whatever of sight, nor conception of it. It is impossible for him to form any idea of what we mean by light or color, consequently he has no cognizance of any object which does not reach his sense of hearing or of touch, though these are so acute as to give a contrary impression sometimes to other people. When he becomes aware of the presence of a person or an object, by means which seem mysterious to outsiders, he can always trace it naturally and legitimately to slight echoes, perceptible only to his keen ears, or to differences in atmospheric pressure, perceptible only to his acute nerves of touch; but with the apparition described, for the only time in his experience, he was aware of presence, size, and appearance, without the use of either of these mediums. The figure never produced the least sound nor came within a number of feet of his person, yet he knew that it was a man, that it moved, and in what direction, even that it wore a full beard, which, like the thick curly hair, was partially gray; also that it was dressed in the style of suit known as 'pepper and salt.' These points were all perfectly distinct and invariable each time. If asked how he perceived them, he will answer he cannot tell, he simply knew it, and so strongly and so distinctly that it is impossible to shake his opinion as to the exact details of the man's appearance. It would seem that in this delusion of the senses he really *saw,* as he has never done in the actual experiences of life, except in the first two years of childhood."

On cross-examining Mr. P., I could not make out that there was anything like visual imagination involved, although he was quite unable to describe in just what terms the false perception was carried on. It seemed to be more like an intensely definite *conception* than anything else, a conception to which the feeling of *present reality* was attached, but in no such shape as easily to fall under the heads laid down in my text.

4. The Hidden Self

1. M. Binet has contributed some of his facts to the Chicago *Open Court* for 1889.

2. M. Janet seems rather to incline to the former view, though suggestion may at times be exclusively responsible, as when he produced what was essentially the same phenomenon by pointing an orange-peel held out on the end of a long stick at the parts!

3. This whole phenomenon shows how an idea which remains itself below the threshold of a certain conscious self may occasion associative effects therein. The skin-sensations, unfelt by the patient's primary consciousness, awaken, nevertheless, their usual visual associates therein.

5. Habit

1. *The Physiology of Mind*, p. 154.
2. J. Bahnsen: *Beiträge zur Charakterologie* (1867), vol. I, p. 209.

7. The Gospel of Relaxation

1. Fleming H. Revell Company, New York [1895].

8. On a Certain Blindness in Human Beings

1. "The Lantern-Bearers," in the volume entitled *Across the Plains*. Abridged in the quotation.

2. *The Religious Aspect of Philosophy* [1885], pp. 157–162 (abridged).

3. De Sénancour: *Obermann* [Brussels, 1837], Lettre XXX.

4. *The Prelude*, Book III.

5. *The Prelude*, Book IV.

6. *Op. cit.* (Boston: Roberts, 1883), pp. 3, 4, 5, 6.

7. "Crossing Brooklyn Ferry" (abridged).

8. *Calamus* (Boston, 1897), pp. 41, 42.

9. *Vita*, lib. 2, chap. iv.

10. *La Guerre et la paix* (Paris, 1884), vol. iii, pp. 268, 275, 316.

11. Quoted by Lotze, *Microcosmus*, English translation, vol. ii, p. 240.

12. *Op. cit.*, pp. 210–222 (abridged).

9. What Makes a Life Significant

1. This address was composed before the Cuban and Philippine wars. Such outbursts of the passion of mastery are, however, only episodes in a social process which in the long run seems everywhere tending towards the Chautauquan ideals.

2. *Ma confession* [Paris, 1887], X (condensed).

3. *Across the Plains:* "Pulvis et Umbra" (abridged).

4. *The Light of the World and Other Sermons*, 5th Series (New York: E. P. Dutton, 1891), pp. 166, 167.

5. Sir James Fitzjames Stephen, *Essays by a Barrister* (London, 1862), p. 318.

10. Philosophical Conceptions and Practical Results

"Philosophical Conceptions and Practical Results" was an address delivered by William James before the Philosophical Union at Berkeley, August 26, 1898.

1. The Foundations of Belief, p. 30.

12. The Sick Soul

1. *Tract on God, Man, and Happiness*, Book ii, ch. x.

2. *A Commentary on Saint Paul's Epistle to the Galatians*, Philadelphia, 1891, pp. 511–512 (abridged).

3. MOLINOS: *The Spiritual Guide Which Disintangles the Soul* [1685], Book II, chaps, xvii, xviii (abridged).

4. I say this in spite of the monistic utterances of many mind-cure writers; for these utterances are really inconsistent with their attitude towards disease, and can easily be shown not to be logically involved in the experiences of union with a higher Presence with which they connect themselves. The higher Presence, namely, need not be the absolute whole of things, it is quite sufficient for the life of religious experience to regard it as a part, if only it be the most ideal part.

5. Cf. J. Milsand: *Luther et le serf-arbitre,* 1884, *passim.*

6. He adds with characteristic healthy-mindedness: "Our business is to continue to fail in good spirits."

7. The God of many men is little more than their court of appeal against the damnatory judgment passed on their failures by the opinion of this world. To our own consciousness there is usually a residuum of worth left over after our sins and errors have been told off—our capacity of acknowledging and regretting them is the germ of a better self *in posse* at least. But the world deals with us *in actu* and not *in posse:* and of this hidden germ, not to be guessed at from without, it never takes account. Then we turn to the All-knower, who knows our bad, but knows this good in us also, and who is just. We cast ourselves with our repentance on his mercy: only by an All-knower can we finally be judged. So the need of a God very definitely emerges from this sort of experience of life.

8. E.g., *Iliad,* XVII, 446: "Nothing then is more wretched anywhere than man of all that breathes and creeps upon this earth."

9. E.g., Theognis: 425–428: "Best of all for all things upon earth is it not to be born nor to behold the splendors of the Sun; next best to traverse as soon as possible the gates of Hades." See also the almost identical passage in *Oedipus in Colonus,* 1225.—The *Anthology* is full of pessimistic utterances: "Naked came I upon the earth, naked I go below the ground—why then do I vainly toil when I see the end naked before me?"—"How did I come to be? Whence am I? Wherefore did I come? To pass away. How can I learn aught when naught I know? Being naught I came to life: once more shall I be what I was. Nothing and nothingness is the whole race of mortals."—"For death we are all cherished and fattened like a herd of hogs that is wantonly butchered."

The difference between Greek pessimism and the oriental and modern variety is that the Greeks had not made the discovery that the pathetic mood may be idealized, and figure as a higher form of sensibility. Their spirit was still too essentially masculine for pessimism to be elaborated or lengthily dwelt on in their classic literature. They would have despised a life set wholly in a minor key, and summoned it to keep within the proper bounds of lachrymosity. The discovery that the enduring emphasis, so far as this world goes, may be laid on its pain and failure, was reserved for races more complex, and (so to speak) more feminine than the Hellenes had attained to being in the classic period. But all the same was the outlook of those Hellenes blackly pessimistic.

10. For instance, on the very day on which I write this page, the post brings me some aphorisms from a worldly-wise old friend in Heidelberg which may serve as a good contemporaneous expression of Epicureanism: "By the word 'happiness' every human being understands something different. It is a phantom pursued only by weaker minds. The wise man is satisfied with the more modest but much more definite term *contentment*. What education should chiefly aim at is to save us from a discontented life. Health is one favoring condition, but by no means an indispensable one, of contentment. Woman's heart and love are a shrewd device of Nature, a trap which she sets for the average man, to force him into working. But the wise man will always prefer work chosen by himself."

11. RIBOT: *La Psychologic des sentiments* [1896], p. 54.

12. A. GRATRY: *Souvenirs de ma jeunesse*, 1897, pp. 119–121, abridged. Some persons are affected with anhedonia permanently, or at any rate with a loss of the usual appetite for life. The annals of suicide supply such examples as the following:

An uneducated domestic servant, aged nineteen, poisons herself, and leaves two letters expressing her motive for the act. To her parents she writes: "Life is sweet perhaps to some, but I prefer what is sweeter than life, and that is death. So good-bye for ever, my dear parents. It is nobody's fault, but a strong desire of my own which I have longed to fulfil for three or four years. I have always had a hope that some day I might have an opportunity of fulfilling it, and now it has come. . . . It is a wonder I have put this off so long, but I thought, perhaps, I should cheer up a bit and put all thought out of my head." To her brother she writes: "Good-bye for ever, my own dearest brother. By the time you get this I shall be gone for ever. I know, dear love, there is no forgiveness for what I am going to do. . . . I am tired of living, so am willing to die. . . . Life may be sweet to some, but death to me is sweeter." S. A. K. STRAHAN: *Suicide and Insanity*, 2d edition, London, 1894, p. 131.

13. ROUBINOVITCH ET TOULOUSE: *La Mélancolie*, 1897, p. 170, abridged.

14. I cull these examples from the work of G. DUMAS: *La Tristesse et la joie*, 1900 [pp. 60, 61, 80, 81].

15. My extracts are from the French translation by 'ZORIA.' In abridging I have taken the liberty of transposing one passage.

16. *Grace Abounding to the Chief of Sinners* [1888]: I have printed a number of detached passages continuously [pp. 43–48, 56, 77].

17. *The Life and Journal of the Rev. Mr. Henry Alline*, Boston, 1806, pp. 25, 26. I owe my acquaintance with this book to my colleague, Dr. Benjamin Rand.

18. Compare BUNYAN: "Then was I struck into a very great trembling, insomuch that at some times I could, for whole days together, feel my very body, as well as my mind, to shake and totter under the sense of the dreadful judgment of God, that should fall on those that have sinned that most fearful and unpardonable sin. I felt also such a clogging and heat at my stomach, by reason of this

my terror, that I was, especially at some times, as if my breast bone would have split asunder. . . . Thus did I wind, and twine, and shrink, under the burthen that was upon me; which burthen also did so oppress me, that I could neither stand, nor go, nor lie, either at rest or quiet" [p. 85].

19. For another case of fear equally sudden, see HENRY JAMES: *Society the Redeemed Form of Man*, Boston, 1879, pp. 43 ff.

20. Example: "It was about eleven o'clock at night . . . but I strolled on still with the people. . . . Suddenly, upon the left side of our road, a crackling was heard among the bushes: all of us were alarmed, and in an instant a tiger, rushing out of the jungle, pounced upon the one of the party that was foremost, and carried him off in the twinkling of an eye. The rush of the animal, and the crush of the poor victim's bones in his mouth, and his last cry of distress, 'Ho hai!' involuntarily re-echoed by all of us, was over in three seconds; and then I know not what happened, till I returned to my senses, when I found myself and companions lying down on the ground, as if prepared to be devoured by our enemy, the sovereign of the forest. I find my pen incapable of describing the terror of that dreadful moment. Our limbs stiffened, our power of speech ceased, and our hearts beat violently, and only a whisper of the same 'Ho hai!' was heard from us. In this state we crept on all-fours for some distance back, and then ran for life, with the speed of an Arab horse, for about half an hour, and fortunately happened to come to a small village. . . . After this every one of us was attacked with fever, attended with shivering, in which deplorable state we remained till morning."—*Autobiography of Lutfullah, a Mohamedan Gentleman*, Leipzig, 1857, p. 112.

14. Does 'Consciousness' Exist?

1. Articles by Baldwin, Ward, Bawden, King, Alexander and others. Dr. Perry is frankly over the border.

2. In my *Psychology* I have tried to show that we need no knower other than the 'passing thought.'

3. G. E. Moore: *Mind*, Vol. XII., N. S., p. 450.

4. Paul Natorp: *Einleitung in die Psychologie*, 1888, pp. 14, 112.

5. "Figuratively speaking, consciousness may be said to be the one universal solvent, or menstruum, in which the different concrete kinds of psychic acts and facts are contained, whether in concealed or in obvious form." G. T. Ladd: *Psychology, Descriptive and Explanatory*, 1894, p. 30.

6. Here as elsewhere the relations are of course *experienced* relations, members of the same originally chaotic manifold of non-perceptual experience of which the related terms themselves are parts.

7. Of the representative function of non-perceptual experience as a whole, I will say a word in a subsequent article: it leads too far into the general theory of knowledge for much to be said about it in a short paper like this.

8. *Grundzüge der Psychologie*, Vol. I., p. 48.

9. Cf. A. L. Hodder: *The Adversaries of the Sceptic*, N.Y., 1899, pp. 94–99.

10. For simplicity's sake I confine my exposition to 'external' reality. But there is also the system of ideal reality in which the room plays its part. Relations of comparison, of classification, serial order, value, also are stubborn, assign a definite place to the room, unlike the incoherence of its places in the mere rhapsody of our successive thoughts.

11. Note the ambiguity of this term, which is taken sometimes objectively and sometimes subjectively.

12. In the *Psychological Review* for July of this year, Dr. R. B. Perry has published a view of Consciousness which comes nearer to mine than any other with which I am acquainted. As present, Dr. Perry thinks, every field of experience is so much 'fact.' It becomes 'opinion' or 'thought' only in retrospection, when a fresh experience, thinking the same object, alters and corrects it. But the corrective experience becomes itself in turn corrected, and thus experience as a whole is a process in which what is objective originally forever turns subjective, turns into our apprehension of the object. I strongly recommend Dr. Perry's admirable article to my readers.

13. I have given a partial account of the matter in *Mind*, Vol. X., p. 27, 1885, and in the *Psychological Review*, Vol. II., p. 105, 1895. See also C. A. Strong's article in the JOURNAL OF PHILOSOPHY, PSYCHOLOGY AND SCIENTIFIC METHODS, Vol. I., p. 253, May 12, 1904. I hope myself very soon to recur to the matter in this JOURNAL.

14. Spencer's proof of his 'Transfigured Realism' (his doctrine that there is an absolutely non-mental reality) comes to mind as a splendid instance of the impossibility of establishing radical heterogeneity between thought and thing. All his painfully accumulated points of difference run gradually into their opposites, and are full of exceptions.

15. I speak here of the complete inner life in which the mind plays freely with its materials. Of course the mind's free play is restricted when it seeks to copy real things in real space.

15. The Energies of Men

"The Energies of Men" was delivered as the presidential address before the American Philosophical Association at Columbia University, December 28, 1906.

1. Thomas De Quincey.
2. This handbook was published last March.
3. *Tour in England, Ireland, and France*, Philadelphia, 1833, p. 435.

16. Concerning Fechner

1. *The Spirit of Modern Philosophy*, pp. 226–227.
2. Fechner: *Über die Seelenfrage*, 1861, p. 170.
3. Fechner's latest summarizing of his views, *Die Tagesansicht gegenüber der*

Nachtansicht, Leipzig, 1879, is now, I understand, in process of translation. His *Little Book of Life after Death* exists already in two American versions, one published by Little, Brown & Co., Boston, the other by the Open Court Co., Chicago.

4. Mr. Bradley ought to be to some degree exempted from my attack in these last pages. Compare especially what he says of non-human consciousness in his *Appearance and Reality,* pp. 269–272.

17. The Moral Equivalent of War

1. *Justice and Liberty,* N. Y., 1909.
2. *First and Last Things,* 1908, p. 215.
3. *Ibid.,* p. 226.

Further Reading

Collected Works

The Works of William James, edited by Frederick H. Burkhardt, Fredson Bowers, and Ignas K. Skrupskelis. 19 vols. Cambridge, Mass.: Harvard University Press, 1975–1988. The individual volumes are *Pragmatism* (1975), *The Meaning of Truth* (1975), *Essays in Radical Empiricism* (1976), *A Pluralistic Universe* (1977), *Essays in Philosophy* (1978), *The Will to Believe* (1979, *Some Problems of Philosophy* (1979), *The Principles of Psychology*, 3 vols. (1981), *Essays in Religion and Morality* (1982), *Talks to Teachers on Psychology: And to Students on Some of Life's Ideals* (1983), *Essays in Psychology* (1983), *Psychology: Briefer Course* (1984), *The Varieties of Religious Experience* (1985), *Essays in Psychical Research* (1986), *Essays, Comments, and Reviews* (1987), *Manuscript Essays and Notes* (1988), *Manuscript Lectures* (1988).

Letters

The Correspondence of William James, edited by Ignas K. Skrupskelis and Elizabeth M. Berkeley. 12 vols. Charlottesville, Va.: University of Virginia Press, 1992–2004.

Selections

The Writings of William James, edited by John J. McDermott. Chicago: University of Chicago Press, 1977. First published 1967 by Random House.

Biographies

Allen, Gay Wilson. *William James*. New York: Viking, 1967.

Lewis, R. W. B. *The Jameses: A Family Narrative*. New York: Farrar, Straus and Giroux, 1991.

Matthiessen, F. O. *The James Family*. New York: Knopf, 1947.

Perry, Ralph Barton. *The Thought and Character of William James*. 2 vols. Boston: Little, Brown, 1935.

Richardson, Robert D. *William James: In the Maelstrom of American Modernism*. Boston: Houghton Mifflin, 2006.

Simon, Linda. *Genuine Reality: A Life of William James*. New York: Harcourt Brace, 1998.

Critical Appraisal

Barzun, Jacques. *A Stroll with William James*. New York: Harper and Row, 1983.

Bjork, Daniel W. *William James: The Center of His Vision*. New York: Columbia University Press, 1988.

Croce, Paul Jerome. *Science and Religion in the Era of William James*. Chapel Hill, N.C.: University of North Carolina Press, 1995.

Feinstein, Howard. *Becoming William James*. Ithaca, N.Y.: Cornell University Press, 1984.

Menand, Louis. *The Metaphysical Club*. New York: Farrar, Straus and Giroux, 2001.

Myers, Gerald E. *William James: His Life and Thought*. New Haven, Conn.: Yale University Press, 1986.

Richardson, Joan. *A Natural History of Pragmatism: The Fact of Feeling from Jonathan Edwards to Gertrude Stein*. Cambridge: Cambridge University Press, 2007.

Santayana, George. "William James." Chap. 3 in *Character and Opinion in the United States*. London: Constable, 1920.

Taylor, Eugene. *William James on Exceptional Mental States*. Amherst, Mass.: University of Massachusetts Press, 1984.

Acknowledgments

Robert Richardson wishes to thank Timothy Seldes, who believed in this book from the start, and Annie Dillard, who suggested the title. He also wishes to thank Lindsay Waters, Hannah Wong, Adriana Kirilova, and all the other helpful, competent, prompt, and cheerful people who make publishing with Harvard University Press a pleasure as well as an honor.

"What Is an Emotion?" is reprinted by permission of the publisher from *The Works of William James—Essays in Psychology*, Frederick Burkhardt, General Editor, Fredson Bowers, Textual Editor, Ignas K. Skrupskelis, Associate Editor, pp. 168–187, Cambridge, Mass.: Harvard University Press, Copyright © 1983 by the President and Fellows of Harvard College.

"The Dilemma of Determinism" is reprinted by permission of the publisher from *The Works of William James—The Will to Believe: And Other Essays in Popular Philosophy*, Frederick Burkhardt, General Editor, Fredson Bowers, Textual Editor, Ignas K. Skrupskelis, Associate Editor, pp. 114–140, Cambridge, Mass.: Harvard University Press, Copyright © 1979 by the President and Fellows of Harvard College.

"The Perception of Reality" is reprinted by permission of the publisher from *The Works of William James—The Principles of Psychology: Volumes I-III*, Frederick Burkhardt, General Editor, Fredson Bowers, Textual Editor, Ignas K. Skrupskelis, Associate Editor, vol. 2, pp. 913–951, Cambridge, Mass.: Harvard University Press, Copyright © 1981 by the President and Fellows of Harvard College.

"The Hidden Self" is reprinted by permission of the publisher from *The Works of William James—Essays in Psychology*, Frederick Burkhardt, General Editor, Fredson Bowers, Textual Editor, Ignas K. Skrupskelis, Associate Editor, pp. 247–268,

Cambridge, Mass.: Harvard University Press, Copyright © 1983 by the President and Fellows of Harvard College.

"Habit" is reprinted by permission of the publisher from *The Works of William James—Psychology: Briefer Course,* Frederick Burkhardt, General Editor, Fredson Bowers, Textual Editor, Ignas K. Skrupskelis, Associate Editor, pp. 125–138, Cambridge, Mass.: Harvard University Press, Copyright © 1984 by the President and Fellows of Harvard College.

"The Will" is reprinted by permission of the publisher from *The Works of William James—Talks to Teachers on Psychology: And to Students on Some of Life's Ideals,* Frederick Burkhardt, General Editor, Fredson Bowers, Textual Editor, Ignas K. Skrupskelis, Associate Editor, pp. 101–114, Cambridge, Mass.: Harvard University Press, Copyright © 1983 by the President and Fellows of Harvard College.

"The Gospel of Relaxation" is reprinted by permission of the publisher from *The Works of William James—Talks to Teachers on Psychology: And to Students on Some of Life's Ideals,* Frederick Burkhardt, General Editor, Fredson Bowers, Textual Editor, Ignas K. Skrupskelis, Associate Editor, pp. 117–131, Cambridge, Mass.: Harvard University Press, Copyright © 1983 by the President and Fellows of Harvard College.

"On a Certain Blindness in Human Beings" is reprinted by permission of the publisher from *The Works of William James—Talks to Teachers on Psychology: And to Students on Some of Life's Ideals,* Frederick Burkhardt, General Editor, Fredson Bowers, Textual Editor, Ignas K. Skrupskelis, Associate Editor, pp. 132–149, Cambridge, Mass.: Harvard University Press, Copyright © 1983 by the President and Fellows of Harvard College.

"What Makes a Life Significant" is reprinted by permission of the publisher from *The Works of William James—Talks to Teachers on Psychology: And to Students on Some of Life's Ideals,* Frederick Burkhardt, General Editor, Fredson Bowers, Textual Editor, Ignas K. Skrupskelis, Associate Editor, pp. 150–167, Cambridge, Mass.: Harvard University Press, Copyright © 1983 by the President and Fellows of Harvard College.

"Philosophical Conceptions and Practical Results" is reprinted by permission of the publisher from *The Works of William James—Pragmatism,* Frederick Burkhardt, General Editor, Fredson Bowers, Textual Editor, Ignas K. Skrupskelis, Associate Editor, pp. 257–270, Cambridge, Mass.: Harvard University Press, Copyright © 1975 by the President and Fellows of Harvard College.

"The Philippine Tangle" is reprinted by permission of the publisher from *The Works of William James—Essays, Comments, and Reviews,* Frederick Burkhardt, General Editor, Fredson Bowers, Textual Editor, Ignas K. Skrupskelis, Associate Editor, pp. 154–158, Cambridge, Mass.: Harvard University Press, Copyright © 1987 by the President and Fellows of Harvard College.

"The Sick Soul" is reprinted by permission of the publisher from *The Works of William James—The Varieties of Religious Experience,* Frederick Burkhardt, General Editor, Fredson Bowers, Textual Editor, Ignas K. Skrupskelis, Associate Editor, pp. 109–138, Cambridge, Mass.: Harvard University Press, Copyright © 1985 by the President and Fellows of Harvard College.

"The Ph.D. Octopus" is reprinted by permission of the publisher from *The Works of William James—Essays, Comments, and Reviews,* Frederick Burkhardt, General Editor, Fredson Bowers, Textual Editor, Ignas K. Skrupskelis, Associate Editor, pp. 67–74, Cambridge, Mass.: Harvard University Press, Copyright © 1987 by the President and Fellows of Harvard College.

"Does 'Consciousness' Exist?" is reprinted by permission of the publisher from *The Works of William James—Essays in Radical Empiricism,* Frederick Burkhardt, General Editor, Fredson Bowers, Textual Editor, Ignas K. Skrupskelis, Associate Editor, pp. 3–19, Cambridge, Mass.: Harvard University Press, Copyright © 1976 by the President and Fellows of Harvard College.

"The Energies of Men" is reprinted by permission of the publisher from *The Works of William James—Essays in Religion and Morality,* Frederick Burkhardt, General Editor, Fredson Bowers, Textual Editor, Ignas K. Skrupskelis, Associate Editor, pp. 129–146, Cambridge, Mass.: Harvard University Press, Copyright © 1982 by the President and Fellows of Harvard College.

"Concerning Fechner" is reprinted by permission of the publisher from *The Works of William James—A Pluralistic Universe,* Frederick Burkhardt, General Editor, Fredson Bowers, Textual Editor, Ignas K. Skrupskelis, Associate Editor, pp. 63–82, Cambridge, Mass.: Harvard University Press, Copyright © 1977 by the President and Fellows of Harvard College.

"The Moral Equivalent of War" is reprinted by permission of the publisher from *The Works of William James—Essays in Religion and Morality,* Frederick Burkhardt, General Editor, Fredson Bowers, Textual Editor, Ignas K. Skrupskelis, Associate Editor, pp. 162–173, Cambridge, Mass.: Harvard University Press, Copyright © 1982 by the President and Fellows of Harvard College.

Index

absolute, the, 282, 283
absolutism, intellectual, 29
action: voluntary, 121, 122, 124; moral, 125; as if, 131
Agassiz, Louis, xii
Aguinaldo, Emilio, 205, 206
Alcoholics Anonymous, x, 210
alcoholism, 125–126, 129
Alexander the Great, 303
Alline, Henry, 233, 329n17
Allport, Gordon, 101
amnesia, 86
anaesthesia, 86
analogy, as method, 290
anhedonia, 223
animal magnetism, 80, 81
Anti-Imperialist League, 203, 208
argumentum ad hominem, 45
Aristotle, 49
Arnold, Matthew, 303
associationist psychology, 120
attention: and effort, 113; voluntary, 126
automatism, 95, 247

Bacon, Francis, 54
Bagehot, Walter, 47; and suspension of belief, 67, 137
Bain, Alexander, 5, 10, 324n31; on belief, 56; on moral habits, 110–111, 200; on genius, 290
Balfour, A. J., 192
belief, psychology of, 46ff.
Bell, Charles, 5
Bergson, Henri, xiii
Berkeley, Bishop, 65; on ideas, 252
Berkeley, University of California at, xiv, 183
Bernheim, Hippolyte, 93

Binet, Alfred, 83, 91, 92, 93, 326n1
Binnenleben, 132
Blood, Benjamin Paul, xv, 318n2
Boer War, ix, 304
Bradley, F. H., 21, 285, 332n4
brain, x, 2–3, 293–294; physiology of, 16–17, 104, 118
Brentano, Franz, 49
Brockton murderer, 20, 31, 42
Brooks, Phillips, 176–177
Browning, Robert, 189
Bryn Mawr College, 238
Buddha, 230
Buddhism, 237
Bunyan, John, 210, 231–232, 329n18

Call, Annie Payson, 130, 140, 142
Calvino, Italo, xvi
Carlyle, Thomas, 39, 72
Carpenter, Edward, 266
Cavour, Camillo Benso, Conte di, 122
Cellini, Benvenuto, 158
chance: and freedom, x; and determinism, 20–21, 23, 27; antipathy to, 26; and pluralism, 42
Chapman, John J., 308
Chautauqua, NY, 166–169, 173
Chesterton, G. K., 266
Chocorua, NH, xiii
choice, x, 247
Christianity, 237, 282
Christian Science, 99, 277
Civilian Conservation Corps, 301
Clouston, Thomas S., 135, 137, 318n3
compensations, 182
consciousness, 247ff.; earth-consciousness, 292